Contents at a Glance

KU-319-013

Table of Contents

Part I   Getting Started with Integration Services

1   Introduction to SQL Server Integration Services

2   Building Your First Package

What do you think of this book? We want to hear from you!

Microsoft is interested in hearing your feedback so we can continually improve our books and learning resources for you. To participate in a brief online survey, please visit:

www.microsoft.com/learning/booksurvey/

Part II   Designing Packages

Part IV   Applying SSIS to Data Warehousing

What do you think of this book? We want to hear from you!

Microsoft is interested in hearing your feedback so we can continually improve our books and learning resources for you. To participate in a brief online survey, please visit:

www.microsoft.com/learning/booksurvey/

Introduction

A complete database solution requires data to be integrated from a variety of sources. One of the greatest challenges facing business today is that important business information exists in multiple locations and in different formats. As an industry, we have empowered business leaders and information workers with access to corporate data and powerful analysis tools. With access to so much information, decision makers need one indisputable version of data. A reliable ETL (extract, transform, and load) process is the backbone of business-critical data consolidation and business intelligence (BI) services used to lead and support business direction. Microsoft SQL Server 2005 Integration Services (SSIS) provides a foundation to design and perform effective ETL processes.

The goal of this book is to help you design and implement ETL solutions as quickly as possible, both in concept and in practice. You will learn and understand the core principles and concepts of effective data transformation. Through simple hands-on exercises, you will quickly learn to design Integration Services packages used to transform data between files and relational databases; handle conditional logic; and to alter, split, match, merge, combine, and join data in a data flow. After completing these exercises, you will know how to use the appropriate tasks, transformations, connection managers, and data source and destination adapters in concert to form SSIS packages. You will learn to deploy, configure, and optimize packages to run on production servers.

This book is written to address the requirements of professionals with different needs. Database administrators and application developers need to transform data to support specific applications. BI system architects require data to be consolidated from multiple source systems to a central data warehouse or data mart. A scheduled ETL package must be flexible enough to handle errors and data anomalies. Whether you need to run a package to perform a quick, one-time data import or you need a scheduled process to populate the corporate data warehouse every night, you will learn to design an Integration Services solution to meet that need.

Finding Your Best Starting Point

Although the range of topics addressed in this book is comprehensive, this book also caters to readers with varying skills who are involved in one or more stages of the data transformation life cycle. Accordingly, you can choose to read only the chapters that apply to the activities for which you are responsible and skip the remaining chapters. If you choose to take this approach, we recommend that you at least review the chapters that apply to other roles in order to obtain a broad exposure to the product. To find the best place to start, use the following table.

If you are	Follow these steps
An information worker who needs to import or export data	1. Install the sample files as described in "Installing and Using the Sample Files." 2. Read Chapter 1, "Introduction to Integration Services," to learn the concepts of data transformation. 3. Work through Chapters 2, "Building Your First Package," 3, "Extracting and Loading Data," 4, "Using Data Flow Transformations," and 5, "Managing Control Flow," to learn the core components of package design. 4. Review Chapter 14, "Applying Best Practices to SSIS Package Design," to understand package design best practices.
An information worker or application developer who needs to build an ETL solution	1. Install the sample files as described in "Installing and Using the Sample Files." 2. Read Chapter 1 to learn the concepts of data transformation. 3. Work through or review Chapters 2, 3, 4, and 5 to learn the core components of package design. 4. Work through Chapters 6, "Scripting Tasks," 7, "Debugging Packages," 8, "Managing Package Execution," and 9, "Detecting and Handling Processing Errors," to learn how to design advanced packages with error handling. 5. Work through or review Chapter 11, "Optimizing SSIS Packages," to learn how to optimize package design and execution. 6. Work through Chapter 14 to understand package design best practices.
A BI architect or solution designer	1. Install the sample files as described in "Installing and Using the Sample Files." 2. Read Chapter 1 to learn the concepts of data transformation. 3. Work through or review Chapters 2, 3, 4, and 5 to learn the core components of package design. 4. Work through Chapters 6, 7, 8, and 9 to learn how to design advanced packages with error handling. 5. Work through or review Chapter 11 to learn how to optimize package design and execution. 6. Work through Chapters 12, "Data Warehouse Concepts," and 13, "Populating Data Warehouse Structures," to learn data warehouse concepts and how to populate data warehouse structures. 7. Work through Chapter 14 to understand package design best practices.
A system or database administrator who needs to configure and optimize a solution	1. Install the sample files as described in "Installing and Using the Sample Files." 2. Work through Chapters 10, "Securing and Deploying SSIS Packages," and 11 to learn how to secure, deploy, and optimize packages. 3. Review other chapters as needed to understand design elements and best practices.

About the Companion CD-ROM

The CD that accompanies this book contains the sample files that you need to follow the step-by-step exercises throughout the book. For each chapter, use the Microsoft Visual Studio solution files that have projects or packages created for you as starting points in preparation for adding other features to the projects or packages. These sample files allow you to build on what you've learned rather than spend time setting up the prerequisites for an exercise. The exercises for each chapter are separate and may be used independently.

System Requirements

To install Integration Services and to use the samples provided on the companion CD, your computer configuration will need to meet the following requirements:

- Microsoft Windows 2000, Windows XP Professional, or Windows Server 2003 with the latest service pack applied.

- Microsoft SQL Server 2005, Developer or Enterprise Edition, with any available service packs applied and using Windows or Mixed Mode authentication. Refer to "Hardware and Software Requirements for Installing SQL Server 2005," listed at *http://msdn2.microsoft.com/en-us/library/ms143506.aspx* to determine which edition is compatible with your operating system.

The step-by-step exercises in this book and the accompanying practice files were tested using Windows XP Professional, Service Pack 2, and Microsoft SQL Server 2005 Developer and Enterprise Editions with Service Pack 1. If you are using another version of the operating system or a different edition of either application, you might notice some slight differences.

Installing and Using the Sample Files

The sample solution and database files require approximately 300 MB of disk space on your computer. To install and prepare the sample files for use with the exercises in this book, follow these steps:

1. Insert the companion CD into your CD-ROM drive.

> **Note**   If the presence of the CD-ROM is automatically detected and a Start window is displayed, you can skip to step 3.

2. Click the Start button, click Run, and then type **D:\startcd** in the Open box, replacing the drive letter with the correct letter for your CD-ROM drive if necessary.

3. Click Install Sample Files to launch the Setup program, and then follow the directions on the screen.

The sample files will be copied from the CD-ROM to your local hard drive. The default installation folder is C:\Documents and Settings\<username>\My Documents \Microsoft Press\is2005sbs, where <username> is the logon name you use to operate your computer. You can change this installation folder to a different location and reference the new location when working through the exercises. For each chapter that uses sample files, you will find a corresponding folder in the is2005sbs folder. You'll be instructed where to find the appropriate sample files when an exercise requires the use of an existing file.

> **Tip**   In the My Documents\Microsoft Press\is2005sbs\Answers folder, you will find a separate folder for each chapter in which you make changes to the sample files. The files in these folders are sample projects in their completed state. You can refer to these files if you want to preview the results of an exercise after the steps have been completed. Because the project files are modified as you work through the chapter exercises, if you ever wish to begin an exercise over again, you will need to restore a backup of the project folder or manually copy and replace these files from the CD.

4. Remove the CD-ROM from the drive when installation is complete.

5. Use Windows Explorer to open My Documents\Microsoft Press\is2005sbs\Setup \Query and double-click to launch the attach_databases.bat file. This will attach three SQL Server 2005 databases used throughout the book.

   This step attaches the SQL Server databases that are the data sources used in packages you will create and use throughout this book.

> **Note**   The attach_databases.bat script will work only if these databases are not previously attached, SQL Server 2005 is running as a local default instance, and the user account you're logged in with has administrative rights on your database server. The student files must also be installed to the default My Documents path in order for this script to run correctly. If any of these conditions don't apply to your environment, you should use SQL Server Management Studio to manually attach all three databases located in the \Setup\Database folder.

You're now ready to get started!

Conventions and Features in This Book

To use your time effectively, be sure that you understand the stylistic conventions that are used throughout this book. The following list explains these conventions:

- Hands-on exercises for you to follow are presented as lists of numbered steps (1, 2, and so on).

- Text that you are to type appears in bold type.

- Properties that you need to set in Visual Studio are sometimes displayed in a table as you work through steps.

- Pressing two keys at the same time is indicated by a plus sign between the two key names, such as Alt + Tab when you need to hold down the Alt key while pressing the Tab key.

- A note that is labeled NOTE gives you more information about a specific topic.

- A note that is labeled IMPORTANT points out information that can help you avoid a problem.

- A note that is labeled TIP conveys advice that you might find useful when using Integration Services.

Part I
Getting Started with Integration Services

In this part:

Chapter 1
Introduction to SQL Server Integration Services

After completing this chapter, you will be able to:

- Understand the purpose of SSIS with data integration applications.
- Understand SSIS objects used to create SSIS applications.
- Understand SSIS performance processing architecture.
- Understand SSIS development, administration, and run-time components.

Microsoft SQL Server 2005 Integration Services (SSIS) is the toolset used to help you implement data integration process applications among your business application system's files and databases. SSIS is much more than a simple extract, transform, and load (ETL) process. SSIS enables database administrators and application developers to design, implement, and manage complex, high-performance ETL applications. Using SSIS, you can select data from one or more sources and standardize, join, merge, cleanse, augment, derive, calculate, and perform just about any other function and operation required for your data integration applications. SSIS also provides procedures to automate many of the administrative functions for SQL Server databases, tables, On-Line Analytical Processing (OLAP) Cubes, and many other functions for components of SQL Server 2005.

The ETL phase of data warehousing, data migration, application integration, and business intelligence projects are commonly from 60 percent to as much as 80 percent of the work effort. Effective deployment of technology such as SQL Server 2005 Integration Services can significantly reduce the time, effort, and cost for this phase. This book is designed to show you how to use the features of SSIS and how best to implement these SSIS features and capabilities with data integration projects for your own application systems environments. Through a series of step-by-step demonstrations and exercises, you will work with common, practical, real-world examples to build SSIS applications. These exercises will show how to work with relational and non-relational data sources, manage referential integrity, handle slowly changing dimensions and other data warehousing and business intelligence challenges, and implement complex transformations. You will also learn how to use the debugging and error-handling features in SSIS to detect, troubleshoot, and recover from errors that might occur during data integration process execution. This book will also show you how to manage SSIS applications as well as provide you with best practices and disciplines for building and maintaining SSIS applications within your business application systems environments.

Common SSIS Applications

One common use for SSIS is to move data from one data source to another. The reasons for moving data are too numerous to count. Some common business reasons for using SSIS include migrating business data from one application to another, extracting data for distribution to external entities, integrating data from external entities, creating sample test data sources for development environments, and extracting and loading data into business intelligence (BI) application systems.

SSIS works extremely well in SQL Server environments, but it can also be used with many non–SQL Server database file types and many of the other database management systems deployed within your Information Technology (IT) environment. SSIS has the ability to read data from other Microsoft products, such as Microsoft Office Excel spreadsheets, as well as text, Extensible Markup Language (XML), and other flat-file types.

One common IT demand in the past few decades has been the need to provide business information to a wider audience within an organization. *Business intelligence* is a relatively new term, but it is certainly not a new concept. The idea is simply to use information already available in your company to help decision makers across the company make decisions better and faster. BI systems can be custom developed or deployed through a variety of packaged reporting and analytic tools. The common component among the various BI systems is the underlying data that drives the information and analysis.

When you need to provide fast-response BI applications for many purposes throughout a large organization, the data that drives such systems most often comes from multiple sources. SSIS provides you with the ability to design and execute data integration operations as simple as moving data between application databases or as complex as consolidating large volumes of data from multiple data sources in different formats, while at the same time applying rules to standardize, modify, and cleanse data content prior to loading into BI data warehouses designed for reporting and analytical applications. You will learn more about data warehouse application characteristics and the role of SSIS within BI and data warehouse applications in Chapter 12, "Data Warehouse Concepts," and Chapter 13, "Populating Data Warehouse Structures," later in this book.

Even if you're not responsible for creating and maintaining a data warehouse, a reporting operational data store, OLAP cubes, or other BI applications, you'll find the features in SSIS quite useful for routine database administrative tasks and many other activities in which you need to move, transform, and load data in any form.

SSIS Objects and Process Control Components

Before you begin learning how to create SSIS applications, it is important to familiarize yourself first with the SSIS process control components and the objects used to create SSIS applications. The first object to note within SSIS is the *package*.

An SSIS package is the highest-level object within an SSIS application. A package is a discrete unit of work that you define for ETL operations or SQL Server Services administration operations or both. It is a collection of SSIS process control components and their objects that define the operations, process dependencies, and sequence flow of activities and operations required for a data integration application. Package objects include *containers, tasks, precedence constraints, variables, data sources, data destinations, SQL Server administration functions*, and *custom tasks* that you can create to address unique requirements for your applications. Package objects are applied to package process control components that include the *control flow, data flow*, and *event handler*.

To control the sequence of activities and operations within a package, you apply the precedence constraint object. Precedence constraints are defined between your package objects and are used to specify the order sequence of operations processing and to control processing branching among optional process flows, dependent data values, and conditions or error conditions.

Another useful object of a package is the container. A container is the package object used to group other objects and other containers. Common uses of containers are for performing iterative processing such as looping through a dataset or processing a set of data files within a directory. Although the container object is within a package, you can consider the SSIS package itself as a special high-level container.

SSIS objects also include a comprehensive set of transformation tasks that are important for data integration and BI solutions. These tasks are designed for merging or aggregating data and for converting and transforming data formats and types. Some new tasks have been provided for handling specialized BI operations such as managing slowly changing dimension data. You can also extend SSIS with your own custom tasks and transformations to handle unique requirements within your business application systems environment.

Perhaps best of all, you will find that with all the SSIS objects available to you for package creation, you can create robust, high-performance ETL and data integration applications with no programming code required. By simply dragging and dropping containers, sources, destinations, transformations, and other objects, the SSIS designer automatically creates all the package executable code for you. Throughout the next several chapters, you will learn more about package objects and control components and practice with many of the objects available to design and develop SSIS packages.

SSIS Process Control

A significant advancement to SSIS is the package architecture design for its process control management. You've already learned that the SSIS process control architecture includes the control flow, data flow, and event handler components. Each of these process control components includes common and unique sets of objects for you to use when designing and creating your packages.

SSIS Control Flow

SSIS package objects (containers, data flow tasks, administration tasks, precedence constraints, and variables) are elements of the control flow component of the process control architecture. The control flow is the highest-level control process. It allows you to orchestrate and manage the run-time process activities of data flow and other processes within a package. In fact, you can design a control flow by using an Execute Package task to manage the sequence of processing for a set of existing packages in a Master Package concept. This capability allows you to combine individual packages into a highly manageable workflow process. Use precedence constraints to set the process rules and to specify sequence within the control flow. An SSIS package consists of a control flow and one or more objects. Data flow and event handler process control components are optional.

SSIS Data Flow

When you want to extract, transform, and load data within a package, you add an SSIS data flow task to the package control flow. Each data flow task creates its own data flow process control component for processing at run time. You configure each data flow to manage data sources, data destinations, and optional data transformations for any kind of data manipulation your packages might require. You can have as many data flow components within a package as you need to handle all the kinds of data sources and destinations you might have.

The SSIS data flow component provides a comprehensive set of pre-defined data sources and destination objects to enable you to design and develop packages easily for most of the databases and data source files you might have within your IT environment. You can add custom data sources if you need them. Data destinations allow you to deliver data from a data flow process in a variety of formats. An SSIS package can even provide data directly to an application by storing it in an ASP.NET *DataReader* destination object. Using this destination-type object, you don't have to place the data in a persistent data store, and you can design application integrations, enabling near real-time data delivery.

A set of data transformation task objects is provided within SSIS data flow. These transformation tasks have been designed to meet most, if not all, of the kinds of data conversion, manipulation, standardization, merging, splitting, fuzzy matching, and other types of transformations without having to write complicated programming code. You will learn about many of these transformation tasks, data sources, and destination objects later, in Part II of this book, "Designing Packages."

SSIS Data Pipeline

The SSIS data flow process control component and its tasks are processed by the *data flow engine* within SSIS. A key feature of the SSIS data flow engine is the *data pipeline*, shown in Figure 1-1, which uses memory buffers to improve processing performance. The data pipeline enables parallel data processing options and reduces or eliminates multiple passes of reading and writing of the data during package execution and processing. This level of efficiency means you can process significantly more data in shorter periods of time than is possible if you rely simply on stored procedures for your ETL processes.

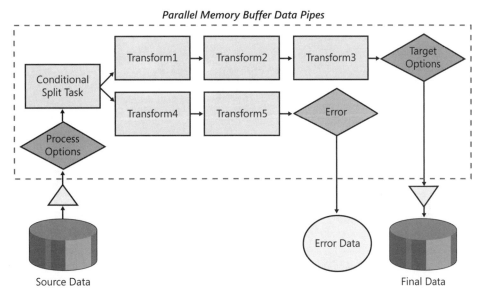

Figure 1-1   The SSIS data flow data pipeline

Maximum data processing performance for SSIS packages is achieved because the data pipeline uses buffers to manipulate data in memory. Source data, whether it's relational, structured as XML data, or stored in flat files like spreadsheets or comma-delimited text files, is converted into table-like structures containing columns and rows and loaded directly into memory buffers without the need of staging the data first in temporary tables. Transformations within a data flow operate on the in-memory buffered data as well as on sorting, merging, modifying, and enhancing the data before sending it to the next transformation or on to its final destination. By avoiding the overhead of re-reading from and writing to disk, the processes required to move and manipulate data can operate at optimal speed.

SSIS Event Handler

The *event handler* process control, unlike the data flow process control, is not managed by the control flow. When you want to control processing at specific occurrences of events during package execution, you use the SSIS event handler process control component. An event handler runs in response to an event raised by the package or by a task or container within the package. Typically, event handlers are created in a package to perform special processing as a result of data anomalies, to trigger other programs, or to launch other packages based upon the event state within the running package. For example, you can create an event handler to send an e-mail alert notification in the event of a task or package for either a success or a failure or simply for a completion state.

You will learn more about SSIS package architecture and its objects and process control components later, in Part II of this book.

SSIS Components

So far, you've learned about SSIS objects and process control architecture. Now you will learn about the SSIS components that you use to design, test, deploy, manage, schedule, and execute SSIS packages. Some of the SSIS components reside on the SSIS server, whereas other components reside on your desktop workstation. A sample configuration scenario is shown in Figure 1-2.

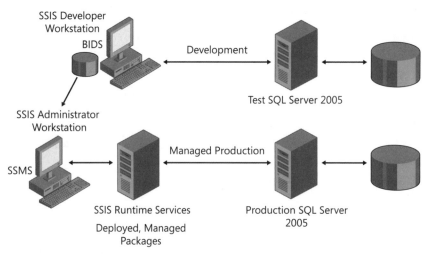

Figure 1-2   Sample SSIS components configuration scenario

SSIS Development Studio

The Business Intelligence Development Studio (BIDS) is the desktop workstation component you use to design, develop, and test SSIS packages. BIDS provides you with a totally graphical-oriented development environment, allowing you to copy, maintain, and create new packages by using a menu and toolbox drag-and-drop method for development. BIDS is a comprehensive development platform that supports collaboration with source code management and version control; provides debugging tools such as breakpoints, variable watches, and data viewers; and includes the *SQL* Server Import and Export Wizard to jump-start package development.

Within BIDS, the SQL Server Import and Export Wizard allows you to generate SSIS packages to copy data from one location to another quickly and easily. The Import and Export Wizard guides you through a series of configuration editor pages that allow you to select the source data, select your target destination, and map source to target data elements. You might find this wizard helpful for creating a starting point for a package. Once a package is generated by the wizard, you can then further enhance the package by using BIDS. You will learn how to use BIDS in Chapter 2, "Building Your First Package."

SSIS Runtime Services

SSIS Runtime Services manages storage of packages in .dtsx (SSIS package system file format) files or in the MSDB database and manages and monitors their execution. SSIS Runtime Services saves your package layout, applies configurations, executes packages, manages data source and destination connection strings and security, and supports logging for tracking and debugging. SSIS Runtime Services executables include the package and all its containers, tasks, custom tasks, and event handlers.

After you design, develop, and complete your testing of SSIS packages from your desktop BIDS, you will want to deploy and implement the packages for scheduled or on-demand processing to the SSIS Runtime Services server. In some companies, the deployment of finished packages is oftentimes performed by a production administrator or other authorized group. At other times, packages can be deployed by the developer. Either way, you can use the graphical interface or a command-line utility to configure and complete the package deployment.

SSIS Package Deployment

The SQL Server Management Studio (SSMS) is a desktop workstation component for the deployment and management of packages into production environments. SSMS connects directly to SSIS Runtime Services and provides access to the Execute Package utility, is used to import and export packages to and from available storage modes (MSDB database or SSIS Package Store), and allows you to view and monitor running packages.

There are also two command-line utilities that you can use to manage, deploy, and execute SSIS packages. Use Dtexec.exe to run a package at the command prompt. An alternative to SSMS, Dtutil.exe, provides package management functionality at the command prompt to copy, move, or delete packages or to confirm that a package exists. You will learn all about the roles of these services and other SSIS application deployment procedures later, in Part III of this book, "Managing Packages."

Finally, a more advanced feature is the Integration Services Object Model that includes application programming interfaces (APIs) for customizing run-time and data flow operations and automating package maintenance and execution by loading, modifying, or executing new or existing packages programmatically from within your business applications.

SQL Server 2000 DTS Migration

SSIS is the next generation of the former Microsoft Data Transformation Services (DTS) that is included within the previous versions of SQL Server. SSIS has been designed with a new, high-performance, and advanced underlying architecture. The good news is that if you already have an inventory of SQL Server Data Transformation Services (DTS) packages, all of these packages will continue to run in SSIS environments without any changes. In addition, SSIS provides the *Package Migration Wizard* that you can use to convert SQL Server 2000 DTS packages to SSIS packages. Because of some of the significant improvements, such as the SSIS control flow and data pipeline architectures, as well as many of the new and enhanced tasks and transformations, DTS package conversion might not always be complete and could require some final manual enhancements. You might also want to redesign some of your existing DTS packages to take advantage of the performance improvements and additional task functionality that is now available within SSIS.

Chapter 1 Quick Reference

This term	Means this
SSIS package	A discrete executable unit of work composed of a collection of control flow and other objects, including data sources, transformations, process sequence, and rules, error and event handling, and data destinations.
Containers	Package objects that provide structure to packages and special services to tasks. Containers are used to support repeating control flows in packages and to group tasks. Containers can include other containers in addition to tasks.
Tasks	Package elements that define activities and processes, including data sources, destinations, transformations, and others.
Precedence constraints	Constraints that link executables, containers, and tasks within the package control flow and specify conditions that determine the sequence and conditions for determining whether executables run.
Variables	Storage for values that an SSIS package and its containers, tasks, and event handlers can use at run time. The scripts in the Script task and the Script component can also use variables.
Control flow	An SSIS package process control component used to control flow elements: the containers that provide structure in packages and services to tasks, tasks that provide functionality in packages, and precedence constraints that connect containers and tasks.
Data flow	An SSIS package data process control component defined from within package control flow that loads data from sources, transforms and routes it through transformations, and saves it to destinations.
Event handler	An SSIS package process control component used to define the process activities to be performed at the time of a specific event state for the package or for any of its tasks or containers.

This term	Means this
Data Pipeline	The memory-based, multithreaded, buffered transformation process flow of data through an SSIS data flow task during package execution.
BIDS	SQL Server Business Intelligence Development Studio. Provides the Integration Services project in which you create packages, their data sources, and data source views.
SSMS	SQL Server Management Studio. Provides the Integration Services service that you use to manage packages and monitor running packages.

Chapter 2

Building Your First Package

After completing this chapter, you will be able to:

- Explore a SQL Server Integration Services project in SQL Server Business Intelligence Development Studio.
- Use the SSIS Import and Export Wizard to create a new Integration Services package.
- Review package elements created by the SSIS Import and Export Wizard.
- Execute a package and view the results.

In this chapter, you'll take a first look at the design environment used to create and manage Microsoft SQL Server Integration Services (SSIS) packages. The tools are significantly different than the design environment for SQL Server 2000 Data Transformation Services, with many improvements.

You will learn to use SQL Server 2005 Business Intelligence Development Studio (BIDS) to create and manage solutions, projects, and SSIS packages. Beginning with using the Import and Export Wizard to create an SSIS package, you will then add it to a BIDS SSIS project. You will look at the objects and elements within the package, which you will learn about in greater detail in Chapter 3, "Extracting and Loading Data."

You'll also learn about several options for executing a package in the design and production environments. Finally, you will view the results of your package execution, which will export data from tables in one database to tables in a new database.

Exploring Business Intelligence Development Studio

SQL Server 2005 Business Intelligence Development Studio is a simplified edition of Microsoft Visual Studio 2005 that is installed with the SQL Server Client Tools. You may install BIDS and the other SQL Server 2005 client tools on any desktop computers with connectivity to your licensed SQL server. No other licensing is required to use this product. BIDS uses the same base application as Visual Studio, but the templates installed with BIDS are used specifically for designing business intelligence (BI) solutions. These templates include Analysis Services, Integration Services, and Reporting Services projects.

The BIDS interface is somewhat similar to SQL Server 2005 Server Management Studio, with docking and autohiding utility windows, but these are two different applications. SQL Server Management Studio (SSMS), with its integrated query windows and object browser, is designed for managing SQL Server and its related services. BIDS is designed to help you manage and develop BI projects and solutions.

You will use the BIDS environment for creating new projects and solutions. Later, you will build on this skill by adding components to existing projects and solutions. A solution is simply a container for managing related projects and really has no other specific functionality. A project consists of several files that define objects such as data connections and SSIS packages.

Different project types are created in BIDS, using specialized templates and designer components that integrate with the BIDS/Visual Studio shell, called the Integrated Development Environment (IDE). The project designers and templates installed with BIDS are used to create SQL Server 2005 Analysis Services, Integration Services, and Reporting Services projects.

Project files should be stored in your local file system or on a network share owned and managed by a specific user. These project files can be shared among multiple project team members by using source and version control software such as Microsoft Visual SourceSafe (VSS) or Visual Studio 2005 Team Foundation Server. These tools allow project files to be locked, checked in, checked out, and explicitly shared by team members from within the BIDS or Visual Studio environment. Third-party source code management software can also be used to perform the same tasks, but it might not integrate as easily into the BIDS environment.

SSIS packages and other object definition files are stored in a standard XML format. BIDS enables you to view and edit the raw XML for an object or to use a graphical designer, with related menus, toolbars, and dialog boxes. In general, it's best to use the graphical designer to make modifications. On occasion, it might be convenient to use a simple Find and Replace command to make changes to the XML file. Just make sure that you always make a backup copy of any file before making changes in this way.

Installing any edition of Visual Studio 2005 will simply add additional templates and designers to the development environment. These project templates will be available by using both the Business Intelligence Development Studio shortcut on the SQL Server program group and the Visual Studio program group. Visual Studio and BIDS use a standard set of menus, toolbars, and utility windows, regardless of the project type. Many of these options are customized and enhanced, depending on the specific project type.

The development environment, illustrated in Figure 2-1, consists of a designer window in the center with utility windows on either side. These windows, such as the Server Explorer, Toolbox, Solution Explorer, and Properties panes, can be set to dock or autohide. When a window is hidden, an icon is displayed on the side bar. When you pass the mouse pointer over this icon, the hidden window will slide over the design surface.

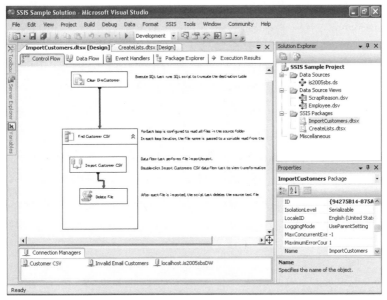

Figure 2-1   The SSIS development environment

Standard and specialized toolbars are available to gain access to many design, development, debugging, and deployment features. These options vary, depending on the project type and the specific object designer you have open. Later, you'll learn to use variables, debugging tools, and deployment configuration settings.

Solution Explorer

The Solution Explorer pane, shown in Figure 2-2, is located in the upper-right area by default. This is used to manage all of the objects and files related to a project.

Figure 2-2   Solution Explorer enables you to manage all of the objects and files in a project

The Properties pane shows a list of all properties for the selected object. Properties can be grouped categorically or sorted alphabetically. Most properties can be set and modified by using this pane. Additionally, many objects have a custom properties interface, accessible by double-clicking the object, that enables you to manage properties by using a dialog box more suited for the object type. The Properties pane contains an object selection drop-down list at the top of the pane, which allows easy selection of all objects, as shown in Figure 2-3.

Figure 2-3   The Properties pane describes the state of an item in BIDS, such as the status of all the properties for a selected object

Other utility panes and windows include SSIS package variables, debugging tools, and the errors window. You will learn to use these in later chapters, including Chapter 7, "Debugging Packages," and Chapter 9, "Detecting and Handling Processing Errors."

When you open BIDS, the Start Page is displayed. This contains a list of the most recently opened projects, getting-started links for new BI developers, and current information about WebCasts, articles, and MSDN educational events. This is a Web page that will be updated if you have Internet connectivity on your development computer.

Docking Utility Windows

The utility windows can be customized to move, hide, show, and dock in the BIDS shell environment. The standard utility windows can be docked to the edges of the BIDS shell window, and a window can be moved to various landing zones in the development environment. Use the mouse to drag a window to view the docking zones before you release it. Once docked, each window can be set to stay or to autohide. In this mode, the window will slide out of the way until you hover the mouse pointer over a corresponding icon. This behavior is controlled by using the pushpin icon in the utility window header bar. Windows can be grouped together to form tab groups. The best way to become acquainted with all of these options is to take some time to work in the development environment and experiment with these features.

Solution Explorer is the master view to a solution and project. When an item is selected in Solution Explorer or selected in a designer window, the properties for that item are available in the Properties pane. You can also use the object drop-down list at the top of the Properties pane to select a specific object or item. When a package is opened in the designer, the Toolbox, displayed on the left side of the BIDS application window, shows available components that can be dropped onto the designer surface.

Exploring an SSIS Project in BIDS

This demonstration introduces you to the SQL Server Business Intelligence Development Studio. You will open an existing package and review key components of the BIDS integrated development environment.

Open SSIS Sample Solution

1. Open Windows Explorer and navigate to the C:\Documents and Settings\<username>\My Documents\Microsoft Press\is2005sbs\Chap02 folder.

2. Double-click the SSIS Sample Solution.sln file. This opens the project in BIDS.

3. Explore the project in Solution Explorer, noting that the Solution Explorer pane is displayed on the right side of the BIDS application window.

4. If only the Solution Explorer icon is visible, the window is probably hidden. In this case, hover the mouse over the icon to show the Solution Explorer pane, and then click the thumbtack icon to pin the window down.

> **Note**   The thumbtack icon in the title bar of the Solution Explorer pane indicates the autohide state of the window. Click the icon to toggle between the autohiding and pinned states. In the pinned position, the thumbtack is pointing down. This indicates that the window will not hide when the mouse pointer is moved away. When the thumbtack points to the side, the window will autohide after the mouse pointer is moved away from it.

5. In Solution Explorer, note the following project elements and their respective object types:

Project Element	Object Type
is2005SbS	Data source
Employee	Data source view
ScrapReason	Data source view
ImportCustomers	Package
CreateLists	Package

View the *ScrapReason* data source view in the Data Source view designer

1. Double-click the *ScrapReason* data source view in Solution Explorer to open the data source view designer. Note that the diagram window contains tables with linked relationships and a named query called *ScrappedProducts*.

   This appears as a virtual table. You can easily navigate to the diagram by left-clicking the mouse over the compass points arrow in the lower-right corner of the designer. Holding the mouse button down allows you to reposition the diagram view in a small thumbnail diagram window. Your screen looks like this:

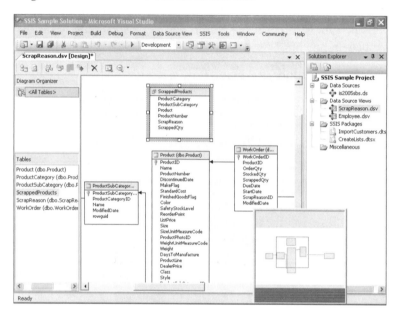

2. Right-click the named query, ScrappedProducts, and choose Edit Named Query to view the Transact-SQL query joining five tables in the Transact-SQL Graphical Query Designer.

   This window is similar to those used in other Microsoft query products such as Microsoft Office Access and Reporting Services.

3. When completed, close the Edit Named Query editor by clicking the Cancel button.

4. Right-click the named query and choose Explore Data to view the results of this query in a separate designer tab. Close this tab (titled Explore ScrappedProducts Table) by clicking the X button on the right of the designer title bar when completed.

   Often, a data source view will contain many tables and queries and can contain tables from multiple data sources.

5. To navigate to tables that are not currently in view, left-click and hold over the compass points icon in the lower-right intersection of the vertical and horizontal scroll bars. A thumbnail view of the diagram appears. Move the pointer over this viewer to navigate the diagram window. Close the data source view designer window when completed.

View the CreateLists package in the package designer

1. Double-click the CreateLists package in Solution Explorer to open the designer. This opens the Control Flow tab showing two data flow tasks with a precedence constraint from the Employee List task to the Scrapped Products task.

2. Double-click the green line to view the precedence constraint properties. The package designer portion of your screen looks like this:

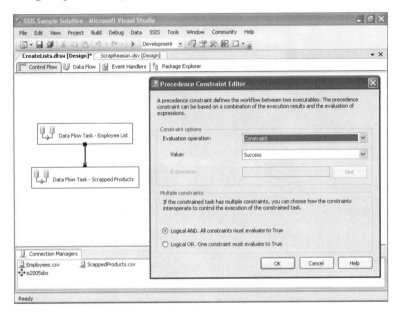

   Note that the Employee List task execution must complete with success before the Scrapped Products task will execute.

3. Click the Cancel button to close the Precedence Constraint Editor when completed.

Open the Data Flow Task – Employee List

A component can be edited by double-clicking its designer shape when it doesn't have focus or clicked on its edge when it does have focus.

1. Open the first task, labeled Data Flow Task – Employee List. This moves to the Data Flow tab and shows all of the components within this task.

Note that you can switch between multiple data flow tasks by using the drop-down list in the Data Flow tab page. The Employee List data flow task consists of the following components:

Component	Component Type
Employee Query	OLE DB data source
FullName	Derived column transformation
Department Shift Employee	Sort transformation
Employees CSV	Flat file destination

Like the control flow components, each element is connected with a green line. On the Data Flow tab, this is a data flow path, which indicates the flow of data as it is read from sources, transformed, and then written to destinations. Your screen looks like this:

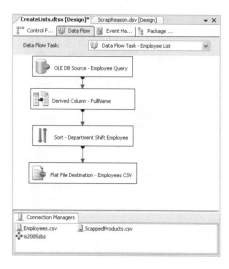

Explore the connection managers

Located at the bottom of the designer window is the Connection Managers pane. A connection manager stores shared data source and destination connection information at the package level. A connection manager can also be derived from a project-level data source.

1. Open each of the connection managers and view the connection properties. In turn, double-click each of the icons in the Connection Managers pane to open the corresponding editor, and then close the editor by clicking the Cancel button.

   The is2005sbs connection manager derives its connection properties from the is2005sbs.ds data source for the project. The two flat file connection managers refer to specific text files located at C:\Documents and Settings\<username>\My Documents\Microsoft Press\is2005sbs\Chap02\Data.

2. In the editor dialog box for the Employees connection manager, view properties in the General properties group. Note the format, header, and delimiter settings used to read the file.

3. The list box on the left side of the connection manager dialog box contains a list of property group icons. Click an item on this list to change the property group page.

    a. View the data and columns read from the text files in the Columns group of properties. Your screen looks like this:

    b. View the properties for each data flow component.

Open the OLE DB Source – Employee Query task

1. Open the OLE DB Source editor for the Employee Query data source, the first component in the data flow designer.

    Note that this source uses the is2005sbs connection manager. This data source retrieves results by using a SQL command with the following Transact-SQL statement:

```
SELECT
  Shift.Name AS Shift
, Department.Name AS Department
, Employee.Title
, Employee.LastName
, Employee.FirstName
FROM Shift
INNER JOIN Employee ON Shift.ShiftID = Employee.ShiftID
INNER JOIN Department ON Employee.DepartmentID = Department.DepartmentID
```

2. Use the Columns page to view the data fields returned by this query.

3. On the Connection Manager page, click the Preview button to view the query results.

4. Close the editor dialog box when completed.

Open the Derived Column – FullName task

1. Double-click the FullName derived column transformation.

   This allows you to define new columns added to the data flow, usually based on existing column values.

   Note that the Employee column is derived from the expression FirstName + " " + LastName, which concatenates the first and last column values separated by a space.

2. Close this editor by clicking the Cancel button.

Open the Sort – Department Shift Employee task

1. Double-click the Department Shift Employee sort transformation to open the editor. This sorts the data flow on specified column values. Each column is listed with a sort order and sort type, either ascending or descending.

   Note that the Title column and the Employee derived column are set to pass through–rather than participate in–the sorting.

2. Close this editor by clicking the Cancel button.

Open the Flat File Destination – Employees CSV task

1. Open the Employees CSV flat file destination.

   This is used to create or overwrite a text file named Employees.csv.

2. Click the Mappings group to see how the columns from the data flow correspond to the columns defined for the destination file.

   Note that only the Department, Shift, and Employee columns are written to the file. Your screen looks like this:

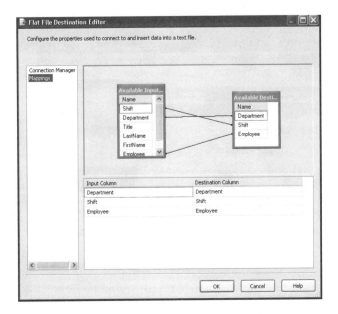

3. Close the Flat File Destination Editor.

View the final output

1. On the Connection Manager page, click the Preview button to view the final output. Close this editor for the Employees CSV flat file destination when completed.

2. Review components of the Scrapped Products data flow task.

3. Using the same pattern as before, use the editors to view properties for each of the transformations in the Scrapped Products data flow task. Starting on the Control Flow tab, edit the Scrapped Products task.

    Note that the connection manager property for the ScrappedProducts data source refers to the data source view ScrapReason, using the reference is2005sbs\ScrapReason.

    By selecting the ScrappedProducts named query in the data source view in Solution Explorer, the original Transact-SQL query is reused.

4. View the properties for the Sum ScrappedQty aggregate transformation.

   This groups values on the ProductCategory, ProductSubCategory, Product, Product-Number, and ScrapReason column values and then applies the Sum aggregation on all detail rows for each grouping.

5. Close any open editor dialog boxes by clicking the Cancel button.

Execute the CreateLists package

The package is complete. All data sources and destinations have been verified, and all tasks and transformations are set and configured. The next step is to execute the package to load and transform the data.

1. In Solution Explorer, right-click the CreateLists package and choose Execute Package. This runs the package in Debug mode, enabling several useful debugging features.

   As the packages execute, each task, connection, and transformation will be displayed in yellow while it executes and then green when completed. When all components are green, the package execution has completed. Your screen looks like this:

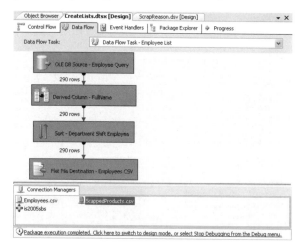

   Because it is running in Debug mode, execution is paused at the end of the operation and must be stopped before returning to the design environment.

2. Terminate execution debugging by clicking Stop Debugging on the Debug menu.

3. Review the destination text files.

View Employees, ScrappedProducts, and customer records files in the data folder

1. In Windows Explorer, view the contents of the C:\Documents and Settings\<user-name>\My Documents\Microsoft Press\is2005sbs\Chap02\Data folder.

The Employees.csv and ScrappedProducts.csv files were created and populated by this package.

2. Use Notepad to view the contents of each file. (You can right-click a file, choose Open With, and then select Notepad.)

3. While viewing the contents of this folder, view the contents of the four files containing customer records. Each contains an alphabetic range of customer names and related demographic information.

Review the ImportCustomers package

1. In SSIS, double-click ImportCustomers in Solution Explorer to open it in the package designer.

   This package contains a Foreach Loop task that can be used to iterate through the members of a variety of different collection types. It is configured to find all comma separated value (CSV) files with names beginning with the word *Customer* in the data folder. For each file, the data flow script tasks (visible in the control flow designer) are executed. You will learn about the mechanics of this process later. For now, just view the related data flow components and their properties.

   This package contains text annotations that explain some of the logic and might be helpful to understand better how the components interact.

2. View the data flow task components of the Data Flow tab.

   Note that the data flow path line has a viewer icon that indicates that it has been configured with a data viewer. This is a debugging tool that effectively works as a breakpoint on each iteration through the file collection loop and displays the records present at that stage in the data flow.

Excute the ImportCustomers package

1. In Solution Explorer, right-click the ImportCustomers package and choose Execute Package.

   The components will display yellow and then green as each task and transformation is completed.

   Partway through the first loop iteration, a grid window will appear with the result from the first customer source file.

2. Resize this window if necessary to view the LastName column.

> **Note**   The data view window has a peculiarity where at times it can't be resized using the lower-right corner. To resize the window if this behavior occurs, resize it vertically and then horizontally.

Your screen looks like this:

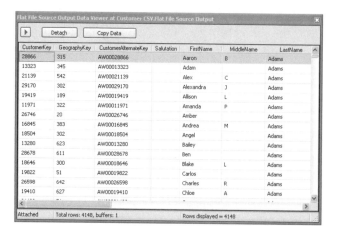

3. Click the green play button to step through the process and view the results of the next loop iteration. Again, note the LastName column values.

4. Repeat this step to display four sets of records.

5. When completed, close the data viewer window, and then click Stop Debugging on the Debug menu.

> **Note**   The script task has deleted each of the source files, so if you would like to repeat this exercise in the future, you can copy these files from the Data_Backup folder to the Data folder.

Using the SSIS Import and Export Wizard

Now let's do something useful with your newfound skills using the BIDS design environment.

The SSIS Import and Export Wizard can be launched from within the SQL Server Management Studio or from a BIDS Integration Services project. The wizard is simple to use when building basic import or export processes but will also allow you to transform data. Depending on which of the two options you choose, either the data source or data destination page will be filled out.

The wizard allows you to save the output to an SSIS package .dtsx file, which can later be added to an SSIS project. You also have the option to execute this package immediately or to save it and execute it later.

Creating Tables in a New Database

In this exercise, you will follow steps to create a new SSIS project and then replace the default package with one generated from the Import and Export Wizard.

You will export product and sales data from the *is2005sbs* database. This is a simplified version of the *Adventure Works Cycles* sample database for SQL Server 2005. It is an operational data store or transactional database system as opposed to a data warehouse or decision support database. The structure of this database is similar to common systems found in many businesses.

You will use the wizard to create a new database called *QuickStartODS* on the local server, and you will import the structure and contents of five tables from the sample database, whose data will be copied to the new database. The wizard can be launched from a database in SQL Server Management Studio or from an SSIS project in BIDS.

Run the wizard in BIDS

1. To run the wizard in BIDS, right-click SSIS Packages in Solution Explorer, and then click SSIS Import and Export Wizard.

Review the *is2005sbs* database by using Management Studio

1. Open SQL Server Management Studio (SSMS):

    a. Click Start, and then click SQL Server Management Studio.

    b. In the Connect to Server dialog box, ensure that the Server Type is Database Engine and the Server Name is localhost, and then click Connect.

2. In Object Explorer, expand the Databases folder.

3. Expand the *is2005sbs* database, and then expand the Tables folder.

    The *is2005sbs* database is a simplified version of the *Adventure Works* sample database provided with SQL Server 2005. It is a transactional or operational database schema rather than a data warehouse schema. You will use this to build your first business intelligence (BI) solution. One of the significant differences between the operational database and the data warehouse database is that there is no Time dimension table in the transaction database.

4. Review the following tables:

    ❑ Customer

    ❑ Product

    ❑ ProductCategory

    ❑ ProductSubcategory

    ❑ SalesOrderDetail

    ❑ SalesOrderHeader

    Later in this exercise, you'll create a working copy of these tables from the *is2005sbs* database.

Create the QuickStart solution to contain the QuickStartIS SSIS project

1. In BIDS, create a new Integration Services project named QuickStartIS by clicking the link to create a project on the BIDS start page (or, from the File menu, click New, and then click Project) and selecting the Integration Services Project template.

2. Change the solution name to **QuickStart**.

3. Browse to C:\Documents and Settings\<username>\My Documents\Microsoft Press\ is2005sbs\Chap02 and select the check box at the bottom of the New Project dialog box to create a directory for the solution.

   A package is automatically created when you start a new Integration Services project. Because you'll use the wizard to create a new package, you don't need the default package.

4. In SSIS, in Solution Explorer, right-click the Package.dtsx file and choose Delete.

   In the following exercise, you'll use the Import and Export Wizard to create a package that imports the listed tables into a new destination database.

Import tables into a new *QuickStartODS* database with a new package

1. Right-click the SSIS Packages folder, and then click SSIS Import and Export Wizard.

2. On the Welcome page, click Next.

3. On the Choose a Data page:

   a. Accept SQL Native Client as the data source.

   b. Accept the default Server Name of (local).

   c. Keep the Use Windows Authentication default authentication.

   d. In the Database drop-down list, change the database to **is2005sbs**.

4. Click Next.

5. Select SQL Server (local) as the destination.

6. Click New, type **QuickStartODS** as the database name, and then click OK to create the new database.

7. Click Next.

   The abbreviation ODS means Operational Data Store. This is an empty database in which to place the copied tables that you'll use later. It will not be a true star schema but a copy of the operational database to use for prototyping.

8. In the Specify Table Copy or Query page, select Copy Data From One Or More Tables Or Views, and then click Next.

9. Select the following tables to copy:

   ❑ [is2005sbs].[dbo].[Product]

   ❑ [is2005sbs].[dbo].[ProductCategory]

   ❑ [is2005sbs].[dbo].[ProductSubcategory]

   ❑ [is2005sbs].[dbo].[SalesOrderDetail]

   ❑ [is2005sbs].[dbo].[SalesOrderHeader]

10. Click Next.

    When you finish the wizard, the package is created but not executed. You can see it added to the SSIS Packages folder.

11. Click Finish, and then click Close to complete the wizard.

12. In Solution Explorer, right-click the new package and choose Rename to change the package name to **QuickStartIS.dtsx**.

    A message box prompts you to synchronize the package file name and the object that it defines. Click Yes to keep these names the same.

> **Note**   Notice the first two tabs: Control Flow and Data Flow. The Control Flow tab handles discrete sequential tasks, with precedence constraints connecting them. The Data Flow tab handles continuous processes that move streams of data from a source to a destination. The second transformation in a complex data flow can often run concurrently with the first. Multiple pipelines can run in parallel within a single data flow task.

Reviewing Package Elements

The SSIS Import and Export Wizard creates a package containing the necessary components to implement an end-to-end data extract, transform, and load (ETL) process. On the surface, this package is very simple because it just moves data from one location to another. Upon closer examination, you'll see that there's a little more to this process.

The QuickStartIS package contains two tasks: one that creates and prepares the destination tables and another task to perform the actual data transformation, called a data flow task. The data flow encapsulates ten different operations, which include reading data from each of the five tables, mapping the columns to the destinations, and then actually writing data to the output tables. In the next exercise, you will review the script used to create the tables and the source and destination data adapters in the data flow task, which are used to perform the data transformation.

Reviewing a Package Created Using the Import and Export Wizard

This exercise reviews the package elements created by the SSIS Import and Export Wizard.

Review the preparation SQL task

1. On the Control Flow tab, double-click the SQL task to display its properties.

2. Click the ellipsis button in the *SQLStatement* property to view the script. Your screen looks like this:

This task contains a script generated by the wizard to build the tables you selected in the wizard.

3. Close the SQL Task Editor.

Review the data flow task

1. Open each data flow task and review each component.

   When you double-click a data flow task, the Data Flow tab is displayed, and you can see the series of five data flows. Each box represents a data flow from a source to a destination.

   Notice that there are multiple transformations or multiple paths. Each of these pipelines can run concurrently. In the designer, you can test the package by running it directly in Debug mode.

2. When completed, close any open dialog boxes by clicking the Cancel button.

Testing a Package

With the data flow task completed, you are ready to execute the package in the Package Designer Debug mode.

Executing the Package in the Designer

This exercise shows you how to execute a package in the BIDS environment. There are actually a few different ways to execute or run a package. You will use the right-click menu from Solution Explorer.

Execute the QuickStartIS.dtsx package

1. Right-click the package in Solution Explorer and click Execute Package.

   While the package is executing, switch between the Control Flow and Data Flow tabs to watch the boxes change from yellow to green as the execution progresses. Green boxes represent tasks that have completed; yellow tasks are still in progress. Notice that the tasks run concurrently.

   When a package finishes, you still have to stop debugging to continue.

Stop debugging and close the package designer

1. Click Stop Debugging on the Debug menu or click the Package Execution Completed link at the bottom of the designer window.

2. Close the package designer.

> **Note**   The color coding of tasks in execution mode is a good visual to remind you to stop debugging before you proceed to the next task. If you can't seem to move forward and can still see the colors on the screen, remember to stop debugging.

Review the *QuickStartODS* database tables by using SSMS

1. In SQL Server Management Studio (SSMS), refresh the list of databases to see the new database.

2. Expand the Tables folder and review the tables that have been created.

3. Right-click dbo.ProductCategory and select Open Table to view the contents of the table.

4. Repeat these steps to open the other tables and to verify that records were appropriately imported.

5. Close each of the table window tabs when completed.

Chapter 2 Quick Reference

This term	Means this
Solution	A container for projects in BIDS. It can contain multiple projects, but at a minimum, a solution contains one project.
Project	Contains all of the files and object definitions for a specific type of business intelligence project (such as Integration Services, Analysis Services, or Reporting Services). All of these files are managed in a file system folder and are referenced in the project definition files.
Business Intelligence Development Studio (BIDS)	A special edition of Visual Studio that is installed with the SQL Server 2005 client tools. No special licensing is required, and it may be distributed freely within the organization for BI and database developers connected to a database server.
SSIS package	Consists of connection managers, control flow tasks, containers, data sources, transformations, and data destinations. These components are used in concert to perform data extract, transform, and load (ETL) operations.
SSIS Import and Export Wizard	Used to create a package from SQL Server Management Studio (SSMS) or from an SSIS project in BIDS. A package and all of its components can also be created manually in an SSIS project within the BIDS environment.
Visual SourceSafe	A version control system similar to Microsoft Team Foundation that is used to manage files and collaborate with other developers. These applications maintain a central copy of the files and allow files to be checked out, checked in, and locked by different developers. A project and all related files should be managed within the developer's personal hard disk or file system. A single project should never be shared between different developers. These files should be backed up regularly regardless of whether they are to be shared with others.
Execute package	In BIDS, a package that can be executed in Debug mode by using the Debug menu or toolbar or from Solution Explorer. In production, the package can be executed from the command line or from a Microsoft Windows utility, or it can be scheduled for automated execution by using the SQL Server Agent.

Part II
Designing Packages

Chapter 3
Extracting and Loading Data

After completing this chapter, you will be able to:

- Understand and create connection managers.

- Extract and load data from different data sources to different destinations.

- Use data sources and data source views to extend the functionality of a regular connection manager.

In Chapter 2, "Building Your First Package," you learned about how to build your first package, and you explored SQL Server Business Intelligence Development Studio (BIDS) and its basic components. In this chapter, you'll learn how to set up a new Microsoft SQL Server Integration Services (SSIS) project, add a data flow task to extract data from a source, and load the results into a destination. Specifically, you'll learn how to create and configure a connection manager for Microsoft Office Excel, SQL DB, and flat files. You will also learn how to use BIDS data sources and data source views to extend the functionality of a regular connection manager.

Connection Managers

A connection manager is an SSIS object that contains the information required to create a physical connection to data stores as well as the metadata describing the structure of the data. In the case of a flat file, a connection manager contains the file path, file name, and metadata identifying rows and columns. A connection manager for a relational data source contains the name of the server, the name of the database, and the credentials for authenticating access to the data. Connection managers are the bridge between package objects and physical data structures. They are used by tasks that require a connection (such as the Execute SQL task), by data adapters that define sources and destinations, and by transformations that perform lookups to a reference table.

Connection Manager Types

A connection manager is a logical representation of a connection. At design time, the properties of a connection manager describe the physical connection that Integration Services creates when the package runs. For example, a connection manager includes the *ConnectionString* property that is set at design time; at run time, a physical connection is created, using the value in the *ConnectionString* property.

Many tasks use connections. For example, an Execute SQL task (that runs SQL statements) requires a connection to a relational database. The sources and destinations in package data flows use connections to extract and load data. Some transformations also require connections to do their work. For example, the Lookup transformation uses a connection to access a reference table to look up and retrieve values. The following is the list of connection managers available in SSIS:

ADO	HTTP	ODBC
ADO.NET	MSMQ	SMOServer
Excel	MSOLAP90	SMTP
File	MultiFile	SQLMobile
FlatFile	MultiFlatFile	WMI
FTP	OLEDB	

This list represents the typical connection managers. However, SSIS gives developers the ability to write source components that can connect to custom data sources and supply data from those sources to other components in a data flow task.

Creating a New Integration Services Project

The process of creating a SQL Server Integration Services project consists of several steps. The first step is to define a name and location for your project and solution. You can also define a new name for the default package that SSIS creates as part of this initial step. The second step in building an SSIS project is to create connection managers for data source and data destinations. You need to know where your data is stored, what the server name that hosts the data is, and which database or file stores the data. Verify that you have all the required credentials to retrieve that data and store the new data in a destination database or file. The third step in creating your new SSIS project is the creation of at least one data flow, for instance, to extract and load data. To create a data flow task to extract and load data, you will need to specify data adapters linked to the source and destination connection managers you define. You can create more than one data flow in a control flow and, indeed, you can connect them in a logical sequence. You will learn more about how to manage a set of data flows in Chapter 5, "Managing Control Flow."

Now you will create a new Integration Services project to which you will add a data flow task. You will create a new package to extract data from a source table and load the data to an Office Excel file. These transformation processes simulate data-delivering routines that you might perform when working in a data warehouse or enterprise environment.

Create a new Integration Services project

1. Start SQL Server Business Intelligence Development Studio. Your screen should look similar to this:

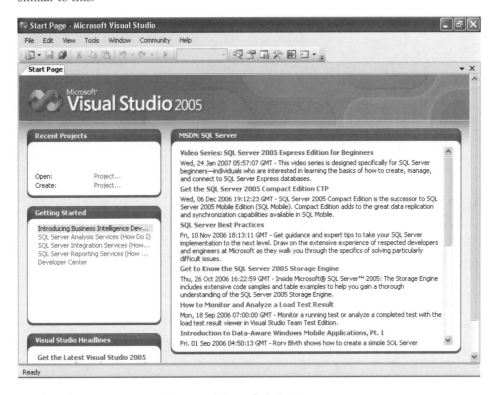

2. On the File menu, point to New, and then click Project.

3. Make sure that the Project Type is set to Business Intelligence Projects, and then click the Integration Services Project template.

4. Type a name for the project: **Chap03**

> **Note**   Notice that the text in the Solution Name box changes automatically to match the project name. You can change the name of the solution, especially when you have a solution with several projects. For now, leave it as Chap03.

5. Change the location for the project to **C:\Documents and Settings\<username> \My Documents\Microsoft Press\is2005sbs\Chap03** and confirm that the Create Directory For Solution check box is selected. The New Project dialog box should look like this:

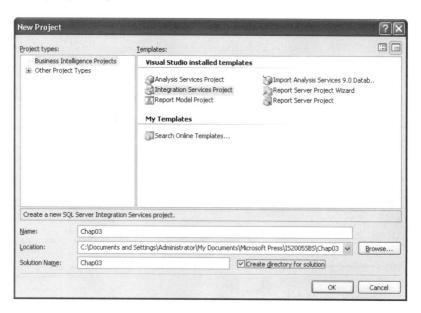

6. Click OK to continue.

7. In Solution Explorer, right-click the package and choose Rename to change the package name to **CopyTable.dtsx**. Click Yes when prompted.

8. Click Yes to rename the package object as well. Now you should see this:

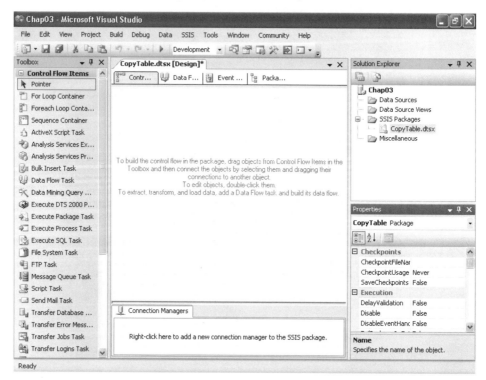

Adding Connection Managers

The second step in building an SSIS project is to create connection managers for data source and data destinations. As described before, connection managers are logical representations of a connection. Connection managers you can add include connections to Oracle, FTP, and HTTP sites; Analysis Services databases; flat files; and more. Each connection manager has its own configuration, depending on the type of connection you want to set.

In the next two procedures, you'll add a connection manager for a SQL Server 2005 database and another connection manager for Office Excel.

Add an OLE DB connection manager for the *is2005sbs* database

1. Right-click anywhere in the Connection Managers pane at the bottom of the Control Flow tab and click New OLE DB Connection.

2. Click New to define a new connection, click the Provider drop-down list to review available providers, and then click Cancel to keep default: Native OLE DB\SQL Native Client.

3. Type **localhost** for the Server Name.

4. Select Use Windows Authentication.

5. Choose is2005sbs as the database.

6. Click the Test Connection button. The following window will appear:

7. Click OK twice.

Add an Office Excel connection manager to the Employee.xls file

1. Create a new folder called **Data** in C:\Documents and Settings\<username>\My Documents\Microsoft Press\is2005sbs\Chap03.

2. Right-click anywhere in the Connection Managers pane at the bottom of the Control Flow tab and click New Connection.

3. In the Add SSIS Connection Manager dialog box, click EXCEL (connection manager for Excel files) and click Add.

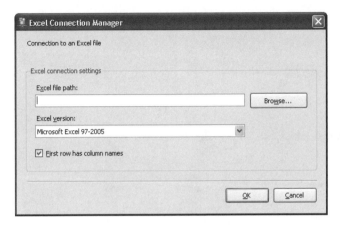

4. Browse to C:\Documents and Settings\<username>\My Documents\Microsoft Press\is2005sbs\Chap03\Data\.

5. Type **Employee** in the File Name box, click Open, and then click OK.

6. Right-click Excel connection manager, select Rename, and rename the connection **Employee**.

Creating a Data Flow

An SSIS package needs at least one component in a control flow. This component could be a data flow task or any component from Control Flow Items or Maintenance Plan Tasks in the Microsoft Visual Studio Toolbox. Basically, you build a control flow by adding tasks or control flow components to the Control Flow tab.

The third step in creating your new SSIS project is the creation of at least one data flow, for instance, to extract and load data. To create a data flow task to extract and load data, you will need to specify data adapters linked to the source and destination connection managers you define. There are different ways to create data flows in a control flow. In this procedure, you'll create a data flow task.

Create a data flow task

1. Click the Data Flow tab.

   Click the message link in the center of the page to add a task.

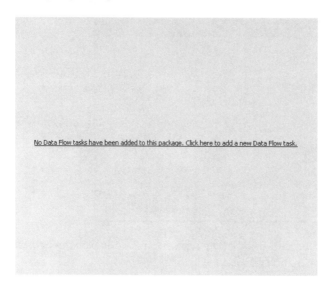

No Data Flow tasks have been added to this package. Click here to add a new Data Flow task.

Tip   If you go to the Data Flow tab right after creating a package, you see a message that no data flow tasks have been added to the package. Clicking the message link adds a new task that you can also access from the Control Flow page.

2. In the Properties pane, change the *Name* property to **Data Flow Task – Copy Employee**.

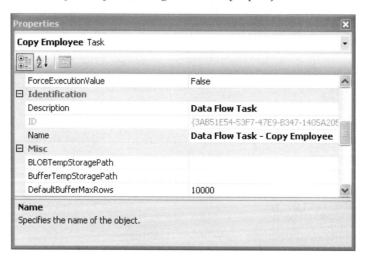

Tip   If the Property panel is not active, press F4 to activate it.

Adding Data Adapters

Now you are ready to add data adapters to your data flow task. The term *data adapter* refers to a set of objects that provide the ability to connect to, and interact with, databases, files, and other resources that provide data storage. Data adapters are used to read, insert, modify, and delete data from these various data storage devices. Within a data flow task, data sources and data destinations are specific implementation types of data adapters.

A data adapter is an object that can be used only in the data flow task and requires a connection manager to be established.

In this procedure, you'll add and map source and destination data adapters.

Add an OLE DB source data adapter

1. Open the Toolbox and review the available objects.

> **Note**   Note that the Toolbox changes. Objects are organized into three main groups in the Toolbox when you are designing a Data Flow: Data Flow Sources, Transformations, and Destinations.

2. Drag OLE DB Source from the Toolbox to the grid.

3. In the Properties pane, change the *Name* property to **OLE DB Source - Employee**.

> **Note** Notice the small red circle with an x inside of it. Integration Services adds an indicator to the object to let you know that it needs a connection manager, which allows tasks to connect to external data sources.

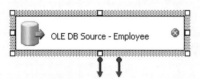

4. On this step, you'll add the connection manager to the source adapter.

Add the localhost.is2005sbs Connection Manager to the OLE DB Source data adapter

1. Double-click the OLE DB Source – Employee data adapter to open the OLE DB Source Editor and click the OLE DB Connection Manager drop-down list.

2. In the drop-down list, select localhost.is2005sbs, and then click OK.

3. Click the Data Access Mode drop-down list to see the different access mode.

4. Select Table Or View.

5. In the Name Of The Table Or The View drop-down list, select the [dbo].[Employee] table.

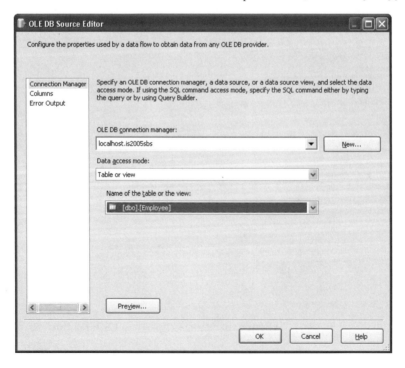

6. Click the Preview button to see sample data of employees, and then click Close.

EmployeeID	FirstName	AddressID	ShiftID	LastNa
1	Terri	1	1	Duffy
2	Jian Shuo	2	1	Wang
3	Michael	3	1	Sullivan
4	Sharon	4	1	Salavari
5	Gail	5	1	Erickson
6	Jossef	6	1	Goldber
7	Ovidiu	7	1	Crăcium
8	Janice	8	1	Galvin
9	Thierry	9	1	D'Hers
10	Brian	10	1	Welcker
14	Stephen	14	1	Jiang
20	Syed	20	1	Abbas
21	Amy	21	1	Alberts

Map the connection manager to the data adapter

1. Click Columns from the left panel of the Editor. This action maps columns from the connection manager to output columns of the adapter.

Note   Mapping between the external column (from the connection manager) and the output column (from the data adapter) is generated automatically when you open this page.

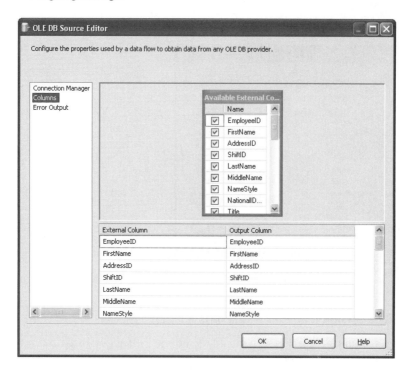

Now you have a data adapter that has been associated with a connection manager and is now ready to be used in a transformation.

2.   Click OK.

> **Note**   Notice that the small red circle on this data adapter has disappeared.

Add an Excel Destination data adapter

1.   Open the Toolbox and expand the Data Flow destinations.

2.   Drag Excel Destination from the Toolbox to the grid.

3.   In the Properties pane, change the *Name* property to **Excel Destination – Employee.**

> **Note**   Notice the small red circle with an x inside of it on this data adapter. Integration Services adds an indicator to the object to let you know that it needs a connection manager.

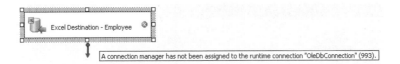

Add the Employee connection manager to the Excel Destination data adapter

1. Double-click the Excel Destination – Employee data adapter.

> **Important**   Note that a warning is displayed. This component has no available input columns. You need to connect the source and the destination.

2. Click No.

3. Click the OLE DB Source – Employee adapter and connect it to the Excel Destination adapter by dragging the green arrow from OLE DB Source – Employee to Excel Destination – Employee.

4. Double-click the Excel Destination – Employee data adapter to open the Excel Destination Editor and verify that Employee is selected in the OLE DB Connection Manager drop-down list.

5. In the Name Of The Excel Sheet drop-down list, click New.

6. Change the name of the sheet to **Employee** by replacing the current name, Excel Destination, next to the CREATE TABLE statement. Keep the quotation marks and change the size of the LoginID column to NVARCHAR(50).

> **Note**   The Excel connection manager will not allow creation of long columns.

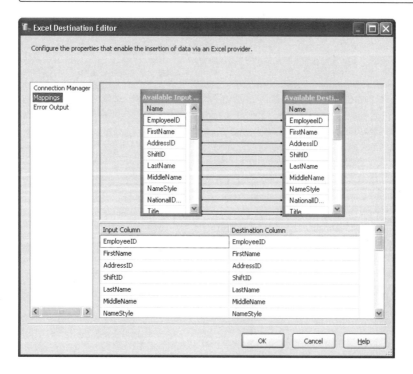

7. Click OK.

8. Click Preview and see that the new table is empty, and then click Close.

9. Click Mappings in the left panel of the Editor.

Note   Mapping between the input column and the destination column (from the Excel data adapter) is generated automatically when you open this page.

10.   Click OK.

> **Note**   Notice the warning icon on the Excel Destination – Employee adapter. Integration Services warns that a Truncation might occur in the LoginID column because the length of the source LoginID column is 256. In this case, it is not a problem because that column has no data larger than 50 characters.

Executing the Package

Once you have created a new SSIS project with connection managers for sources and destinations, created a data flow task with source and destination data adapters, and mapped the columns that you want to transfer from your source table to your destination Office Excel file, you are ready to run this package.

When you execute a package, Integration Services validates the package and executes the tasks defined in the control flow. You can change certain properties to optimize the processing time. You can learn more about optimization in Chapter 11, "Optimizing SSIS Packages." In this procedure, you'll execute the package you have built.

Execute the package

1.   Right-click the CopyTable.dtsx package and choose Execute Package.

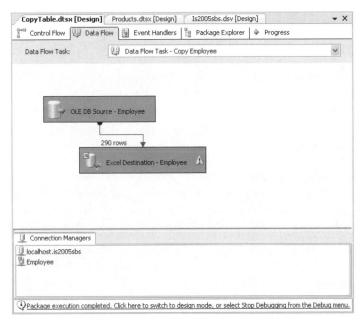

2.   Click the Stop Debugging button on the Debug toolbar.

3. Using Windows Explorer, navigate to the C:\Documents and Settings\<username> \My Documents\Microsoft Press\IS2005sbs\Chap03\Data\ folder.

4. Open the Employee.xls file to confirm that data appears in the file.

5. Click the Employee tab, and data should appear.

Using Data Sources and Data Source Views

A data source is a connection that represents a simple connection to a data store; it includes all tables and views in the data store. A data source has project scope, which means that a data source created in an Integration Services project is available to all the packages in the project. A data source can be defined and then referenced by connection managers in multiple packages. This makes it easy to update all connection managers that use that data source. A project can have multiple data sources, just as it can have multiple connection managers.

Although a data source includes all tables and views, a data source view selects specific database objects (such as tables and views) or adds new relationships between objects. You can extend a data source view by adding calculated columns that are populated by custom expressions, adding new relationships between tables, replacing tables in the data source view with queries, and adding related tables. You can also apply a filter to a data source view to specify a subset of the data selected.

The objective of the next exercise is to load data from a new table, Products, to a flat file. You will create the product's table by defining a named query in a data source view. In addition, you will create a new data source, as source for the data source view, in the connection manager.

 Note   Use the previous project as the source.

Creating a Data Source

In this step, you make your decision about how to define the connection string for your data source. You can create a new connection, a data source based on an existing connection, a data source based on another object, such as an existing data source in your solution, or an Analysis Services project.

In this procedure, you'll create a data source based on a new connection.

Create a data source

1. In Solution Explorer, right-click the Data Sources folder, and then click New Data Source.

2. On the Welcome To The Data Source Wizard page, click Next.

3. On the Select How To Define the Connection page, verify that Create A Data Source Based On An Existing Or New Connection is selected, and then click New.

4. The connection manager dialog box appears with Native OLE DB\SQL Native Client selected in the Provider drop-down list.

5. Leave the Native OLE DB\SQL Native Client provider selected.

6. Type **localhost** in the Server Name box.

7. Select Use Windows Authentication.

8. Select is2005sbs as the database from the drop-down list. Your screen looks like this:

9. Click the Test Connection button and verify that it is successful. Then click OK twice.

> **Note** The New Connection localhost.is2005sbs should now appear in the Data Connections pane.

10. Click Next. The Completing The Wizard page will appear, and a default data source name is displayed in the Data Source Name box.

11. Click Finish. The new data source will appear in the Data Sources folder in Solution Explorer.

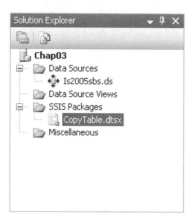

Creating a Data Source View

In this step, you select objects from the relational database to be included in the data source view. You can also include system objects or select one table and automatically add related tables to that one.

In this procedure, you'll specify a data source and select tables to define a new data source view.

Create a data source view

1. In Solution Explorer, right-click the Data Source Views folder, and then click New Data Source View.

2. On the Welcome To The Data Source View Wizard page, click Next.

3. On the Select A Data Source page, in the Relational Data Sources list, click the existing data source Is2005sbs as the primary data source for the data source view. The properties of the selected data source appear in the Data Source Properties pane.

4. Click Next.

5. On the Select Tables And Views page, select:

    ❑ dbo.Product.

    ❑ dbo.ProductCategory.

    ❑ dbo.ProductSubCategory.

6. Click the right arrow to include them in the Included Objects.

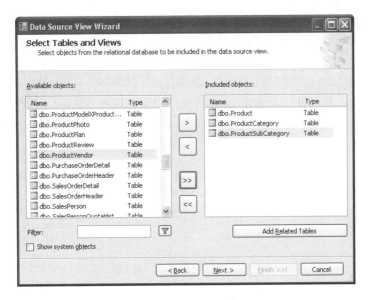

7. Click Next. Leave Is2005sbs as a name for this data source view. This is the default data source view name, which is the name of the data source for which you are creating the data source view. The Preview pane displays a tree view of the objects in your new data source view.

8. Click Finish. The new data source view will appear in the Data Source Views folder in Solution Explorer.

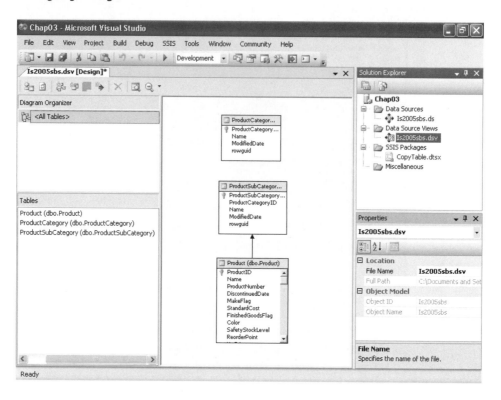

Creating a New Named Query

A named query is a table based on a SQL Expression. In this SQL Expression, you can specify columns and rows from more than one table even from different data sources. You can expand a relational schema by using named queries without modifying the original data source. You can split tables or join tables into a single data source views table.

 Note You cannot base a named query on a table that contains a named calculation.

Create a named query

1. In Solution Explorer, expand the Data Source Views folder, and then open the .dsv file in Data Source View Designer by doing one of the following:

   a. Double-click the .dsv file.

   b. Right-click the .dsv file and click Open.

   c. Select the .dsv file, and then, on the View menu, click Open.

2. In the Tables pane, right-click an open area, and then click New Named Query.

3. In the Create Named Query dialog box, do the following:

   a. In the Name text box, type **Products**.

   b. In the Data Source drop-down list, verify that Is2005sbs (primary) is selected.

   c. Type or copy the next query in the bottom pane. Replace the current statement.

   SELECT * FROM Product
   INNER JOIN ProductSubCategory **ON**
   Product.ProductSubCategoryID =
   ProductSubCategory.ProductSubCategoryID
   INNER JOIN ProductCategory   **ON**
   ProductSubCategory.ProductCategoryID = ProductCategory.ProductCategoryID

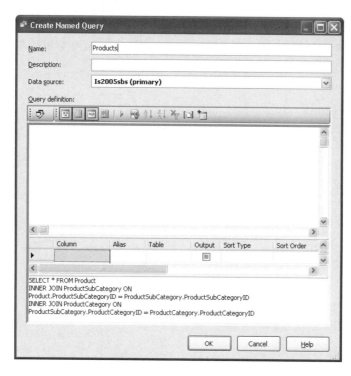

4. Under Query Definition, click the Run icon.

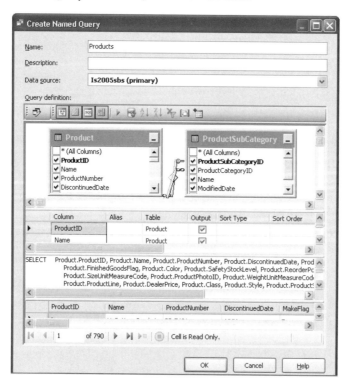

5. Click OK.

6. Click OK. A new table will appear in the design pane with the name Products.

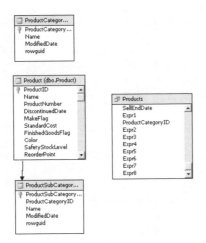

Copying Data from a Named Query to a Flat File

Once you have created a new table by defining a named query, you are ready to use it in a data flow. Then, the next steps are to create a new data flow, create source and destination data adapters, and map the flow of data.

In this next procedure, you'll create a new data flow task, create and configure an OLE DB Source adapter using the named query created in the previous step, and create and configure a destination flat file data adapter.

Copy data from a named query products table to a flat file

1. In Solution Explorer, right-click SSIS Packages, and then select New SSIS Package.

2. Right-click Package1.dtsx, select Rename, and name the new package **Products**.

3. Click Yes to also rename the package object.

4. In the designer, drag a Data Flow Task from the Control Flow Items group of the Toolbox to the Control Flow design area.

5. In the Properties pane, change the *Name* property to **Data Flow Task – Copy Products**.

6. In the designer, double-click in the Data Flow Task component to open the Data Flow design area.

7. In the designer, drag an OLE DB Source from the Data Flow Sources group of the Toolbox to the Data Flow design area.

8. In the Properties pane, change the *Name* property to **OLE DB Source – Products**.

> **Tip**   Note the warning icon that appears in the OLE DB Source. You can hover your mouse over it to read the text of the warning.

9. In the Connection Managers pane, right-click an open area, and then click New Connection From Data Source.

10. In the Select Data Source dialog box, ensure that Is2005sbs is selected, and then click OK.

11. Note that a new connection manager icon appears in the Connection Managers pane.

12. Double-click the OLE DB Source – Products component. Select Connection Manager, and then expand Is2005sbs from the OLE DB Connection Manager drop-down list. Select Is2005sbs Data Source View from the tree and click OK.

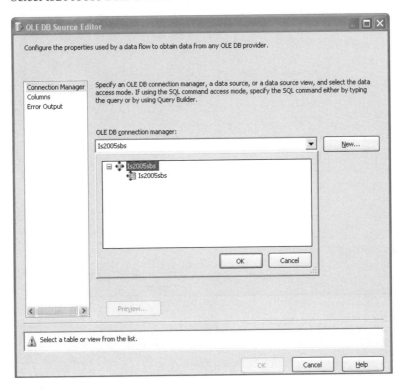

13. Now, in the Data Access Mode drop-down list, select Named Query. The named query products will be displayed. Click the Preview button to check the data.

14. Click the Close button, and then click OK to finish.

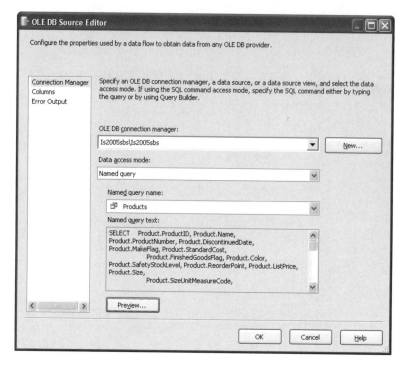

Connect to a flat file destination

1. In the designer, drag a Flat File Destination from the Data Flow Destinations group of the Toolbox to the Data Flow design area.

2. In the Properties pane, change the *Name* property to **Flat File Destination – Products**.

> **Note**   Note the warning icon that appears in the Flat File Destination. You can hover your mouse over it to read the text of the warning.

3. Link OLE DB Source – Products and Flat File Destination – Products by dragging the green arrow from OLE DB Source – Products to Flat File Destination – Products.

4. Double-click Flat File Destination – Products to open the Flat File Destination Editor.

5. Ensure that Connection Manager is selected. Click the New button in the Flat File Connection Manager to open the Flat File Format window. Select Delimited and click OK.

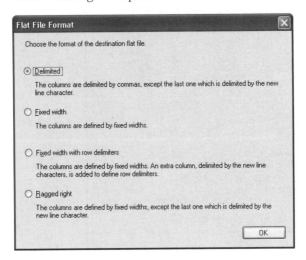

6. In the Connection Manager Name, change the *Name* property to **Products**.

7. In the Flat File Connection Manager Editor, click the Browse button and type **Products** in the File Name text box. Click Open.

   Be sure that the folder is C:\Documents and Settings\<username>\My Documents \Microsoft Press\is2005sbs\Chap03\Data.

8. In the Flat File Connection Manager Editor, click OK.

Note   Note that the OK button is disabled in the Flat File Destination Editor. It is because mappings columns have not yet been set.

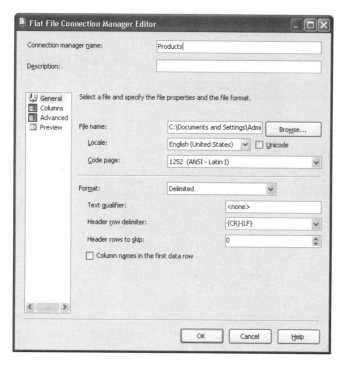

9. In the Flat File Destination Editor, click Mappings in the left pane. Verify that the columns are mapped correctly and click OK.

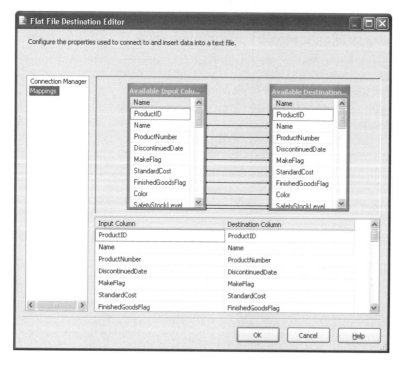

10. Now you are ready to execute your package (Products.dtsx). Your package should look like this:

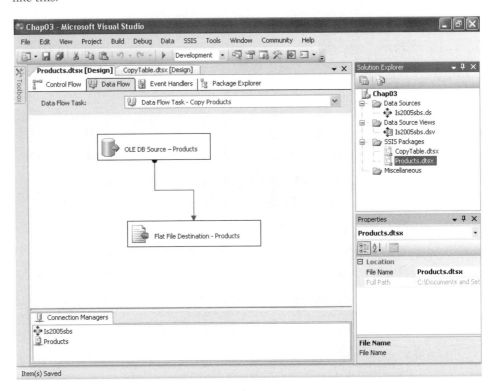

Executing the Package

This package is a very simple one that includes only one data flow. You have configured an OLE DB source based in a named query created in a data source view. When this package is executing, the data flow reads a buffer of data from the data source view and loads the data defined to the Named Query Products to a Products.txt file.

To execute this package, you can go to the Debug menu and select the Start Debugging button, press the F5 key, or right-click the package and choose Execute Package.

When the Data Flow is complete, all the components in the Data Flow change color from yellow to green. It means that they have all completed successfully. The last view will look like this:

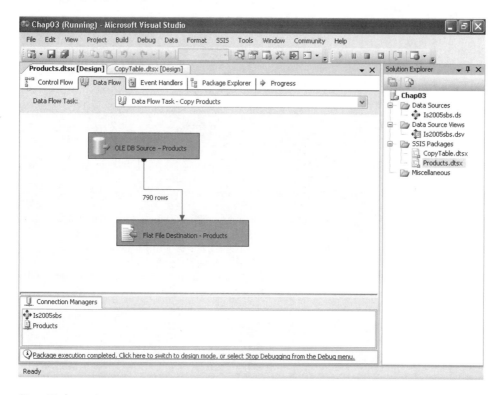

Stop Debugging

1. Click the Stop Debugging button on the Debug toolbar.

2. Using Windows Explorer, navigate to the C:\Documents and Settings\<username>\My Documents\Microsoft Press\IS2005SBS\Chap03\Data\ folder.

3. Open the Products.txt file to confirm data appears in the file.

4. Save the solution.

Chapter 3 Quick Reference

To	Do this
Create an Integration Services package	Start SQL Server Business Intelligence Development Studio. On the File menu, point to New, and then click Project. Make sure that the Project Type is set to Business Intelligence Projects, and then click the Integration Services Project template. Type a name for the project. Specify the location folder for the project and confirm that the Create Directory For Solution check box is selected. Click OK.
Add an OLE DB connection manager	Right-click anywhere in the Connection Managers pane at the bottom of the Control Flow tab and click New OLE DB Connection. Click New to define a new connection. Keep the default: Native OLE DB\SQL Server Native Client. Type localhost for the Server Name. Select Use Windows Authentication and choose the desired database.
Review available connection manager types	Right-click anywhere in the Connection Managers pane at the bottom of the Control Flow tab and explore the list of connections available: Flat File Connection, ADO.NET Connection, Analysis Services Connection, and so on.
Add an Excel connection manager	Right-click anywhere in the Connection Managers pane at the bottom of the Control Flow tab and click New Connection. In the SSIS connection manager, click EXCEL (connection manager for Excel files) and click Add. Type a name for the Excel file and specify an Office Excel file path.
Create a data flow task	Click the Data Flow tab. If you go to the Data Flow page right after creating a package, you will see a message stating that no data flow tasks have been added to the package. Click the message link to add a new task. You can also access it from the Control Flow page.
Add an OLE DB Source data adapter	Drag OLE DB Source from the Toolbox to the grid. The small red circle on this data adapter means that it needs a connection manager.
Add a connection manager to the OLE DB Source data adapter	Double-click the OLE DB Source data adapter to open the Editor and click OLE DB Connection Manager. In OLE DB Connection Manager, select a connection manager. In the Data Access Mode, select Table Or View and choose the desired table.
Map the connection manager to the data adapter	Click columns from the left panel of the OLE DB Source Editor. This action maps columns from the connection manager to output columns of the adapter.
Add an Excel Destination data adapter	Open the Toolbox and expand Data Flow Destinations. Drag Excel Destination from the Toolbox to the grid. The small red circle on this data adapter means that it needs a connection manager.

To	Do this
Add an Excel connection manager to the Excel Destination data adapter	Double-click the Excel Destination data adapter. This is a destination component that needs to be connected to the input source component. Click the OLE DB Source adapter and connect it to the Excel Destination adapter by dragging the green arrow from OLE DB Source to Excel Destination. Double-click the Excel Destination data adapter to open the Editor and verify that the connection manager is selected. In the Name text box of the Excel sheet, click New. Change the name of the sheet and change the size of long columns. The Excel connection manager will not allow creation of long columns. Finally, click Mapping in the left panel of the Editor.
Execute the package	Right-click the desired package and choose Execute Package.
Create a data source	In Solution Explorer, right-click the Data Sources folder, and then click New Data Source. On the Welcome To The Data Source Wizard page, click Next. On the Select How To Define The Connection page, verify that Create A Data Source Based On An Existing Or New Connection is selected, and then click New. Leave the Native OLE DB\SQL Native Client provider selected. Type **localhost** in the Server Name text box, select Use Windows Authentication, and select a database. Click OK, and then click Finish twice.
Create a data source view	In Solution Explorer, right-click the Data Source Views folder, and then click New Data Source View. Click Next on the Welcome To The Data Source View Wizard page. Select a data source and click Next. Select the objects you want to include in your data source view. Click next, and then click Finish.
Create a new Named Query	In Solution Explorer, expand the Data Source Views folder, and then open the data source view. In the Tables pane, right-click an open area, and then click New Named Query. Type a name for the new named query and specify a SQL statement in the bottom pane to define your named query. Click OK.
Add a connection manager from Data Source	In the Connection Managers pane, right-click an open area, and then click New Connection from Data Source. In Select Data Source, choose a data source that you created.
Set an OLE DB Source from a Named Query	In the designer, drag a Data Flow task from the Control Flow, open the Data Flow, and drag an OLE DB Source from the Data Flow Sources tab. Double-click the OLE DB Source component. Then, select and expand the data source you created from the OLE DB connection manager list. Select the data source view from the tree and click OK. In data access mode, select Named query and click OK.

Chapter 4

Using Data Flow Transformations

After completing this chapter, you will be able to:

- Understand how data flow is constructed in a package.

- Understand the function of data flow transformations and when to use them.

- Create a new SSIS project and add a data flow task to it.

- Use Conditional Split, Derived Column, and Multicast transformations to aggregate, merge, distribute, and modify data.

- Configure how a component handles errors.

In Chapter 3, "Extracting and Loading Data," you learned how to create and configure connection managers, how to use data flow sources to extend the functionality of connection managers, and how to add a data flow task to extract data from a source and then load the results into a destination.

In this chapter, you'll take a closer look at how Microsoft SQL Server Integration Services (SSIS) can be used to transform data. As you work through the series of procedures in this chapter, you'll learn how to develop packages that use a data flow task and a variety of data flow transformations to extract data from a data source, perform transformations, and load the transformed data into a destination table or file.

Creating Data Flow in a Package

The data flow in an SSIS package is constructed by using different types of data flow elements: data flow sources that extract data, transformations that modify and aggregate data, destinations that load data, and paths that connect the outputs and inputs of data flow components into a data flow. To build the data flow in a package, you drag objects from the Data Flow Items group in the Toolbox onto the Control Flow designer in SQL Server Business Intelligence Development Studio (BIDS). This section discusses these data flow objects in more detail.

Data Flow Sources

Data flow sources are the data flow objects that make data from different types of data sources available to the data flow. Sources have one regular output, and many have one error output.

A data flow source reads the metadata from a connection manager and sets up a data flow pipeline in the computer's memory. It then reads the data from the source and feeds it through the pipeline's starting point.

Data Flow Transformations

SSIS transformations are the components in the data flow of a package that aggregate, merge, distribute, and modify data. Transformations also perform lookup operations and generate sample datasets.

A data flow transformation modifies data as it flows through the pipeline. As a data record flows through the pipeline, transformations might:

- Modify the fields in the record.
- Add new fields to the record.
- Aggregate records.
- Create new pipelines and send each record down every pipeline.
- Create new pipelines and, based on the data in the record, determine to which pipeline to send the record.
- Read data from multiple pipelines and send them into a single pipeline.
- Perform many other types of transformations.

Data Flow Destinations

Destinations are the data flow components that flow the data into different types of data sources or create an in-memory dataset. Destinations have one input and one error output.

A data flow destination maps the pipeline metadata to the data destination metadata stored in a connection manager. The data flow destination then reads the transformed data from the end of the pipeline and writes it to the data destination.

Data Source Connections

Connection managers contain metadata about data flow sources and data flow destinations. An Open Database Connectivity (ODBC) connection manager enables a package to connect to a variety of database management systems by using the ODBC specification.

When you add an ODBC connection to a package and set the connection manager properties, SSIS creates a connection manager and adds the connection manager to the *Connections* collection of the package. At run time, the connection manager is resolved as a physical ODBC connection.

You create the data flow in a package by using the Data Flow designer, the design surface on the Data Flow tab in BIDS. Creating a data flow includes the following steps:

- Adding one or more sources to extract data from files and databases.

- Adding the transformations that meet the business requirements of the package.

- Connecting data flow components by connecting the output of sources and transformations to the input of transformations and destinations.

- Adding one or more destinations to load data into data stores such as files and databases.

- Configuring error outputs on components to handle problems such as errors or data values that are truncated.

- Adding connection managers to the package if the data flow includes components that connect to data sources. You can add connection managers while working in the Data Flow designer, but you can also add them when the Control Flow or Event Handlers tab is active.

 Note   The key information to remember is that data flows from top to bottom, and it is occasionally split (or sometimes merged) but never looped. Data flow always starts with a data source and ends with a destination data store.

SSIS Transformations

Most transformations have one input, one regular output, and one error output. Some transformations have multiple inputs to consolidate data from separate pipelines, and some transformations have multiple outputs to separate data into separate pipelines. Not all transformations have error output.

The types of transformations in the pipeline affect the data flow engine's management of memory buffers. Row transformations, such as Data Conversion or Derived Column, are very efficient at reusing existing buffers. Multiple rows are received into the buffer from an upstream component in batches, data in the buffer is manipulated on a row-by-row basis, and then these rows in the buffer are operated on by the next component. This process continues until all rows from the source have been transformed.

Other transformation types must create new buffers to store output before allowing the next component access to the data and, consequently, place the greatest demands on system resources. Transformations operating on rowsets, such as Aggregate or Sort, must read all input before creating any output. Transformations that combine input, such as Merge or Union All, are somewhere in between the other transformation types, reading some input before creating output, but they do copy that output to a different buffer and thus have greater resource requirements. The following section describes the transformations that SSIS includes.

Row Transformations

The following transformations update column values and create new columns. The transformation is applied to each row in the transformation input.

- **Character Map**   This transformation maps characters in a string into different characters—for example, a lowercase-character mapping changes ASCII 64 (A) into ASCII 97 (a). It overwrites the column with the new string or adds a column to the output row.

  - ❑ Full-width <-> half-width characters

  - ❑ Hiragana <-> Katakana characters

  - ❑ Simplified Chinese <-> Traditional Chinese

  - ❑ Lowercase

  - ❑ Uppercase

  - ❑ Reverse byte order (order of the bytes in each character reversed)

  - ❑ Apply linguistic casing (simple case mapping for Turkic and other locales)

- **Copy Column**   This transformation creates new columns in the output row from existing columns in the input row for subsequent transformation.

- **Data Conversion**   This transformation applies data conversion functions to change data type, column length, or precision and scale to an input column and adds a column with the new data to the output row.

- **Derived Column**   This transformation applies expressions to an input column to create a new value for a new column in the output row or as a replacement value for the existing column.

- **Script Component**   This transformation runs custom code against data in the pipeline.

- **OLE DB Command**   This transformation runs a SQL statement (optionally parameterized) for each row in the pipeline.

Rowset Transformations

The following transformations create new rowsets. The rowset can include aggregate and sorted values, sample rowsets, or pivoted and unpivoted rowsets.

- **Aggregate**   This transformation applies an aggregate function (Sum, Minimum, Maximum, and so on) to grouped records and produces new output records from aggregated results. Output records contain only the columns used for grouping and the aggregated values.

- **Sort**   This transformation applies an ascending or descending sort to one or more columns and optionally removes rows with duplicate values in the sort columns.

- **Percentage Sampling**   This transformation creates a random sample set of output rows by selecting a specified percentage of input rows, commonly used for data mining.

- **Row Sampling**   This transformation creates a random sample set of output rows by selecting a specified number of input rows, primarily used for testing packages with a subset of representative data.

- **Pivot**   This transformation converts rows into columns. For example, suppose your input rows contain CustomerName, Product, and Quantity. If you pivot on Product, the resulting output will have CustomerName and one column for each product. The output product columns will contain the values that were in the input Quantity column.

- **Unpivot**   This transformation converts columns into rows. For example, suppose your input has a CustomerName column and a column for each product your company sells. The product columns contain the quantity that the customer purchased. If you unpivot on the product columns, your output row will have CustomerName, Product, and Quantity rows. The Product column will contain the names of the product columns in the input rows.

Split and Join Transformations

The following transformations distribute rows to different outputs, create copies of the transformation inputs, join multiple inputs into one output, and perform lookup operations.

- **Conditional Split**   This transformation separates input rows into separate output pipelines based on a Boolean expression configured for each output. A single input row is passed to the first output row for which the condition is true or to a default output defined for rows that meet no conditions.

- **Multicast**   This transformation copies all input rows to two or more outputs.

- **Merge**   In this transformation, input rows are interleaved. Merges combine two sorted datasets with the same column structure into a single output. The output will be sorted in the same order as the two inputs.

- **Merge Join**   In this transformation, input rows are combined side by side. Merge Join combines two sorted datasets, using a FULL, LEFT, or INNER join.

- **Union All**   In this transformation, input rows are stacked. Union All combines two or more datasets with the same column structure into a single output.

- **Lookup**   This transformation joins input rows with columns in a reference dataset (from a table, view, or SQL statement) to add one or more columns to the output row.

Data Quality Transformations

The following transformations perform data quality operations such as standardizing values and looking up values in a reference table.

- **Fuzzy Lookup**   This transformation finds close or exact matches between two or more columns (DT_WSTR and DT_STR data types only) in the input row and a row in a reference table and adds selected columns from the matched row and columns for fuzzy matching metrics.

- **Fuzzy Grouping**   This transformation finds close or exact matches between input rows based on one or more columns and adds columns to the output, identifying matches and similarity scores.

Data-Mining Transformations

The following transformations perform data-mining operations:

- **Data-Mining Query**   Uses data from the input rows to execute prediction queries on a SQL Server Analysis Services data-mining model and creates output rows from the query result set.

- **Term Extraction**   Extracts nouns or noun phrases (or both) from an input column containing English text, places the extracted terms in a column in the output row, and adds another column for the score. Multiple output rows per input row are created when multiple terms are extracted from an input column.

- **Term Lookup**   Matches text in an input column with a reference table, counts the number of occurrences of the term in the dataset, and adds a term and frequency column to the output row. As with Term Extraction, multiple output rows per input row can be created.

Other Transformations

SSIS includes the following transformations to export and import data, add audit information, count rows, and work slowly with changing dimensions.

- **Export Column**   This transformation reads a file name from an input column and inserts data from another column in the same row into the specified file.

- **Import Column**   This transformation reads a file name from an input column and inserts data from the specified file into a new output column for the same row.

- **Audit**   This transformation adds the value of a system variable, such as *MachineName* or *ExecutionInstanceGUID*, to a new output column.

- **Row Count**   This transformation counts the number of rows currently in the data flow and stores the value in a variable.

- **Slowly Changing Dimension**   This transformation manages inserts and updates in a data warehouse for Type 1 and Type 2 changes.

Synchronous and Asynchronous Transformations

The following transformations determine how rows are processed.

- **Synchronous transformations**   These transformations process data row by row. They manipulate data that already exists in a memory buffer. Transformations that use data already contained in the row are the fastest (for instance, Derived Column). Transformations that process data row by row but must interact with an external data source will be slower (Lookup, Object Linking and Embedding (OLE) DB Command).

- **Asynchronous transformations**   These transformations cause SSIS to copy and manipulate data from one memory buffer to another. Asynchronous transformations potentially have more or fewer output rows than input rows.

- **Partially blocking transformations**   These transformations join datasets (Merge) or create a dataset that is dissimilar to the source dataset. (Pivot output has different columns from its input.) Data flows through these transformations more slowly than it flows through non-blocking transformations.

- **Blocking transformations**   These transformations cannot send a row on to the next transformation until all of the input rows have been read.

Using Expressions in Packages

An *expression* is a combination of symbols—identifiers, literals, functions, and operators—that yields a single data value. Simple expressions can be a single constant, variable, or function. More frequently, expressions are complex, using multiple operators and functions and referencing multiple columns and variables. The key information to remember is that expressions always return a single value.

Expression Usage in SSIS

In SSIS, expressions can be used to implement a decision-based condition, create and update values in data columns, assign values to variables, define constraints in precedence constraints, and provide the expressions used by the For Loop container. This section describes the elements in SSIS that can use expressions.

Conditional Split Transformation

The Conditional Split transformation implements a decision structure based on expressions to direct data rows to different destinations. Expressions used in a Conditional Split transformation must evaluate to *true* or *false*. For example, rows that meet the condition in the expression "Column1 > Column2" can be routed to a separate output.

Derived Column Transformation

The Derived Column transformation uses values created by using expressions either to populate new columns in a data flow or to update existing columns. For example, the expression Column1 + "ABC" can be used to update a value or to create a new value with the concatenated string.

Variables

Variables can be referenced in expressions. A SSIS package supports the following two types of variables:

- **System variables**   These variables contain package, task, and transformation metadata such as name, ID, start time, version, creation date, machine name, user name, and so on.

- **User variables**   These variables are created by the package designer and can contain any desired data stored in a variety of data types.

Expressions reference variables using @[System::*VariableName*] or @[User::*VariableName*] syntax.

Precedence Constraints

Precedence constraints can use expressions to specify the conditions that determine whether the constrained task or container in a package runs. Expressions used in a precedence constraint must evaluate to *true* or *false*. For example, the expression @[*User::A*] > @[*User::B*] compares two user-defined variables to determine whether the constrained task runs.

The For Loop Container

The For Loop container repeats a set of tasks until an expression evaluates to *false*. The For Loop container uses the following three expressions:

- The first expression initializes the variable.

- The second expression determines whether the set of tasks should be repeated.

- The third expression determines how the variable should be changed each time the set of tasks is repeated.

Expressions Elements

Expressions are based on an expression language, which is similar to C or C#. This language includes the following three elements:

- **The expression grammar**   Defines expression syntax and the operators, functions, and data types available for use in expressions

- **The expression evaluator**   Parses expressions and determines whether expressions adhere to the rules of the expression grammar

- **The expression builder**   Provides a list of available data columns and system and user variables and a list of functions and operators that is used to build expressions

> **More Info**   You can learn more about the language on which expressions are based in the SQL Server Books Online article, "Integration Services Expression Concepts" at the following URL: *http://msdn2.microsoft.com/en-us/library/ms141827.aspx.*

Building Expressions

The expression builder is a graphical tool for building expressions and is available in the dialog boxes for the Conditional Split and Derived Column transformations. To build expressions, you can drag and then drop items from either list onto the expression column. The expression builder automatically adds needed syntax elements, such as the @ prefix, on variable names.

Using Data Flow Transformations

The objective of the following set of procedures is to extract data from a source table and then load the data into a Microsoft Office Excel file. These transformation processes simulate data-delivering routines that you might perform when working in a data warehouse or enterprise environment.

Specifically, you'll first create a package for cleansing data from a flat file source and then place the results in a separate flat file destination. After this is accomplished, you'll use the Conditional Split transformation to extract specific rows from the source and then use the Derived Column transformation to trim the extracted rows. Finally, you will add a Multicast transformation to send the same output to two different destinations: a text file and a SQL Server 2005 database table.

Opening and Exploring the SSIS Project

Before you create a new package, it's important to open and explore the Chap04_Project SSIS project so that you become familiar with the packages that have been created for this project. The SSIS Packages folder contains two packages: LookupGeography and NewProducts. The following steps will walk you through a preview of these packages.

Open and explore the SSIS project

1. In Windows Explorer, navigate to the C:\Documents and Settings\<username>\ My Documents\Microsoft Press\is2005sbs\Chap04\ folder.

2. Double-click the Chap04_Project.sln file.

   The project opens in SQL Server Business Intelligence Development Studio (BIDS).

3. In BIDS, locate the Solution Explorer window on the right side of the design surface.

   Make sure this window is visible and not set to Auto-Hide, so you can see all of the files in the project.

4. In Solution Explorer, if necessary, expand the SSIS Packages folder.

   Notice that two packages have been created: LookupGeography and NewProducts.

5. Double-click NewProducts.dtsx to open this package in design mode.

   Your screen looks similar to this:

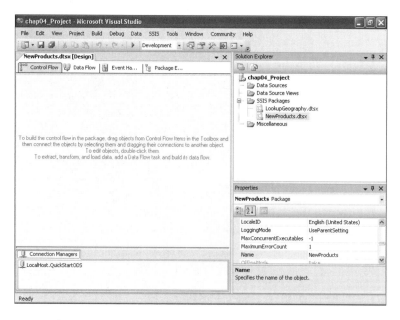

6. Locate the Connection Managers pane in the lower-left pane.

   Notice that the NewProducts package already contains an OLE DB connection manager called LocalHost.QuickStartODS.

7. Right-click LocalHost.QuickStartODS, and then click Edit.

    The Connection Manager dialog box appears.

    Your screen now looks like this:

8. Verify that the connection manager references the *QuickStartODS* database on the local-host:

    ❑ Verify that in the Server Name box, LocalHost is selected.

    ❑ Verify that in the Connect To A Database frame, in the Select Or Enter A Database drop-down list, QuickStartODS is selected.

    ❑ Click OK.

Preview the NewProducts.txt file

1. In Windows Explorer, navigate to the C:\Documents and Settings\<username>\ My Documents\Microsoft Press\is2005sbs\Chap04\Data folder.

2. Double-click the NewProducts.txt file to open it in Notepad.

    Your screen looks like this:

Notice that the NewProducts.txt file contains a list of product names and attributes. There is a header row containing column names, and there are sub-header rows containing product subcategories.

3. Close the NewProducts.txt file.

Creating the Data Flow Task

A Data Flow task encapsulates the data flow engine that moves data between sources and destinations, providing the facility to transform, clean, and modify data as it is moved. Creating a Data Flow task and adding it to a package control flow makes it possible for the package to extract, transform, and load data.

In this procedure, you will create the data flow task named Data Flow Task – Import Products. To build the control flow in a package, you drag objects from the Control Flow Items group in the Toolbox onto the Control Flow designer. To edit the object, you double-click it and then change various properties, such as its name.

Create the Data Flow task

1. In BIDS, on the left side of the screen, click Toolbox. The Toolbox menu appears.

   Your screen looks like this:

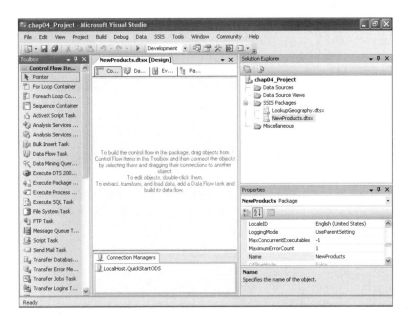

Scroll through the list and note the number and types of objects that are available in the Toolbox.

2. On the Toolbox menu, in the Control Flow Items group, drag Data Flow Task onto the Control Flow design surface. The new data flow task appears on the Control Flow designer.

Your screen should look similar to this:

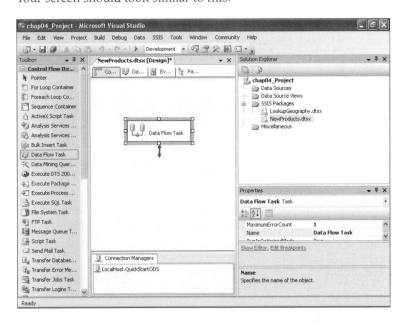

3. In the Properties pane, located on the right side of the screen, make sure that Data Flow Task is selected.

4. Click the Alphabetical button to alphabetize the Properties list.

5. In the Properties list, locate Name, and then change the name property from Data Flow Task to **Data Flow Task – Import Products**.

Your screen now looks like this:

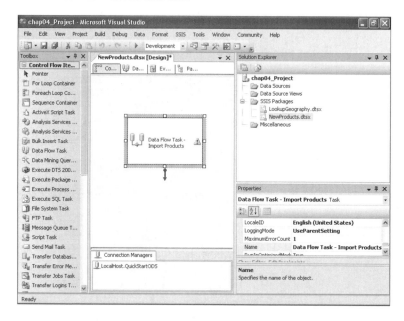

Notice that the name of the data flow task in the Data Flow designer is now Data Flow Task – Import Products.

Using a Flat File Source

A Flat File source reads data from a text file. The text file can be in delimited, fixed-width, or ragged-right format.

■ **Delimited format**   This format uses column and row delimiters to define columns and rows.

■ **Fixed-width format**   This format uses width to define columns and rows.

■ **Ragged-right format**   This format uses width to define all columns except for the last column, which is delimited by the row delimiter.

Configuring a Flat File Source

You can configure the Flat File source in the following ways:

- Add a column to the transformation output that contains the name of the text file from which the Flat File source extracts data.

- Specify whether the Flat File source interprets zero-length strings in columns as null values.

In the following procedure, you will create a data adapter named Flat File Source – NewProducts.

Create a data adapter

1. In BIDS, on the Toolbox menu, in the Data Flow Sources group, drag Flat File Source onto the Data Flow design surface. The new data adapter appears on the Data Flow designer.

   Your screen looks like this:

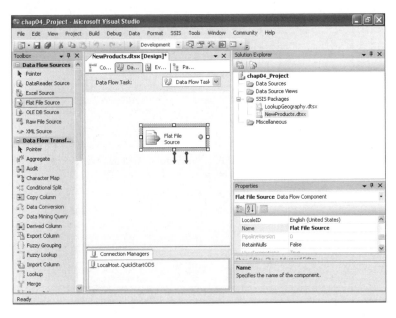

2. In the Properties list, locate Name, and then change the name property from Flat File Source to **Flat File Source – NewProducts**.

Your screen now looks like this:

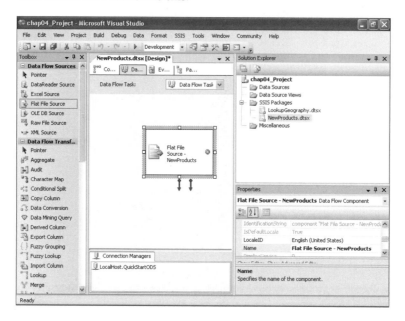

Notice that the name of the data adapter in the Data Flow designer is now Flat File Source – NewProducts.

Adding a Connection Manager

Now that you have created the Flat File Source – NewProducts data adapter, you are ready to create a new connection manager. You use the Flat File Source Editor to create the new connection manager. After you have created the connection manager, you will specify its properties and file format. Finally, you will define the columns for the connection manager.

Add a connection manager

1. In BIDS, on the Data Flow designer, double-click the Flat File Source – NewProducts data adapter. The Flat File Source Editor dialog box appears.

2. In the Flat File Source Editor dialog box, click New to create a new connection manager.

3. In the Connection Manager Name box, type **NewProducts**.

4. Next to the File Name box, click Browse and navigate to C:\Documents and Settings\ <username>\My Documents\Microsoft Press\is2005sbs\ Chap04\Data\.

5. Click NewProducts.txt, and then click Open.

Your screen looks like this:

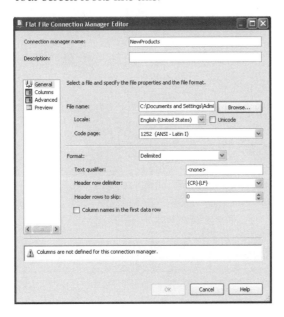

Notice the message at the bottom of the Flat File Connection Manager Editor box that reads "Columns are not defined for this connection manager."

In the Flat File Connection Manager Editor box, you can specify file properties and the file format.

6. Ensure that the default values in the following table are selected.

The default value for the other properties is correct for NewProducts.txt.

Property	Default Value
Locale	English (United States)
Code Page	1252 (ANSI – Latin I)
Format	Delimited
Text Qualifier	<none>
Header Row Delimiter	{CR}{LF}
Header Rows To Skip	0

7. At the bottom of the editor box, select the Column Names In The First Data Row check box.

8. In the left pane, click Columns.

Your screen now looks like this:

Notice that a table appears with three columns and data for rows 1–81. Rows 1–81 are a preview of the rows to be extracted from the file.

Notice that in the Specify The Characters That Delimit The Source File frame, you can change the row and column delimiters, if necessary.

9. In the left pane, click Advanced.

Your screen now looks like this:

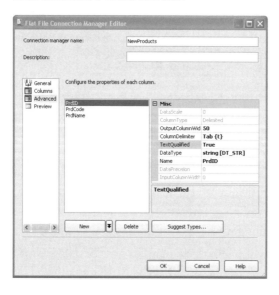

10. In the Configure The Properties Of Each Column pane, click PrdID, and then, in the right pane in the second column, change PrdID to **ProductID**.

11. Click PrdCode, and then, in the right pane in the second column, change PrdCode to **ProductCode**.

12. Click PrdName, and then, in the right pane in the second column, change PrdName to **ProductName**.

    Notice the other default values for a column. You can change these properties if needed.

13. Click OK to close the Flat File Connection Manager Editor.

14. In the Flat File Source Editor, click Preview to see sample rows from the source data file. The Data View dialog box opens.

    Your screen looks like this:

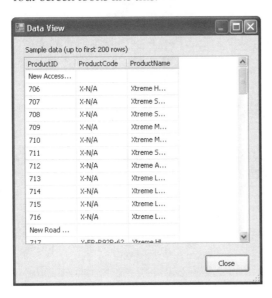

15. Click Close to close the Data View box.

16. Click OK to close the Flat File Source Editor.

Adding a Conditional Split Transformation

In this procedure, you will add a Conditional Split transformation named Conditional Split – Valid Product Rows. The first step you must perform is separating the rows you want to keep from the rows you want to discard. In this procedure, you will discard the subcategory sub-header rows (ProductID begins with New) and the rows where the product is not available (ProductCode begins with X-N/A). The best tool to perform this job is the Conditional Split transformation. Conditional Split transformations determine from input which output channel to use, based on the result of an expression.

Add a Conditional Split transformation

1. In BIDS, on the Toolbox menu, in the Data Flow Transformations group, drag Conditional Split onto the Data Flow design surface. The new Conditional Split transformation appears on the Data Flow designer.

2. In the Properties list, locate Name, and then, in the right column, change the name property from Conditional Split to **Conditional Split – Valid Product Rows**.

3. In the Data Flow designer, click the Flat File Source – NewProducts data adapter to select it and then drag its output (green arrow) onto the destination Conditional Split – Valid Product Rows.

   Your screen looks like this:

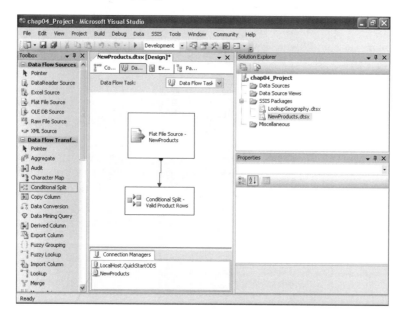

   This sets the Flat File Source – NewProducts data adapter as the input for the Conditional Split – Valid Product Rows transformation. Now you're ready to configure the output channels of the Conditional Split.

4. Double-click Conditional Split – Valid Product Rows. The Conditional Split Transformation Editor opens.

5. At the bottom of the editor, change the Default output name from Conditional Split Default Output to **DiscardRows**.

Your screen now looks like this:

Note   All rows that don't meet one of the conditions go to the default output. In this case, it's worth giving the default output a meaningful name.

6. To create an additional output, in the middle pane, click the column under Output Name, and then type **ValidRows**.

Note   With Conditional Split, you get multiple output channels (green arrows). Giving names to the output channels makes it easier to choose the right one.

7. Click the column under Condition, and then type **SUBSTRING([ProductID],1,3) != <;$QD>New<;$QD> && SUBSTRING([ProductCode],1,5) != <;$QD>X-N/A<;$QD>**.

You can copy the preceding expression, or you can copy the expression from C:\Documents and Settings\<username>\My Documents\MicrosoftPress \is2005sbs \Chap04\Expressions\ConditionalSplit.txt and then paste it in the text area under the Condition column.

Your screen now looks like this:

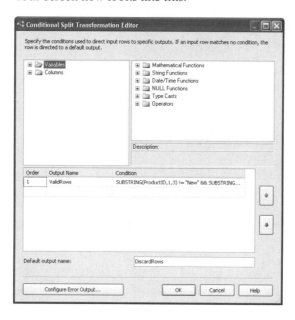

This expression includes two data-cleansing filters. The first is used to evaluate whether the first three characters of ProductID indicate a sub-header row. If the row is a sub-header row, the row is sent to the default output that you named DiscardRows. The second expression filters rows in which the Product Code indicates a product that is not available.

> **Tip**   To help you type expressions, you can expand the folders in the upper-left pane of the editor to access functions and type casts and operators. The expression syntax is similar to C and C#. For a full description, see the SQL Server 2005 Books Online topic, "Integration Services Expression Reference" at the following URL: *http://msdn2.microsoft.com/en-us/library/ms141232.aspx.*

8. Click OK to close the Conditional Split Transformation Editor.

Adding a Derived Column Transformation

After you have separated the rows you want to keep, the next step is to discard part of the product name data (the size value) in those rows. In this procedure, you'll add a Derived Column transformation named Derived Column – Replace ProductName, using ValidRows output from ConditionalSplit – Valid Product Rows.

Add a Derived Column transformation

1. In BIDS, on the Toolbox menu, in the Data Flow Transformations group, drag Derived Column onto the Data Flow design surface. The new Derived Column transformation appears on the Data Flow designer.

> **Note**   The Derived Column transformation applies transformations to an existing column or creates a new column.

2. In the Properties list, locate Name, and then, in the right column, change the name property from Derived Column to **Derived Column – Replace ProductName**.

3. In the Data Flow designer, click Conditional Split – Valid Product Rows to select it, and then drag its output (green arrow) to the destination Derived Column – Replace ProductName.

> **Tip**   Even though you defined two outputs, the Conditional Split transformation shows only one output (green arrow). If you later click Conditional Split again, you will notice a new green arrow that you could use to connect an unassigned output to another destination.

The Input Output Selection dialog box opens to let you choose which output to connect to the input of the destination component.

Your screen should look similar to this:

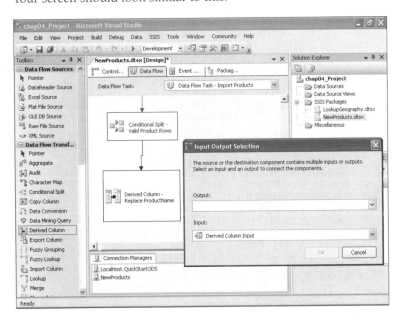

4. In the Input Output Selection dialog box, in the Output drop-down list, select Valid-Rows.

5. Click OK to close the Input Output Selection dialog box.

6. In the Data Flow designer, double-click Derived Column – Replace ProductName. The Derived Column Transformation Editor opens.

7. In the editor, in the left pane, expand the Columns folder.

8. Click ProductName and drag it to the first row of the Derived Column Name list.

9. Click the first row under Derived Column and select Replace ProductName.

> **Tip**   You can make the results of an expression transform an existing column or create a new column. In this case, the source is not worth keeping. In reality, even when you "replace" a column, it creates a new space in the buffer and simply maps the name of the column to the new space.

10. Click the first row under Expression, and then type: **SUBSTRING(Product-Name,1,(FINDSTRING(ProductName,"Size",1) - 2))**.

Your screen now looks like this:

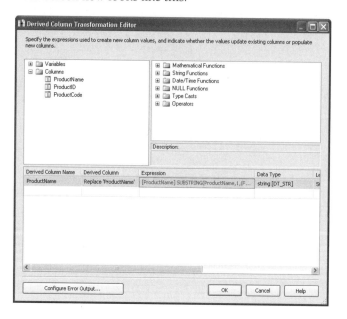

11. This expression is used to strip off the size portion of the product name. You can copy the preceding expression, or you can copy the expression from C:\Documents and Settings\<username>\My Documents\Microsoft Press\is2005sbs\Chap04\ Expressions\DerivedColumn.txt and paste it into the Expression text box.

12. Click OK to close the Derived Column Transformation Editor.

Viewing the Properties of the Derived Column Transformation

Now that you have added the Derived Column transformation named Derived Column – Replace ProductName and used it to discard part of the product name data, you are ready to view the properties of the new transformation. In this procedure, you will use the Advanced Editor to view the properties of the Derived Column transformation. This editor enables you to view or change advanced properties of the component.

View the properties of the Derived Column transformation

1. In BIDS, in the Data Flow designer, right-click Derived Column – Replace ProductName, and then click Show Advanced Editor. The Advanced Editor For Derived Column – Replace ProductName dialog box opens.

    This editor enables you to view or change advanced properties of the component.

2. In the editor, click the Input And Output Properties tab.

3. In the left pane, expand Derived Column Input, expand the Input Columns folder, and then click the ProductName column.

    Your screen looks like this:

Notice the Expression versus FriendlyExpression custom properties. Expression uses the lineage identifier to create an internal representation of the column. FriendlyExpression is the string value that you provided in the Expression text box.

4. Click OK to close the editor.

Adding a Flat File Destination Data Adapter and Executing the Package

The final step of this data-cleansing process is to write the results to a text file. In the first procedure, you will add a flat-file destination data adapter named Flat File Destination – Products Destination with a new connection manager named ProductsDestination. After you have added the flat-file destination data adapter, you will execute the package and view the results.

Add a flat-file destination data adapter

1. In BIDS, on the Toolbox menu, in the Data Flow Destinations group, drag Flat File Destination onto the Data Flow design surface. The data adapter appears on the Data Flow designer.

2. In the Properties list, locate Name, and then, in the right column, change the name property from Flat File Destination to **Flat File Destination - ProductsDestination**.

3. In the Data Flow designer, click Derived Column – Replace ProductName to select it, and then drag its output (green arrow) to Flat File Destination – ProductsDestination.

   Your screen should look similar to this:

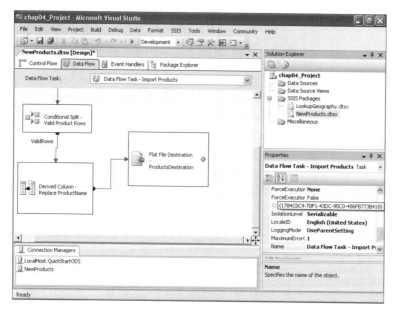

4. In the Data Flow designer, double-click Flat File Destination – ProductsDestination. The Flat File Destination Editor opens.

5. In the editor, click New to create a new connection manager. The Flat File Format dialog box opens.

6. In the Flat File Format dialog box, ensure that the Delimited option is selected, and then click OK.

7. In the Flat File Connection Manager Editor, in the File Name box, type **Products-Destination**.

    Notice that the other fields in the editor box populate (that is, Locale, Code Page, and so on).

8. Next to the File Name box, click Browse.

9. In the Open box, navigate to C:\Documents and Settings\<username>\My Documents\ Microsoft Press\is2005sbs\Chap04\Data.

10. In the File Name box, type **ProductsDestination.txt,** and then click Open.

11. At the bottom of the Flat File Connection Manager Editor box, select the Column Names In The First Data Row check box.

12. In the left pane, click Columns.

    Notice that the data flow metadata is used to set the column names of the output file.

13. Click OK to close the Flat File Connection Manager Editor.

14. In the Flat File Destination Editor, ensure that the Overwrite Data In The File check box is selected.

15. In the left pane, click Mappings to associate the input columns with the destination columns.

    Your screen looks like this:

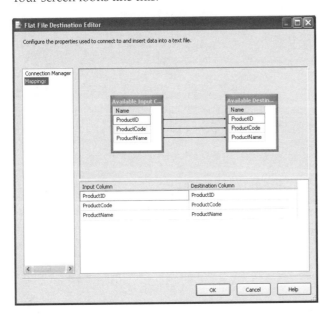

16. Click OK to close the Flat File Destination Editor.

Execute the package

1. In BIDS, in Solution Explorer, right-click NewProducts.dtsx and click Execute Package.

   The package is saved and executed in debug mode.

   In the designer, notice that the task blocks turn green as each task is successfully completed. When the package has successfully executed, it should read, "Package execution completed. Click here to switch to design mode, or select Stop Debugging from the Debug menu at the bottom of the screen."

   Your screen looks similar to this:

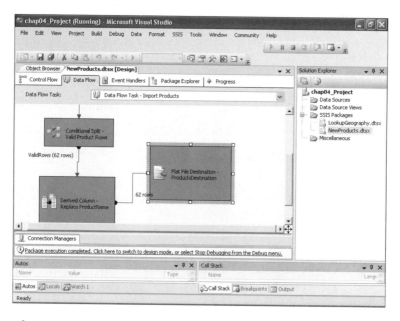

2. After execution is complete, on the Debug menu, click the Stop Debugging button.

3. In Windows Explorer, navigate to the C:\Documents and Settings\<username>\My Documents\Microsoft Press\is2005sbs\ Chap04 \Data folder.

4. Double-click the ProductsDestination.txt file to open it.

Your screen now looks like this:

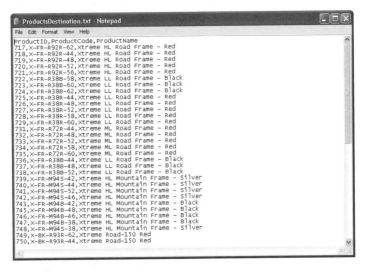

5. In the ProductsDestination.text file, confirm that the correct rows with properly transformed data (product names without size) appear in the file.

6. Close the ProductsDestination.text file.

Sending Output to Different Destinations

Now you're ready to send the results of the Derived Column transformation to two destinations: a database table and the existing flat-file destination. In the first procedure, you will add a Multicast transformation named Multicast – File and Database to the NewProducts package. Then you will add a SQL Server destination data adapter named SQL Server Destination – ProductNames and create a database table named ProductNames. Finally, you will create the Execute SQL Task – Delete From ProductNames task that deletes the data from the ProductNames table and then execute the package and evaluate the results.

Add a Multicast transformation

1. In BIDS, on the Toolbox menu, in the Data Flow Transformations group, drag Multicast onto the Data Flow design surface. The Multicast transformation appears on the Data Flow designer.

> **Note**   Both Multicast transformations and Conditional Split transformations have multiple outputs; however, with Multicast transformations, each output gets all the rows.

2. In the Properties list, locate Name, and then change the name property from Multicast to **Multicast – File and Database**.

3. Delete the connector (green arrow) between Derived Column – Replace ProductName and Flat File Destination – ProductsDestination.

4. Drag the output (green arrow) from Derived Column – Replace ProductName onto the Multicast – File and Database transformation.

5. Drag the output (green arrow) from the Multicast – File and Database transformation onto Flat File Destination – ProductsDestination.

   Your screen now looks similar to this:

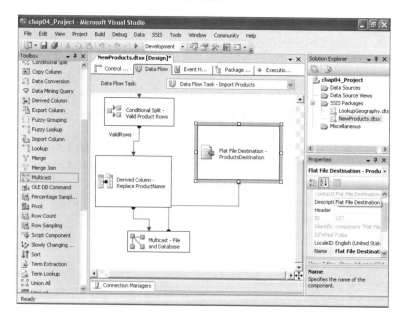

> **Note**   As long as you don't do anything to change the lineage of the columns, you can break and read flows without remapping. If you do anything that might affect the columns, you must discard the mapping and re-create it.

Add a SQL Server destination data adapter

1. In BIDS, on the Toolbox menu, in the Data Flow Transformations group, drag SQL Server Destination onto the Data Flow design surface. The Destination data adapter appears on the Data Flow designer.

2. In the Properties list, locate Name, and then change the name property from SQL Server Destination to **SQL Server Destination – ProductNames**.

3. Drag the output (green arrow) from Multicast – File and Database Transformation onto SQL Server Destination – ProductNames.

   Your screen now looks similar to this:

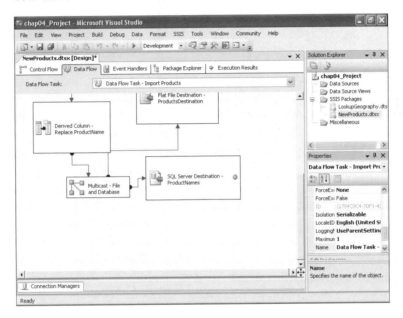

   Now that you have added the SQL Server Destination data adapter, you will create a new table named ProductNames.

4. In the Data Flow designer, double-click the new data adapter named SQL Server Destination – ProductNames. The SQL Destination Editor dialog box opens.

5. In the editor, ensure that the LocalHost.QuickStartODS is selected as the OLE DB connection manager.

6. To create a new table:

    ❑   To the right of the Use A Table Or View drop-down list, click New. The Create Table dialog box opens.

    ❑   In the Create Table dialog box, delete the text between the two brackets that reads SQL Server Destination – Product Names and replace it with **ProductNames**.

Your screen looks like this:

    ❑   Click OK to close the Create Table dialog box.

The connection manager will create a table for you, but it defaults to the name of the data adapter.

> **Note**   Notice that you don't have the option to overwrite the data as you had when you added the Flat File Destination data adapter. Therefore, in the following procedure, you will delete the data from the ProductNames table.

7. In the SQL Destination Editor, in the left pane, click Mappings to create mappings between the input and destination columns.

Your screen now looks like this:

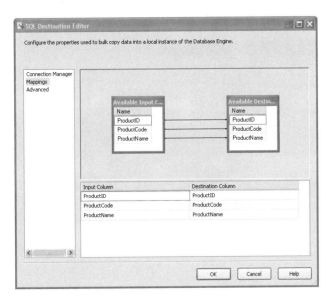

8. Click OK to close the SQL Destination Editor.

> **Important**   Before loading the ProductNames table, be aware that this task will delete any records that it might already contain.

Create the task that deletes data from the table

1. On the Toolbox menu, in the Control Flow Items group, drag Execute SQL Task onto the Control Flow design surface. The new Execute SQL task appears on the Control Flow designer.

2. In the Properties list, locate Name, and then change the name property from Execute SQL Task to **Execute SQL Task – Delete From ProductNames**.

3. In the Control Flow designer, double-click Execute SQL Task – Delete From Product-Names. The Execute SQL Task Editor opens.

4. In the Execute SQL Task Editor, in the right pane, under SQL Statement, click Connection, and then, in the right box, select LocalHost.QuickStartODS.

5. Under SQL Statement, click SQLStatement, and then click the ellipses button in the right box. The Enter SQL Query dialog box opens.

6. In the Enter SQL Query box, type **Delete From ProductNames**.

7. Click OK to close the Enter SQL Query box.

Your screen now looks like this:

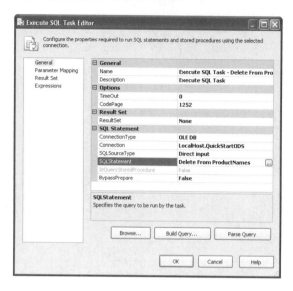

8.   Click OK to close the Execute SQL Task Editor.

9.   In the Control Flow designer, click the Execute SQL Task – Delete From ProductNames task, and then drag the precedence constraint (green arrow) onto Data Flow Task – Import Products.

Your screen looks similar to this:

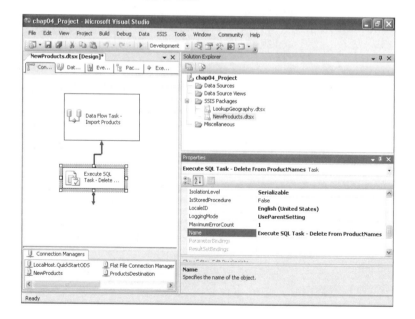

The precedence constraint ensures that Execute SQL Task – Delete From ProductNames successfully deletes the data in the ProductNames table before Data Flow Task – Import Products populates the table.

Execute the package and check the results

1. In BIDS, in Solution Explorer, right-click NewProducts.dtsx, and then click Execute Package.

2. After the execution is complete, on the Debug menu, click Stop Debugging.

3. Open Microsoft SQL Server Management Studio.

4. In SQL Server Management Studio, in the left pane, in Object Explorer, expand the Databases folder, expand QuickStartODS, and then expand the Tables folder.

5. In the Tables folder, right-click dbo.ProductNames, and then click Open Table.

> **Tip**   If you don't see dbo.ProductNames listed, right-click the Tables folder, and then click Refresh.

The Table – dbo.ProductNames tab appears in the right pane, and the table populates with data.

6. Confirm that the table includes the correct rows with properly transformed data (product names without size).

Your screen now looks like this:

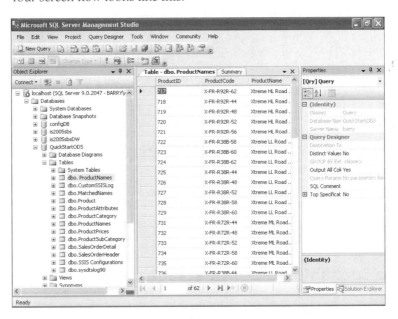

Configuring Error Output

When a data flow component applies a transformation to column data, extracts data from sources, or loads data into destinations, errors can occur. Errors usually occur because of unexpected data values, such as when an expression fails to evaluate because a column value is zero.

Types of Errors

Errors fall into one of the following two categories:

- **Errors**   An error indicates an unequivocal failure and generates a NULL result.
- **Truncation**   A truncation is less serious than an error. You can elect to treat truncations as errors or as acceptable conditions.

Error Options

Many data flow components support error outputs that enable you to control how the component handles errors. You have the option to ignore the error, redirect the row to the component's error output, or fail the component. The following list describes these options.

- **Fail Component**   When this option is chosen, the data flow task fails when an error or truncation occurs.
- **Ignore Failure**   When this option is chosen, the error or truncation is ignored, and the data row is directed to continue on to the next transformation. For example, if a Lookup transformation fails, you can have a Derived Column transformation set the failed lookup column to Unknown.
- **Redirect Row**   This option allows you to continue processing successfully transformed rows and to redirect error rows to a data destination where they can be examined and perhaps reprocessed.

> **Note**   By default, all components are configured to fail on error or truncation.

The following set of procedures shows you how to create a package that will read a file containing customer data and then look up geography data from the *is2005sbsDW* database Dim-Geography table. It is important to track the rows of data where the lookup is unsuccessful. You will configure the lookup task to redirect lookup error rows to a file for later investigation.

Exploring the LookupGeography Package

Before you begin the process of configuring error output, it's important to open and explore the LookupGeography package. You will use the Flat File Connection Manager Editor to preview the data in the CustomerList.txt file and to verify that the correct database is selected. The following steps will walk you through the procedure.

Open and explore the package

1. In BIDS, in Solution Explorer, double-click LookupGeography.dtsx. The package opens in design mode.

> **Note** The LookupGeography package already contains a flat file and an OLE DB connection manager.

2. In the Connection Managers pane, right-click CustomerList, and then click Edit. The Flat File Connection Manager Editor opens.

3. In the Flat File Connection Manager Editor, in the left pane, click Preview.

4. The data contained in the CustomerList.txt file, which is located in the C:\Documents and Settings\<username>\My Documents\Microsoft Press\is2005sbs\Chap04\Data folder, is displayed.

    Your screen now looks like this:

5. Click OK to close the editor.

6. In the Connection Managers pane, right-click LocalHost.is2005sbsDW, and then click Edit. The Connection Manager dialog box opens.

7. In the Connection Manager dialog box, in the Connect To A Database frame, in the Select Or Enter A Database Name drop-down list, verify that is2005sbsDW is selected.

8. Click OK to close the Connection Manager dialog box.

Creating a Task

Before you can configure error output, you need to create a task that can be used to read a file containing customer data. In this procedure, you will create a new Data Flow task named Data Flow Task – Lookup Geography.

Create the Data Flow Task – Lookup Geography task

1. On the Toolbox menu, in the Control Flow Items group, drag Data Flow Task onto the Control Flow design surface. The new Data Flow task appears on the Control Flow designer.

2. In the Properties list, locate Name, and then change the name property from Data Flow Task to **Data Flow Task – Lookup Geography**.

3. In the Control Flow designer, double-click Data Flow Task – Lookup Geography.

    Notice that the Data Flow tab is now selected, and you have switched from the Control Flow designer to the Data Flow designer.

Creating and Naming a Flat File Source

Now that you have created the Data Flow Task – Lookup Geography task, you can create the flat-file source that will be used to read the file containing customer data. In this procedure, you will create a flat-file source and name it Flat File Source – CustomerList. You will then map the Connection Manager columns to the Flat File Source columns.

Create a flat file

1. On the Toolbox menu, in the Data Flow Sources group, drag Flat File Source onto the Data Flow design surface. The new Flat File Source appears on the Data Flow designer.

2. In the Properties list, locate Name, and then change the name property from Flat File Source to **Flat File Source – CustomerList**.

3. In the Data Flow designer, double-click Flat File Source – CustomerList. The Flat File Source Editor dialog box opens.

4. In the Flat File Source Editor, in the Flat File Connection Manager drop-down list, ensure that CustomerList is selected.

5. In the left pane, click Columns to map the Connection Manager columns to the Flat File Source columns.

Your screen looks like this:

6.   Click OK to close the Flat File Source Editor.

Adding a Data Conversion Transformation

In this procedure, you'll create a Data Conversion transformation named Data Conversion – NumGeographyKey.

To use the Lookup transformation, the source column and the lookup column must have the same data type. In this procedure, you'll use a Data Conversion transformation to convert the GeographyKey column in the source file to an integer.

Convert the GeographyKey column to an integer

1.   On the Toolbox menu, in the Data Flow Transformations group, drag Data Conversion onto the Data Flow design surface. The new Data Conversion transformation appears on the Data Flow designer.

2.   In the Properties list, locate Name, and then change the name property from Data Conversion to **Data Conversion – NumGeographyKey**.

3.   In the Control Flow designer, click Flat File Source – CustomerList, and then drag its output (green arrow) onto Data Conversion – NumGeographyKey.

4.   Double-click Data Conversion – NumGeographyKey. The Data Conversion Transformation Editor opens.

5. In the Data Conversion Transformation Editor, in the Available Input Columns table, select the CustomerKey check box.

   Notice that a row was added to the table in the bottom pane.

6. In the bottom pane, in the Output Alias column, type **NumGeographyKey**.

7. In the Data Type column, select four-byte signed integer [DT_I4].

   Your screen looks similar to this:

8. Click OK to close the Data Conversion Transformation Editor.

Adding a Lookup Transformation

Now that the GeographyKey in the source file matches the data type of the key column of the lookup table, you can add the Lookup transformation to obtain additional columns of data. In this procedure, you will add a Lookup transformation named Lookup – Geography.

Add a Lookup transformation

1. On the Toolbox menu, in the Data Flow Transformations group, drag Lookup onto the Data Flow design surface. The new Lookup transformation appears on the Data Flow designer.

2. In the Properties list, locate Name, and then change the name property from Lookup to **Lookup Geography**.

3. In the Control Flow designer, click Data Conversion – NumGeographyKey, and then drag its output (green arrow) to Lookup – Geography.

4. Double-click the Lookup – Geography transformation. The Lookup Transformation Editor opens with the Reference Table tab selected.

5. In the Lookup Transformation Editor, in the OLE DB Connection Manager drop-down list, ensure that LocalHost.is2005sbsDW is selected.

6. Ensure that the Use A Table Or View option is selected, and then select [dbo].[Dim-Geography].

    The [dbo].[DimGeography] table is now selected.

7. Click the Columns tab.

8. In the Available Input Columns table, drag NumGeographyKey and drop it on GeographyKey in the Available Lookup Columns table.

    The lookup join is now established.

9. In the Available Lookup Columns table, select the City, StateProvinceName, and CountryRegionName check boxes.

10. In the bottom pane, in the Output Alias column, click StateProvinceName and rename it **StateProvince**.

11. In the Output Alias column, click CountryRegionName and rename it **CountryRegion**.

    Your screen looks like this:

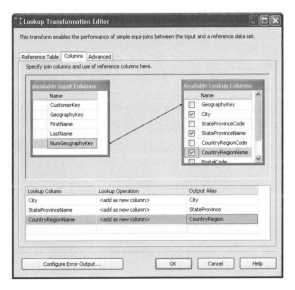

12. At the bottom of the screen, click Configure Error Output. The Configure Error Output dialog box opens.

13. In the first row, click the Error column, and then select Redirect Row.

14. Click OK to close the Configure Error Output dialog box.

15. Click OK to close the Lookup Transformation Editor.

Adding a Flat File Destination for Lookup Errors

In this procedure, you will write lookup errors to a file for later investigation and possible reprocessing. First, you will create a flat-file destination and name it Flat File Destination – Lookup Errors. Then, you will drag Lookup – Geography error output to Flat File Destination – Lookup Errors and create a new connection manager named LookupErrors. Finally, you will use the Flat File Destination Editor to associate the input columns with the destination columns.

Write lookup errors to a file

1. On the Toolbox menu, in the Data Flow Destinations group, drag Flat File Destination onto the Data Flow design surface.

2. In the Properties list, locate Name, and then change the name property from Flat File Destination to **Flat File Destination – Lookup Errors**.

3. In the Control Flow designer, click Lookup – Geography, and then drag its error output (red arrow) to Flat File Destination – Lookup Errors. The Configure Error Output box opens.

4. Click OK to close the Configure Error Output dialog box.

5. Double-click Flat File Destination – Lookup Errors. The Flat File Destination Editor opens.

6. In the Flat File Destination Editor, click New to create a new connection manager. The Flat File Format dialog box opens.

7. In the Flat File Format box, ensure that the Delimited option is selected, and then click OK.

8. In the Flat File Connection Manager Editor box, in the File Name box, type **Lookup-Errors**.

9. Click Browse. The Open dialog box appears.

10. Navigate to C:\Documents and Settings\<username>\My Documents\Microsoft Press\is2005sbs\Chap04\Data.

11. Select **LookupErrors.txt**, and then click Open.

12. In the Flat File Connection Manager Editor, at the bottom of the box, select the Column Names In The First Data Row check box.

13. Click OK to close the Flat File Connection Manager Editor.

14. In the Flat File Destination Editor, ensure that the Overwrite Data In The File option is selected.

15. In the left pane, click Mappings.

The input columns are now associated with the destination columns.

Your screen looks like this:

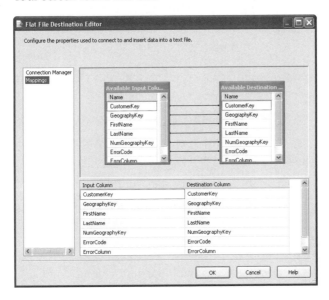

16. Click OK to close the Flat File Destination Editor.

Adding a Flat File Destination for Successful Lookups

In this procedure, you'll write successful rows to another flat file. First, you will create a flat-file destination and name it Flat File Destination – NewCustomerList. Then, you will drag Lookup – Geography successful lookup output to Flat File Destination – NewCustomerList and create a new connection manager named NewCustomerList. Finally, you will use the Flat File Destination Editor to associate the input columns with the destination columns.

Write successful rows to another flat file

1. On the Toolbox menu, in the Data Flow Destinations group, drag Flat File Destination onto the Data Flow design surface.

2. In the Properties list, locate Name, and then change the name property from Flat File Destination to **Flat File Destination – NewCustomerList**.

3. In the Control Flow designer, click Lookup – Geography, and then drag its successful lookup output (green arrow) to Flat File Destination – NewCustomerList.

4. Double-click Flat File Destination – NewCustomerList. The Flat File Destination Editor opens.

5. In the Flat File Destination Editor, click New to create a new connection manager. The Flat File Format dialog box opens.

6. In the Flat File Format dialog box, ensure that the Delimited option is selected, and then click OK.

7. In the Flat File Connection Manager Editor, in the File Name box, type **NewCustomerList**.

    The connection manager is now named NewCustomerList.

8. Click Browse. The Open dialog box appears.

9. Navigate to C:\Documents and Settings\<username>\My Documents\Microsoft Press\is2005sbs\Chap04\Data.

10. In the File name box, type **NewCustomerList.txt**, and then click Open.

11. In the Flat File Connection Manager Editor, at the bottom of the box, select the Column Names In The First Data Row check box.

12. Click OK to close the Flat File Connection Manager Editor.

13. In the Flat File Destination Editor, ensure that the Overwrite data in the file check box is selected.

14. In the left pane, click Mappings.

    The input columns are now associated with the destination columns.

15. Click OK to close the Flat File Destination Editor.

Executing the Package and Checking the Results

In the previous exercises, you created the task named Data Flow Task – Lookup Geography and the flat-file source named Flat File Source – CustomerList to read data from a text file. You then created a Data Conversion transformation named Data Conversion – NumGeographyKey to convert the data in an input column and copy it to a new output column. You added a Lookup transformation named Lookup – Geography to perform lookups. After this was completed, you wrote lookup errors to a file. Finally, you added a flat-file destination for successful lookups. Now that you have completed these steps, you are ready to execute the package and review the results. The following steps will show you how to accomplish this.

Execute the package and check the results

1. In BIDS, in Solution Explorer, right-click LookupGeography.dtsx, and then click Execute Package.

2. After the execution is complete, on the Debug menu, click Stop Debugging.

3. In Windows Explorer, navigate to C:\Documents and Settings\<username>\My Documents\Microsoft Press\is3005sbs\Chap04\Data.

4. In the Data folder, open the file named NewCustomerList.txt and verify that it contains customer and geography data.

    Your screen looks like this:

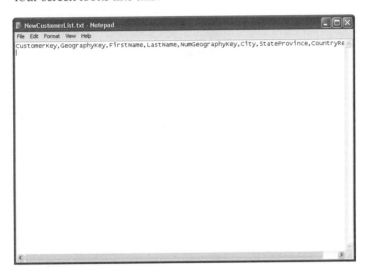

5. In the Data folder, open the file named LookupErrors.txt and verify that it contains lookup failures with customer data but that it doesn't contain any geography data.

    Your screen looks like this:

Chapter 4 Quick Reference

To	Do This
Open the SSIS project	In Windows Explorer, navigate to the project, and then double-click the file to open it in BIDS. In Solution Explorer, double-click a package to open it in design mode.
Create a data flow task	In BIDS, on the Toolbox menu, in the Control Flow Items group, drag Data Flow Task onto the Control Flow design surface.
Edit an object	In BIDS, on the design surface, double-click the object, and then change its properties as needed.
Create a data adapter	In BIDS, on the Toolbox menu, in the Data Flow Sources group, drag Flat File Source onto the Data Flow design surface.
Add a connection manager	In BIDS, on the Data Flow designer, double-click the data adapter. In the Editor dialog box, click New to create a new connection manager. Specify the file name, the file properties, and the file format.
Add a Conditional Split transformation	In BIDS, on the Toolbox menu, in the Data Flow Transformations group, drag Conditional Split onto the Data Flow surface.
Add a Derived Column transformation	In BIDS, on the Toolbox menu, in the Data Flow Transformations group, drag Derived Column onto the Data Flow design surface.
Add a Multicast transformation	In BIDS, on the Toolbox menu, in the Data Flow Transformations group, drag Multicast onto the Data Flow design surface.
Add a Destination data adapter	In BIDS, on the Toolbox menu, in the Data Flow Transformations group, drag SQL Server Destination onto the design surface.
Create a task	In BIDS, on the Toolbox menu, in the Control Flow Items group, drag Data Flow Task onto the design surface.
Create a flat file	In BIDS, on the Toolbox menu, in the Data Flow Sources group, drag Flat File Source onto the design surface.
Add a lookup transformation	In BIDS, on the Toolbox menu, in the Data Flow Transformations group, drag Lookup onto the design surface.

Chapter 5
Managing Control Flow

After completing this chapter, you will be able to:

- Understand control flow management.

- Group and organize tasks in a control flow, using different types of containers.

- Use Fuzzy Lookup and the Foreach Loop container to extend the functionality of cleaning data and repeating control flow in a package.

- Design the flow of a package, applying precedence constraints between components of a package.

In Chapter 4, "Using Data Flow Transformations," you learned how to develop packages that use a data flow task and a variety of data flow transformations to extract data from a data source, perform transformations, and load the transformed data into a destination table or file. In this chapter, you'll learn how to design a control flow of tasks, group data flow tasks to organize and structure your package, and define an order of execution by defining precedence and conditions between tasks or groups of tasks. You'll also learn how to use Fuzzy Lookup to perform data cleaning and a Foreach Loop container for repetition of a specific task. Specifically, you'll learn how to group, organize, and arrange tasks into a control flow. You will also learn how to use a Foreach Loop container to extend the functionality of a regular container.

Control Flow Elements

Microsoft SQL Server Integration Services (SSIS) is a tool to move data between different systems; it's also an effective and complete tool to extract, transform, process, and clean data and perform maintenance. In general, SSIS is a set of components to create complex solutions organized in a controlled work flow.

When you create a package, you use a set of control flow items and maintenance tasks in the control flow pane. Then you need to specify how they will be related to each other. Figure 5-1 is an example of this basic architecture.

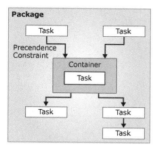

Figure 5-1   Package control flow architecture

A package consists of a control flow and, optionally, one or more data flows. SSIS provides three different types of control flow elements:

- Containers that provide structures in packages

- Tasks that provide functionality

- Precedence constraints that connect the executables, containers, and tasks into an ordered control flow

Tasks are control flow elements that define units of work to be performed in a package control flow. An SSIS package is composed of one or more tasks. If the package contains more than one task, they are connected and sequenced in the control flow by precedence constraints. A control flow can consist of more than one level of nested containers. For instance, in this chapter, you will create a container that contains a Foreach Loop container to perform a specific task.

Control Flow Components

The SSIS Designer provides a toolbox that contains all the control flow items and maintenance plan tasks. You can find more specific and detailed information about each component in Microsoft SQL Server 2005 Books Online at *http://msdn2.microsoft.com/en-us/library /ms130214.aspx*. The following is a list of the control flow components available in SSIS:

- Data flow tasks

- SQL Server tasks

- Data preparation tasks

- Workflow tasks

- Scripting tasks

- Analysis Services tasks

- Maintenance tasks

- Containers

This list represents the typical control flow components. However, SSIS gives developers the ability to write custom tasks by using a programming language such as Microsoft Visual Basic.NET or C#.NET.

Now you will learn how to use some of these components in a workflow. The first exercise will show you the *DelayValidation* property.

Note   *DelayValidation* is an important property used to delay the validation of an SSIS object until run time. This property exists on all SSIS components.

When this property is set to *False*, which is its default value, it can help you find problems prior to execution. These errors or warnings can be real or potential issues. Thus, when you know that they are related to objects that haven't been created but will be created later as part of the process, you can ignore them by setting the *DelayValidation* property to *True*.

For example, it is common to create a complex extract, transform, and load (ETL) process with several packages that need to run in sequence. They could consume considerable time and fail after several hours of execution because one of the packages needs objects that haven't been created yet. Even if you tested this ETL process in the development environment and did not encounter errors, it can fail in the production environment. This occurs because, in development, you have all the objects you need, but in the production environment, you don't necessarily have all the objects. They are created when the process runs.

In this scenario, you probably want to use the *DelayValidation* property. Setting this property to *True* in the objects that could potentially have issues allows you to skip pre-execution validation, and your package can start running without errors. In the following procedure, you'll set the *DelayValidation* property.

Note   At execution, SSIS checks or validates all objects that were not validated in the pre-execution phase.

Work with tasks and *DelayValidation*

1. Open Microsoft SQL Server Management Studio, connect to your Database Engine server, and verify that the Employee table is deleted from the *QuickStartODS* database.

2. Navigate to C:\Documents and Settings\<username>\My Documents\Microsoft Press\is2005sbs\Chap05 and double-click Chap05.sln to open the solution in Microsoft Visual Studio.

3. Notice that the Error List pane is empty.

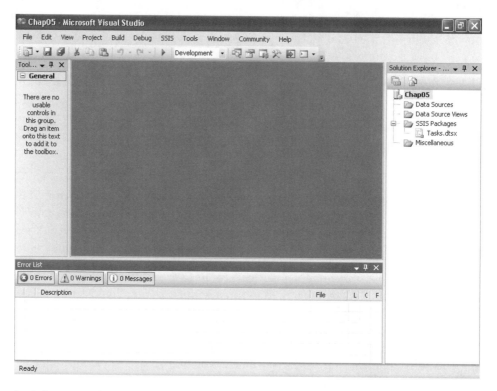

4. In Solution Explorer, in the SSIS Package folder, double-click Tasks.dtsx.

5. In the Control Flow pane, right-click an open area and click Properties to display the Properties pane.

6. In the Execution group, verify that *DelayValidation* is set to *False*.

7. Click the Execute SQL Task – Create Employee Table task and notice that the Properties pane changes. In the Execution group, verify that *DelayValidation* is *False*.

8. Do the same to Data Flow Task – Employee Excel to QSODS. Verify that *DelayValidation* is *False*.

   You can also see that the Error List pane shows two errors. In the last sentences of their descriptions, they say "Invalid object name 'dbo.Employee'" and "Check that the object exists in the database." In fact, the object, which is the Employee table, hasn't been created yet.

9.   Your screen should look similar to this:

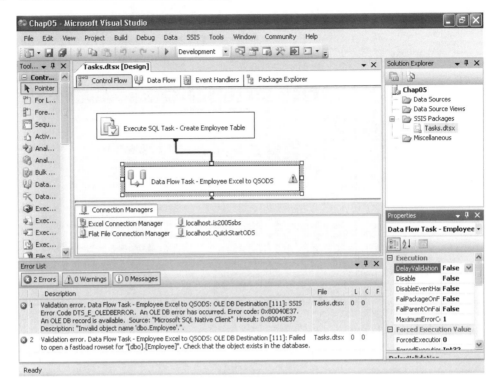

10.   Right-click Tasks.dtsx and choose Execute Package. A Package Validation Error is displayed.

> **Note**   It is a valid error because the destination table has not been created yet.

11. Your screen should look similar to this:

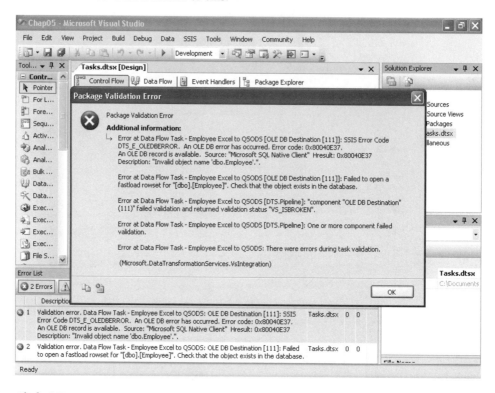

12. Click OK.

13. Select the Tasks Package in the Properties pane and change the *DelayValidation* setting to *True* for the package.

14. Execute the package again and verify that it finishes successfully.

15. In SQL Server Management Studio (SSMS), verify that the Employee table has been created with data in the *QuickStartODS* database.

16. On the Debug menu, click the Stop Debugging button to stop the executed package, and then close Visual Studio.

Using Containers

SSIS contains four types of containers. They are objects that give structure to packages and additional functionality to tasks. They support repeating control flows in packages, and they group tasks and containers into meaningful units of work. Containers can include other containers in addition to tasks. The following is a list of container types available in SSIS.

■ **Foreach Loop container**   Defines a control flow repeatedly by using an enumerator. The Foreach Loop container repeats the control flow for each member of a specified enumerator. For example, if you want to read all the files that have the *.log file name extension located in a specific folder, use the Foreach file enumerator.

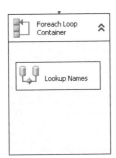

■ **For Loop container**   Evaluates an expression and repeats its workflow until the expression evaluates to *False*. For example, you can define an initial expression as @iCounter=0, an evaluation expression as @iCounter<5, and the iteration expression as @iCounter=@iCounter + 1, and the task will run five times. The expressions must be valid SSIS expressions. You can build nested loops and implement complex looping because For Loop containers can include other For Loop containers.

- **Sequence container**   Groups tasks and containers into control flows that are subsets of the package control flow. That is, sequence containers group the package into multiple separate control flows. It gives you such benefits as the ability to disable groups for debugging, to manage properties on multiple tasks instead of on just individual tasks, and to provide scope for variables that are used by components in the sequence container.

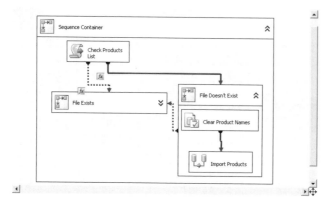

- **Task Host container**   The nested-container architecture of Integration Services enables all containers to include other containers except for the Task Host container, which encapsulates only a single task. The Task Host container services a single task.

Note   Packages and Event Handlers are also types of containers.

The next exercise uses sequence containers to link groups of tasks. The objective is to test whether the output file already exists. A script task is used to verify whether the file exists. If it does, then only a portion of the package needs to execute, but if the file does not exist, the entire package needs to run.

Note   The next exercise uses the solution described in Chapter 4, "Using Data Flow Transformations," as the source.

Add sequence containers

1. Navigate to C:\Documents and Settings\<username>\My Documents\Microsoft Press\is2005sbs\Chap05\Chap05(b) and double-click Chap05(b).sln to open the solution in Visual Studio.

2. Open the NewProducts.dtsx package.

3. On the Control Flow page, drag a Sequence Container object from the Control Flow Items group Toolbox to the grid.

4. In the Properties window, in the Name box, change the name of the sequence container to **Sequence Container – File Doesn't Exist**.

> **Tip**   Alternatively, you can right-click the sequence container and choose Rename.

5. Drag existing tasks into the sequence container.

   To do this, you must select and drag Execute SQL Task – Delete From ProductNames and Data Flow Task – Import Products together rather than individually. Your screen should look similar to this:

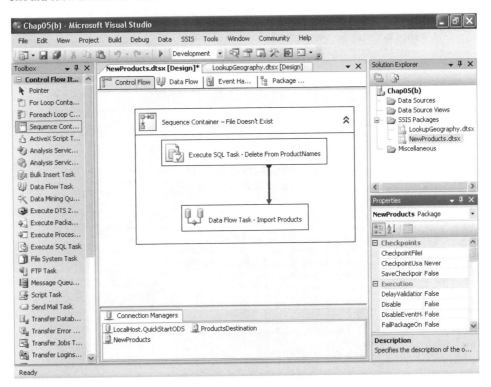

Now you need a way to test whether the output file is found and, if not found, to jump to the sequence container. The first step is to create a variable for the package.

Test whether the output file is found

1. Right-click the background of the Control Flow pane and choose Variables.

   This brings up a window that you can dock on the side.

2. Click the Add Variable button in the Variables toolbar.

3. In the Name column, change the name to **FileFound**. In the Data Type column, change the type to **Boolean**.

> **Note** The scope for a variable is the container that is active when you create the variable. In this case, it is the package.

Your screen should look similar to this:

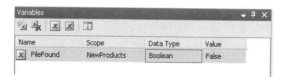

Next, assign a value to the variable. You can use a script task to do this.

Assign a value to the variable

1. Drag Script Task from the Control Flow Items group Toolbox to the grid.

2. Double-click Script Task to open the Script Task Editor.

3. On the General page, in the Name property box, change the *Name* property to **Script Task – Check Products List**.

4. On the Script page, notice that the default language is Visual Basic .NET. Click the Design Script button to add the following non-bold code to the *Main()* subroutine. You can also copy the script from the Script file in the Data folder.

```
Public Sub Main()
    Try
        Dim myVariable as Variables
        Dts.VariableDispenser.LockOneForWrite("FileFound", myVariable)
        myVariable("FileFound").Value =
        System.IO.File.Exists(Dts.Connections( _
        "ProductsDestination").ConnectionString)
        Dts.TaskResult = Dts.Results.Success
    Catch
    Dts.TaskResult = Dts.Results.Failure
    End Try

    Dts.TaskResult = Dts.Results.Success
End Sub
```

The VariableDispenser belongs to the task, not to the package. If you have multiple variables to acquire, you add each one independently to the VariableDispenser, using LockForRead and LockForWrite and only the variable name as an argument. This does not actually lock the variable but puts it in a list to lock. Once all the variables are in the dispenser, you call GetVariables to put the array of variables into the local variable (*myVariable* in this example). If you need only one variable, the *LockOne* functions are a shortcut.

Use System.IO to test for the existence of the output file. Rather than hard-code the path and filename, use the connection. The *FileFound* variable will contain the result of the test. Whether the file is found or not, the task will return Success.

You don't need to release the variable at the end of the function. It will be done automatically at the end of the package. Your code should look like this:

```vb
' Microsoft SQL Server Integration Services Script Task
' Write scripts using Microsoft Visual Basic
' The ScriptMain class is the entry point of the Script Task.

Imports System
Imports System.Data
Imports System.Math
Imports Microsoft.SqlServer.Dts.Runtime

Public Class ScriptMain

    ' The execution engine calls this method when the task executes.
    ' To access the object model, use the Dts object. Connections, variables,
    ' and logging features are available as static members of the Dts class.
    ' Before returning from this method, set the value of Dts.TaskResult to i
    '
    ' To open Code and Text Editor Help, press F1.
    ' To open Object Browser, press Ctrl+Alt+J.

    Public Sub Main()
        '
        Try
            Dim myVariable As Variables
            Dts.VariableDispenser.LockOneForWrite("FileFound", myVariable)
            myVariable("FileFound").Value = System.IO.File.Exists(Dts.Connect
            Dts.TaskResult = Dts.Results.Success
        Catch
            Dts.TaskResult = Dts.Results.Failure
        End Try

        '
        Dts.TaskResult = Dts.Results.Success
    End Sub

End Class
```

5. Close the Design Script window and click OK to close the Script Task Editor.

   The next step is to create a placeholder for the tasks to be performed if the file is found.

Create a placeholder

1. On the Control Flow page, drag Sequence Container from the Control Flow Items group Toolbox to the grid.

2. Right-click the name of the container and rename the sequence container **Sequence Container – File Exists**.

3. Using Windows Explorer, navigate to the C:\Documents and Settings\<username>\My Documents\Microsoft Press\is2005sbs\Chap05\Chap05(b)\Data\ folder.

4. Open the FuzzyInputA.txt file to review its contents.

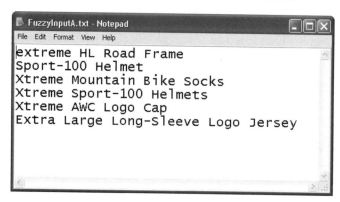

5. On the Control Flow page, drag a Data Flow Task from the Control Flow Items group Toolbox to the Sequence Container – File Exists container.

6. Right-click the new task, select Rename, and change the name of the task to **Data Flow Task – Lookup Names.**

7. Double-click Data Flow Task – Lookup Names to open the Data Flow page.

8. Drag Flat File Source from the Data Flow Sources group Toolbox to the grid. Rename this task **Flat File Source – FuzzyInput.**

9. Double-click the Flat File Source – FuzzyInput data adapter, and then click the New button to open the Flat File Connection Manager Editor to create a new connection manager.

10. Enter a name for the connection manager: **Product Input Names**.

11. Use the Browse button to navigate to the source text file: C:\Documents and Settings\<username>\My Documents\Microsoft Press\is2005sbs\Chap05\Chap05(b)\Data\FuzzyInputA.txt.

12. Click Advanced to edit the following properties:

   a. Name: **ProductName**

   b. OutputColumnWidth: **50**

13. Click OK.

> **Note**   Fuzzy Lookup gives a warning if the column width of the source is different from the reference column.

14. In the Flat File Source Editor, click Columns. This will set the mapping between the External Column and the Output Column. Click OK.

Adding a Fuzzy Lookup Transformation

The Fuzzy Lookup transformation performs data cleaning tasks. Fuzzy Lookup enables you to match input records with clean, standardized records in a reference table. This transformation finds the closest match and indicates the quality of the match. The reference data must be a table in a SQL Server 2005 database. The match between the value in an input column and the value in the reference table can be an exact match or an approximate match. However, if you want an exact match, it is better to use a Lookup transformation instead. The transformation requires at least one column match to be configured for fuzzy matching.

Because Fuzzy Lookup transformation needs a reference table, it could sometimes consume time and resources, especially in large environments. Fuzzy Lookup uses temporal index tables to store the data for easy access and to enhance performance, which can consume a large amount of memory. You can make adjustments in the advance properties to optimize the performance within your specific environment. It is good practice to use non-production servers to run large and complex fuzzy transformation tasks.

> **Note**   Columns that participate in the join between the input and the reference table must have compatible data types.

Now you're ready to match the list of names in the input file to the master list of new product names.

Add a Fuzzy Lookup transformation

1. Drag a Fuzzy Lookup transformation from the Data Flow Transformations group Toolbox to the grid. Rename it **Fuzzy Lookup – Product Names**.

2. Connect the output from Flat File Source – FuzzyInput to Fuzzy Lookup – Product Names by clicking and dragging the green arrow.

3. Double-click the Fuzzy Lookup task to open the Fuzzy Lookup Transformation Editor and set the properties to Connection manager: localhost.QuickStartODS.

4. Generate a new index, using Reference Table [dbo].[ProductNames].

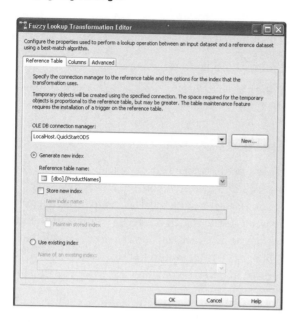

> **Tip**   Fuzzy Lookup creates a sophisticated index on the lookup table. It can create the index each time, or it can store the index in the database. For a large lookup table that doesn't change frequently, you should store the indexes.

5. Click the Columns tab, and then create a join between ProductName in the Available Input Columns and ProductName in the Available Lookup Columns by clicking and dragging ProductName from the Input Columns to ProductName in the Lookup Columns.

6. Check the Pass Through checkbox in the Available Input Columns table so that the source file name is included in the output file.

7. Select the ProductName column as the Lookup Column.

8. Click OK.

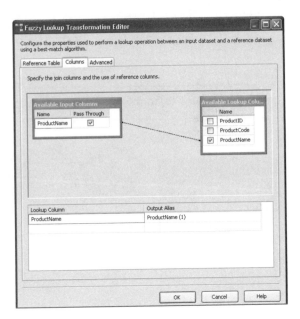

Now you are ready to put the results of the lookup into a database table.

Add a SQL Server destination

1. Drag SQL Server Destination from the Data Flow Destinations group Toolbox to the grid. Rename it **SQL Server Destination – MatchedNames**.

2. Drag an output arrow from the Fuzzy Lookup transformation to the SQL Server destination.

3. Double-click the SQL Server Destination – MatchedNames data adapter.

4. Select the connection manager: localhost.QuickStartODS.

5. Click the New button to create a new table.

6. Replace the default table name SQL Server Destination – MatchedNames with **Matched-Names**.

7. Click OK.

> **Note** Notice the extra columns created to hold statistics for the transformation.

Your screen should look similar to this:

8. Click Mappings in the SQL Destination Editor to set the correct mappings between the input and destination columns.

9. Click OK.

Now you should have a screen that looks like this:

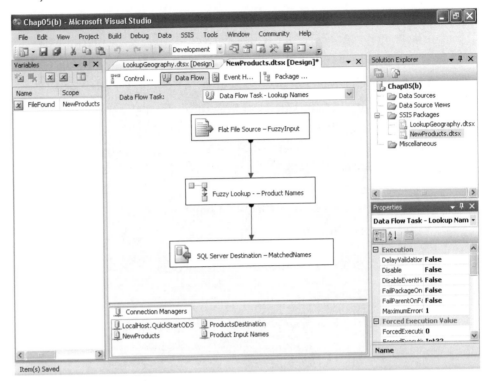

If you run the task a second time, the same rows will be added twice to the Matched-Names table. You can add a step that clears out the destination table before executing the lookup.

Add an Execute SQL task

1. On the Control Flow page, add a new Execute SQL Task to the File Exists container. Double-click the new task and set the following properties:

    ❏ Name: **Execute SQL Task – Clear Matched Names**

    ❏ Connection: localhost.QuickStartODS

    ❏ SQL Statement: Delete from MatchedNames

2. Click OK.

Adding a Foreach Loop Container

The next step is to loop through multiple input files. In this demonstration, you will use the default enumerator Foreach File. The Foreach Loop container provides several other enumerators that you can review by clicking the list box.

Add a Foreach Loop container to Sequence Container – File Exists

1. Drag Foreach Loop Container from the Control Flow Items group Toolbox into the Sequence Container – File Exists container.

2. Double-click the new container to open the editor, and then click Collection to change the following properties:

   ❏ Folder: **C:\Documents and Settings\<username>\My Documents\Microsoft Press\is2005sbs\Chap05\Chap05(b)\Data**

   ❏ Files: **FuzzyInput*.txt**

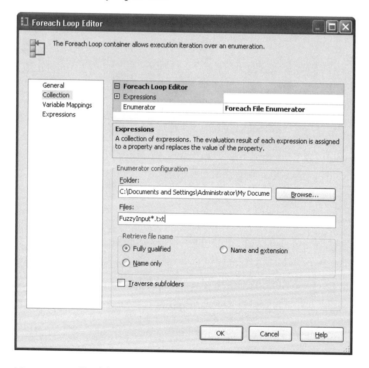

Now you will add a variable that will change the connection string for each iteration of the loop so that each input file in the specified folder will be read.

3. Click Variable Mappings in the Foreach Loop editor.

4. In the Variable drop-down list box, select <New Variable...>.

5. Change the *Container* property to the name of the package, NewProducts (at the top of the hierarchy), to set the scope of the variable to the entire package.

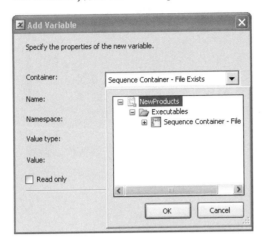

6. Change the variable's *Name* property to **InputFile**.

7. Click OK twice.

8. Click the Product Input Names connection to display its Properties pane.

9. Click the ellipsis in the *Expressions* property.

10. In the Property drop-down list, select ConnectionString and add the following expression: **@[User::InputFile]**. (This expression references the user variable called *InputFile*.)

11. Click OK.

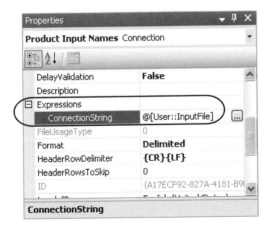

12. Clear Precedence Constraint between Execute SQL Task – Clear Matched Names and Data Flow Task – Lookup Names.

13. Drag Data Flow Task – Lookup Names into the Foreach Loop container. Now the Sequence Container – File Exists should look like this:

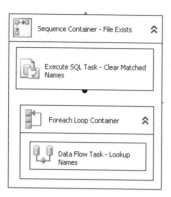

Applying Precedence Constraints

Precedence constraints connect executables into a control flow. An executable is an SSIS object in a control flow. For example, an executable could be a For Loop, a Foreach Loop or Sequence container, a task, or an event handler.

Precedence constraints specify conditions that determine whether executables run. Basically, you can control the sequence or execution order based on restrictions, expressions, or both. The constraint values are Success, Failure, or Completion. The expression has to be a Boolean expression, and you can combine expressions and constraints, for instance, Expression-and-Constraint or Expression-or-Constraint. When you have a task that has more than one precedence executable or precedence task, you can decide to evaluate each precedent constraint to *True*, or you can choose to evaluate only one constraint to *True*. You can set all these options in the Precedence Constraint Editor.

In the next steps, you will learn how to use and set constraints, use Evaluation Operation and Expressions in constraints, and, finally, set logical AND and OR statements to set multiple constraints.

Apply precedence constraints

1. Drag the output arrow from Script Task – Check Products List to Sequence Container – File Doesn't Exist.

2. Double-click the constraint to open the Precedence Constraint Editor and modify the following options:

   ❑ Evaluation Operation: Expression and Constraint

   ❑ Expression: @FileFound == False

Your screen should look similar to this:

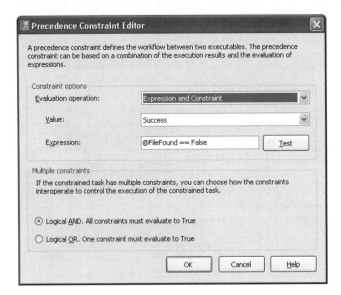

 Note   Use the @ symbol in front of a variable to reference it in an expression.

3.   Click OK.

4.   Drag the output arrow from Script Task – Check Products List to Sequence Container – File Exists.

5.   Double-click the constraint to edit the Precedence Constraint options:

   ❑   Evaluation Operation: Expression and Constraint

   ❑   Expression: @FileFound == True (It means that the file exists.)

6.   Click OK.

7.   Drag the green arrow from the Execute SQL Task – Clear Matched Names task to the Foreach Loop container.

8.   Delete the ProductsDestination.txt file from C:\Documents and Settings\<user-name>\My Documents\MicrosoftPress\is2005sbs\Chap05\Chap05(b)\Data.

9.   Right-click the NewProducts.dtsx package and choose Execute Package. Only the File Doesn't Exist branch should execute.

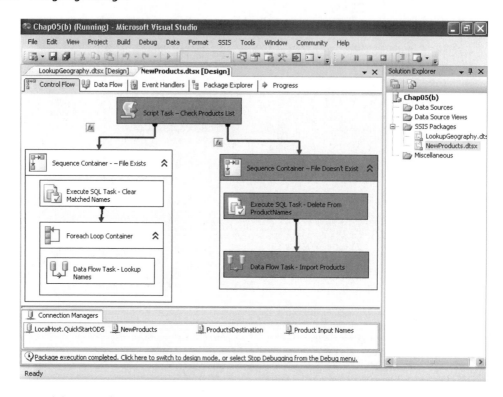

10. Stop debugging from the Debug menu, and then re-execute the package. Only the File Exists branch should execute.

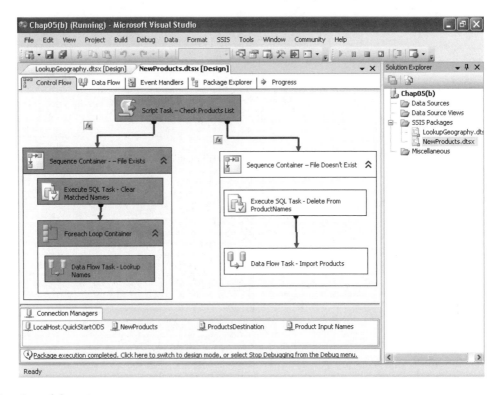

11. Stop debugging.

    Now only one branch will be taken. However, even if the File Doesn't Exist branch runs, the File Exists branch will still need to run. You can add a Precedence Constraint between the two containers to trigger the execution of the File Exists branch.

12. Add a Precedent Constraint from the Sequence Container – File Doesn't Exist container to the Sequence Container – File Exists container.

13. Select the logical OR constraint option for this new constraint.

> **Caution**   Because there are multiple constraints on the Sequence Container – File Exists container, you need to determine whether both constraints (logical AND) or just one constraint (logical OR) needs to be satisfied to execute the tasks within the container. In this case, only one constraint will be executed, never both, so you need to use the OR constraint option.

Your screen should look similar to this:

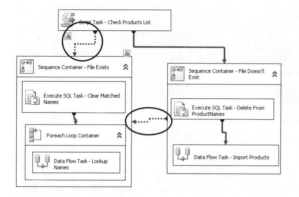

> **Note**   The precedence constraint with a logical OR condition appears as a dotted green arrow.

14. Delete the ProductsDestination.txt file.

15. Execute the package. Both branches should execute.

16. Stop debugging the package and close the solution.

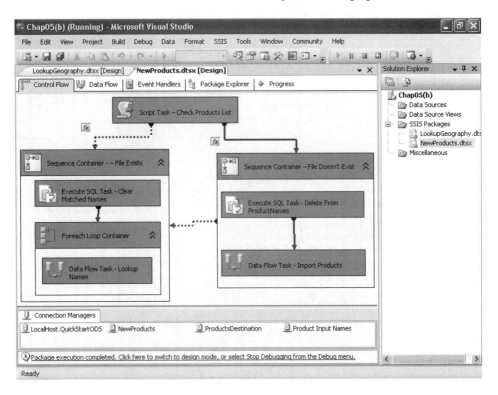

Chapter 5 Quick Reference

To	Do this
Change *DelayValidation* property	In the Control Flow pane, right-click an open area and click Properties to open the Properties pane. In the Execution set, change *DelayValidation* to *True* or *False*.
Add a Sequence Container control flow item	On the Control Flow page, drag Sequence Container from the Toolbox to the grid. Drag existing tasks into Sequence Container. Drag tasks together.
Add a variable	Right-click the background of the package and choose Variables. This brings up a window that you can dock on the side. Click the Add Variable button in the Variables toolbar. Change the Name and Data Type as necessary. Note that the scope for a new variable is the container that is active when you create the variable; in this case, it is the package.
Add a Script Task	Drag Script Task from the Toolbox to the grid. Double-click the Script Task to assign its properties. Click the Design Script button to add code to the *Main()* function.

To	Do this
Add a connection manager for Fuzzy Lookup input	Create a new Data Flow, and then double-click to open it. Drag Flat File Source from the Toolbox to the grid. Double-click the Flat File Source data adapter, and then click the New button to create a new connection manager. Use the Browse button to navigate to the source text file. You have to verify that the column width of the source is not different from the reference column because Fuzzy Lookup gives a warning if the column width of the source is different from the reference column. Click Advanced in the Flat File Connection Manager Editor to change the OutputColumnWidth to a value equal to the reference column in the lookup table. Then, in the Flat File Source Editor, click Columns. This will set the mapping between the External Column and the Output Column. Click OK.
Add a Fuzzy Lookup transformation	Drag a Fuzzy Lookup transformation from the Toolbox to the grid. Connect the output from the Flat File Source to the Fuzzy Lookup by clicking and dragging the green arrow. Double-click the Fuzzy Lookup task to open the transformation editor and set the properties for Connection Manager and Reference Table Name. Click the Columns tab, and then create a join by clicking and dragging the Input Columns to the Lookup Columns. Check Pass Through in the Available Input Columns box so that the source file name is included in the output file. Finally, select the Lookup Column and click OK.
Add a SQL Server Destination	Drag SQL Server Destination from the Toolbox to the grid. Drag an output arrow from the Fuzzy Lookup transformation to the SQL Server Destination. Double-click the SQL Server Destination and select a connection manager. Create a new table and notice that extra columns are created to hold statistics for the transformation. Click Mappings in the SQL Destination Editor to set the correct mappings between the input and destination columns, and then click OK.
Add an Execute SQL task	On the Control Flow page, add a new Execute SQL task to the container and set properties for Name, Connection, and SQL Statement. Click OK.
Add a Foreach Loop container to a Sequence container	Drag Foreach Loop Container from the Toolbox into Sequence Container. Double-click the new container to open the editor, and then click Collection to change the properties for Folder and Files (Ex. FuzzyInput*.txt). Click Variable Mappings in the Foreach Loop Editor and, in the Variable list box, select <New Variable...>. Change the *Container* property to the name of the package (at the top of the hierarchy) to set the scope of the variable to the entire package. Change the variable's *Name* property and click OK twice. Click Connection Manager for the input files and display its properties window. Click the ellipsis in the *Expressions* property and set Property to *ConnectionString*; add the following expression: @[User::<variable name>. This expression references the user variable you specified when you set up the Variable Mappings in the Foreach Loop Editor.
Apply Precedence constraints	Drag the output arrow from Script Task to Sequence Container. Double-click the constraint to edit the Precedence constraint options: Evaluation Operation, Value, and Expression. When you have more than one constraint on a task, you will need to specify the Multiple Constraints option.

Chapter 6
Scripting Tasks

After completing this chapter, you will be able to:

- Create, modify, and execute custom behaviors, using the Script Task, Script Component, and ActiveX Script Task.

- Write custom code in the Microsoft Visual Studio for Application (VSA) development environment, using Microsoft Visual Basic .NET.

- Incorporate external Microsoft .NET assemblies and COM into the Script Task and Script Component.

- Implement error-handling code, using TRY...CATCH...FINALLY statements.

- Access SSIS built-in capabilities such as Variables, Events, and Logs from custom code in the Script Task and Script Component.

In the previous chapters, you learned how to create a package by using Control Flow tasks and containers as well as Data Flow components. However, you might discover that Microsoft SQL Server Integration Services (SSIS) built-in items do not satisfy complicated requirements in some cases. For example, how can you get rid of unnecessary lines in a comma-separated-value (CSV) file before you import the file? What if you need to look up employees' information in Active Directory directory services while you are loading data from a flat file?

To support these kinds of complicated requirements, SSIS provides a way to implement custom script code in your package to extend its abilities. SSIS provides three options to implement script code: the Script Task, Script Component, and ActiveX Script Task. In this chapter, you will learn the differences among them and how to implement them in your package. SQL Server Business Intelligence Development Studio (BIDS) provides you with a special development environment to implement script code, called Microsoft Visual Studio for Applications (VSA). Throughout this chapter, you will also learn how to use VSA to implement script code.

Understanding Scripting Tasks

You can use the Script Task in Control Flow. If you know ActiveX Script Task in SQL Server 2000 Data Transformation Services (DTS), you can regard Script Task as the next version of ActiveX Script Task. Script Task is now integrated with Microsoft .NET Framework to offer you the powerful features .NET Framework provides.

Figure 6-1 shows a basic programming model of the Script Task. When you create a new Script task in Control Flow, SSIS Designer generates a skeleton code of the *ScriptMain* class as well as of the *Main* method. All you have to do is write business logic inside the *Script-Main.Main* method, using VSA and Code Editor. When the containing package is executed, the SSIS engine calls this *Main* method at first. You can also create your own method in the *ScriptMain* class and call it from the *Main* method, or you can create your own custom classes and modules.

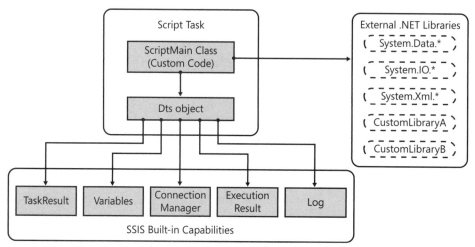

Figure 6-1   Script Task programming model

Note   As you can see in the skeleton code, you need to use Visual Basic .NET to implement a Script task. Although .NET Framework itself provides several kinds of programming languages, such as Visual C# .NET, Visual Basic .NET is the only option for the current version of SSIS.

The script often needs to work with a *Data Transformation Services (DTS)* global object. The *DTS* object provides a way to access SSIS built-in capabilities such as variables, event messages, and logs. You can use objects defined in external .NET assemblies. For example, if you would like to inspect the content of an XML file, add reference to System.Xml.dll and parse the file by using the *XmlDocument* class. You can also use your custom libraries or COM libraries in a Script task.

The rest of this section will show you how the Script task programming model that was discussed previously works and how you can implement custom code through the model. You will also learn the basic features of VSA and Code Editor through exercises.

> **More Info**   Because this book focuses on the features of SSIS 2005, the exercise doesn't provide much information about the Visual Basic .NET language or .NET libraries. If you need detailed information about them, please refer to the MSDN Web site at *http://msdn2.microsoft.com/*.

Implementing a Script Task

Let's assume that you need to export all employees' information from your database to a text file. The format of the text file is a little tricky. One record is split into multiple lines, and each line contains a column name and the value concatenated by a colon. Each record should be separated by a dashed line. The Flat File destination in the Data Flow task doesn't support this requirement because it allows you to choose only character-delimited or fixed-length formats. Instead of using a Data Flow task, you will use a Script task to retrieve the data from the database and write out the data to the text file with a specified format. Because the Script task is so powerful and versatile, it often incorporates multiple tasks into a single one.

Creating a New Script Task and Initiating Code

First, you will learn how to write code in the Script task by using the VSA environment. In the following procedure, you will create a new package and a new Script task in the new package; then you will implement your code in the task, using Code Editor in VSA. Through this procedure, you will also review the basic features of VSA.

Create a new project and add a Script task

1. Start SQL Server Business Intelligence Development Studio (BIDS).

2. On the File menu, point to New, and then select Project.

3. Select Integration Services Project and type **Chapter06_01** in the Name text box.

4. In the Location text box, specify **C:\Documents and Settings\<username>\My Documents\Microsoft Press\is2005SbS\Chap06**. Make sure the Create directory for the solution option is checked and click OK.

5. In the Toolbox, in the Control Flow Items group, select Script Task and drag it to the design surface of the Control Flow tab.

6. Double-click the new Script task.

7. In the Script Task Editor dialog box, change Name to **Script Task – Export Employees**.

8. On the Script page, click Design Script. Your screen looks like this:

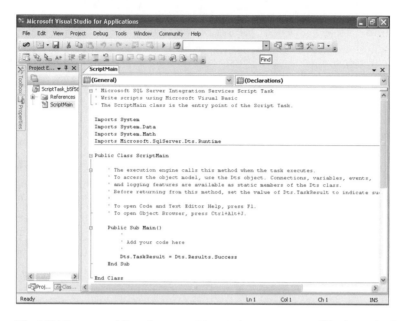

The VSA Integrated Development Environment (IDE) will be launched, and it shows the skeleton code of the *ScriptMain* class and *Main* method. By default, the *Main* method has just one statement: Dts.TaskResult = Dts.Results.Success. This statement returns the overall success result to the SSIS engine. You need to add your custom code before this statement.

9. In Project Explorer, right-click the References folder and select Add Reference.

10. In the Add Reference dialog box, select Sytem.Xml.dll in the .NET list box, and then click Add. System.Xml.dll appears in the Selected Projects And Components list box on the bottom.

11. Click OK.

    Ensure that System.Xml was added under the References folder. This allows you to use objects defined in System.Xml.dll. This process is necessary to use *DataSet* in your code because *DataSet* refers to one of the objects defined in the System.Xml.dll.

12. In the Code Editor, remove all comment lines that start with an apostrophe (').

13. Insert a new line before the Dts.TaskResult = Dts.Results.Success line.

14. Type the following code in the new line:

    ```
    Dim fileName as String = "C:\Employees.txt"
    ```

    Notice that a small window pops up with a list of candidates for the keyword when you press the space key after the AS statement. This is called *IntelliSense*. When you type some of the characters you want to write, IntelliSense suggests candidates that start with the character you have typed. If you find a word you want to type, select the word from the list with the up or down arrow keys and press the Tab key to complete the word. This will reduce typing and help cut down on mistakes.

15. Place the cursor on the word *Class* in the editor and press F1.

> **Note**   If the Online Help Setting dialog box displays, select "Use local help as primary source" and click OK.

Microsoft Document Explorer appears on the screen with the appropriate help content for the CLASS statement. When the F1 key is pressed, the Code Editor detects the word under the cursor and launches Microsoft Document Explorer, passing the word as a parameter.

16. Append the following lines under the last line of IMPORTS statements. (It should be *Imports Microsoft.SqlServer.Dts.Runtime.*)

```
Imports Microsoft.SqlServer.Dts.Runtime
Imports System.IO Imports System.Data.SqlClient

Public Class ScriptMain
```

These IMPORTS statements allow you to use classes defined under the specified namespaces without specifying a fully qualified name. This statement makes your script code shorter and easier to read. A namespace is a context for naming items such as classes, modules, and interfaces. For example, you will use the *DataSet* class in the following procedure; *DataSet* is defined under the *System.Data* namespace. If you declare *Imports System.Data* at the beginning of your script, you can simply write your code as:

```
Dim ds As DataSet
```

It is not mandatory to have IMPORTS statements in your script. If you don't have an IMPORT SYSTEM.DATA statement, you have to write as follows:

```
Dim ds As System.Data.DataSet
```

17. Insert the following code in the *Main* method before the *Dts.TaskResult = Dts.Results.Success* line:

```
Public Sub Main()
    Dim fileName as String = "C:\Employees.txt"

    Const CONNECTION_STRING As String = _
        "Data Source=localhost;" & _
        "Initial Catalog=is2005sbsDW;Integrated Security=SSPI;"
    Const SQL_SELECT_EMPLOYEE As String = _
        "SELECT" & _
        " FirstName, LastName, MiddleName, Gender, Title, " & _
        " DepartmentName, HireDate, LoginID, EmailAddress, Phone " & _
        "FROM DimEmployee " & _
        "ORDER BY LastName"
    Const RECORD_SEPARATOR As String = _
        "-----------------------------------------------------------"
```

```vbnet
    Dim writer As StreamWriter
    Dim con As SqlConnection = New SqlConnection(CONNECTION_STRING)
    Dim adapter As New SqlDataAdapter(SQL_SELECT_EMPLOYEE, con)
    Dim ds As New DataSet
    adapter.Fill(ds)

    writer = New StreamWriter (fileName, False)
    writer.AutoFlush = True
    With ds.Tables(0)
        For row As Integer = 0 To .Rows.Count - 1
            For col As Integer = 0 To .Columns.Count - 1
                writer.WriteLine("{0}: {1}", _
                    .Columns(col).ColumnName, .Rows(row)(col))
            Next col

            writer.WriteLine(RECORD_SEPARATOR)
        Next row
    End With

    writer.Close()

    Dts.TaskResult = Dts.Results.Success
End Sub
```

> **Note** This script is also available in the text file saved under the C:\Documents and Settings\<username>\Microsoft Press\is2005SbS\Chap06\Chapter06_01_Script.txt.

The following is a pseudocode rendering of the preceding script code. Refer to the MSDN Web site if you would like to know the details of each statement.

Declare resources, which will be used later in the method (e.g. filename).

Retrieve all data from DimEmployees table in *is2005sbsDW* database and store it in the DataSet.

Open a text stream for the result file.

Look into each column in each row and write out all column name and value to the text stream.

Write out the separator (dash line) at the end of each record.

Return the overall result to SSIS engine.

18. Close VSA by clicking the Close box in the window title bar.

> **Tip** You don't need to select Save on the File menu. VSA will automatically save all updates when it is closed.

19. Click OK to close the Script Task Editor dialog box.

20. On the Control Flow tab, press F5 to execute the package. Ensure that the Script Task – Export Employees turns green.

21. Start Windows Explorer and open the root folder for drive C.

> **Note**   Throughout this chapter, you will copy files to the root folder of your drive C. To open an Explorer window to this location, choose Start, Run, and then type **drive C**, and click OK. You may delete these files at the end of the exercise.

Notice that Employees.txt has been generated. Double-click to open the text file in Notepad and confirm that the employee data has been successfully exported with the expected format.

22. On the Debug menu, click the Stop Debugging button.

Handling Errors

When you implement the Script Task, you might need to incorporate some error-handling behaviors in your script code. For example, if you're expected to register the result of the script in the database, you need to update the database when the script displays an unexpected error, such as File Not Found or Destination Database Is Not Available. If you don't implement error-handling code, the execution will be terminated when it encounters an unexpected error, and you will not register the result in the database.

You can use a TRY...CATCH...FINALLY statement to trap errors and implement alternative behaviors in your script code. A basic TRY...CATCH...FINALLY statement looks like this:

```
Try
    (regular code)
Catch ex As Exception
    (error handling code)
End Try
```

If the code encounters an error somewhere inside the *Try* block (between the TRY and CATCH statements), the execution enters the *Catch* block (between the CATCH and END TRY statements) and executes the alternative code implemented in the block. If you would like to know the details of the error, you can refer to the *Exception* object (defined as *ex* in the preceding example) inside the *Catch* block.

You can also implement extra behaviors inside the *Finally* block. The code in the *Finally* block will be executed regardless of whether an error has occurred in the *Try* block. It will be executed after the code in the *Try* or *Catch* block has been executed. The statement in the *Finally* block looks like this:

```
Try
    (regular code)
Catch ex As Exception
    (error handling code)
Finally
    (finalization code)
End Try
```

When you implement code in the *Finally* block, you need to be careful to handle the error that might occur inside the block. If an error occurs in the *Finally* block and you don't have a TRY...CATCH...FINALLY statement inside the *Finally* block, the execution will be terminated, and the rest of the code in the *Finally* block won't be executed.

Whether the TRY...CATCH...FINALLY statement enables you to switch the behavior depends on what kind of error has occurred. You can create multiple *Catch* blocks with different types of exceptions in their parameters. For example:

```
Try
    (regular code)
Catch ioex As IOException
    (error handling code for I/O related errors)
Catch sqlex As SqlException
    (error handling code for database related errors)
Catch ex As Exception
    (error handling code for all other errors)
End Try
```

In the following procedure, you will add the TRY...CATCH...FINALLY statement inside your code and add a simple behavior in the *Finally* block to close the *StreamWriter* object before the script returns a failure as the overall result. It is common and always good to have this kind of resource-release code in your script.

> **Note** You can use the TRY...CATCH...FINALLY statement when you implement the Script component as well.

Add error-handling code in the Script Task

1. On the Control Flow tab, double-click the Script Task – Export Employees.

2. In the Script Task Editor dialog box, on the Script page, click Design Script.

3. In the Code Editor, insert a new line *before* the Dim Adapter As New SqlDataAdapter line.

4. Type **Try** in the new line and press Enter.

> **Note** VSA will automatically add a CATCH...END TRY statement after a TRY statement. This is another user-aid functionality of the Code Editor.

5. Cut all existing code that follows the END TRY statement and paste it in the *Try* block.

6. Type the following code in the *Catch* block.

```
Dts.TaskResult = Dts.Results.Failure
```

This code will signal the failure of the procedure to the containing package when an unexpected error occurs inside the *Try* block.

7. Remove the following lines in the *Try* block:

```
writer.Close()
```

8. Insert a new line right before the END TRY statement and type **Finally** in the new line.

9. Insert the following code in the *Finally* block:

```
If writer IsNot Nothing Then
    writer.Close()
End If
```

This code closes the *StreamWriter* object used in the *Try* block, regardless of whether an error has occurred in the *Try* block. The purpose of having an IF statement before you close the *StreamWriter* object is to avoid an unexpected error in the *Finally* block. If the *writer* variable is null for some reason, the WRITER.CLOSE() statement fails, and the execution will be terminated.

Now your code looks like this:

```
Dim writer As StreamWriter
Dim con As SqlConnection = New SqlConnection(CONNECTION_STRING)

Try
    Dim adapter As New SqlDataAdapter(SQL_SELECT_EMPLOYEE, con)
    Dim ds As New DataSet
    adapter.Fill(ds)

    writer = New StreamWriter (fileName, False)
    writer.AutoFlush = True

    With ds.Tables(0)
        For row As Integer = 0 To .Rows.Count - 1
            For col As Integer = 0 To .Columns.Count - 1
                writer.WriteLine("{0}: {1}", _
                    .Columns(col).ColumnName, .Rows(row)(col))
            Next col

            writer.WriteLine(RECORD_SEPARATOR)
        Next row
    End With

    Dts.TaskResult = Dts.Results.Success

Catch ex As Exception
    Dts.TaskResult = Dts.Results.Failure
Finally
    If writer IsNot Nothing Then
        writer.Close()
    End If
End Try
End Sub
```

10. Close VSA and the Script Task Editor dialog box.

11. Press F5 to execute the package. Make sure the updated code still works.

12. On the Debug menu, click Stop Debugging.

13. Open Microsoft SQL Server Management Studio (SSMS) and connect to localhost.

14. In the Object Explorer, expand Databases and right-click is2005sbsDW, point to Tasks, and select Take Offline. A progress dialog box appears, and the database will soon go offline.

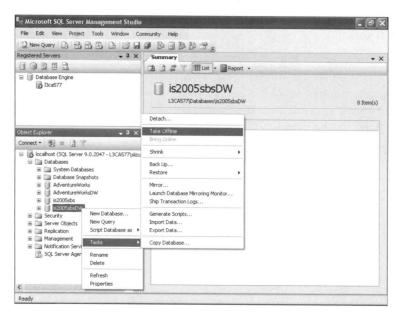

15. Go back to BIDS and press F5 to execute the package again. Because you took the source database offline, the Script Task − Export Employees fails and turns red.

16. Click the Progress tab.

Notice that an error message has been logged with a white and red exclamation icon next to the message Error: The Script returned a failure result.

17. On the Debug menu, select Stop Debugging.

> **Note**   Please keep the database offline for the next section.

Providing a Message to the Progress Tab

In the previous section, you successfully handled the error in the *Try* block. You could see that the error occurred in the Progress tab as you expected. However, you did not have enough information to know exactly what happened in the script.

The messages on the Progress tab are derived through each component's event. The *Dts.Events* object enables you to raise various kinds of events such as Information, Progress, and Error. In the following procedure, you will add code to provide the following events to the Progress tab:

- Open a destination file as an *Information* event (with file name).

- Process employee data as a *Progress* event.

- Detect errors as *Error* events (with detail error messages).

More Info   Messages on the Progress tab will be discussed in more detail in Chapter 7, "Debugging Packages."

Modify the script to fire an event

1. Double-click Script Task – Export Employees.

2. In the Script Task Editor dialog box, click Design Script on the Script page.

3. In the Code Editor, append the following code in the *Main* method:

```
Public Sub Main()
    Dim fileName As String = "C:\Employees.txt"
    Const COMPONENT_NAME As String = "Export Employees"
    Const CONNECTION_STRING As String = _
        "Data Source=localhost;" & _
        "Initial Catalog=is2005sbsDW;Integrated Security=SSPI;"
    ...
    Try
        ...
    Catch ex As Exception
        Dts.Events.FireError(0, COMPONENT_NAME, ex.Message, "", 0)
        Dts.TaskResult = Dts.Results.Failure
    Finally
        If writer IsNot Nothing Then
            writer.Close()
        End If
    End Try
End Sub
```

The *Dts.Events.FireError* method requires five parameters. The first parameter is an arbitrary error code by which you can identify this error, which is not necessary to specify this time. The second parameter is the name of the source component, which should be the name of this script task. The third parameter is a message text that will be displayed on the Progress tab. You specify the error message derived by the *Exception* object here. The fourth and fifth parameters are the information to incorporate help, which is also not necessary this time.

Important   If *Dts.Events.FireError* has been executed in the script, the final result of the Script Task will always be failure even if you are specifying *Dts.Results.Success* to *Dts.TaskResult*.

---

4. Close VSA and the Script Task Editor dialog box.

5. Press F5 to execute the package. Your package fails again because the *is2005sbsDW* database is offline.

6. Click the Progress tab. Your screen looks like this:

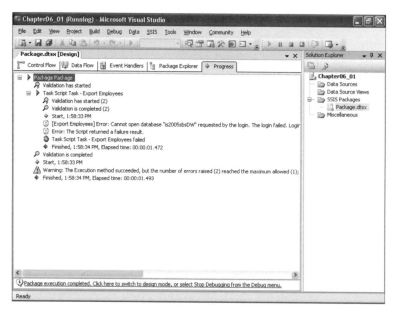

Notice that an event message with a red exclamation mark appears with a verbose error message on the Progress tab. This event message was derived by the *Dts.Events.FireError* method, which you implemented in the previous step.

7. On the Debug menu, click Stop Debugging.

8. On the Control Flow tab, double-click Script Task – Export Employees. In the Script Task Editor dialog box, click Design Script on the Script page.

9. In the Code Editor, append the following code in the *Main* method:

```
Dim writer As StreamWriter
Dim con As OleDbConnection = New OleDbConnection(CONNECTION_STRING)

Try
    Dim adapter As New OleDbDataAdapter(SQL_SELECT_EMPLOYEE, con)
    Dim ds As New DataSet
    adapter.Fill(ds)

    Dts.Events.FireInformation(0, COMPONENT_NAME, _
        String.Format("Opening output file '{0}'", fileName), _
        "", 0, True)
```

```
        writer = New StreamWriter (fileName, False)
        writer.AutoFlush = True

        With ds.Tables(0)
            For row As Integer = 0 To .Rows.Count - 1
                For col As Integer = 0 To .Columns.Count - 1
                    writer.WriteLine("{0}: {1}", _
                        .Columns(col).ColumnName, .Rows(row)(col))
                Next col

                writer.WriteLine(RECORD_SEPARATOR)

                Dts.Events.FireProgress("Exporting Employee", _
                    CInt((row + 1) / .Rows.Count * 100), row + 1, _
                    .Rows.Count, COMPONENT_NAME, True)
            Next row
        End With

        Dts.TaskResult = Dts.Results.Success
    Catch ex As Exception
        Dts.Events.FireError (0, COMPONENT_NAME, ex.Message, "", 0)
        Dts.TaskResult = Dts.Results.Failure
    Finally
        ...
    End Try
End Sub
```

The parameters for the *Dts.Events.FireInformation* method are almost the same as for the *FireError* method. The last parameter of *FireInformation* determines whether the SSIS engine suppresses the event when the second execution comes to the same statement. If the value is *False*, the SSIS engine doesn't raise the event for the rest of the execution. This sometimes increases the performance cost of package execution because firing an event is expensive.

The *FireProgress* method requires six parameters. The first parameter is the description of the *Progress* event. The second through fourth parameters determine the percentage of the progress. The fifth parameter is the name of the component, and the last parameter is the same as the one in the *FireInformation* method.

10. Close VSA and the Script Task Editor dialog box.

11. In SSMS, right-click is2005sbsDW, point to Tasks, and select Bring Online. A small progress dialog box appears, and the database goes online.

12. Go back to BIDS and press F5 to execute the package. This time, the package is complete without errors.

13. Click the Progress tab. Your screen now looks like this:

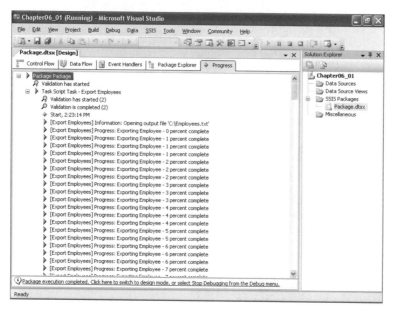

Notice that messages starting with [Export Employees] have been added to the Progress tab. The first message beginning with [Export Employees] Information is generated by the *Dts.Events.FireInformation* method, and following messages beginning with [Export Employees] Progress are generated by the *Dts.Events.FireProgress* method. The percentage shown in the message is calculated by the parameters of the *Dts.Events.FireProgress* method.

14. On the Debug menu, click Stop Debugging.

Providing Verbose Information to the Log File

If your Script Task has a complicated process, you might want to write out verbose information to a log file for debugging purposes. It is especially useful when the package has been deployed to the production environment, and you cannot use BIDS and VSA to debug the package.

SSIS enables you to implement logging code through the *Dts.Log* method. When the *Dts.Log* method is called in the script, the SSIS engine will route the message to the log providers that are configured in the containing package. You can set up different kinds of providers such as text file, SQL Server, and Windows Event Log. This logging capability will be discussed in more detail in Chapter 8, "Managing Package Execution."

In the following procedure, you will add script code to provide verbose information to the SSIS engine and configure the log settings of the containing package to route the message to a text file.

Configure package log settings

1. On the Control Flow tab, select Script Task – Export Employees.

2. In the Properties pane, change the *LoggingMode* property to *Enabled*.

   By default, the Script Task is designed to inherit the log settings of the containing package. This step enables you to configure the task's log setting apart from the settings of the containing package.

3. Right-click anywhere on the design surface of the Control Flow tab and select Logging.

4. In the Containers pane, select the check box next to Package to enable logging.

5. On the Providers and Logs tab, select SSIS Log Provider For Text Files from the Provider Type drop-down list and click Add. A new entity appears in the list box.

6. Click the *Configuration* field in the new entity. Click the drop-down list box that appears in the *Configuration* field and select <New connection...>. The File Connection Manager Editor dialog box appears.

7. In the Connection Manager Editor dialog box, select Create File from the Usage Type drop-down list.

8. Click Browse, navigate to the root folder of the drive C, type **Script Task Log.txt**, and click Open. Your screen looks like this:

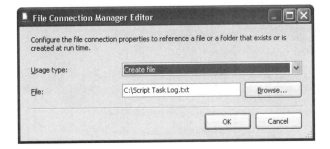

9. Click OK.

10. Select the check box next to SSIS Log Provider For Text Files. This will configure the package to use this log file.

> **Important**   Make sure that you are still selecting Package in the rightmost tree view. If you have selected Export Employee when you select the check box, select Package in the Containers pane tree view and check the SSIS Log Provider For Text Files entity again.

11. In the tree-view on the left side of the Configure SSIS Logs: Package dialog box, select the Script Task – Export Employees node. If the check box next to the node is not checked, click the check box to select this item.

12. Select the check box next to the SSIS Log Provider For Text Files entity again. Your screen now looks like this:

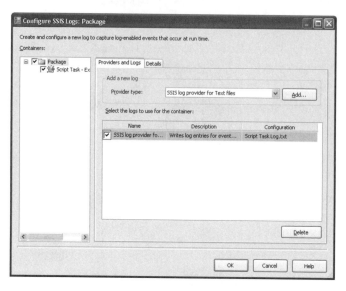

13. Click the Details tab and select the check box in the ScriptTaskLogEntry row. This allows SSIS to listen and log the message coming up from the *Dts.Log* method in Script Task – Export Employees. Your screen looks like this:

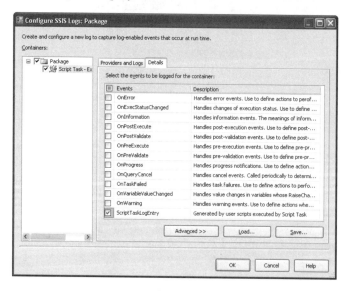

14. Click OK.

Notice that the connection named Script Task Log.txt has been created in the Connection Managers pane. This object contains a path to the log file that you specified in the previous steps. If you double-click it, you can see the dialog box that you saw in the previous step.

The package log configuration is all set. In the following procedure, you will add custom code to invoke the *Dts.Log* method.

15. Double-click the Script Task – Export Employees. In the Script Task Editor dialog box, click Design Script on the Script page.

16. In the Code Editor, insert the following code in the *Main* method:

```
Try
        Dts.Log("Opening database connection: " & _
            con.ConnectionString, 0, Nothing)
        Dim adapter As New SqlDataAdapter(SQL_SELECT_EMPLOYEE, con)
        Dim ds As New DataSet
        adapter.Fill(ds)

        Dts.Log(String.Format( _
            "Retrieving {0} data, opening output file '{1}'", _
            ds.Tables(0).Rows.Count, _
            fileName), _
            0, Nothing)

        Dts.Events.FireInformation(0, COMPONENT_NAME, _
            String.Format("Opening output file '{0}'", fileName), _
            "", 0, True)

        writer = New StreamWriter (fileName, False)
        writer.AutoFlush = True

        With ds.Tables(0)
            For row As Integer = 0 To .Rows.Count - 1
                For col As Integer = 0 To .Columns.Count - 1
                    writer.WriteLine("{0}: {1}", _
                        .Columns(col).ColumnName, .Rows(row)(col))

                Next col

                writer.WriteLine(RECORD_SEPARATOR)
                Dts.Events.FireProgress("Exporting Employee", _
                    CInt((row + 1) / .Rows.Count * 100), row + 1, _
                    .Rows.Count, COMPONENT_NAME, True)
            Next row
        End With

        Dts.TaskResult = Dts.Results.Success
Catch ex As Exception
        Dts.Events.FireError (0, COMPONENT_NAME, ex.Message, "", 0)
        Dts.Log("Exception detected: " & ex.ToString(), 0, Nothing)
        Dts.TaskResult = Dts.Results.Failure
Finally
        If writer IsNot Nothing Then
            Dts.Log("Closing output file", 0, Nothing)
            writer.Close()
```

```
            End If
        End Try
    End Sub
```

17. Close VSA and the Script Task Editor dialog box.

18. Press F5 to execute the package. Confirm that the task turns green.

19. Start Windows Explorer and open the root folder of the drive C.

    The Script Task Log.txt should be created in the root folder of the drive C. Double-click the text file to open it in Notepad and confirm that the verbose messages are logged in the file.

20. Go back to BIDS and click Stop Debugging on the Debug menu.

Using Variables

Passing information from one task to the other is a common necessity. SSIS provides a temporary data storage called *Variables*; it is the most common way to pass information between tasks. Variables will be discussed in more detail in Chapter 8.

In the following procedure, you will add a variable to the package that holds the name of the result file and then modify the existing script to incorporate it. It is common to use a variable to output file names because you might need to change an output file name when you deploy the package to the production environment. This also applies to the database connection string settings.

Configure variable settings

1. Right-click anywhere on the design surface of the Control Flow tab and select Variables.

2. In the Variables pane, click the Add Variable button (in the top-left corner of the window). A new variable appears in the Name list.

> **Note**   Make sure the scope of the variable is displayed as Package. If it is Script Task – Export Employees, you selected the Script Task – Export Employees task when you clicked the Add Variables button. Delete the new variable (the delete button is the second one from the left), deselect the Script task, and then create the variable again.

3. Change the name of the new variable to **ExportFileName**.

4. Change the data type from Int32 to **String**.

5. Click the *Value* field and type **C:\Employees_Default.txt**. Your Variables window looks like this:

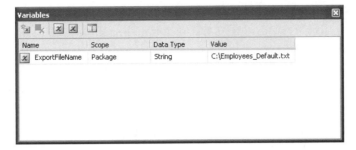

The value you specified in the *Value* field is going to be a default value of the variable. This default value is valid until this variable is updated by package configurations or other tasks.

Now the package variable is ready to use. To access this variable from the Script Task, you need to configure the *ReadOnlyVariables* property in the task by performing the following steps.

6. Double-click the Script Task – Export Employees. The Script Task Editor dialog box appears.

7. On the Script page, click the field next to the *ReadOnlyVariables* property and type **ExportFileName.**

This allows you to access the *ExportFileName* variable from your script code. Your screen looks like this:

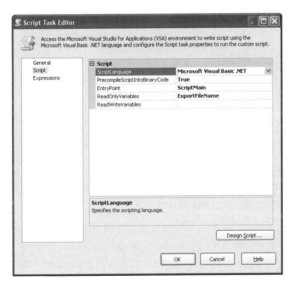

Now the *ExportFileName* variable is ready to use. In the following procedure, you will modify the script code to look up this variable as a file name for the output file.

Modify the script to read variables

1. Open VSA. If necessary, open the Script Task Editor dialog box and click Design Script on the Script page. Otherwise, double-click Script Task – Export Employee and click Design Script on the Script page in the Script Task Editor dialog box.

2. Replace the first line of the *Main* method, starting from Dim fileName As String ..., with the following code:

```
Dim fileName As String = Dts.Variables("ExportFileName").Value
```

Notice that your script code now has a blue wavy underline at *Dts.Variables(ExportFile-Name).Value*. This is the other user-aid function of the Code Editor. The underline indicates that something is wrong with the code. Place your mouse pointer over the blue wavy underline. A smart tag with a red exclamation mark appears. If you click the smart tag, the Code Editor shows the details of the error in the pop-up window, as shown below:

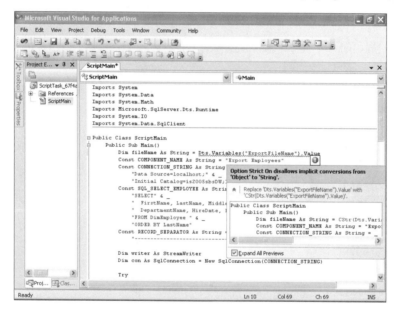

The message in the pop-up window shows that SSIS cannot convert *Dts.Variables(Export-FileName).Value* to the String type implicitly. Because the type of variable is *System.Object*, you have to cast it explicitly into the expected type.

The pop-up window also suggests a resolution if one is available. Click the Replace the Dts.Variables("ExportFileName").Value with . . . hyperlink that appears in the pop-up window. The Code Editor automatically replaces the target code with the appropriate code.

Now your code looks like this:

```
Public Sub Main()
    Dim fileName As String = CStr(Dts.Variables("ExportFileName").Value)
```

```
Const COMPONENT_NAME As String = "Export Employees"
…
Try
    …
Catch ex As Exception
    …
Finally
    …
End Try
End Sub
```

The replaced code is casting *Dts.Variables("ExportFileName").Value* into the String type, using the *CStr* function. There are plenty of functions for data type conversion. Refer to MSDN for details.

3. Close VSA and the Script Task Editor dialog box.

4. Start Windows Explorer, open the root folder of the drive C, and delete the Employees.txt file.

5. Go back to BIDS and press F5 to execute the package. Confirm that the Script Task – Export Employees turns green.

6. Go back to Windows Explorer and ensure that Employees_Default.txt has been created in the root folder of the drive C. This means the new script in Script Task – Export Employees looked up the *ExportFileName* variable to obtain the export file name. Because no other tasks updated the variable before Script Task – Export Employees was executed, the variable remained the default value.

7. Go back to BIDS and click Stop Debugging on the Debug menu.

Modifying a Variable at Run Time

A run-time variable is often changed to a designated value from outside of the package during execution. There are several ways to change package variables at run time; using Configurations is the most common way to do it. Configurations will be discussed in Chapter 8. In the following procedure, you will add another Script task to update the *ExportFileName* variable before Script Task – Export Employees is executed.

Add a new Script task and update variables at run time

1. In the Toolbox, in the Control Flow Items group, select Script Task and drag it to the design surface of the Control Flow tab.

2. Select the new Script task in Control Flow and drag the green arrow to Script Task – Export Employees. Your screen should look like this:

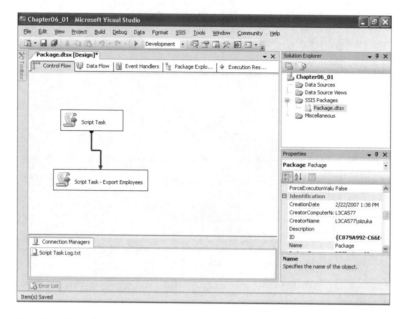

3. Double-click the new Script task. In the Script Task Editor dialog box, change the name to **Script Task – Export Employees.**

4. On the Script page, type **ExportFileName** in ReadWriteVariables. This allows you to update variables in your code.

5. Click Design Script and open VSA.

6. In the Code Editor, add the following row in the *Main* method:

```
Public Sub Main()
    '
    ' Add your code here
    '
        Dts.Variables("ExportFileName").Value = "C:\Employees_Runtime.txt"
    Dts.TaskResult = Dts.Results.Success
End Sub
Close VSA and the Script Task Editor dialog box.
```

7. Press F5 to execute the package. Observe that both Script Task – Set ExportFileName and Script Task – Export Employees turn green.

8. Open the root folder of the drive C in Windows Explorer and confirm that the Employees_Runtime.txt file has been created instead of Employees_Default.txt. This means your package used a file path updated by Script Task – Set ExportFileName instead of using the variable's default value. Double-click to open C:\Employees_RunTime.txt in Notepad and verify that the result was exported correctly.

Understanding the Script Component

The Script component allows you to implement custom behaviors in Data Flow. As you have already learned in the last few chapters, SSIS provides three kinds of Data Flow components: Source, Transformation, and Destination. The Script component can be used as any of these types.

The Script component is often useful in the following cases:

- You would like to process a custom-format flat file as a data source.

- You would like to validate a value in a certain row while loading data to your database.

- You would like to feed data to a custom destination such as Web Services.

To use the Script component with other components, you need to define inputs and outputs of the Script component. When you use it as the source component, you have to define outputs, so you can connect to a downstream component such as a transformation or destination component. If you would like to use the Script component as a destination component, you have to define inputs. Otherwise, you have to define both inputs and outputs.

Figure 6-2 shows a basic programming model of the Script component. The way you implement it is slightly different from how you implement the Script task.

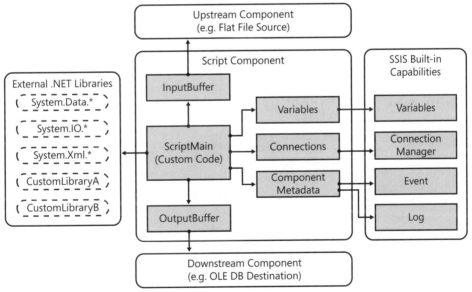

Figure 6-2   The Script component programming model

The Script component has unique objects called *InputBuffer* and *OutputBuffer*. *InputBuffer* provides a method to read data from an upstream component, and *OutputBuffer* provides a method to feed data to a downstream component. You will write a custom code working with these buffer objects to process the data in the Script component. Each buffer object has a set of properties synchronized with the definition of the inputs and outputs.

The number of buffers in the Script component varies by the number of inputs and outputs. The name of each buffer will be synchronized with the names of the inputs and outputs. For example, if you define two inputs, CustomerInput and OrderInput, you will have two *Input-Buffer* objects, named *CustomerInputBuffer* and *OrderInputBuffer*, in the Script component.

Like the *Dts* object in the Script task, SSIS offers you some objects with which to access SSIS built-in capabilities from the Script component. The *Me.Variables* object provides access to package variables. The *Me.ComponentMetadata* object provides several methods to raise events from the Script component, as with the methods defined under the *Dts.Event* object in the Script task. The *Me.ComponentMetadata* object also provides the *Log* method, which works like the *Dts.Log* method in the Script task.

The other rules are the same as with the Script task. As you have learned in the previous section, you can incorporate other objects that are defined in external .NET assemblies in your Script component.

Implementing the Script Component

Let's assume that you are going to import customer data from a CSV file into a DimCustomer table in the *is2005sbsDW* database. While you're importing the data, you need to validate each customer's e-mail address and store the validation result in an additional column in the Dim-Customer table. The Script transformation component is often useful for validating data in Data Flow.

Reviewing a Sample Project

First, let's look through the sample project you will work with in the following procedure.

Start BIDS and open the solution file saved under C:\Documents and Settings\<username>\My Documents\Microsoft Press\is2005SbS\Chap06_02-InitialCode \Chapter06_02.sln. In Solution Explorer, double-click Package.dtsx. Your screen should like this:

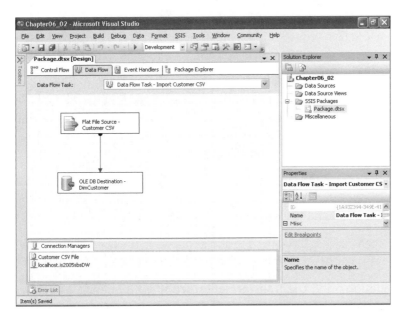

The main stream of the package is quite simple: Truncate the destination table and import the CSV file. Executing SQL Task – Clear DimCustomer truncates the DimCustomer table before the CSV file is loaded into DimCustomer. Data Flow – Import Customer CSV is a Data Flow task to import a CSV file into a DimCustomer table.

Double-click the Data Flow – Import Customer CSV to see the inside of the task. Your screen will be switched to the Data Flow tab like this:

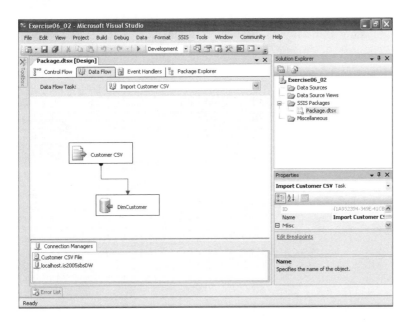

Flat File Source – Customer CSV is mapped to a CSV file that holds source customer data. The file name and the schema of the CSV file are defined in the Customer CSV File connection, which you can see in the connection managers. OLE DB Destination – DimCustomer is mapped to the DimCustomer table in the *is2005sbsDW* database.

Before executing the package, you need to copy a source CSV file into the root folder of the drive C. Start Windows Explorer, copy Customers.csv, saved under the C:\Documents and Settings\<username>\My Documents\Microsoft Press\is2005SbS\Chap06_02-InitialCode \Data folder, to the root folder of the drive C. Open the CSV file in Microsoft Office Excel and review the customer data in the file.

Go back to BIDS. Press F5 to execute the package. All the items on the Control Flow tab and Data Flow tab turn green, and you should be able to see the row count in the Data Flow tab.

Before you modify the package, you need to add a column to the DimCustomer table to hold the validation result. The new column is called IsValidEmail, and the data type is Boolean.

Implement validation using the Transformation script component

1. Start SSMS and connect to localhost.

2. In Object Explorer, select the *is2005sbsDW* database in the Databases folder and click the New Query button on the Standard toolbar.

3. In the Query Editor, type the following SQL code:

   ```
   ALTER TABLE is2005sbsDW.dbo.DimCustomer ADD IsValidEmail bit NULL DEFAULT 0
   ```

4. Press F5 to execute the query. Ensure that the Command(s) Completed Successfully message is displayed on the Messages tab.

   Now you are ready to modify the package. You will add a new Script component in the Data Flow – Import Customer CSV and implement validation code in the new component.

5. In BIDS, click the Data Flow tab.

6. In the Toolbox, expand the Data Flow Transformations group, and then drag Script Component to the design surface of the Data Flow tab. The following dialog box appears on the screen:

In this dialog box, you will define which type of Script component you are going to use. As you learned at the beginning of this section, the Script component can be used as a source, destination, and transformation component. In this procedure, select Transformation.

7. Select Transformation and click OK.

8. Select the green arrow between Flat File Source – Customer CSV and OLE DB Destination – DimCustomer and press Delete to remove the path.

9. Select Flat File Source – Customer CSV, and then drag the green arrow to the new Script component.

10. Double-click the new Script component. The Script Transformation Editor dialog box appears.

11. On the Input Columns page, select the check box next to EmailAddress in the Available Input Columns table. Notice that the *Input Column*, the *Output Alias*, and *Usage Type* fields are automatically completed in the following list. This step enables you to declare which input fields you would like to access in your code. Your screen looks like this:

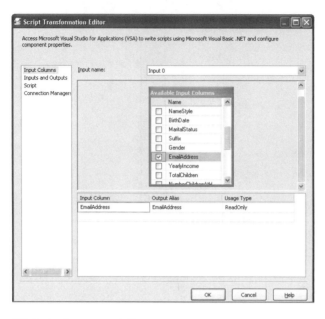

12. Click the Inputs and Outputs page.

13. In the tree view in the middle of the dialog box, expand Output 0 and select Output Columns. Click Add Column.

14. Rename the new column **IsValidEmail**.

15. In Data Type Properties, change the *DataType* property to **Boolean [DT_BOOL]**. You screen looks like this:

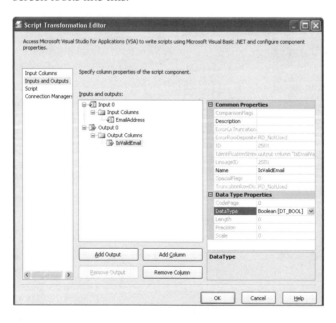

16. Click the Script page. In the right-side pane, change the *Name* property to **Script Component – Validate Email.**

17. Click Design Script. The VSA IDE appears on the screen.

18. In the Code Editor, insert the following code in your script:

```
Imports System
Imports System.Data
Imports System.Math
Imports Microsoft.SqlServer.Dts.Pipeline.Wrapper
Imports Microsoft.SqlServer.Dts.Runtime.Wrapper
Imports System.Text.RegularExpressions

Public Class ScriptMain
    Inherits UserComponent

    Public Overrides Sub Input0_ProcessInputRow(ByVal Row As Input0Buffer)
        '
        ' Add your code here
        '
        Const EMAIL_PATTERN As String = _
            "^\w+([-+.]\w+)*@\w+([-.]\w+)*\.\w+([-.]\w+)*$"
        If Row.EmailAddress_IsNull Then

            Row.IsValidEmail = False
                Exit Sub
        End If

        Row.IsValidEmail = Regex.IsMatch(Row.EmailAddress, _
            EMAIL_PATTERN)
    End Sub

End Class
```

The *Input0_ProcessInputRow* method will be invoked when SSIS inserts each row into this Script transformation component. For example, if an upstream component inserts five rows into this component, SSIS will call this method five times.

The *Row* parameter object contains all the information for each row's inputs and outputs, which you defined in the previous steps. Each column is defined as a member property of the *Input0Buffer* class. If you type **Row** in the Code Editor and type a dot (.), you can browse through the properties that you can access in the IntelliSense window.

The preceding code validates a given e-mail address by using Regular Expressions. Regular Expressions is a string pattern matching functionality, often used to examine whether the given text is following certain patterns. Regular Expressions is also useful for extracting certain patterns of string from the given text. In this code, *EMAIL_PATTERN* holds the regular expressions for the generic e-mail address. The *Regex.IsMatch* method returns *True* if the e-mail address matches the e-mail address pattern; otherwise, it returns *False*. For more information about Regular Expressions, refer to the "NET Framework Regular Expressions" section on the MSDN Web site at *http://msdn.microsoft.com/library/default.asp?url=/library/en-us/cpguide/html/cpcon-COMRegularExpressions.asp.*

19. Close VSA and the Script Transformation Editor dialog box.

20. Select the Script Component – Validate Email component and drag the green arrow to OLE DB Destination – DimCustomer.

21. Double-click OLE DB Destination – DimCustomer. The OLE DB Destination Editor dialog box appears. On the Mappings page, scroll down the grid and find IsValidEmail under Destination Column. Under Input Column should be <Ignore>. Change it to **IsValidEmail**, which you created in the previous steps.

22. Click OK. Your screen now looks like this:

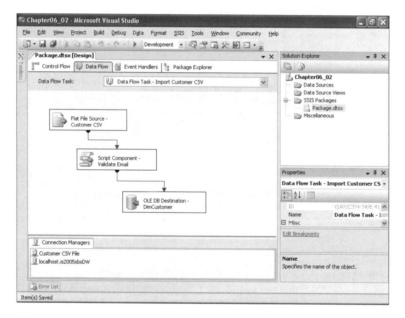

23. If you have not copied Customer.csv to the root folder of the drive C in the previous step, start Windows Explorer, copy Customers.csv, saved in the C:\Documents and Settings\<username>\My Documents\Microsoft Press\is2005SbS\Chap06_02-InitialCode\Data folder to root folder of the drive C.

24. Press F5 to execute the package. Make sure all components turn green and that the row count is displayed in the Data Flow.

25. Go back to SSMS, expand databases *is2005sbsDW* and *Tables*, and right-click the dbo.DimCustomer table. Select Open Table. Verify that the IsValidEmail column is all *True*.

26. Let's make sure validation code is working as you expect. Start Notepad, open C:\Customers.csv, and modify the e-mail address of the first customer (jon24@adventure-works.com) to an improper address, such as ABC.

27. Save your changes.

28. Go back to BIDS and press Shift+Ctrl+F5 to restart the package.

29. Go back to SSMS and select Execute SQL on the Query Designer menu to refresh the result grid. Ensure that the first customer's *IsValidEmail* value changed to *False*. This indicates that your validation code is working as you expect.

30. In Object Explorer, select the *is2005sbsDW* database and click New Query on the Standard toolbar.

31. In the Query Editor, type the following SQL code:

```
ALTER TABLE is2005sbsDW.dbo.DimCustomer DROP COLUMN IsValidEmail
```

32. Press F5 to execute the query. Make sure that the message Command(s) Completed Successfully appears on the Messages tab.

Understanding an ActiveX Script Task

The ActiveX Script task has been retained in SSIS 2005 for backward compatibility purposes. If you don't have any script code that you have to migrate from SQL Server 2000 DTS, you should use the Script task rather than the ActiveX Script task. The Script task provides you with a sophisticated way to implement such code as IntelliSense and integrated help, and it provides step-through debugging capability, which will be discussed in Chapter 7. The ActiveX Script task may be deprecated in a future release of SQL Server, so as a rule, it should not be used to implement new code.

The major component, called DTSGlobalVariables.Parent in SQL Server 2000 DTS, is no longer available in SSIS 2005. If you have an ActiveX task that manipulates package and task settings at run time, using the *DTSGlobalVariables.Parent* object, you cannot migrate it straight to the SSIS 2005 ActiveX Script task. SSIS 2005 suggests that you use Property Expressions and Package Configurations as the alternative for *DTSGlobalVariables.Parent*. These functionalities will be discussed in Chapter 8.

In SSIS 2005, you can still use ADO, FileSystemObject, and other COM objects. You can access variables through the *DTSGlobalVariables* object.

Implementing an ActiveX Script Task

In the following procedure, you will create a new package with a single ActiveX Script task, which will perform the same procedure that you implemented in the "Implement a Script Task" section. Retrieve the data from DimEmployee and export it to the custom format file. The ActiveX Script task also looks up the ExportFileName variable for the file name of the output file.

Create a new package with a single ActiveX Script task

1. Start BIDS.

2. On the File menu, point to New and select Project.

3. Select Integration Services Project and type **Chapter06_03** in the Name text box.

4. In the Location text box, specify **C:\Documents and Settings\\<username>\My Documents\Microsoft Press\is2005SbS\Chapter06_03-ActiveX**. Make sure that the Create Directory For A Solution option is selected and click OK.

5. Right-click anywhere on the design surface of the Control Flow tab and select Variables.

6. Click the Add Variables button (in the top-left corner of the variables window).

7. Rename the new variable **ExportFileName.**

8. Change the new variable's Data Type from Int32 to String and type **C:\Employees_AX.txt** in the Value column.

9. In the Toolbox, in the Control Flow Items group, select ActiveX Script Task and drag it to the design surface of the Control Flow tab.

10. Double-click the new ActiveX Script task. The ActiveX Script Task Editor dialog box appears.

11. On the General page, change the *Name* property to **ActiveX Script Task – Export Employees.**

12. On the Script page, select the *Script* property in the property grid and click the ellipsis button displayed on the right side of the grid. The ActiveX Script dialog box appears.

13. Insert the following script in the ActiveX Script dialog box:

```
Option Explicit

Function Main()
   Const RECORD_SEPARATOR = _
      "---------------------------------------------------------"
   Dim filename
   Dim con, rs
   Dim fso, writer
   Dim col, row
   Dim connectionString
   Dim sqlSelectEmployee
```

```
connectionString = _
    "Provider=SQLOLEDB;Data Source=localhost;" & _
    "Initial Catalog=is2005sbsDW;Integrated Security=SSPI"

sqlSelectEmployee = _
    "SELECT FirstName, LastName, MiddleName, " & _
    "Gender, Title, DepartmentName, HireDate, LoginID, " & _
    "EmailAddress, Phone FROM DimEmployee ORDER BY LastName"

fileName = DTSGlobalVariables("ExportFileName")

Set con = CreateObject("ADODB.Connection")
con.Open connectionString
Set rs = con.Execute(sqlSelectEmployee)

Set fso = CreateObject("Scripting.FileSystemObject")
Set writer = fso.CreateTextFile(fileName, True)

Do Until rs.EOF
    For col = 0 To rs.Fields.Count - 1
        writer.WriteLine rs.Fields(col).Name & ": " _
            & rs.Fields(col).Value
    Next

    writer.WriteLine RECORD_SEPARATOR
    rs.MoveNext
Loop

writer.Close
rs.Close
con.Close
End Function
```

This script is available in the text file saved in C:\Documents and Settings\<user-name>\My Documents\Microsoft Press\Chap06\Chapter06_03-ActiveX \Chapter06_03 _AXScript.txt.

The basic structure of the script is very similar to the one in the Script task exercise, although the script here doesn't have error-handling and logging code. The script retrieves data from DimEmployee in the *is2005sbsDW* database, using ADO, and writes out the text using FileSystemObject, with a result file name from the *ExportFileName* variable, using the *DTSGlobalVariables* object.

Your screen looks like this:

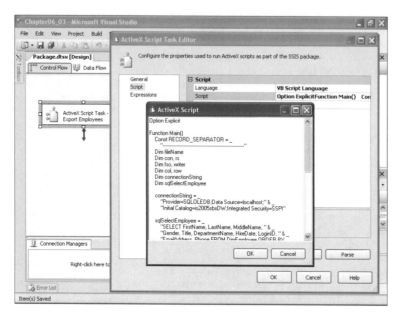

14. Click OK.

15. In the ActiveX Script Task Editor dialog box, on the Script page, type **Main** in EntryMethod.

    The *EntryMethod* property is to point the function, which should be called first. If you don't have function in your script, this property doesn't need to be specified.

16. Click OK to close the ActiveX Script Task Editor dialog box.

17. Press F5 to execute the package. Confirm that the ActiveX Script Task – Export Employees turns green.

18. Open the root folder of the drive C in Windows Explorer and verify that Employees_AX.txt has been created. In Notepad, open C:\Employees_AX.txt and verify that the employee data has been exported correctly.

19. On the Debug toolbar, click Stop Debugging.

> **Note** If the ActiveX Script task fails due to an [ActiveX Script Task] Error: Retrieving The File Name For A Component Failed With Error Code 0x0147763C error, open the script and replace *localhost* with the name of your computer.

Chapter 6 Quick Reference

To	Do This
Implement custom code in Control Flow	In the Toolbox, drag the Script Task to the design surface of the Control Flow tab. Double-click the Script task and click Design Script on the Script page in the Script Task Editor dialog box. In the VSA Code Editor, implement your own code in the *Main* method and set the overall result to the *Dts.TaskResult* property. The Code Editor provides you with several features to make your coding work easy.
Implement custom data processing code inside of the Data Flow	In the Toolbox, expand Data Flow Transformations and drag Script Component to the design surface of the Data Flow tab. In the Select Script Component Type dialog box, select Source, Transformation, or Destination as the situation demands. On the Input page and the Inputs and Outputs page in the Script Transformation Editor dialog box, define the inputs and outputs of the Script component. Select the Script page and click Design Script. In the VSA Code Editor, implement a script code to work with the *InputBuffer/OutputBuffer* object.
Implement error-handling code in the script	Implement the TRY...CATCH...FINALLY statement inside your script code. If an error occurred in the Try block, the alternative code implemented in the *Catch* block will be executed. You can specify multiple *Catch* blocks, based on the type of *Exception* object. You can also create the *Finally* block to implement finalization code.
Provide messages to the Progress tab	From the Script task, call the appropriate method defined under the *Dts.Events* object. The *Dts.Events* object allows you to raise several kinds of events, such as *Information*, *Progress*, and *Errors*. From the Script component, use methods defined under the *Me.ComponentMetadata* object.
Write out verbose information to a log file	From the Script task, call the *Dts.Log* method with appropriate parameters. From the Script component, call the *Me.ComponentMetadata.Log* method inside the script code. To configure the log settings, change the *LoggingMode* property of the Script task to *Enable*. Right-click anywhere on the design surface of the Control Flow tab and select Logging. In the Configure SSIS Logs dialog box, select the check box next to the package and the Script task to activate logging. On the Providers and Logs tab, add a log provider for text files and specify the file name. Select the check box to activate the provider. On the Details tab, select the check box next to the *ScriptTaskLogEntry* event so the SSIS engine listens to the message derived by the *Dts.Log* method.

To	Do This
Access the package variables	Right-click the design surface of the Control Flow tab and select Variables. Create a new variable in the Variables window. In the Script task, access the *Dts.Variables* object with the appropriate parameter name. You also need to set the variable name in either the *ReadOnlyVariables* property or the *ReadWriteVariables* property of the Script task. In the Script component, access the *Me.Variables* object. You also need to set the *ReadOnlyVariables* or *ReadWriteVariables* properties to use variables in the Script component.
Validate string data such as e-mail addresses	Use Regular Expressions. Call the *Regex.IsMatch* method with the string you would like to examine and the character patterns defined by Regular Expressions. If the string matches the patterns, the *IsMatch* method returns *True*. The *Regex* class is defined under the *System.Text.Regular-Expressions* namespace. Refer to the MSDN Web site to obtain detailed information about Regular Expressions.
Implement custom code using the ActiveX Script task	Create a new ActiveX Script task and implement script in the *Script* property. Specify the *EntryMethod* property if the script has a starter method. The ActiveX Script task is currently retained for backward compatibility, but use Script task if possible.

Chapter 7
Debugging Packages

After completing this chapter, you will be able to:

- Create breakpoints on packages, containers, and tasks in Control Flow and suspend execution at different kinds of events.

- Inspect the current state of execution, using debug windows such as Locals, Autos, and Watch.

- Understand progress messages logged on the Progress and Execution results tabs.

- Partially execute packages by disabling tasks and containers in Control Flow.

- Set data viewers in Data Flow tasks to preview data between transformation components.

- Create breakpoints in a Script task and inspect code line by line, using VSA debugging capabilities.

In the past few chapters, you learned how to create a package by using several kinds of tasks and Data Flow components. Perhaps you have already built a complicated package on your own.

In general, the more complicated your program is, the more chance you have of implanting defects in the program. When you execute a package in Microsoft SQL Server Business Intelligence Development Studio (BIDS), you might have to debug the package because it fails, or the result is not what you intend. BIDS, SQL Server Integration Services (SSIS) Designer, and Microsoft Visual Studio for Applications (VSA) provide powerful features and tools to diagnose the problem precisely and quickly. The Control Flow, Data Flow, and Script features require different tools for debugging due to the difference of architectures. In this chapter, you will learn what options you have to debug a package, and then you will learn how to use them through exercises.

Debugging Control Flow

If you have one of the following issues in your package, this section will give you an idea of how to troubleshoot it:

- A certain task that works with a resource external to the package (for instance, files, database, Web services, and so on) fails. You would like to check its state immediately before the task is executed.

- A package variable is changed to an unexpected value under certain conditions. You would like to find out which task is updating the variable.

- A Foreach Loop container or For Loop container doesn't work as you intend (for example, the loop never ends, the loop doesn't pick up the correct set of sources, and so on). You would like to know what is happening inside the loop.

These problems generally happen in tasks and containers in Control Flow. BIDS and SSIS Designer allow you to suspend execution by using breakpoints and allow you to browse the state through debug windows. Also, progress messages appearing on the Progress tab help you understand details of the execution status. The goal of debugging Control Flow is to discover which tasks, settings, or resources are causing the issue and to find out the reason for the defects.

Understanding Breakpoints

A breakpoint is a marker for where you would like to pause package execution. When the package is executed in BIDS, it suspends package execution at the breakpoint you have specified and enables you to investigate the state of the package. SSIS Designer allows you to set breakpoints on events that a package, container, and task provide. Events are essentially messages derived by a component, such as "I'm starting," "I'm done now," or "I have a problem." You can set breakpoints on multiple events and on the different items at the same time. The following table shows common events that most components provide:

Event	Description
OnPreExecute	This event is raised by a package, task, or container immediately before it runs, when the execution logic begins.
OnPostExecute	This event is raised by a package, task, or container immediately after it runs, immediately after the execution logic of the task completes.
OnError	This event is raised by a task or container when an error occurs.
OnWarning	This event is raised any time the task is in a state that does not justify an error but does warrant alerting the client.
OnInformation	This event is raised any time the task is to provide information.
OnTaskFailed	This event is raised by the task host when it fails.
OnProgress	This event is raised any time a task experiences measurable progress.
OnQueryCancel	This event is raised by tasks and containers to determine whether they should stop running at any juncture in task processing where it is feasible to cancel execution.
OnVariableValueChanged	This event is raised by a variable whenever its value is changed.
OnCustomEvent	This event is raised by tasks to raise custom task-defined events.

The *OnPreExecute* event is usually used to suspend execution before the component in question is executed. The *OnPostExecute* event is also useful if you would like to see what the target component has done immediately after the execution. If you would like to suspend execution when an error occurs anywhere inside the package, you can set a breakpoint on the *OnError* event at the package level.

Some components have their own events. For example, on the For Loop and Foreach Loop containers, you can set a breakpoint at the beginning of each iteration of the loop.

SSIS Designer also enables you to specify Hit Count Type and Hit Count options on each breakpoint. You can choose Always, Hit Count Equals, Hit Count Greater Than Or Equal To, or Hit Count Multiple from Hit Count Type and specify the hit count. Always will be used by default if you don't specify this option. This can be used with loop iteration events. For example, if your package loads multiple comma separated value (CSV) files into a database and it keeps failing at the third file, you can suspend execution when the Foreach Loop container comes to the third loop. You set a breakpoint at the loop iteration event on the container by specifying Hit Count Equals on Hit Count Type and 3 on Hit Count.

In the following procedure, you will learn how to set breakpoints and suspend execution in Control Flow by using BIDS and SSIS Designer.

Set breakpoints and suspend package execution

1. Start BIDS.

2. On the File menu, point to Open, and then select Project/Solution.

3. In the Open Project dialog box, specify C:\Documents and Settings\<username>\My Documents\Microsoft Press\is2005SbS\Chap07\Chapter07.sln and click Open.

4. In Solution Explorer, double-click DebuggingControlFlow.dtsx to open the package.

5. Right-click Execute SQL Task – Clear DimCustomer and select Edit Breakpoints.

   The Set Breakpoints <*container name*> dialog box appears with the list of breakpoints that you can set on the task. You can also specify the Hit Count Type and Hit Count options through this dialog box. Here, you will set a breakpoint on the *OnPreExecute* event by selecting the Enabled check box by the break condition.

6. Select the check box next to the break condition Break When The Container Receives The OnPreExecute Event. Your screen looks like this:

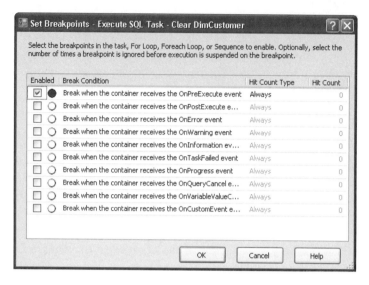

7. Click OK.

    Notice that a red dot is displayed on Execute SQL Task – Clear DimCustomer, as shown in the following illustration. This indicates that a breakpoint has been set on this task.

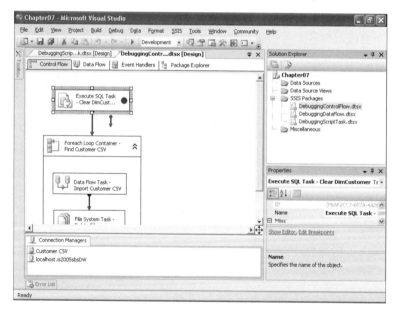

    Select Foreach Loop Container – Find Customer CSV and press F9.

8. F9 is a shortcut key to set a breakpoint on the *OnPreExecute* event. Press F9 again and observe that the breakpoint is removed.

9. Right-click anywhere on the design surface of the Control Flow tab and select Edit Break-points. This allows you to set breakpoints at the package level.

10. Select the check box next to the break condition Break When The Container Receives The OnPostExecute Event.

11. Click OK.

12. Right-click Foreach Loop Container – Find Customer CSV and select Edit Breakpoints.

    Verify that the dialog box shows the Foreach Loop container–specific break condition Break When The Beginning Of Every Iteration Of The Loop at the end of the list.

13. Select the check box next to the break condition Break At The Beginning Of Every Iteration Of The Loop.

14. Select Hit Count Equals from the Hit Count Type drop-down list and type **3** in the *Hit-Count* field. Your screen looks like this:

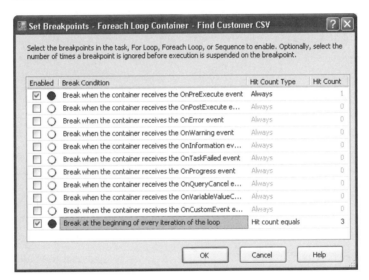

15. Click OK.

16. Before you execute the package, you need to copy the source CSV files to a designated location. Start Windows Explorer and open C:\Documents and Settings\<user-name>\My Documents\Microsoft Press\is2005SbS\Chap07\Data. Copy all CSV files in the folder to the root folder of the C drive.

17. Go back to BIDS and press F5 to execute the package.

    The first breakpoint is the *OnPreExecute* event of Execute SQL Task – Clear DimCus-tomer. Notice that a yellow arrow appears on the red dot, as shown in the following illus-tration. This arrow indicates the current location of execution.

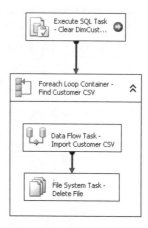

Also, be aware that the Execute SQL Task – Clear DimCustomer task is colored yellow. SSIS Designer changes the color of tasks and containers to depict the current state of each item. The following table shows the meanings of each color:

Color	Execution Status
White	The item is waiting for execution; it has not executed yet.
Yellow	The item is currently running.
Green	The item ran successfully.
Red	The item ran and encountered errors.
Gray	The item is being disabled (will be skipped).

18. Start SQL Server Management Studio (SSMS) and connect to localhost.

19. In Object Explorer, expand Databases, is2005sbsDW, and Tables. Right-click the dbo.DimCustomer table, and then click Open Table. Verify that the table holds data.

20. Go back to BIDS and press F5 to resume execution. Notice that the yellow arrow stops at Foreach Loop Container – Find Customer CSV.

21. Go back to SSMS and select Execute SQL on the Query Designer menu. Notice that data in DimCustomer has been truncated by the Execute SQL Task – Clear DimCustomer task.

22. Go back to BIDS and press F5.

    Because you have set the condition Hit Count = 3 at the loop iteration event, SSIS Designer executes Data Flow Task – Imports Customer CSV and File System Task – Delete File for the first two files and then breaks execution before the container enters the third iteration. Open the root directory of the C drive in Windows Explorer and verify that the first two CSV files (Customer_A-F.csv and Customer_G-L.csv) have been processed and deleted.

23. Select File System Task – Delete File and press F9.

    A red dot is now displayed on the File System Task – Delete File task. As you can see here, you can set and remove breakpoints while the execution is suspended.

24. Press F5. Once you have verified that execution has been suspended at File System Task – Delete File, press F5 to resume execution.

    Now the yellow arrow appears on the Control Flow tab. This indicates that the package execution has reached the end, and the *OnPostExecute* event was fired.

25. Press F5 to complete execution.

26. On the Debug menu, click Stop Debugging.

27. On the Debug menu, select Delete All Breakpoints. Click Yes in the alert message box.

> **Tip** As you can see in the menu caption, you can also delete all breakpoints by pressing Shift+Ctrl+F9.

Reviewing Debug Windows

As you go through the procedure in the previous section, you might want to look into such details as package variables. You might have noticed that a set of small windows docked in the BIDS window appear while you are executing a package. These windows provide information about the package or about each item in Control Flow while execution is suspended by breakpoints. BIDS provides several kinds of windows for debugging, and the following windows are useful when you debug Control Flow. These windows are available on the Debug menu in BIDS.

Call Stack

■ The Call Stack window provides a hierarchy and sequence of the package execution. You can view the names of containers and tasks invoked in the execution. A yellow arrow in the window identifies the task or container currently running.

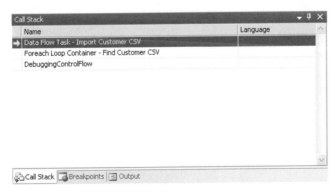

Breakpoints

- The Breakpoints window provides a list of the breakpoints currently set in the package. You can activate, deactivate, and delete breakpoints by using this window. You can also modify the break condition of each breakpoint through this window.

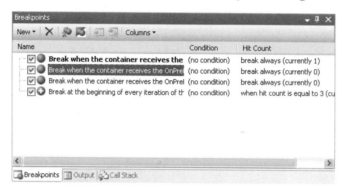

When a package is executed, the Breakpoint window shows how many times the breakpoint is passed in the Hit Count column.

❑ **Locals**   The Locals window is the primary tool for browsing variables. Under the *Variables* node in the list, you can view all system variables and user variables available in the current package. You can also modify the value of variables through this window while the execution is suspended.

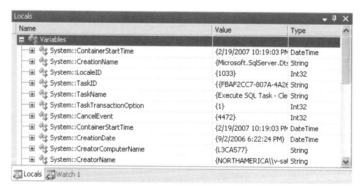

In the following procedure, you will see how you can browse and modify the variables through the Locals window.

Tip   Most debug windows are available only while you are executing the package in BIDS. If you would like to review the final state of the package, you need to set a breakpoint at the *OnPostExecute* event at the package level.

Execute package and review debug windows

1. On the Control Flow tab, right-click Foreach Loop Container – Find Customer CSV and select Edit Breakpoints.

2. Select the check box next to the break condition Break When The Beginning Of Every Iteration Of The Loop.

3. Click OK.

4. Start Windows Explorer and navigate to C:\Documents and Settings\<username>\ My Documents\Microsoft Press\is2005SbS\Chap07\Data. Copy all CSV files in the root folder of the C drive.

5. Press F5 to execute the package. Verify that the package is suspended at the Find Customer CSV container.

6. On the Debug menu, select Breakpoints to open the Breakpoints window.

   Ensure that all the breakpoints you have set are listed in the window. You might notice that one of the breakpoints is marked with a red dot and a white plus sign. This indicates the breakpoint has an additional condition such as Hit Count Type and Hit Count.

7. On the Debug menu, point to Windows, and then select Locals. Expand the *Variables* node in the Locals window.

   Verify that all system variables and user variables are listed in the *Variables* node. Find *User::FileName* variables in the list. The value of the variable now should be *C:\Customer_A-F.csv*. This variable holds a CSV file name that will be provided to the Flat File source component in Data Flow Task – Import Customer CSV.

8. Press F5 to process the first CSV file.

   Foreach Loop Container – Find Customer CSV found the second CSV file and updated User::FileName to C:\Customers_G-L.csv.

9. In the Locals window, expand User::FileName and change the value in the *Value* property to an incorrect file name, such as **ABC**.

10. Press F5.

    The package fails because it tries to find the given, but inappropriate, file name.

11. On the Debug menu, select Stop Debugging.

12. On the Debug menu, select Delete All Breakpoints. Click Yes to confirm.

13. In Windows Explorer, delete any CSV files remaining in the root folder of the C drive.

Understanding Progress Messages

When a package is executed, SSIS Designer logs events and messages raised by packages and components on the Progress tab. This helps you understand package execution precisely.

After you stop debugging a package, these messages remain available on the Execution Results tab, so you can refer to them later.

The messages on the Progress tab usually appear in the following form:

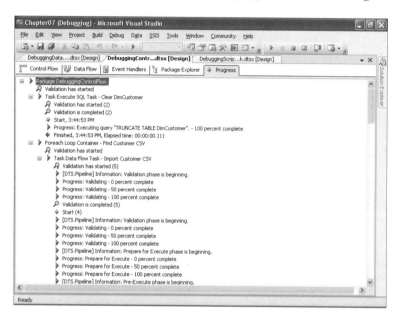

A Progress message starts with the top-level package name, and all tasks and containers defined in the package appear under that package name. Tasks and containers are alphabetical, not chronological.

Event messages derived by each component appear under the component name. The messages of each component usually start with a validation message such as Validation Has Started, Progress:Validating, and Validation Is Complete. This is because the SSIS engine validates all components defined in the package before the package is actually executed. If you suspend the package at its *OnPreExecute* event and look on the Progress tab, you can see that the message tree is structured, and the validation of each item is complete.

After the validation, the SSIS engine logs the package's *start* event as Start under the top-level package name with the current time stamp. After the package is executed, the SSIS engine logs each component's *start* event and *interim* event such as the *information*, *progress*, *error*, and *complete* (logged as *Finished*) events. The messages under each component appear in chronological order.

To find an active task, find a task that has a Start message but doesn't have a Finished message at the end of the message set. If you would like to know the total execution time or the execution time for each component, refer to the elapsed time logged with the Finished message under the component.

Executing a Package Partially

If you have a long series of tasks and containers in your package, you might want to execute the package only partially to save you debugging time.

BIDS and SSIS Designer provide two options to execute packages partially. The first option is to right-click a task or container and select Execute Task or Execute Container. The SSIS engine executes the specified task or container and then terminates package execution without executing other tasks and containers. If breakpoints are set in the task and container, they will be ignored.

The other option is to disable tasks and containers that you would like to skip during the execution. This can be helpful if you would like to investigate more than one task or container. Breakpoints work well for this.

In the following procedure, you will learn how to execute a package partially by using the features previously discussed.

Disable a task and execute a package partially

1. Start Windows Explorer and navigate to C:\Documents and Settings\<username>\My Documents\Microsoft Press\is2005SbS\Chap07\Data. Copy all CSV files in the folder to the root folder of the C drive.

2. In Control Flow, right-click Execute SQL Task – Clear DimCustomer and select Execute Task.

   The SSIS engine executes the specified task (Execute SQL Task – Clear DimCustomer) and terminates execution before it begins the next task.

3. On the Debug menu, select Stop Debugging.

4. Right-click File System Task – Delete File and select Disable.

   Notice that the task has been grayed out. This indicates that the task is disabled and never runs.

5. Press F5 to execute the package.

   The package runs and executes all tasks and containers in Control Flow. Start Windows Explorer and open the C folder. Observe that the CSV files remain in the folder because you disabled the delete task (File System Task – Delete File) in the last step.

6. On the Debug menu, select Stop Debugging.

7. Right-click File System Task – Delete File and select Enable.

Debugging Data Flow

When your package encounters the following issues, you need to investigate the Data Flow task:

- A Data Flow task produces no result data, or it produces the wrong number of records. You would like to discover the component that is causing the issue.

- In a Data Flow task, unexpected data is produced during the transformation. You would like to suspend the data flow and look into the passed data.

You might have noticed that SSIS Designer doesn't allow you to set breakpoints to Data Flow components. This is because the breakpoints and debug windows might not be efficient tools when you inspect data flowing inside the Data Flow task. Instead of the breakpoints and debug windows, SSIS Designer provides you with a tool called data viewers.

Browsing Data By Using Data Viewers

A data viewer is a browser that you can attach to paths between two Data Flow components. You can set data viewers before or after the component in question to see whether the component is working as you intend. For example, you might set a data viewer right after the Lookup Transformation component to monitor whether the component retrieves appropriate values from a designated data source.

SSIS Designer provides four different types of viewers: Grid, Histogram, Scatter Plot, and Chart Format. You can set different types of viewers for each data flow path. The following illustration shows a Grid data viewer working on SSIS Designer.

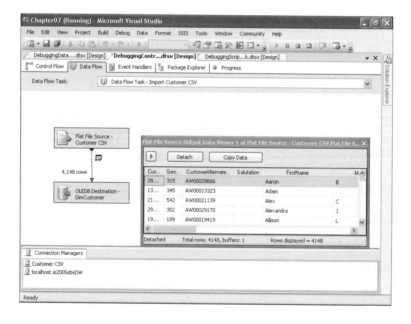

You might need to choose an appropriate viewer as the situation demands. Usually, the Grid viewer is the first option to inspect data because of its versatility. The rest of the viewers help you understand what kind of data is flowing or how the data is spread.

Data viewers work like a composite tool of the breakpoints and debug windows. The SSIS engine suspends data flow execution while you are browsing through a data viewer. SSIS Designer allows you to detach and attach data viewers during the execution, just like the breakpoints in Control Flow. If you are finished browsing through the data, you can simply detach the data viewer to let the rest of the data go through.

In the following procedure, you will learn how to browse through data flowing inside the Data Flow task by using data viewers.

Set data viewers and browse data

1. If you haven't opened Chapter07.sln yet, start BIDS and open the solution file saved in C:\Documents and Settings\<username>\Microsoft Press\is2005SbS\Chap07\Chapter07.sln.

2. In Solution Explorer, double-click DebuggingDataFlow.dtsx.

3. In SSIS Designer, click the Data Flow tab.

4. Right-click the green arrow between OLEDB Data Source – vProductProfitability and Flat File Destination – ProductProfitability CSV and select Data Viewers.

5. In the Data Flow Path Editor dialog box, click Add. The Configure Data Viewer dialog box appears on the screen.

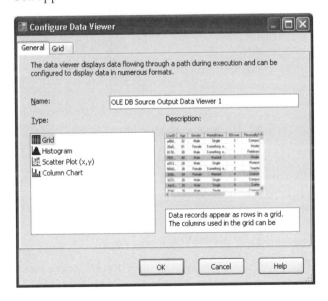

This dialog box allows you to configure a data viewer directly on the data path. In the General tab, you can select a data viewer from four types and specify a name for the data viewer. The name specified here will be used as a caption of the data viewer.

The second tab is aligned with the data viewer you have selected on the General tab. The second tab enables you to configure the appearance of the data viewer.

6. In the Configure Data Viewer dialog box, select Grid in the Type list and change Name to **Grid – ProductProfitability Output Summary**.

7. On the Grid tab, click the double left-arrow button to move all columns into the Unused Columns list on the left side.

8. In the Unused Columns list, double-click the following columns to move them to the Displayed Columns list on the right side: Year, Month, Product, OrderQuantity, and SalesAmount. Your screen looks like this:

9. Click OK. Verify that the new data viewer is added in the list.

10. Click Add.

11. In Configure Data Viewer, select Column Chart and change the name to **Column Chart – SubCategory**.

12. In the Column Chart tab, select SubCategory in the Visualized Column list and click OK.

13. Click OK to close the Data Flow Path Editor dialog box.

    SSIS Designer shows an eyeglasses icon next to the path to specify that the path contains data viewer settings.

14. Make sure you are on the Data Flow tab, and then press F5 to execute the package. Your screen looks like this:

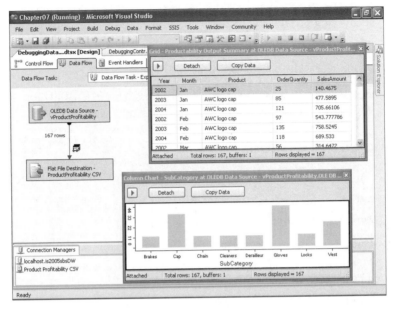

Two data viewer windows appear over BIDS and, soon, the process will be suspended at the path between OLEDB Data Source – vProductProfitability and Flat File Destination – ProductProfitability CSV. The Grid – ProductProfitability Output Summary window shows the first data block from the data source in the grid, and the Column Chart – Sub-Category window shows a column chart based on the SubCategory data.

Also, notice that SSIS Designer displays the record count of the current data block near the data flow path. You can use this number to make sure the data flowing through each path is as you expect it to be.

15. Click the green arrow button in the Grid – ProductProfitability Output Summary window.

The first data block has been processed, and the next data block appears in the Grid – ProductProfitability Output Summary window. Also, the column chart in the Column Chart – SubCategory window has been updated by the new data. Click the green arrow button in the data viewer window several times and review the data flow.

When you have finished reviewing data, you can detach data viewers to let the process go through without detouring through the data viewers.

16. Click Detach in the Grid – ProductProfitability Output Summary window and Column Chart – SubCategory window.

The two data viewers are now detached from the path, and data flows freely. You can re-attach the data viewer while execution is active.

17. While SSIS Designer is processing data, click Attach in the Grid – ProductProfitability Output Summary window. Notice that the data viewer is now attached on the path again and shows the current data block in the grid. Click the green arrow button in the window several times to review the data.

18. Click Detach in the Grid – ProductProfitability Output Summary window.

19. After all files are processed, select Stop Debugging on the Debug menu.

20. On the Debug menu, select Delete All Breakpoints. This deletes all data viewers set in the Data Flow task.

Understanding Other Options

Along with the data viewers, the following tools also help you debug data flow.

- **Progress Messages**   If an error occurred inside the data flow, the messages on the Progress tab are the first place to investigate the error.

- **Error Output**   If the error occurred inside your Data Flow task, the Error Output feature helps you identify the record causing the error. Error Output is discussed in Chapter 4, "Using Data Flow Transformations."

- **Row Count**   As you have seen in the previous exercise, SSIS Designer shows you the number of processed records in the Data Flow tab. If the resulting data count is incorrect, this might be one of the clues for debugging.

Debugging Script Task

Once you have identified that a Script task is causing an issue, you need to look into the code defined in it. The concept of debugging script code is similar to what you learned in the "Debugging Control Flow" section: you set breakpoints to suspend execution and look at the state of script through debug windows. The difference is that you can set breakpoints at each line of code and walk through the code line by line using VSA. VSA also provides extra tools to inspect the state of script. The rest of this section will show you how to debug a Script task by using these tools.

Walk Through Code by Using Breakpoints

To debug code defined in your Script task, you need to set at least one breakpoint in the code by using the VSA Code Editor. To create the breakpoint, place the cursor on the line in which you want to create a breakpoint and press F9. When the package is executed and execution reaches the breakpoint in the Script task, VSA appears and highlights the statement in the Code Editor, as shown here:

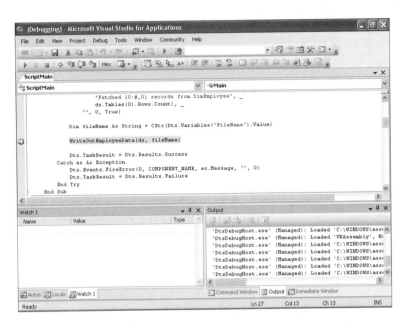

At this point, the highlighted statement is not executed yet. While the execution is suspended, you can inspect elements in the state of the script, such as variables and properties, using debug windows (discussed later in this section). Once you complete the inspection, you can advance to the next statement. VSA provides you with the following options to manage code execution:

- **Continue (assigned to F5)**   The Continue command executes the rest of the code, including the current statement, and breaks execution at the next breakpoint.

- **Step Into (assigned to F11)**   The Step Into command executes the current statement and breaks execution at the next statement. If the current statement calls a user-defined method, the Step Into command enters the method and breaks execution at the first line of the method.

- **Step Over (assigned to F10)**   The Step Over command executes the current statement and breaks execution at the next statement. If the current statement calls a user-defined method, the Step Over command executes the entire method and breaks execution at the next statement in the current method.

- **Step Out (assigned to Shift + F11)**   The Step Out command executes the rest of the statement in the current method, including the current statement, and then breaks execution at the statement where the current method has been invoked. This command is often used with the Step Into command.

- **Run To Cursor**   The Run To Cursor command executes the current statement as well as the rest of the statement in the current method defined before the specified line.

Set breakpoints and walk through code

1. If you haven't opened Chapter07.sln yet, start BIDS and open the solution file saved in C:\Documents and Settings\<username>\Microsoft Press\is2005SbS\Chap07\Chapter07.sln.

2. In Solution Explorer, double-click DebuggingScriptTask.dtsx.

3. Double-click Script Task – Export Employees.

4. In the Script Task Editor, select the Script page and click the Design Script... button. VSA appears on the screen.

5. In the Code Editor, place the cursor on the Dim ds As DataSet = GetEmployeeData() line, and then press F9.

   The line is highlighted in red, and a red dot appears in the right-side gray band. This indicates that you have set a breakpoint in the statement.

6. Place the cursor on the WriteOutEmployeeData(ds, fileName) line and press F9. Your screen looks like this:

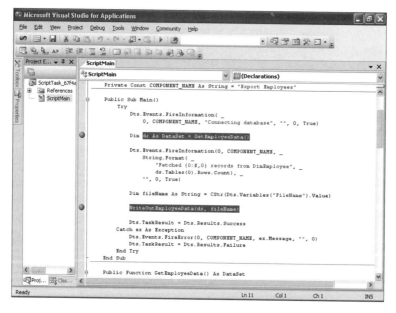

7. Close the VSA code editor window, and then click OK to close the Script Task Editor dialog box.

   Notice that a red dot appears on Script Task – Export Employees. This also indicates that you have set breakpoints inside the task.

8. Press F5 to execute the package.

VSA appears and highlights the first line of code that has a breakpoint. Your screen should look like this:

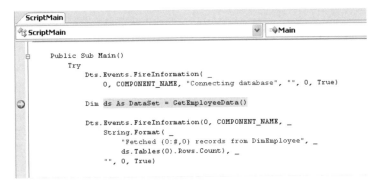

The current statement is not executed yet. You will execute the entire *GetEmployeeData* method with the Step Over command because you're not interested in each statement in the method.

9. Press F10.

   F10 is a shortcut key assigned to the Step Over command. Notice that execution didn't go through the *GetEmployeeData* method and breaks at the next statement in the *Main* method.

10. Press F5.

    When you press F5, the execution resumes and executes the rest of the statement until it encounters the next breakpoint. Now, execution should break at the *WriteOutEmployeeData* method line. You will review the method to see its details.

11. Press F11.

    Execution enters the *WriteOutEmployeeData* subroutine and breaks at the first line of the method. Press F11 several times to walk through the statement.

12. Right-click the writer.WriteLine(RECORD_SEPARATOR) line and select Run To Cursor.

    Execution resumes and executes the rest of the statement, then breaks at the specified line. This command is often useful if the method needs to go through long statements before it comes to the statement you are interested in.

13. Press Shift + F11.

    Shift + F11 is a shortcut key assigned to the Step Out command. Now execution exits the *WriteOutEmployeeData* method and breaks at the statement that invoked it.

14. Press F5 to exit the Script task.

15. On the Debug menu, select Stop Debugging.

> **Note**   Leave the breakpoints in the Script task for the next procedure.

Reviewing State by Using VSA Features

While you are walking through code inside the Script task, you can review the current state by using debug windows, as you learned in the "Debugging Control Flow" section. In addition to the windows discussed in that section, VSA provides others to help debug a Script task.

- **Autos**   The Autos window has functionality similar to the Locals window. It helps you look into variables or properties that are referred to by the current statement in the Code Editor. The difference between the Locals window and the Autos window is that the Autos window automatically picks up relevant objects according to the current statement.

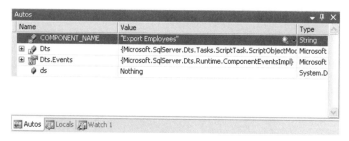

- **Watch**   Whereas the Autos window varies its content during execution, the Watch window allows you to track specific items persistently throughout the execution. The Watch window also allows you to specify expressions such as Dts.Variables.Count > 0. To add an item in the Watch window, either right-click an object and select Add Watch or type expressions in the window directly.

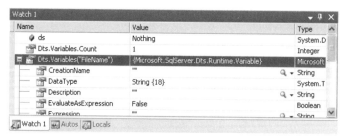

- **QuickWatch**   QuickWatch is a dialog box used to examine an object without adding it to the Watch window. QuickWatch allows you to specify expressions such as Watch window. To launch the QuickWatch dialog box, right-click an object and select QuickWatch.

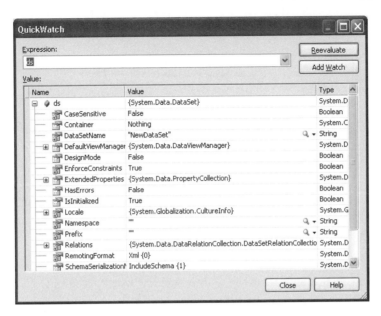

- **Immediate**   The Immediate window is a command-line tool window to examine objects or expressions. To examine an object, type expressions after the ? command, such as ? Dts.Variables(<;$QD>ABC<;$QD>).Value. The result appears as text after the command line. IntelliSense helps you type expressions in the Immediate window.

- **DataTip**   DataTip allows you to inspect objects without adding them to the Watch window, just like the QuickWatch dialog box. DataTip is an easier tool to use. If you hover the mouse pointer over the variables in the code, DataTip shows the content in a small tips window by the line. If the target is an object (an instance of class), you can inspect its member values by expanding the plus sign that appears in the small window.

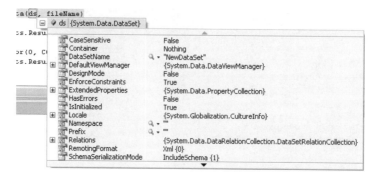

- **Output** The Microsoft .NET Framework enables you to provide information to the Output window through the *System.Diagnostics.Debug* class or *System.Diagnostics.Trace* class, for example, if you have the following code in your Script task:

```
Debug.WriteLine("Varibles Count: " & Dts.Variables.Count)
```

The following text appears in the Output window when it's executed:

```
Variables Count: 1
```

This is often useful when you would like to leave the result in text and compare the intermediate results side by side.

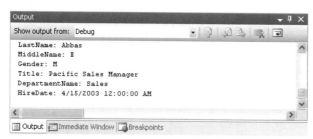

In the following procedure, you will set breakpoints in the code and see the steps through the debugging by using VSA. You will also learn how to use the debug windows for scripts.

Review state, using debug windows

1. Double-click Script Task – Export Employees.

2. In the Script Task Editor, select Script Page and click Design Script. VSA appears on the screen.

3. In the Code Editor, find the Next col statement in the *WriteOutEmployeeData* subroutine. Insert the following code before the Next col line:

```
Debug.WriteLine(String.Format("{0}: {1}", _ .Columns(col).ColumnName,
.Rows(row)(col)))
```

4. Close VSA and click OK to close the Script Task Editor dialog box.

5. Press F5 to execute the package. Execution breaks at the first breakpoint.

6. On the Debug menu, point to Windows, and then select Autos.

   Verify that the Autos window shows objects related to the current statement. Make sure that the *ds* variable is currently *Nothing*. Press F10 to execute the *GetEmployeeData* subroutine, and then notice that the *ds* variable has been initialized by the *GetEmployeeData* subroutine. Also, the Autos window now shows the other objects related to the next statement. When you look at the *ds.Tables(0).Rows.Count* entity, you can see the number of records that have been retrieved from the database.

7. Hover the mouse cursor over the *ds* variable in the following line:

   ```
   WriteOutEmployeeData(ds, fileName)
   ```

   The DataTip window appears by the line and shows the *ds* variable in the window. If you click the plus sign in the window, you can see all the properties of the *ds* variable.

8. On the Debug menu, point to Windows, and then select Immediate.

9. In the Immediate window, type the following command, and then press Enter:

   ```
   ?Dts.Variables("FileName").Value
   ```

   The content of the *FileName* variable appears in the next line.

10. Press F5.

11. Find the line you have inserted in the previous step (starts with *Debug.WriteLine*). Right-click the line and select Run To Cursor.

12. On the Debug menu, point to Windows, point to Watch, and then select Watch 1.

13. In the Watch 1 window, type **col** in the *Name* field of the blank line. The value should be *0*.

14. Press F10 several times to run through a loop a couple of times. Observe that the *col* variable is incremented each time the execution passes the For statement.

15. On the View menu, select Output. In the Output window, observe that the field name and value are logged by the *Debug.WriteLine* method.

16. Press F5 to execute the rest of the statement.

17. On the Debug menu, select Stop Debugging.

How Can I Debug the Script Component?

Unfortunately, breakpoints are not supported in the Script component. However, it is still possible to write the state out of the component to understand what is happening inside the Script component. First, create a new Output in the Script component to write intermediate data or invalid data out of the component. Connect the Output to an arbitrary destination component, such as Flat File. You can set a data viewer between these two components to review the data while you're executing the package. Another option is to use the *Me.Log* method to write out to Microsoft Windows Event Log, to SQL Server, or to a text file. You can also use event methods (for instance, *FireInformation*) defined under *Me.ComponentMetadata* to write a message to the Progress tab. Refer to Chapter 6, "Scripting Tasks," for details.

Chapter 7 Quick Reference

To	Do this
Create a breakpoint and review variable status in Control Flow	On the Control Flow tab, right-click a task or component and select Set Breakpoints. Select the check box next to the appropriate break condition. Set Hit Count Type and Hit Count if it is necessary. If you would like to create a breakpoint at the package level, right-click the background of the Control Flow pane and select Set Breakpoints. Once you execute the package, the yellow arrow depicts the current location. On the Debug menu, point to Windows and select Locals to open the Locals window. Expand the *Variables* node in the Locals window to review system and user variables. When you have finished reviewing the status, press F5 to continue execution.
Execute Package Partially	Right-click a task or container and select Execute Task or Execute Container. This allows you to execute a specific item in Control Flow. Right-click the task or container you would like to skip during the execution and select Disable. Press F5 to execute the package. The SSIS engine executes the package, skipping disabled tasks and containers.
Review data flow between Data Flow components	On the Data Flow tab, right-click a data flow path and select Data Viewers. In the Data Flow Path Editor dialog box, click Add to add a new data viewer. In the Configure Data Viewer dialog box, select the appropriate type of viewer and modify the viewer properties on the second tab. Data will be displayed in the data viewer once the execution reaches the path. Review the data and click the green arrow or Detach in the data viewer window to process execution.

To	Do this
Create a breakpoint and step through code in the Script task	In Control Flow, double-click a Script task. In the Script Task Editor dialog box, click Design Script on the Script page. In the Code Editor, place the cursor on the statement and press F9.
	Once execution reaches the breakpoint, press F10, F11, or Shift+F11 to continue execution. Right-click the statement and select Run To Cursor to process statements defined before the line.
Review variables while suspending execution in the Script task	While execution is suspended, go to the Debug menu, point to Windows, and select Autos. Review objects related to the current statement in the Autos window.
	Right-click the target variable and select Add To Watch. Watch 1 allows you to track changes in the variable.
	Hover the mouse pointer over the object. The DataTip window displays information about the object under the mouse pointer.
	On the Debug menu, point to Windows and select Immediate. In the Immediate window, type expressions after the ? command and press Enter. The Immediate window displays the result of the expression in the next line.

Chapter 8
Managing Package Execution

After completing this chapter, you will be able to:

- Understand package configurations and create and edit an XML configuration file.

- Create multiple configuration files, including environment variable, SQL Server, and parent package variable configurations.

- Configure and execute logging.

In the previous chapters, you learned how to create a package. Now it's time to learn how to manage package execution. In this chapter, you'll learn how package configurations can be used to develop packages that are flexible and easy to deploy and distribute. In addition, you'll learn how to create an XML configuration file. Finally, you'll learn how to configure and execute logging.

Understanding Package Configurations

Microsoft SQL Server 2005 Integration Services (SSIS) provides package configurations that you can use to update the values of properties at run time. A *package configuration* is a property and the value assigned to the property that you add to a completed package. This enables you to modify package property values without having to modify the actual package. Some examples of package configurations include file paths, user logon information, server names, database connections strings, variable values, and so on. A common use of package configurations is to enable the server name and user logon information to be applied dynamically at run time.

Configuration Benefits

Package configurations provide the following benefits:

- Configurations make it easier to move packages in development, test, and production environments. For example, a configuration can update the path of a source file or change the name of a database or server to a new resource location without modifying the actual package.

- Configurations are useful when you deploy packages to many different servers. For example, a variable in the configuration for each deployed package can contain a different disk space value and, if the available disk space does not meet this value, the package will not run.

- Configurations make packages more flexible. For example, a configuration can update the value of a variable that is used in a property expression.

Configuration Types

Before you can create a package configuration, you must specify the configuration type. SSIS supports several different methods of storing package configurations. Table 8-1 briefly describes the package configuration types supported by SSIS. In this section, you will learn how to configure an XML file. The following sections will show you how to configure environment variable, SQL Server, and parent package variable configurations.

Table 8-1   Package Configuration Types Supported by SSIS

Configuration Type	Description
XML	An XML file can contain a single or multiple configurations.
Environment variable	An environment variable contains the configurations.
Registry entry	The registry entry contains the configurations.
Parent package variable	A variable in the package contains the configuration. This configuration type is typically used to update properties in child packages.
SQL Server table	A table in a SQL Server database can contain either single or multiple configurations.
Direct and indirect	SSIS provides direct and indirect configurations. Indirect configurations use environment variables.

Understanding the XML Configuration File

XML is the preferred format for a configuration file because it can be read by many different technologies. An XML configuration file can contain configurations for multiple properties. It contains both the property path (for instance, \Package.Connections[CustomerList].Properties[ConnectionString]) and the configured value (for instance, C:\Temp\Integration Services Project1\Data\CustomerList.txt). XML configurations are simple to read and modify. They are also easy to keep together with the package (*.dtsx) file.

Specifying a New XML Configuration File Location

If you use a direct XML configuration file and move your package to a new environment, you must edit the package to specify the new location of the XML configuration file. If you use indirect configurations, you must specify one environment variable for each configuration. Using direct and indirect configurations are discussed later in this chapter.

Creating and Editing an XML Configuration File

As you've seen, creating and editing an XML configuration makes your package deployment more flexible. In the following procedures, creating an XML configuration file entails extracting data from a source table and then loading the data into a Microsoft Office Excel file. These transformation processes simulate the data-delivering routines that you might perform when working in a data warehouse or an enterprise environment.

Opening the SSIS Project and Executing the Package

You cannot run the Package Installation Wizard until you create an SSIS project. In this procedure, you'll create a new SSIS project to which you will add a data flow task.

Create a new SSIS project

1. To open the SSIS project, in Windows Explorer, navigate to C:\Documents and Settings\<username>\My Documents\Microsoft Press\is2005sbs\Chap08\.

2. Double-click Chap08.sln. The project opens in Business Intelligence Development Studio (BIDS).

3. In BIDS, locate the Solution Explorer window on the right side of the design environment. Make sure this window is visible and not autohidden so you can see all of the files in the project.

4. Find the NewProducts.dtsx file under the SSIS Packages folder. Double-click NewProducts.dtsx to open this package in the designer.

   You have now opened the project. It's time to execute the project.

5. In Solution Explorer, right-click NewProducts.dtsx, and then click Execute Package.

   Wait until the package has executed successfully before starting the next step.

   Notice that in the design window, as each task is completed successfully, the color of the task blocks changes from yellow to green. When the package has executed successfully, the task blocks should be green, and the bottom of the screen should read "Package execution completed. Click here to switch to design mode, or select Stop Debugging from the Debug menu." Your screen should resemble the following illustration:

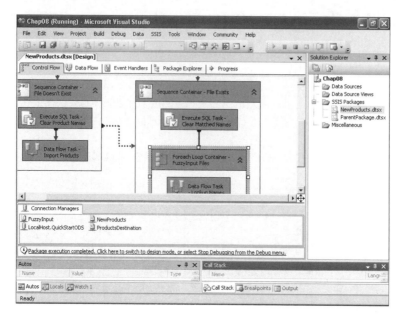

When a package is executed, it creates an output file.

6. To view the output file, switch to Windows Explorer.

7. Navigate to C:\Documents and Settings\<username>\My Documents\Microsoft Press\is2005sbs\Chap08\Data.

8. Double-click ProductsDestination.txt.

   Notice that there are 62 records in the *QuickStartODS* database ProductNames table.

9. Switch to BIDS.

10. On the Debug menu, click Stop Debugging.

Creating an XML Configuration File

In this procedure, you'll create an XML configuration file named NewProducts.dtsConfig. You'll then configure the XML configuration file to store the *ConnectionString* property.

Create an XML configuration file

1. In BIDS, on the SSIS menu, click Package Configurations. The Package Configurations Organizer opens.

2. In the Package Configurations Organizer, select the Enable Package Configurations check box.

> **Note**   Configurations can be enabled or disabled for a package configuration. If you disable a package configuration, the property values stored in the package are used, and the property values in the configurations are ignored.

3. Click Add to start the Package Configuration Wizard. The Welcome To The Package Configuration Wizard page appears.

4. On the Welcome To The Package Configuration Wizard page, click Next. The Select Configuration Type page appears.

5. On the Select Configuration Type page:

    a. In the Configuration Type drop-down list, select XML Configuration File.

    b. Ensure that the Specify Configuration Settings Directly option is selected.

    c. In the Configuration File Name text box, type **C:\Documents and Settings\ <username>\My Documents\Microsoft Press\is2005sbs\Chap08\New-Products.dtsConfig**.

    Your screen should look similar to this:

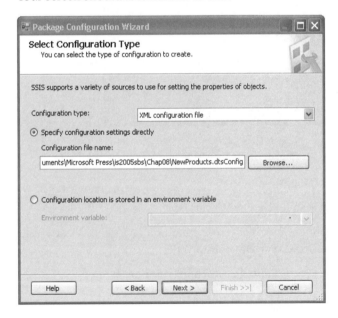

    You have now selected the type of configuration to create.

6. Click Next. The Select Properties To Export page appears.

7. On the Select Properties To Export page:

   a. In the Objects pane, locate the Connection Managers folder, expand Products-Destination, and then expand the Properties folder.

   b. Select the ConnectString check box.

   You have now selected the properties that will be exported to the configuration file.

   Your screen looks like this:

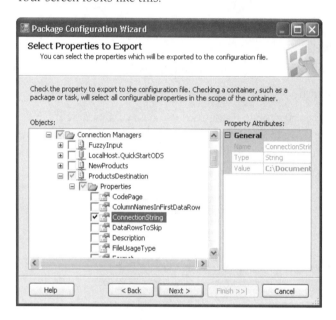

   Notice that in the Property Attributes pane, the Name, Type, and Value of the Products-Destination connection manager connection string is displayed. These values will be written to the XML configuration file.

8. Click Next. The Completing The Wizard page appears.

9. To specify the configuration name, on the Completing The Wizard page, in the Configuration Name text box, type **DestinationFile**.

10. Click Finish to close the Completing The Wizard page.

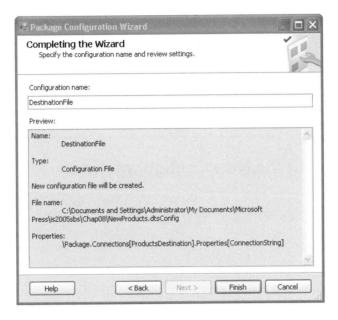

11. Click Close to close the Package Configurations Organizer.

Editing the XML Configuration File

In this procedure, you'll edit the XML configuration file by replacing the ProductDestination.txt file with the XMLProductDestination.txt file. This change will enable the package to write product records to the XMLProductsDestination.txt file.

Edit the XML configuration file

1. In Windows Explorer, navigate to C:\Documents and Settings\<username>\My Documents\Microsoft Press\is2005sbs\Chap08\NewProducts.dtsConfig.

2. Right-click NewProducts.dtsConfig, click Open With, select Microsoft Visual Studio Version Selector, and then click OK.

3. In SSIS, on the NewProducts.dtsConfig tab, find <ConfiguredValue> in the XML file:

    a. On the Edit menu, click Find and Replace, and then click Quick Find.

    b. In the Find and Replace box, in the Find What box, type **<ConfiguredValue>**.

    c. Click Find Next.

    d. <ConfiguredValue> is highlighted in the XML file.

    Notice the values of the attributes contained in the <Configuration> tag.

4. Between the <ConfiguredValue> tags, locate the destination file named ProductsDestination.txt.

5. Rename the destination file ProductsDestination.txt **XMLProductsDestination.txt**.

6. On the File menu, click Save NewProducts.dtsConfig.

7. Close the SSIS file.

> **Note**   When this configuration is enabled, the package writes product records to the XMLProductsDestination.txt file.

Testing the Package with the New Configuration

Now that you have created and edited the XML file, you need to test the package to ensure that it is functioning properly and that it created the correct .txt file.

Test the package

1. Switch to BIDS.

2. In BIDS, in the Solution Explorer pane, right-click NewProducts.dtsx, and then click Execute Package.

3. Wait until the package has executed successfully.

4. Switch to Windows Explorer.

5. In Windows Explorer, navigate to C:\Documents and Settings\<username>\My Documents\ Microsoft Press\ is2005sbs \Chap08\Data.

6. In the Data folder, verify that the package created the XMLProductsDestination.txt file.

Multiple Configuration Files

Now that you understand how to create and edit a configuration file, you are ready to learn how to create multiple configuration files. This section will discuss the other configuration types supported by SSIS, including the environment variable, registry entry, parent package variable, SQL Server table, and direct and indirect configuration types.

Environment Variable

An environment variable configuration sets a package property equal to the value in an environment variable. You must create and set the environment variable value by using the Microsoft Windows–based operating system. Only one package property can be configured per environment variable configuration. Environmental configurations are useful for configuring properties that are dependent on the computer that is executing the package. The environment variable contains only a value. The Package Configuration Organizer must contain information about the package property that is going to be set equal to the environment variable.

Registry Entry

A registry entry configuration is similar to an environment variable configuration. Registry entries are more difficult to create but more secure than environment variables.

Parent Package Variables

A parent package can contain an Execute Package task that executes a child package. The child package can contain a parent package variable configuration that sets a child package property equal to the value of a parent package variable. For example, a child package could extract data from the Employees table for one department and write it to a text file. A parent package could contain a *Department* variable that the child package reads to determine the set of employee data to write to the text file.

SQL Server Tables

SQL Server configurations contain both the package property path and the value. A single SQL Server configuration can contain multiple package properties and values. SQL Server configurations are useful for large-scale SSIS implementations and when a single configuration can be used by multiple packages. For example, you might have a configuration that contains your data warehouse server name and database name. Multiple packages could then read this configuration as they update the data warehouse.

Direct and Indirect Configurations

When you create a configuration in the Package Configuration Wizard, you can specify the location of the configuration (direct), or you can specify an environment variable that contains the location of the configuration (indirect). Indirect configurations can be created for XML configuration files, registry entries, and SQL Server configurations. Indirect configurations require one environment variable for each configuration, but they allow XML configuration locations to be changed without editing a package.

Using Configuration Files

If you use indirect configurations, you must specify one environment variable for each configuration. Using direct and indirect configurations is discussed later in this chapter.

Typically, the most flexible way to use configurations is to use an environment variable or registry entry that contains a connection string to a SQL Server database containing SQL Server configurations. You should list this configuration first in the Package Configuration Organizer, and then the remaining configurations should use SQL Server or parent package variable configurations.

Determining Configuration Order

Configurations are applied in the order in which they are listed in the Package Configuration Organizer with one exception: Parent package variable configurations are always applied last. If multiple configurations contain the same package property, the property is set to the value in the last applied configuration. Because parent package variable configurations are applied last, you should ensure that other configurations are not dependent on them.

Evaluating Configuration Failure

If a configuration fails (for example, you give the wrong location for an XML configuration file), the package will continue to execute using the values set for the properties in the package. Configuration failure generates a warning but not an error. Package execution is momentarily slowed by a configuration error.

Using Multiple Configurations

XML configuration files and SQL Server configurations can contain multiple package properties. For example, a single configuration can contain the connection strings to all of the source and target files and databases. All the packages can then read this configuration. However, because not all packages use all of the sources and targets, warnings are generated when the packages read the configuration. It is better to create multiple XML or SQL Server configurations, one configuration per set of related properties. For example, you could create one configuration that contains the connection string and text qualifier for a source text file and another configuration containing the connection string for a target database. This way, each package reads only the configurations it needs.

Creating Multiple Configuration Files

In the following procedures, you'll create SQL Server configurations. To use SQL Server configurations, first you must designate a SQL Server database to contain the configurations table. After you have created the database, you'll use environment variable configurations to designate this database. Finally, you'll create parent package variable configurations.

Creating the Database and the OLE DB Connection Manager

In this procedure, you'll create a new database named *ConfigDB*, and then create a connection manager named LocalHost.ConfigDB.

Create a new database

1. In SQL Server Management Studio, create a new database named *ConfigDB*:

    a. In Object Explorer, right-click the Databases folder, and then click New Database.

    b. In the New Database dialog box, in the Database Name text box, type **ConfigDB**.

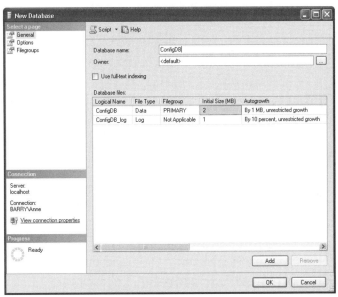

    Notice that in the New Database dialog box, in the Database Files pane, the new database *ConfigDB* is listed.

    c. Click OK to close the New Database dialog box.

2. In BIDS, create a connection manager named LocalHost.ConfigDB:

    a. In Solution Explorer, double-click NewProducts.dtsx to open the package designer.

    b. In the design environment, in the Connection Managers pane, right-click anywhere, and then click New OLE DB Connection. The Configure OLE DB Connection Manager dialog box appears.

    c. In the Configure OLE DB Connection Manager dialog box, click New. The Connection Manager dialog box appears.

    d. In the Connection Manager dialog box, in the Server Name drop-down list, type **LocalHost**.

    e. In the Connect To A Database frame, ensure that the Select Or Enter A Database Name option is selected, and then select configDB.

f. Click OK to close the Connection Manager dialog box.

g. In the Configure OLE DB Connection Manager dialog box, click OK.

h. Notice that LocalHost.ConfigDB appears on the Connection Managers pane in BIDS.

Creating the Environment Variable

In this procedure, you'll create a database environment variable named *ConfigDBName*.

Create a database environment

1. Click Start, click My Computer, right-click anywhere in the window, and then click Properties. The System Properties dialog box opens.

2. In the System Properties dialog box, at the bottom of the Advanced tab, click Environment Variables. The Environment Variables dialog box opens.

3. In the Environment Variables dialog box, in the System Variables frame, click New. The New System Variable dialog box opens.

4. In the New System Variable dialog box, in the Variable name box, type **ConfigDBName**.

5. In the Variable value box, type **ConfigDB**.

   Your screen should look like this:

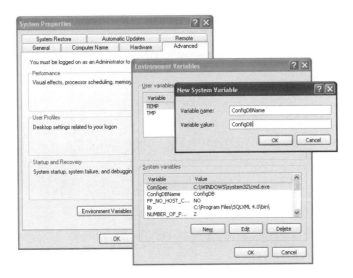

6. Click OK to close the New System Variable dialog box.

7. Click OK to close the Environment Variables dialog box.

8. Click OK to close the System Properties dialog box.

> **Tip**   You can verify that you have successfully created the environment variable by running the SET command in a Windows Command Prompt window. This command enables you to view all the Windows environment variables and their values.

9. In BIDS, on the File menu, click Save All, and then close BIDS.

10. In Windows Explorer, go to C:\Document and Settings\<username>\My Documents\ Microsoft Press\is2005sbs\Chap08 and double-click Chap08.sln to restart BIDS. BIDS opens.

11. In Solution Explorer, double-click NewProducts.dtsx to open the package designer.

> **Tip**   Restarting refreshes the list of environment variables in BIDS.

Creating the Environment Variable Configuration

In this procedure, you'll configure the environment variable named *ConfigDBName* that you created in the previous procedure.

Configure the environment variable

1. In BIDS, on the SSIS menu, click Package Configurations. The Package Configurations Organizer opens.

2. In the Package Configurations Organizer, ensure that the Enable Package Configurations check box is selected.

3. Click Add to start the Package Configuration Wizard. The Welcome To The Package Configuration Wizard page appears.

4. On the Welcome To The Package Configuration Wizard page, click Next. The Select Configuration Type page appears.

5. On the Select Configuration Type page, in the Configuration Type drop-down list, select Environment Variable.

6. In the Environment Variable drop-down list, select ConfigDBName.

   Your screen should look like this:

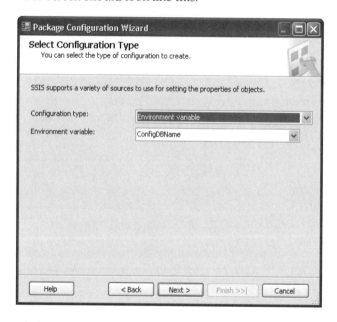

7. Click Next. The Select Target Property page appears.

8. On the Select Target Property page, in the Objects pane, locate the Connection Managers folder, expand LocalHost.ConfigDB, expand the Properties folder, and then click Initial-Catalog.

   Notice that on the right side of the screen, in the Property Attributes pane, the Name, Type, and Value of the *LocalHost.ConfigDB connection manager InitialCatalog (database name)* property is displayed.

9. Click Next. The Completing The Wizard page appears.

10. On the Completing The Wizard page, in the Configuration Name text box, type **ConfigDBName**.

11. Click Finish to close the wizard.

12. Leave the Package Configurations Organizer open.

Creating the SQL Server Configuration

In this procedure, you'll create a SQL Server table in the *ConfigDB* database SSIS configurations table, and then change NewProducts.txt to NewProductsShortList.txt.

Create a SQL Server table

1. In the Package Configurations Organizer, ensure that the Enable Package Configurations check box is selected.

2. Click Add to start the Package Configuration Wizard. The Welcome To The Package Configuration Wizard page appears.

3. On the Welcome To The Package Configuration Wizard page, click Next. The Select Configuration Type page appears.

4. On the Select Configuration Type page, in the Configuration Type drop-down list, select SQL Server.

5. Ensure that the Specify Configuration Settings Directly option is selected.

6. In the Connection drop-down list, select LocalHost.ConfigDB.

7. Next to the Configuration Table drop-down list, click New. The Create Table box opens.

Your screen should look similar to this:

8. Click OK. The Package Configuration Wizard page appears.

9. In the Package Configuration Wizard, verify that a table named [dbo].[SSIS Configurations] was created in the *ConfigDB* database and listed in the Configuration Table dropdown list.

10. In the Configuration Filter drop-down list, type **ProductsShortListFilter**, and then click Next. The Select Properties To Export page appears.

11. On the Select Properties To Export page, in the Objects pane, locate the Connection Managers folder, expand NewProducts, and then expand the Properties folder.

12. Select the ConnectionString check box, and then click Next. The Completing The Wizard page appears.

13. On the Completing The Wizard page, in the Configuration Name text box, type **ProductsShortList**.

14. Click Finish to close the wizard.

15. Close the Package Configurations Organizer.

16. In SQL Server Management Studio, open the *ConfigDB* database SSIS Configurations table:

a. On the left side of the screen, in Object Explorer, right-click the Databases folder, and then click Refresh.

   b. Expand the configDB folder, expand the Tables folder, right-click dbo.SSIS Configurations, and then click Open Table.

Notice that the tab in the middle of the screen changes to read dbo.SSIS Configurations.

17. On the Table – dbo.SSIS Configurations tab, in the ConfiguredValue column, click NewProducts.txt, and then change the name to **NewProductsShortList.txt**.

18. Click the next record to save your changes.

Testing the Package with the New Configuration

Now that you have created and configured the package, it's time to test the new configuration.

Test the new configuration

1. In Windows Explorer, delete the file named C:\Documents and Settings\<username>\My Documents\Microsoft Press\is2005sbs\Chap08\Data\XMLProducts-Destination.txt.

2. In BIDS, in the Connection Managers pane, right-click the LocalHost.ConfigDB connection manager, and then click Edit. The Connection Manager dialog box appears.

3. In the Connect To A Database frame, in the Select Or Enter A Database Name drop-down list, select is2005sbsDW, and then click OK.

The LocalHost.ConfigDB connection manager now points to the wrong database. When the package runs, the *ConfigDBName* configuration will change the LocalHost.ConfigDB connection manager so that it points to the *ConfigDB* database.

4. In Solution Explorer, right-click NewProducts.dtsx, and then select Execute Package. Wait until the package has executed successfully.

5. On the Debug menu, click Stop Debugging.

6. Switch to SQL Server Management Studio.

7. In SQL Server Management Studio, in Object Explorer, expand QuickStartODS, expand Tables, and then right-click dbo.ProductNames and click Open table.

Notice that the tab in the middle of the screen changes to read dbo.ProductNames.

8. On the toolbar, click the red exclamation mark (!) (Execute SQL).

On the Table – dbo.ProductNames tab, SQL populates the table with data.

9. Verify that the table contains only 42 records, as shown in the following screen shot.

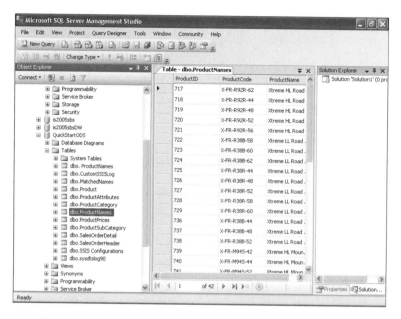

10. Switch to Windows Explorer.

11. Navigate to C:\Documents and Settings\<username>\My Documents\Microsoft Press\is2005sbs\Chap08\Data.

12. Ensure that the file named XMLProductsDestination.txt was created in the Data folder.

Exploring the Parent Package

Before you create the parent package variable configuration, it's important to view the Parent-Package.dtsx package, which contains an Execute Package task that runs the NewProducts.dtsx package.

View the ParentPackage.dtsx package

1. In BIDS, in Solution Explorer, double-click the ParentPackage.dtsx package to open the package designer.

2. In the Connection Managers pane, right-click NewProducts.dtsx, and then click Edit. The File Connection Manager Editor box appears.

3. In the File Connection Manager Editor box, view the Usage Type and File properties of NewProducts.dstx.

   The NewProducts.dtsx file connection manager references the NewProducts.dtsx package.

4. Click OK to close the File Connection Manager Editor box.

5. In the package designer, right-click Execute Package Task – NewProducts, and then click Edit. The Execute Package Task Editor appears.

6. In the Execute Package Task Editor box, view its properties, such as General, Package, and Expressions.

    The Execute Package Task – NewProducts task executes the package referenced by the NewProducts.dtsx connection manager.

7. Click OK to close the Execute Package Task Editor.

8. Right-click anywhere in the package designer, click Variables, and then view the *ParentProductsDestination* variable properties.

9. The *ParentProductsDestination* variable contains a fully qualified file name. You might need to expand the Variables pane to view the variable properties.

Creating the Parent Package Variable Configuration

In this procedure, you'll create the ParentProductsDestination parent package variable configuration.

Create the ParentProductsDestination parent package

1. In BIDS, in Solution Explorer, double-click the NewProducts.dtsx package to open the package designer.

2. On the SSIS menu, click Package Configurations. The Package Configurations Organizer opens.

3. In the Package Configurations Organizer, ensure that the Enable Package Configurations check box is selected.

4. Click Add to start the Package Configuration Wizard. The Welcome To The Package Configuration Wizard appears.

5. On the Welcome To The Package Configuration Wizard page, click Next. The Select Configuration Type page appears.

6. On the Select Configuration Type page, in the Configuration Type drop-down list, click Parent Package Variable.

7. Ensure that the Specify Configuration Settings Directly option is selected.

8. In the Parent Variable text box, type **ParentProductsDestination**.

9. Click Next. The Select Target Property page appears.

10. On the Select Target Property page, in the Objects pane, expand the Connection Managers folder, expand ProductsDestination, expand the Properties folder, and then click ConnectionString.

11. Click Next. The Completing The Wizard page appears.

12. On the Completing the Wizard page, in the Configuration name box, type **ParentDestinationFile**.

    Your screen should look similar to this:

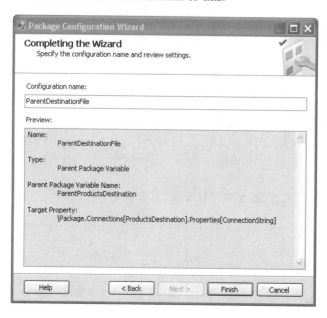

13. Click Finish to close the Package Configuration Wizard.

    The package now has two configurations that modify the destination file name. The last configuration to modify a property is applied to the package.

14. Click Close to close the Package Configurations Organizer.

15. On the File menu, click Save All.

Test the package with the new configuration

1. In Windows Explorer, delete the file named C:\Documents and Settings\<username>\My Documents\Microsoft Press\is2005sbs\Chap08\Data\XMLProductsDestination.txt.

2. In BIDS, in Solution Explorer, right-click ParentPackage.dtsx, and then click Execute Package. Wait until the package has executed successfully.

3. In Windows Explorer, navigate to C:\Documents and Settings\<username>\My Documents\Microsoft Press\is2005sbs\Chap08\Data.

4. In the Data folder, verify that the package created the ParentProductsDestination.txt file.

5. In BIDS, on the Debug menu, click Stop Debugging.

Exploring Package Execution Options

Packages can be run in various wizards and applications; however, packages are most often run in SQL Server Business Intelligence Development Studio (BIDS) during the development, debugging, and testing of packages. The Execute Package task extends the enterprise capabilities of SSIS by enabling packages to run other packages as part of a workflow. A package that runs another package is generally referred to as a *parent package*, and the packages that a parent workflow runs are called *child packages*. This section discusses the various methods for creating and executing packages.

Using the SQL Server Import and Export Wizard to Execute Packages

The SQL Server Import and Export Wizard provides the simplest method for creating and executing a simple package. You can start the SQL Server Import and Export Wizard from an Integrations Services package in BIDS, or you can start the wizard from SQL Server Management Studio; however, you can execute a package only if you start the SQL Server Import and Export Wizard in SQL Server Management Studio.

Start the SQL Server Wizard from BIDS

1. In BIDS, create an SSIS project by performing the following steps:

    a. On the File menu, click New, and then click New Project.

    b. In the New Project dialog box, provide a name, location, and solution for your project, and then click OK.

2. In Solution Explorer, right-click the SSIS packages folder, and then click SSIS Import And Export Wizard. The SQL Server Import And Export Wizard appears.

3. Follow the wizard steps, and then save the package in your project.

> **Note** A package cannot be executed if you start the SQL Server Import And Export Wizard from an Integrations Services package in BIDS.

Start the SQL Server Wizard from Management Studio

1. In Management Studio, connect to a database engine by performing the following steps:

    a. On the File menu, click Connect Object Explorer. The Connect to Server dialog box appears.

    b. Click Connect.

2. In Object Explorer, expand the Databases folder.

3. Right-click the name of the database you created earlier (configdb), click Tasks, and then click either Import Data or Export Data. The SQL Server Import And Export Wizard appears.

4. Follow the wizard steps, save the package, and then decide whether to execute the package.

Using DTExecUI to Execute Packages

Another effective tool for executing packages is the SSIS package execution utility DTExecUI. DTExecUI is a command prompt utility that enables you to run packages from a command prompt or from within SQL Server Management Studio.

Run a package by using the DTExecUI utility

1. To open a command prompt window, click Start, and then click Run. The Run box appears.

2. In the command prompt window, type **dtexecui**, and then press Enter. The Execute Package Utility dialog box opens.

3. In the Execute Package Utility dialog box, specify any of the following:

   ❑ Package to execute

   ❑ XML configuration files

   ❑ Connection Manager connection strings

   ❑ Variables

   ❑ Other package properties

4. Click Execute to run the package. Wait until the package has executed successfully.

Using DTExec to Execute Packages

The DTExec utility provides access to all the package configuration and execution features, such as connections, properties, variables, logging, and progress indicators. It enables you to load packages from three sources: a SQL Server database, the SSIS service, and the Windows file system.

The DTExec utility proceeds through four phases as it executes:

- Command sourcing phase
- Package load phase
- Configuration phase
- Validation and execution phase

DTExec enables you to run packages from a command prompt. The basic syntax is dtexec /option [value] [/option [value]]. The Execute Package Utility contains a command-line window. This window contains the /option [value] part of the dtexec syntax. The dtexec command can be saved in a *.bat or *.cmd file, and then the package can be run by executing one of these files. This is particularly useful with enterprise job-scheduling software. The SSIS developers can create the *.cmd files, and then the job-scheduling software needs only to execute the *.cmd files.

On a 64-bit server, the 64-bit version of dtexec.exe is located at \Program Files\Microsoft SQL Server\90\DTS\Binn\DTExec.exe. The 32-bit version of dtexec.exe is located at \Program Files\Microsoft SQL Server (x86)\90\DTS\Binn\DTExec.exe. It is sometimes useful to execute SSIS in 32-bit mode on a 64-bit server. For example, there is no 64-bit Microsoft Access OLE DB (Jet engine) driver.

> **More Info**   For more information about the DTExec utility, see the SQL Server 2005 Books Online article titled "dtexec Utility" at *http://msdn2.microsoft.com/en-us/library/ms162810.aspx*.

Run a package by using the DTExec utility

1. Open a command prompt window.

2. In the command prompt window, type **dtexec /** followed by the DTS, SQL, or File option and the package path, including package name.

3. If the package encryption level is EncryptSensitiveWithPassword or EncryptAllWith-Password, use the Decrypt option to provide the password. If no password is included, dtexec will prompt you for the password.

4. Optionally, provide additional command-line options.

5. Press Enter.

6. Optionally, view logging and reporting information before closing the Command Prompt window. The Execute Package Utility dialog box opens.

7. In the Execute Package Utility dialog box, click Execute Package. Wait until the package has executed successfully.

Using SQL Server Management Studio to Execute a Package

In SQL Server Management Studio, in Object Explorer, you can connect to an SSIS server, expand the Stored Packages folder, and then expand either the File System or MSDB folder.

Run a package by using SQL Server Management Studio

1. In SQL Server Management Studio, right-click a package, and then click Run Package. Execute Package Utility opens.

2. Execute the package as described previously.

Extending Package Execution Options

You can extend the enterprise capabilities of SSIS by using the Execute Package and Execute Process tasks.

Execute Package tasks

The Execute Package task enables packages to run other packages as part of a workflow. You can use the Execute Package task for the following general purposes:

- Breaking down complex package workflow
- Reusing parts of packages
- Grouping work units
- Controlling package security

For example, you can use the Execute Package task to modularize your packages. Each child package can perform a small, well-defined unit of work, and then a parent package can contain multiple Execute Package tasks to execute all of the child packages. One common use is to have one package per data warehouse dimension and then have a parent package that executes all of the dimension packages.

A child package can be executed by a parent package, using an Execute Package task. The child package can use a configuration to read the parent package variables.

Execute Process tasks

The Execute Process task can execute any file that can be executed from the command prompt. This includes the SSIS Command Line Utility (DTExec). You can specify the executable and command-line arguments. You can also execute a *.bat or *.cmd file that contains a dtexec command.

Using SQL Server Agent

SQL Server Agent is a Windows service that executes scheduled administration tasks, which are called *jobs*. It uses SQL Server to store job information. Jobs contain one or more job steps. Each step contains its own task, for example, backing up a database. SQL Server Agent can run a job on a schedule, in response to a specific event, or on demand.

SQL Server Agent can be configured to execute an SSIS package. It can also be configured to modify the package XML configuration files, connection manager strings, variables, and other package properties.

Execute tasks and containers and then disable the task and execute the package

1. In BIDS, in Solution Explorer, double-click NewProducts.dtsx to open the package designer.

2. On the Control Flow tab, right-click Execute SQL Task – Clear Product Names, and then click Execute Task.

3. In SQL Server Management Studio, in the *QuickStartODS* database, click the Table – dbo.ProductNames tab, and then, on the Query Designer toolbar, click the exclamation mark (!) (Execute SQL).

   Verify that the *QuickStartODS* database ProductNames table is empty.

4. In BIDS, on the Debug menu, click Stop Debugging.

5. Right-click Sequence Container – File Doesn't Exist, and then click Execute Container.

6. In SQL Server Management Studio, click the Table – dbo.ProductNames tab, and then click the exclamation mark (!) (Execute SQL).

   Verify that the *QuickStartODS* database ProductNames table now contains data.

7. In BIDS, on the Debug menu, click Stop Debugging.

8. On the Control Flow tab, right-click Foreach Loop Container – FuzzyInput Files, and then click Disable.

9. In Solution Explorer, right-click NewProducts.dtsx, and then click Execute Package. Wait until the package has executed successfully. Your screen should resemble this:

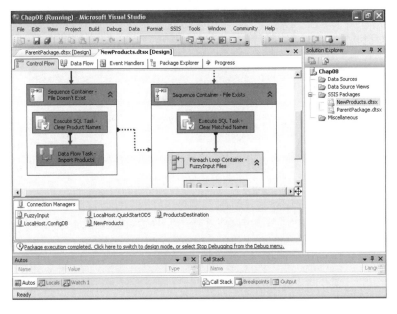

10. In SQL Server Management Studio, in Object Explorer, expand QuickStartODS, expand the Tables folder, right-click dbo.MatchedNames, and then click Open Table.

    Notice that the tab in the middle of the screen changes to read dbo.MatchedNames.

11. Click the Table – dbo.MatchedNames tab, and then click the exclamation mark (!) (Execute SQL).

12. On the Table – dbo.MatchedNames tab, verify that the table is empty.

13. In BIDS, on the Debug menu, click Stop Debugging.

14. On the File menu, click Save All.

15. Close the NewProducts.dtsx package.

Using the Execute Package Utility

In this procedure, you'll learn how to use the Execute Package Utility.

Use the Execute Package Utility

1. In Windows Explorer, navigate to C:\Documents and Settings\<username>\My Documents\Microsoft Press\is2005sbs\Chap08\XPkgUNewProducts.dtsConfig.

2. Right-click XPkgUNewProducts.dtsConfig, click Open With, and then click Microsoft Visual Studio Version Selector.

   In BIDS, on the XPkgUNewProducts.dtsConfig tab, between the <ConfiguredValue> tags, notice that the name of the destination file has been changed to XPkgUProducts-Destination.txt.

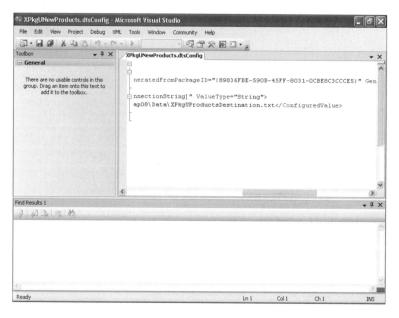

3. In Windows Explorer, double-click the C:\Documents and Settings\<username>\My Documents\Microsoft Press\is2005sbs\Chap08\NewProducts.dtsx file. Execute Package Utility opens.

4. In Execute Package Utility, in the left pane, click Configurations, and then click Add. The Open dialog box appears.

5. In the Open dialog box, browse to C:\Documents and Settings\<username>\My Documents\Microsoft Press\is2005sbs\Chap08\XPkgUNewProducts.dtsConfig, and then click Open.

6. In the Execute Package Utility dialog box, in the left pane, click each option to see the changes that can be made to a package when it is executed using Execute Package Utility.

7. Click Execute. The Package Execution Progress dialog box opens. This dialog box shows event log entries as the package executes.

8. When package execution completes, click Close to close the Package Execution Progress dialog box.

9. Leave the Execute Package Utility dialog box open.

10. In Windows Explorer, verify that the NewProducts package created the C:\Documents and Settings\<username>\My Documents\Microsoft Press\is2005sbs\Chap08\Data\XPkgUProductsDestination.txt file.

Use the command-line utility

1. In the Execute Package Utility dialog box, in the left pane, click Command Line.

2. Copy all of the text in the Command Line box.

3. In Windows Explorer, right-click C:\Documents and Settings\<username>\My Documents\Microsoft Press\is2005sbs\Chap08\ExecuteNewProducts.cmd, and then click Edit.

4. In ExecuteNewProducts.cmd – Notepad, replace *<paste here>* with the text you copied from the Command Line box.

5. On the File menu, click Save.

6. Close the file, and then close Execute Package Utility.

7. In Windows Explorer, double-click C:\Documents and Settings\<username>\My Documents\Microsoft Press\is2005sbs\Chap08\ExecuteNewProducts.cmd.

   The command-line utility executes the NewProducts package.

8. When package execution completes, press any key to close the command-line window.

Executing a package by using SQL Agent

1. In SQL Server Management Studio, verify that you are connected to the SQL Server database engine. (If you are not connected, on the File menu, click Connect Object Explorer, and then, in the Connect to Server box, click Connect.)

2. In the left pane, toward the bottom of the tree, right-click the SQL Server Agent folder, and then click Start.

> **Note** By default, the SQL Server Agent service is stopped. To start the service, in Object Explorer, right-click the SQL Server Agent folder, and then click Start.

3. Right-click the Jobs folder (located under the SQL Server Agent folder), and then click New Job. The New Job dialog box opens.

4. In the New Job dialog box, in the left pane, click General, and then, in the Name text box, type **ExecutePackageJob**.

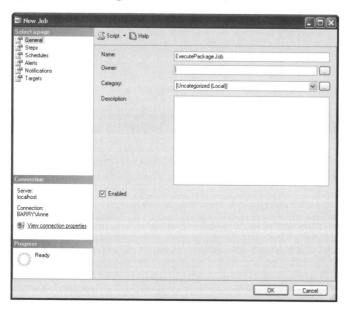

5. In the left pane, click Steps, and then click New. The New Job Step dialog box opens.

6. In the New Job Step dialog box, in the Step Name text box, type **ExecutePackageStep**.

7. In the Type drop-down list, select SQL Server Integration Services Package.

8. In the Package Source drop-down list, select File System.

9. In the Package text box, navigate to C:\Documents and Settings\<username>\My Documents\Microsoft Press\is2005sbs\Chap08\NewProducts.dtsx, and then click Open.

10. Click OK to close the New Job Step dialog box, and then click OK to close the New Job dialog box.

11. In SQL Server Management Studio, in the left pane, expand the Jobs folder, right-click ExecutePackageJob, and then click Start Job At Step. SQL Server Agent executes the NewProducts package.

12. After the package executes, click Close to close the Start Jobs dialog box.

    Now that the SQL Server Agent job is created, the package can be executed on a periodic basis by using the scheduling features in SQL Server Agent.

Understanding Package Logging

In Chapter 7, "Debugging Packages," you learned that there are several options for monitoring the progress of package execution during the development cycle. However, these options are useful only when executing a package manually. After a package is placed into production, a different method is required to monitor the package's progress. SSIS includes logging features that write log entries when run-time events occur and provides a schema of commonly logged information to include in log entries.

A *log* is a collection of information about the package that is collected when the package runs. For example, a log can provide the start and finish times for a package run. A *log provider* defines the destination type and the format that the package and its container and tasks can use to log run-time information. The logs are associated with the package, but the tasks and containers in the package can log information to any package log. This means that an object can use the same logging configuration as its parent, use a different logging configuration, or not generate log entries.

SSIS supports a diverse set of log providers and enables you to create custom log providers such as a SQL Server database or text file. SSIS includes the following log providers:

- The Text File log provider
- The SQL Server Profiler log provider
- The SQL Server log provider
- The Windows Event log provider
- The XML File log provider

The Text File, SQL Server Profiler, and XML File log providers require a file connection manager. The SQL Server log provider requires an OLE DB connection manager.

Multiple logging destinations can be configured. An object can log to one or many of these destinations.

> **Important**   Use caution when selecting the events to log. Because logging all events can create a very large log file, you should log only a few important events at once, such as *OnError* and *OnFailure*.

Implementing Package Logging

The following procedures will teach you how to log events as a package executes.

Configuring Package Logging

The first step in implementing package logging is to configure logging for the package. In this procedure, you will use the SSIS Log Provider for SQL Server to configure the package.

Configure package logging

1. In BIDS, in Solution Explorer, double-click NewProducts.dtsx to open the package designer.

2. On the SSIS menu, click Logging. The Configure SSIS Logs: NewProducts dialog box opens.

3. In the Configure SSIS Logs: NewProducts dialog box, in the Containers pane, select the NewProducts check box.

4. Expand all the nodes of the tree, and then clear all the check boxes.

5. Click NewProducts.

6. On the Providers And Logs tab, in the Provider Type drop-down list, verify that SSIS Log Provider For Text Files is selected, and then click Add. In the Select The Logs To Use For The Container list, a new entry is added to the table.

7. Select the new entry check box and rename it **PackageTextLog**.

8. Click the field in the Configuration column, and then select <New Connection...>.

    The File Connection Manager Editor opens.

    Your screen should look similar to this:

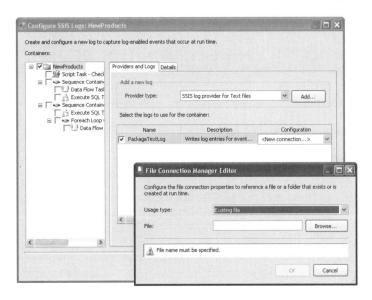

9. In the File Connection Manager Editor dialog box, in the Usage Type drop-down list, select Create File.

10. In the File text box, navigate to C:\Documents and Settings\<username>\My Documents\Microsoft Press\is2005sbs\Chap08\Logs\PackageText.log.

11. Click OK to close the editor.

12. In the Configure SSIS Logs: NewProducts dialog box, in the Provider Type drop-down list, select SSIS Log Provider For SQL Server, and then click Add. In the Select The Logs To Use For The Container list, a new entry is added to the table.

13. Select the new entry check box and rename it **PackageSQLLog**.

14. Click the field in the Configuration column, and then select LocalHost.QuickStartODS.

Note   Log entries are written to the sysdtslog90 table. This table is created the first time the package is executed with logging enabled.

15. On the Details tab, select the OnError, OnPreExecute, and OnTaskFailed check boxes.

16. Click OK to close the Configure SSIS Logs: NewProducts dialog box.

Logging is now configured for the package. No log entries will be created for the containers or tasks.

Note   An object can write log entries to multiple log providers, but the same entries will be written to all of the log providers.

Executing the Package and Viewing the Logs

Now that you have configured the package for logging, you are ready to execute the package and view the logs. In the following procedures, you will execute the NewProducts.dtsx package and view its log entries. You will then configure container and task logging for the New-Products.dtsx package and then again execute the package and view its log entries.

Execute the package and view the logs

1. In BIDS, right-click NewProducts.dtsx, and then click Execute Package. Wait until the package has executed successfully.

2. In Windows Explorer, open the C:\Documents and Settings\<username>\My Documents\Microsoft Press\is2005sbs\Chap08\Logs\PackageText.log file and view the log entries.

3. In SQL Server Management Studio, in the left pane, expand Databases and QuickStart-ODS. Expand the Tables folder, and then right-click dbo.sysdtslog90 and click Open table. View the log entries.

4. In BIDS, on the Debug menu, click Stop Debugging.

Configure container and task logging

1. In BIDS, in Solution Explorer, double-click NewProducts.dtsx.

2. On the SSIS menu, click Logging. The Configure SSIS Logs: NewProducts dialog box opens.

3. In the Configure SSIS Logs: NewProducts dialog box, on the Providers And Logs tab, in the Provider Type drop-down list, verify that SSIS Log Provider For Text Files is selected, and then click Add.

4. In the Select The Logs To Use For The Container list, a new entry is added to the table.

5. Rename the new entry **ClearMatchedNamesLog** and ensure that the new entry is not selected.

6. Click the field in the Configuration column, and then select <New connection...>. The File Connection Manager Editor opens.

7. In the Usage Type drop-down list, select Create File.

8. In the File text box, navigate to C:\Documents and Settings\<username>\My Documents\Microsoft Press\is2005sbs\Chap08\Logs\ClearMatchedNames.log.

9. Click OK to close the editor.

10. In BIDS, in Solution Explorer, double-click NewProducts.dtsx to open the project designer.

11. On the SSIS menu, click Logging. The Configure SSIS Logs: NewProducts dialog box opens.

12. In the Configure SSIS Logs: NewProducts dialog box, in the Containers pane, expand all the nodes of the tree.

13. Select the Script Task – Check Products List check box twice.

    When the Script Task – Check Products List check box is selected twice, the check mark should be grayed (dimmed). This means that the Script Task – Check Products List task will inherit its logging settings from its parent (NewProducts package). Notice that you cannot change the content of the Providers and Logs tab or the Details tab.

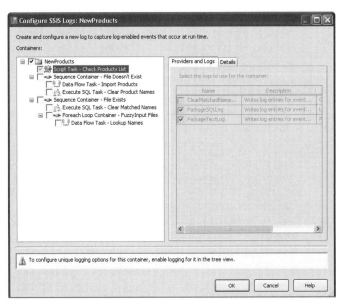

14. Select the Execute SQL Task – Clear Matched Names check box.

    A black check mark means the object has its own log settings.

15. On the Providers And Logs tab, select the ClearMatchedNamesLog and the Package-SQLLog check boxes. (The PackageTextLog check box should be cleared.)

16. On the Details tab, select the Events check box.

    All Execute SQL Task – Clear Matched Names events will be logged.

17. Click OK to close the Configure SSIS Logs: NewProducts dialog box.

Execute the package and view the logs

1. In BIDS, in Solution Explorer, right-click NewProducts.dtsx, and then click Execute Package. Wait until the package has executed successfully.

2. In Windows Explorer, open the C:\Documents and Settings\<username>\My Documents\Microsoft Press\is2005sbs\Chap08\Logs\PackageText.log file and view the log entries.

3.   Open the C:\Documents and Settings\<username>\My Documents\Microsoft Press\is2005sbs\Chap08\Logs\ClearMatchedNames.log file and view the log entries.

4.   Open the *QuickStartODS* database sysdtslog90 table and view the log entries.

Chapter 8 Quick Reference

To	Do This
Create a new SSIS project	In Windows Explorer, navigate to the project, and then double-click the file to open it in BIDS. In BIDS, in Solution Explorer, double-click the file to open the package in design mode.
Execute a project	In BIDS, in Solution Explorer, right-click the project, and then click Execute Package.
Create an XML configuration file	In BIDS, on the SSIS menu, click Package Configurations. In the Package Configurations Organizer, select the Enable Package Configurations check box, and then click Add to start the Package Configuration Wizard. Follow the steps of the wizard to create the XML configuration file.
Edit an XML configuration file	Right-click the project file name, click Open With, select Microsoft Visual Studio Version Selector, and then click OK. In SSIS, on the Project tab, find <Configured Value> in the XML file. Between the <Configured Value> tags, locate the destination file and rename it.
Create an environment variable	Click Start, click My Computer, right-click the background, and then click Properties. In the System Properties dialog box, on the Advanced tab, click Environment Variables, and then click New.
Configure an environment variable	In BIDS, on the SSIS menu, click Package Configurations, and then click Add to start the Package Configuration Wizard. Follow the wizard steps to configure the environment variable.
Create a SQL Server configuration	In BIDS, on the SSIS menu, click Package Configurations, and then click Add to start the Package Configuration Wizard. In the Package Configuration Wizard, on the Select Configuration Type, select SQL Server and follow the wizard steps to create the SQL Server configuration.
Create a parent package variable configuration	In BIDS, on the SSIS menu, click Package Configurations, and then click Add to start the Package Configuration Wizard. In the Package Configuration Wizard, in the Select Configuration Type drop-down list, select Parent Package Variable, and then follow the wizard steps to create the Parent Package Variable configuration.
Execute a package using the DTExecUI utility	Open a Command Prompt window, type dtexecui, and then press Enter.
Execute a package using the DTExec utility	Open a Command Prompt window, type **dtexec /** followed by **DTS, SQL,** or file option and the package path.
Configure package logging	In BIDS, on the SSIS menu, click Logging.

Part III
Managing Packages

Chapter 9
Detecting and Handling Processing Errors

After completing this chapter, you will be able to:

- Understand basic methods of error detection and handling.
- Create and configure event handlers to respond to events that are raised at run time.
- Use transactions to maintain data integrity.
- Use checkpoint restarts to restart failed packages.

In Chapter 8, "Managing Package Execution," you learned how to monitor and update the values of properties at run time without having to modify the actual package. You also learned several ways to execute a package and how to use Microsoft SQL Server Integration Services (SSIS) logging to monitor package execution. In this chapter, you'll learn how to detect and handle the processing errors that can occur when packages are designed and executed. You'll also learn how to create and configure event handlers to develop control flow that responds to events as a package executes, including how to provide more sophisticated error handling. Finally, you'll learn how to use transactions to maintain data integrity and checkpoint restarts to restart failed packages.

In the beginning of this chapter, the exercises will show you how to use event handlers to perform custom logging, one of many possible uses for event handlers. You'll learn how to create an event handler and then add an Execute SQL Task to it, which will be used to log pre-execute events. You'll then create additional event handlers to log post-execute and error events. In the exercises later in the chapter, you'll test the package with invalid data, create an event handler to fix the problem, and then, once again, execute the package. Finally, you'll learn how to send files with incorrectly formatted data into an Error folder without disrupting the execution of the rest of the package.

Basic Error Detection and Handling

Before you begin to use event handlers for custom logging, it's important for you to understand the basic methods that SSIS provides for detecting and handling errors. You can perform basic error detection by maintaining and detecting changes in metadata. You can also use validation to verify package properties and configuration during package design and during package execution. SSIS also provides failure precedence constraints that can be used to determine the tasks that execute when an error occurs. Data flow transformations can be configured to fail on error, re-route error-causing records, or to ignore errors. This section describes these basic methods of error detection and handling.

Understanding Metadata Lineage

In a data flow task, upstream and downstream transformations establish a *metadata contract* with each other. If a column is modified in an upstream transformation, the downstream transformations recognize that the column's metadata has changed and require the metadata contract to be refreshed. The downstream transformation can then determine whether it is still valid, given the change in the column. For example, if a column in a data source transformation is changed from a numeric data type to a character data type, all downstream transformations will require their metadata contracts to be refreshed. As the metadata contracts are refreshed, downstream transformations become aware that the column has a character data type. Any transformation that performs a numeric operation on the column will then raise an error in the Data Flow designer.

Understanding Validation

SSIS provides validation to ensure that a package will not execute if a task or transformation is configured incorrectly. Validation verifies that SSIS can connect to all of the data sources and destinations, that component property values are valid and within range, that all metadata is correct, and so on. By default, all package components are validated twice:

- Before package execution begins
- Before individual components are executed

A package might fail the validation that occurs before package execution begins, even though the package can execute successfully. For example, a data source might not be available until after a package begins executing. Consider a package in which the first task copies a file into a folder and then a second task extracts data from the file. The package will raise an error when it is validated before package execution because the file is not in the folder. In such instances, packages and components have a *DelayValidation* property that can be set to *True*. The component will not be validated until just before it is executed.

Understanding Precedence Constraints

A *precedence constraint* is used to link two tasks (or containers) in a package. If it is a success precedence constraint, the first task must execute successfully before the second task will run. If it is a failure precedence constraint, the second task will execute only if the first task fails. You can use failure precedence constraints to execute a task that handles the error that occurred in the preceding task or to send a notification that an error occurred.

Understanding Data Flow Transformations

Data flow transformations are the components in the data flow of a package that aggregate, merge, distribute, and modify data. They can also perform lookup operations and generate sample datasets.

You can configure data flow transformations to fail when an error occurs, send an error-causing record to the transformation's error output, or ignore errors and send all records to the transformation's output.

Configuring a Transformation to Fail When an Error Occurs

When a data flow transformation is configured to fail when an error occurs, it causes the data flow task to fail also. When this occurs, you can use a failure precedence constraint to execute a task, or you can use an event handler to handle the error. (Event handlers are discussed later in this chapter.)

Configuring a Transformation to Re-route Error-Causing Records

Configuring a transformation to send error-causing records to the transformation's error output allows you to split the data flow pipeline so that successfully transformed data follows one branch of the pipeline, and data that generates errors follows a different branch of the pipeline. The error-causing records can then be subject to additional transformations or be sent to a file or database table for review and reprocessing. For example, records that fail to find a match in a Lookup transformation can be directed into the error output and routed into another Lookup transformation that applies a different matching logic. Records that fail to find a match in the second Lookup transformation can be written to a text file for manual review.

Configuring a Data Flow Transformation to Ignore Errors

You can configure a transformation to ignore errors and send all records to the transformation's output if an error can safely be ignored. When a transformation is configured as such, you might also want to use a derived column transformation to perform inline error handling or use a conditional split transformation to apply more sophisticated logic to re-route the error-causing records.

Understanding Event Handlers

Now that you understand some of the basic methods provided by SSIS for detecting and handling errors, it's time to learn how you can use event handlers to perform some of these tasks. *Event handlers* are workflows that enable SSIS packages to respond programmatically to events that are raised at run time by a package, container, or task. Events signal a number of different states, including error conditions when a task starts, when a task completes, or when a change occurs in variable status. For example, an *OnError* event is raised when an error occurs.

Using Event Handlers to Perform Tasks

Event handlers can perform tasks such as the following:

- Clean up temporary data storage when a package or task finishes running
- Retrieve system information to assess resource availability before a package runs
- Refresh data in a table when lookup in a reference table fails
- Send an e-mail message when an error or warning occurs or when a task fails

Event handlers eliminate redundancy by providing the same functionality for an event regardless of which task or container generated the event. For example, if you want to send an e-mail message when any task fails, you can put a Send Mail task in an *OnError* event handler. This is significantly less work than having a failure precedence constraint and a Send Mail task associated with every task or container that might generate an error.

Triggering an Event Handler

Because a task is part of a container and a container is part of a package, when a task generates an error event, its containers and package also generate an error event. Likewise, when an event occurs, it can cause additional tasks to execute. In fact, event handlers can cause other event handlers to execute.

When an event occurs and it does not have an event handler, the event is raised to the next container up the container hierarchy in a package. If this container has an event handler, the event handler runs in response to the event. If not, the event is raised to the next container up the container hierarchy and so on up to the package.

If an *OnError* event handler is configured for multiple tasks and containers, unexpected behavior can arise, and events appear to *bubble up*. To prevent an event from bubbling up, set the event handler's *Propagate* property to *False*.

 Note   Individual data flow transformations cannot trigger an event handler. If a transformation fails, the entire data flow task fails and generates an event.

Using the Event Handlers Provided by SSIS

For detecting and handling errors, the most important event handlers are *OnPreExecute*, *OnPostExecute*, *OnWarning*, *OnError*, and *OnTaskFailed*. Table 9-1 describes some of the event handlers that SSIS provides and describes the run-time events that cause event handlers to run.

Table 9-1   **Predefined Events**

Event	Description
OnPreExecute	Writes a log entry immediately before the executable runs
OnPostExecute	Writes a log entry immediately after the executable has finished running
OnWarning	Writes a log entry when a warning occurs
OnError	Writes a log entry when an error occurs
OnTaskFailed	Writes a log entry when a task fails

Creating Event Handlers

The Event Handlers design surface is similar to the Control Flow design surface. In fact, creating an event handler is similar to building a package; an event handler has tasks and containers, which are sequenced into a control flow, and an event handler can also include data flows.

In SSIS, each event has its own event handler design surface for implementing compound workflows, including, but not limited to:

- Tasks.
- Precedences.
- Expressions.
- Viewers.

You create event handlers by using the design surface of the Event Handlers tab in SSIS Designer. When the Event Handlers tab is active, the *Control Flow Items* and *Maintenance Plan Tasks* groups of the Toolbox in SSIS Designer contain the task and containers for building the control flow in the event handler. To build an event handler, drag objects onto the designer from the Control Flow Items group in Toolbox.

The *Data Flow Sources*, *Transformations*, and *Data Flow Destinations* groups contain the data sources, transformations, and destinations for building the data flows in the event handler.

The Event Handlers tab also includes the Connection Managers pane, where you can create and modify the connection managers that event handlers use to connect to servers and data sources.

Creating the *QuickStartODS* Database

The procedures in this chapter assume that the *QuickStartODS* database exists on your computer in Microsoft SQL Server. The *QuickStartODS* database was created in Chapter 4, "Using Data Flow Transformations." If you haven't done the exercises in Chapter 4, the database might not exist on your computer.

Determine whether the *QuickStartODS* database is on your computer

1. In SQL Server Management Studio, in Object Explorer, right-click the Databases folder, and then click Refresh.

2. Expand the Databases folder and see whether *QuickStartODS* is listed. If it is not listed in the Databases folder, you must create the database by using the following instructions.

Create the *QuickStartODS* database

1. In SQL Server Management Studio, create a new database named *QuickStartODS*:

   a. In Object Explorer, right-click the Databases folder, and then click New Database.

   b. In the New Database dialog box, in the Database Name text box, type **QuickStartODS**.

   c. Click OK.

Accessing the SSIS Design Environment

You must create an event handler before you can use it to respond to an event. The first step is to open the solution so that you can access the designer in which the event handler is created.

Open the NewProducts.dtsx package

1. Using Windows Explorer, navigate to the C:\Documents and Settings\<username>\My Documents\Microsoft Press\is2005sbs\Chap09\ folder.

2. Double-click Chap09.sln to open the project. The Chap09 project opens in SQL Server Business Intelligence Development Studio (BIDS).

3. In BIDS, locate the Solution Explorer pane on the right side of the design environment. Make sure this pane is visible and not set to Auto-Hide, so you can see all of the files in the project.

4. In the SSIS Packages folder, double-click NewProducts.dtsx. The package opens in the designer.

Your screen should look similar to this:

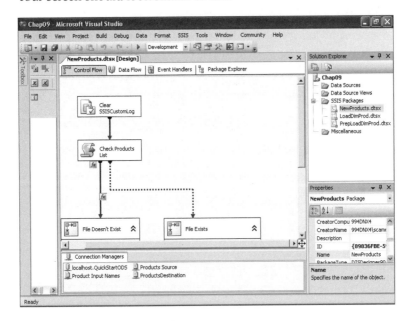

Creating an *OnPreExecute* Event Handler

The *OnPreExecute* event handler is used to indicate that an object is about to start executing.

In this procedure, you'll open the Event Handlers design environment in which you create event handlers and then create the *OnPreExecute* event handler.

Create an *OnPreExecute* event handler

1. In the design environment, on the NewProducts.dtsx [Design]* tab, click the Event Handlers tab. The Event Handlers design environment opens.

2. In the Executable drop-down list, select NewProducts, and then click OK.

3. In the Event Handler drop-down list, select OnPreExecute.

4. In the Event Handlers design environment, click the blue text that reads "Click here to create an OnPreExecute event handler for executable NewProducts."

   The Event Handlers control flow design environment appears and contains text that now reads "Event handlers are containers of workflow. They are executed when the selected event occurs. To build an event handler, drag objects here from the Control Flow Items toolbox."

Your screen should look similar to this:

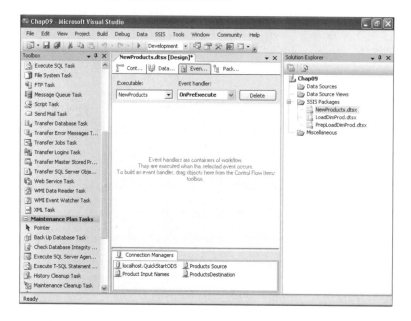

Adding a Task to an Event Handler

Now that you have created an event handler, you must add the Execute SQL task to it. The Execute SQL task runs SQL statements or stored procedures from a package. The task can contain either a single SQL statement or multiple SQL statements that run sequentially. There are a variety of purposes for using the Execute SQL task, including using it to insert log records.

In this procedure, you'll add the Execute SQL task to the event handler you created in the previous procedure.

Add an Execute SQL task to the *OnPreExecute* event handler

1. On the left side of the screen, click Toolbox. The Toolbox menu appears.

2. On the Toolbox menu, in the Control Flow Items group, drag Execute SQL Task onto the Event Handlers design environment. The Execute SQL Task box appears on the Event Handlers designer.

Your screen should look similar to this:

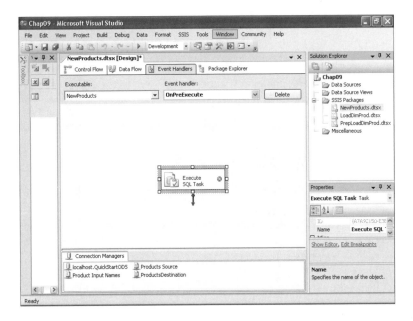

Configuring the Task

After you add the Execute SQL task to the event handler, you must configure the task. This procedure shows you how to access the SQL Task Editor, where you can modify the task properties.

Configure the Execute SQL task

1. In the design environment, double-click Execute SQL Task to open its editor. The Execute SQL Task Editor opens.

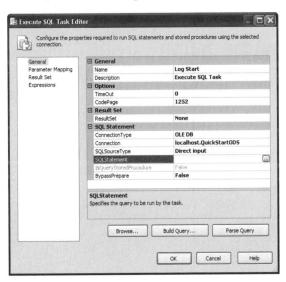

2. In the left pane, click General.

3. In the right pane, under General, click Name, and then, in the right column, type **Log Start**.

4. Under SQL Statement, click Connection, and then, in the right column drop-down list, select localhost.QuickStartODS.

5. Under SQL Statement, click SQL Statement, and then, in the right column, click the ellipses button.

    The Enter SQL Query dialog box appears.

6. Copy the following query:

```
Insert into [dbo].[CustomSSISLog]
([PackageName]
,[SourceName]
,[SourceDescription]
,[Event]
,[EventDate])
VALUES
(?
,?
,?
,'Start'
,GetDate())
```

7. In the Enter SQL Query dialog box, paste the copied query.

> **Note** Initially, the dbo.CustomSSISLog table doesn't exist in the *QuickStartODS* database. The ClearSSISCustomLog task drops and then re-creates the table each time the package is executed.

Your screen should look like this:

Click OK to close the Enter SQL Query dialog box.

8. Leave the Execute SQL Task Editor open.

Mapping SSIS Variables to SQL Statement Parameters

You can use parameter mapping to map parameters to a SQL INSERT statement or stored procedure. You use the Parameter Mapping page of the Execute SQL Task Editor to map variables to parameters in the SQL statement.

The following steps show you how to configure the Execute SQL task to run parameterized SQL statements. The parameters in the SQL statement are populated by system variables that are auto-generated when a package, container, or task is executed. When you assign a system variable to a parameter, you must configure it as an input or output parameter, select the data type, and give the parameter a name. When using an OLE DB connection, because the parameters are designated by their ordinal position in the SQL statement, they must be named 0, 1, 2, and so on.

Configure the Execute SQL task to run parameterized SQL statements

1. In Execute SQL Task Editor, in the left pane, click Parameter Mapping.

2. Click Add.

   A new variable is added to the editor. You will add three variables to the editor.

   For the first variable:

   a. In the right pane, in the Variable Name column drop-down list, select System::PackageName.

   b. In the Direction column drop-down list, select Input.

   c. In the Data Type column drop-down list, select NVARCHAR.

   d. In the Parameter Name column, type 0.

3. Click Add to add a new variable.

4. For the second variable:

   a. In the Variable Name column drop-down list, select System::SourceName.

   b. In the Direction column drop-down list, select Input.

   c. In the Data Type column drop-down list, select NVARCHAR.

   d. In the Parameter Name column, type 1.

5. Click Add to add a new variable.

6. For the third variable:

   a. In the Variable Name column drop-down list, select System::SourceDescription.

   b. In the Direction column drop-down list, select Input.

   c. In the Data Type column drop-down list, select NVARCHAR.

   d. In the Parameter Name column, type **2**.

Your screen should look like this:

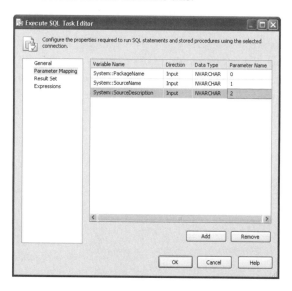

7. You have now modified the properties of the Execute SQL task.

8. Click OK to save your changes and close Execute SQL Task Editor.

Creating a Log Finish Event Handler

In the previous exercise, you created an *OnPreExecute* event handler that writes log entries immediately before the executable runs, and then you added a Log Start Execute SQL task to it. Now you'll create an *OnPostExecute* event that writes log entries immediately after the executable has finished running, and you'll add a Log Finish Execute SQL task to it.

In this exercise, you'll copy the Log Start Execute SQL task and then create an *OnPostExecute* event handler to which you'll add the Log Finish Execute SQL task.

Add a Log Finish Execute SQL task to an *OnPostExecute* event handler

1. In the Event Handlers design environment, right-click Log Start and click Copy to copy the Log Start Execute SQL task.

2. Create a new event handler:

    a. In the Executable drop-down list, select NewProducts, and then click OK.

    b. In the Event Handler drop-down list, select OnPostExecute.

3. Click the blue text that reads "Click here to create an OnPostExecute event handler for executable NewProducts."

4. In the Event Handlers design environment, right-click and paste the Log Start Execute SQL task that you copied in the previous step. The Log Start task appears in the design environment.

5. Right-click Log Start and rename the task **Log Finish**.

6. Double-click Log Finish to open its properties. The Execute SQL Task Editor opens.

7. In the right pane, under General, click Name, and then ensure that the name was changed to **Log Finish**.

8. Under SQL Statement, click SQL Statement, and then, in the right column, click the ellipses button.

    The Enter SQL Query dialog box appears.

9. In the Enter SQL Query dialog box, change the SQL Statement from Start to **Finish** (located toward the bottom of the code).

    Your screen looks like this:

10. Click OK to close the Enter SQL Query dialog box.

11. Click OK to close the Execute SQL Task Editor.

Creating a Log Error Event Handler

In the previous exercises, you created an *OnPreExecute* event handler and an *OnPostExecute* event handler. Now you'll create an *OnError* event handler that writes log entries when an error occurs. After you have done this, you'll add a Log Error Execute SQL task to it.

In this exercise, you'll copy the Log Start Execute SQL task and then create an *OnError* event handler to which you'll add the Log Error Execute SQL task.

Add a Log Error Execute SQL task to an *OnError* event handler

1. In the Event Handlers design environment, in the Event Handler drop-down list, select OnPreExecute.

   Log Start Execute SQL Task appears in the design environment.

2. Right-click Log Start and click Copy to copy Log Start Execute SQL Task.

3. Create a new event handler:

   a. In the Executable drop-down list, select NewProducts, and then click OK.

   b. In the Event Handler drop-down list, select OnError.

4. Click the blue text that reads "Click here to create an 'OnError' event handler for executable NewProducts."

5. In the Event Handlers design environment, right-click and paste the Log Start Execute SQL task that you copied in the previous step. Log Start Task appears in the design environment.

6. Right-click Log Start and rename the task **Log Error**.

7. Double-click Log Error to open its properties. The Execute SQL Task Editor opens.

8. Under SQL Statement, click SQL Statement, and then, in the right column, click the ellipses button.

   The Enter SQL Query dialog box appears.

9. In the Enter SQL Query box, change the SQL Statement from Start to **Error** (located toward the bottom of the code).

The screen looks like this:

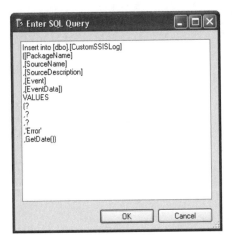

10. Click OK to close the Enter SQL Query dialog box.

11. Click OK to close the Execute SQL Task Editor.

Executing the Package

Now that you have created the three event handlers that will be raised when errors occur, you can execute the package. You double-click NewProducts.dtsx to execute the package in BIDS, and then you switch to SQL Server Management Studio to view the records in the log table.

Execute the NewProducts.dtsx package and view the results in Management Studio

1. In BIDS, in the design environment, on the NewProducts.dtsx [Design]* tab, click the Control Flow tab.

    You are now in the Control Flow design environment.

2. On the right side of the screen, in Solution Explorer, right-click NewProducts.dtsx and click Execute Package.

    Wait until the package has executed successfully before starting the next step. The package has successfully executed when, at the bottom of the screen, it reads "Package execution completed. Click here to switch to design mode, or select Stop Debugging from the Debug menu."

Your screen should look similar to this:

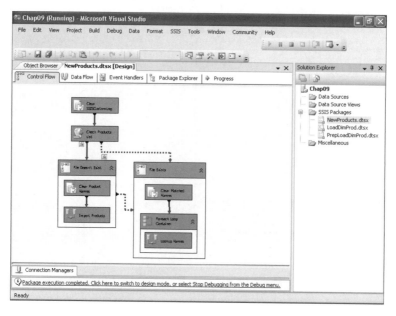

3. On the Debug menu, click Stop Debugging.

4. Click Start, click SQL Server Management Studio, and then, in the Connect to Server dialog box, click Connect to open SQL Server Management Studio.

5. In SQL Server Management Studio, in the left pane, expand the Databases folder, expand QuickStartODS, expand the Tables folder, and then right-click dbo.CustomSSISLog and select Open Table. The log records contained in dbo.CustomSSISLog are displayed.

6. If dbo.CustomSSISLog is not listed in the Tables folder, right-click the Tables folder, and then click Refresh. The dbo.CustomSSISLog table now appears in the Tables folder list.

7. Compare the log entries to the containers and tasks in the NewProducts package. In the log table, the SourceName column contains the name of the task or container, and the SourceDescription column contains the name of the event.

   When the package starts, the Clear SSISCustomLog task executes and clears the custom log table. This deletes the start event for the package and the start event for the Clear SSISCustomLog task. This means that the first event in the log table is the *Clear SSISCustomLog* finish event. Under normal circumstances, you would not have the first task in your package clear the log, so the first event in the log would be the package start event.

   The second and third records in the log table are the start and finish events for the Check Products List script task. These records are followed by the File Doesn't Exist sequence container start event and then the start and finish events for the Clear Product Names execute SQL task and Import Products data flow task. Then the finish event for the File

Doesn't Exist record appears. If you look farther down in the table, you will see four sets of start and finish events for the Lookup Names data flow task. These are generated when the Foreach Loop container iterates over the FuzzyInput*.txt files in the Data folder. The last record is the finish event for the NewProducts package.

Testing the Package with Invalid Data

Now that you have created event handlers and executed the package, you are ready to test the package with invalid data. One of the files (FuzzyInputC.txt) includes incorrectly formatted data, which causes your package to fail when executed.

Test the NewProducts.dtsx package with invalid data

1. In Windows Explorer, navigate to the C:\Documents and Settings\<username>\My Documents\Microsoft Press\is2005sbs\Chap09\Data\ folder.

2. Rename the file FuzzyInputC.txt.error **FuzzyInputC.txt** (delete the .error extension).

3. Double-click FuzzyInputC.txt to view its contents in Notepad.

    Your screen should look similar to this:

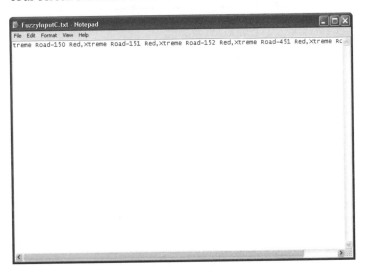

> **Note**   Instead of one product name per line, product names are separated by commas. This will cause an error.

4. Close Notepad.

5. In BIDS, in Solution Explorer, ensure that you are in the Control Flow designer. (Click the Control Flow tab.)

6. Right-click NewProducts.dtsx, and then click Execute Package.

Your screen should look similar to this:

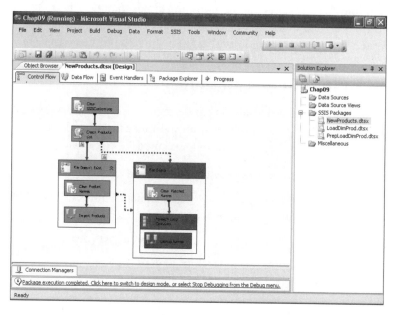

7. On the Debug menu, click Stop Debugging.

   On the Control Flow tab, notice that the Lookup Names error has escalated up to the Foreach Loop container and the File Exists container. (The Output window also shows that the package has failed.)

8. Switch to SQL Server Management Studio.

9. In SQL Server Management Studio, in the right pane, click the Table – dbo.CustomSSIS-Log tab to ensure that the log data is displayed.

10. On the Query Designer toolbar, click the Execute SQL button (exclamation point) to refresh the displayed data.

> **Note** If the data in CustomSSISLogKey is not displayed in ascending order, click the Show SQL Pane button, change the SQL query to SELECT * FROM CustomSSISLog ORDER BY 1, and then click the Execute SQL button (exclamation mark). You can then click the Show SQL Pane button to hide the SQL statement.

> **Note** In the CustomSSISLog table, Lookup Names has two start and finish events and a third start event followed by multiple failure events caused by the incorrectly formatted data in FuzzyInputC.txt. This is followed by a Lookup Names finish event. The NewProducts.dtsx package doesn't attempt to open FuzzyInputD.txt and Fuzzy-InputE.txt, so there are no more Lookup Names events. The Foreach Loop and File-Exists containers finish, and then the NewProducts package finishes.

Creating an Event Handler to Fix the Problem

In the previous exercise, incorrectly formatted data in the FuzzyInputC.txt file caused the NewProducts.dtsx package to fail when it was executed. In this exercise, you'll create a new event handler with the following properties:

- Executable: Lookup Names
- EventHandler: OnTaskFailed

Create an *OnTaskFailed* event handler for executable lookup names

1. In BIDS, click the Event Handlers tab.

2. In the Executable drop-down list, expand NewProducts, expand Executables, expand File Exists, expand Executables, expand Foreach Loop Container, expand Executables, and then select Lookup Names.

   Your screen looks like this:

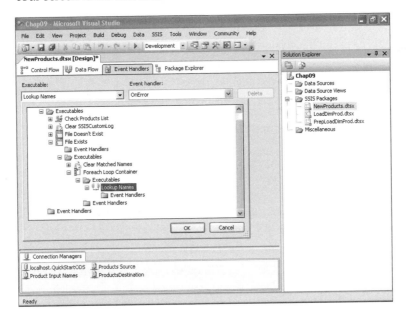

3. Click OK.

4. In the Event Handler drop-down list, select OnTaskFailed.

   You are going to create an event handler that, when the Lookup Names task fails, the current input file is copied to the Errors folder. When the *OnError* event occurs because the Lookup Names task still has a lock on the file, preventing it from being copied, you'll use the *OnTaskFailed* event handler.

Creating a Task to Move the File with Invalid Data

After you create the *OnTaskFailed* event handler for executable Lookup Names, you'll create a File System task to move the invalid data to an Errors folder.

In this procedure, you'll move the file that caused the errors to a different folder. Finally, you'll create a file connection manager named Error.

Create a File System task and a new connection manager

1. In BIDS, in the Event Handlers design environment, click the blue text that reads "Click here to create an OnTaskFailed event handler for executable Lookup Names."

2. On the left side of the screen, click Toolbox.

> **Tip**   If the toolbox has disappeared from your screen, click the View menu, and then click Toolbox.

3. In the Toolbox, select File System Task and drag it onto the Event Handler designer.

4. Double-click the File System Task box. The File System Task Editor opens.

5. In the right pane, under General, click Name, and then, in the right column, type **Copy to Errors Folder**.

6. Under Source Connection, click Source Connection, and then, in the right column drop-down list, click Product Input Names.

7. Under Destination Connection, click Destination Connection, and then, in the right column drop-down list, select <New Connection>. The File Connection Manager Editor appears.

8. In the File Connection Manager Editor, in the Usage Type drop-down list, select Existing folder.

9. In the Folder box, browse to C:\Documents and Settings\<username>\My Documents\Microsoft Press\is2005sbs\Chap09\Errors, and then click OK.

10. Click OK to close the File Connection Manager Editor.

    This will create a new connection manager named Errors.

    Your screen looks like this:

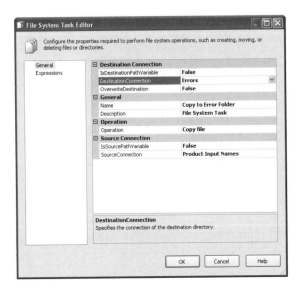

11. Click OK to close the File System Task Editor.

    Your screen now looks like this:

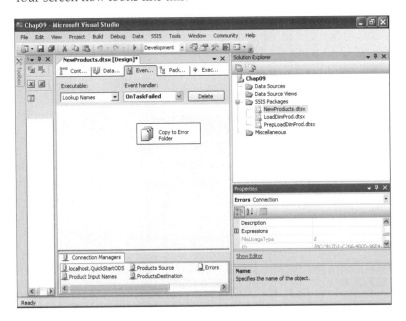

Setting Connection Manager Settings

After you create the new connection manager named Errors, you need to configure it.

In this procedure, you'll configure the settings for the Errors folder.

Set connection manager settings

1. In BIDS, in the Connection Managers pane (located on the bottom of the screen), right-click the new file connection manager named Errors and click Properties.

2. In the Properties pane, located on the right side of the screen, click Alphabetical (the AZ button) to sort the properties alphabetically.

3. In the Properties list, expand Expressions, and then, in the right column, click the ellipses button.

   The Property Expressions Editor opens.

4. In the Property Expressions Editor, in the Property column drop-down list, select ConnectionString.

5. In the Expression column drop-down list, click the ellipses button.

   The Expression Builder opens.

6. In the Expression Builder, in the Expression pane located near the bottom of the window, type **"C:\\Documents and Settings\\<username>\\My Documents\\Microsoft Press\\is2005sbs\\Chap09\\Errors\\"+@[User::InputFile]**.

7. Click Evaluate Expression.

   The value you typed in the Expression pane is evaluated by SSIS and displayed in the Evaluated value pane. It's OK that there isn't a file name at the end of the file path—the variable User::InputFile is not populated until the Foreach Loop container executes.

   Your screen looks like this:

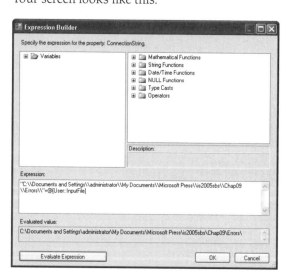

8. Click OK to close the Expression Builder.

9. Click OK to close the Property Expressions Editor.

Preventing Events from Escalating to Containers and Packages

You have configured an error handler to copy the invalid file to the Errors folder. Because this event is "handled," you want the package to move on to the next file and continue executing. To do this, you need to prevent the error from escalating to the Foreach Loop container, the File Exists container, and the NewProducts package. You also need to configure the package to allow a limited number of errors to occur before the package fails.

Prevent the *OnTaskFailed* event from escalating from the Lookup Names task to the Foreach Loop container

1. In BIDS, click the Event Handlers tab, then, on the SSIS menu, click Variables.

2. On the upper-left side of the screen, click the Show System Variables button (the shaded X). The Variables list appears.

3. Extend the window so that you can see all four columns.

4. Click the Name column to sort the variables alphabetically.

5. Find the *Propagate* variable.

6. In the Value column drop-down list, change the *Propagate* variable value from True to **False**.

> **Note**   This prevents the *OnTaskFailed* event from escalating from the Lookup Names task to the Foreach Loop container.

Your screen now looks like this:

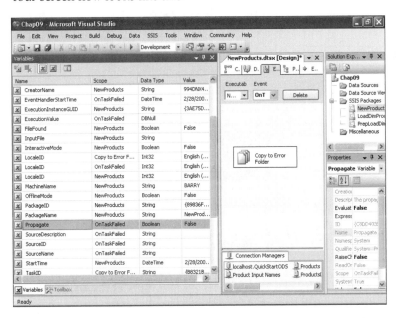

7. Close the Variables list.

Changing Error Count Properties

After you have prevented the *OnTaskFailed* event from escalating from the Lookup Names task to the Foreach Loop container, you need to configure the package to allow a limited number of errors to occur before the package fails.

In this procedure, you'll change the maximum number of errors before the executable fails from 1 to 100.

Change the *MaximumErrorCount* property from 1 to 100

1. In BIDS, on the Control Flow tab, right-click anywhere in the design area, and then click Properties.

2. In the Properties pane, on the right side of the screen, make sure that NewProducts Package is displayed in the drop-down list.

3. In the Properties list, locate MaximumErrorCount, and then change the value from 1 to **100**. (When the value is changed, the number becomes bold.)

> **Note**   The *MaximumErrorCount* property specifies the maximum number of errors before the executable fails.

Your screen looks like this:

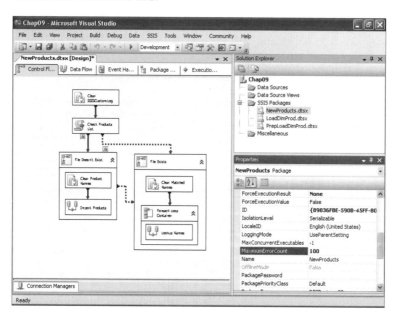

4. In the package designer, click File Exists, and then, in the Properties list, locate MaximumErrorCount and change the value from 1 to **100**.

5. In the package designer, click Foreach Loop Container, and then, in the Properties list, locate MaximumErrorCount and change the value from 1 to **100**.

> **Note**   This prevents the Lookup Names task error from causing the containers and package to fail.

Executing the Package

Now that you have created a method for sending files with incorrectly formatted data to an Error folder without disrupting the package, you are ready to execute the NewProducts.dtsx package once again.

Execute the NewProducts.dtsx package

1. In Solution Explorer, right-click NewProducts.dtsx, and then click Execute Package.

2. Notice that all the tasks in the package successfully execute except for the Lookup Names task, which fails.

   Your screen should look like this:

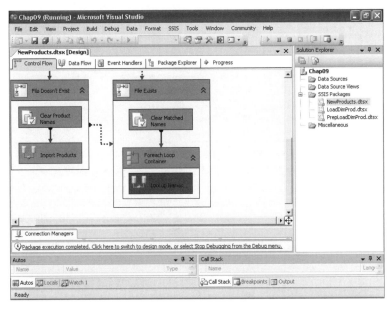

3. On the Debug menu, click Stop Debugging.

4. Switch to SQL Server Management Studio.

5. In SQL Server Management Studio, in the right pane, click the Table – dbo.CustomSSIS-Log tab to ensure that the log data is displayed.

6. In the left pane, above Object Explorer, click the Execute SQL button (exclamation point) to refresh the displayed data.

> **Note** The previous two steps assumed that you had the Table – dbo.CustomSSISLog table open. If the table wasn't open, in Object Explorer, right-click QuickStartODS, and then click Refresh. Right-click dbo.CustomSSISLog, and then click Open Table.

Your screen looks like this:

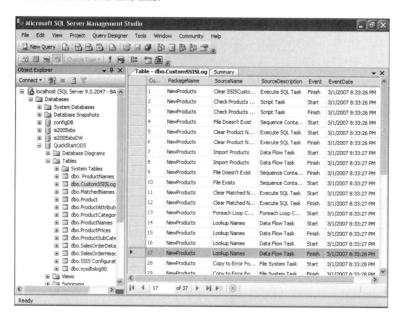

> **Note** In the CustomSSISLog table, the Lookup Names task has two sets of start and finish event records as it processes FuzzyInputA.txt and FuzzyInputB.txt, and a third start event record (FuzzyInputC.txt) followed by multiple error events. The Copy to Errors Folder task has a start and finish event (the events associated with the error handler copying FuzzyInputC.txt to the errors folder), and the Lookup Names task has two start and finish events as it processes FuzzyInputD.txt and FuzzyInputE.txt. The error handler allowed the package to handle the error and continue executing.

7. In Windows Explorer, navigate to the C:\Documents and Settings\<username>\My Documents\Microsoft Press\is2005sbs\Chap09\Errors folder and ensure that the FuzzyInputC.txt file has been copied to this location.

8. In BIDS, on the File menu, click Close to close the New Products package, and then close BIDS.

9. In SQL Server Management Studio, on the File menu, click Close to close the Custom-SSISLog table, and then close Management Studio.

Maintaining Data Consistency with Transactions

Transactions are used to maintain data integrity by ensuring that a database remains in a consistent state even if a package fails. They accomplish this by binding the database actions that tasks perform into units, which either succeed or fail together. Because all the database actions that are part of a transaction are either committed or rolled back together, you can ensure that data remains in a consistent state. For example, if you have a package with multiple data flow tasks, each updating and inserting data into a different database table, and the package fails, all of the database update actions performed by the data flow tasks are rolled back together, thereby ensuring a consistent state. If all the data flow tasks succeed, the changes performed are committed together.

Configuring Transactions

Transactions can be enabled for all SSIS container types, including tasks, containers, and packages. You configure transactions by using the container's *TransactionOption* property, which is set in the SSIS design environment. The *TransactionOption* property supports the following values:

- **Not Supported**   The container does not start a transaction and will not join an existing transaction even if it has already started.

- **Supported**   The container does not start a transaction but will join an existing transaction that has already started.

- **Required**   The container starts a new transaction. If an existing transaction has already been started by the parent container, the container will join it.

Using Checkpoint Restarts

If a package contains components that require a lot of resources to execute, you might not want to rerun the entire package when a single component fails. Checkpoints enable SSIS to restart failed packages from the point of failure instead of rerunning the whole package. If a package is configured to use checkpoints, information about package execution is written to a checkpoint file. When the failed package is rerun, the checkpoint file is used to restart the package from the point of failure. If the package is run successfully, the checkpoint file is deleted and then re-created the next time the package is run.

Understanding the Benefits of Checkpoints

Using checkpoints can provide the following benefits:

- Avoid repeating the downloading and uploading of large files.

- Avoid repeating the loading of large amounts of data.

- Avoid repeating the aggregation of values.

When using checkpoints, entire containers or tasks are re-executed. For example, if a Foreach loop fails on the third item of its enumerator, when it restarts, it starts on the first item of the enumerator. If a file contains a faulty record and causes an error, the whole file is read when package execution resumes.

Configuring Packages for Checkpoints

A package must be configured to provide checkpoint functionality. This entails the following:

- Configuring the package to save checkpoints.

- Giving the package the location of the checkpoint file.

- Configuring checkpoint usage. *Always* means the package will not execute unless a checkpoint file is available. *IfExists* means the package will use a checkpoint file if it exists; otherwise, the entire package will execute.

Individual checkpoints are configured by setting a task or container's *FailPackageOnFailure* property to *True*. If a container is configured as a checkpoint, all tasks within the container will execute when the package is restarted.

Using Checkpoints and Transactions

The purpose of this exercise is to show how to use checkpoints and transactions. In the first set of exercises, you'll simply load the necessary data into the *is2005sbsDW* and *QuickStartODS* database tables in preparation for fixing the error that was created in the previous exercises.

Preparing to Use Checkpoints and Transactions to Fix the Error

Before you can use checkpoint files and transactions to fix the error, you need to execute the PrepLoadDimProd.dtsx package and view the data in SQL Server Management Studio.

In this procedure, you'll execute the PreLoadDimProd.dtsx package and then view the dbo.ProductAttributes, dbo.ProductPrices, and dbo.DimProd tables in SQL Server Management Studio.

Open the PrepLoadDimProd.dtsx package and view the tables in Management Studio

1. In Windows Explorer, navigate to the C:\Documents and Settings\<username>\My Documents\Microsoft Press\is2005sbs\Chap09 folder.

2. Double-click Chap09.sln to open the solution file in BIDS.

3. In BIDS, in Solution Explorer, right-click PrepLoadDimProd.dtsx, and then click Execute Package.

   Wait until the package has executed successfully before starting the next step.

Notice that in the design window, as each task is successfully completed, the color of the task blocks changes from yellow to green. When the package has successfully executed, the task blocks should be green and, at the bottom of the screen, it should read, "Package execution completed. Click here to switch to design mode, or select Stop Debugging from the Debug menu."

Your screen should look like this:

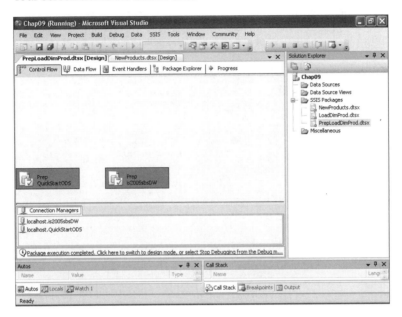

4. On the Debug menu, click Stop Debugging.

5. Open SQL Server Management Studio.

6. In the Connect to Server box, ensure that the Server name is localhost, and then click Connect. Management Studio opens.

7. To view the data in the dbo.ProductAttributes table:

   a. In the left pane, in Object Explorer, expand the Databases folder, expand Quick-StartODS, and then expand the Tables folder.

   b. Right-click dbo.ProductAttributes, and then click Open Table.

> **Note**   If you don't see dbo.ProductAttributes in the Table folder, in Object Explorer, right-click the *QuickStartODS* database, and then click Refresh.

   c. Wait for the table to populate in the right pane.

   Your screen should look like this:

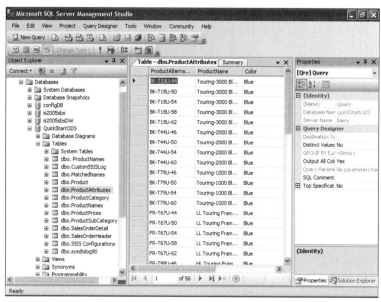

d. Horizontally scroll through the table and notice that the Color column doesn't contain Silver/Blk.

8. To view the data in the dbo.ProductPrices table:

a. In the left pane, in Object Explorer, right-click dbo.ProductPrices, and then click Open Table.

b. Wait for the table to populate in the right pane.

Your screen now looks like this:

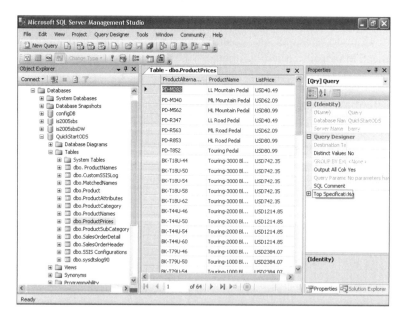

Notice that values in the ListPrice column are prefixed by USD.

9. To view the table in dbo.DimProd:

   a. In the left pane, in Object Explorer, expand the *is2005sbsDW* database, and then expand the Tables folder.

   b. Right-click dbo.DimProd, and then click Open Table.

   c. Wait for the table to populate in the right pane.

   Your screen now looks like this:

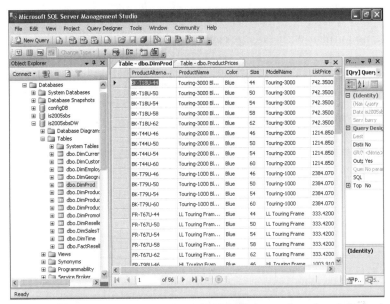

   d. Horizontally scroll through the table and notice that the Color column doesn't contain Silver/Blk. Also, notice that the ListPrice column contains numeric data.

Becoming Familiar with the LoadDimProd Package

In this procedure, you'll familiarize yourself with the four tasks on the Control Flow tab (Delete Staging Tables, Delete DimProd, LoadStaging Tables, and Load DimProd) and the properties associated with each. You'll then execute the LoadDimProd.dtsx package and discover that the Load DimProd task failed because the ListPrice column was incorrectly formatted.

You'll then switch to SQL Server Management Studio and view and refresh the data in the ProductAttributes, ProductPrices, and DimProd tables. The DimProd table is empty because the LoadDimProd task failed and left the data in an inconsistent state.

In BIDS, on the Control Flow tab, you'll create a Sequence container named Process DimProd and then move the Delete DimProd and Load DimProd tasks into this container. You'll also delete the precedence constraint between the Load Staging Tables task and the Load Dim-Prod task and then create a precedence constraint between the Load Staging Tables task and the Process DimProd sequence container.

You'll then execute the PrepLoadDimProd.dtsx package and find that the package executes successfully. When you switch to SQL Server Management Studio to view the DimProd table, you find that it now has data.

You return to BIDS and execute the LoadDimProd.dtsx package again, and the Load DimProd task fails again. You discover that because Process DimProd ran as a transaction, Delete Dim-Prod was rolled back, so the table still contained data.

Become familiar with the package

1. In BIDS, in Solution Explorer, double-click LoadDimProd.dtsx to open the package in the design environment.

> **Note**   The LoadDimProd package already exists. In this exercise, you will configure only transactions and checkpoints.

2. In the Control Flow designer, double-click each task to open its editor, and then view the various properties for each task.

> **Important**   Be sure that you click Cancel to close the editor so that you don't actu-ally make any changes to the tasks.

The following table lists and describes the function of each task:

Task	Function
Delete staging tables	Deletes the records from dbo.ProductAttributes and dbo.Product-Prices tables
Delete DimProd	Deletes the records from the DimProd table
Load staging tables	Reads data from the \Chap09\Data\ProductAttributes.csv file and inserts it into the dbo.ProductAttributes table
	Reads data from the \Chap09\Data\ProductPrice.csv file and inserts it into the dbo.ProductPrices table
Load DimProd	Joins data in dbo.ProductAttributes and dbo.ProductPrices tables and inserts it into the dbo.DimProd table

3. In Solution Explorer, right-click LoadDimProd.dtsx, and then click Execute Package.

Your screen looks similar to this:

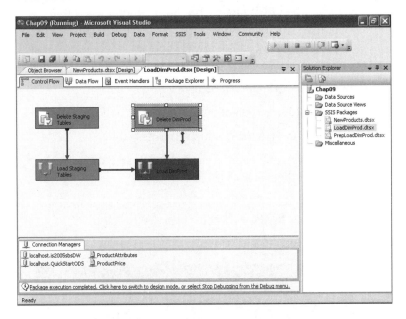

Notice that the tasks that delete the records in the staging tables and the DimProd table and the task that loads the staging tables succeed, but the Load DimProd task fails.

4. Double-click Load DimProd.

Your screen looks similar to this:

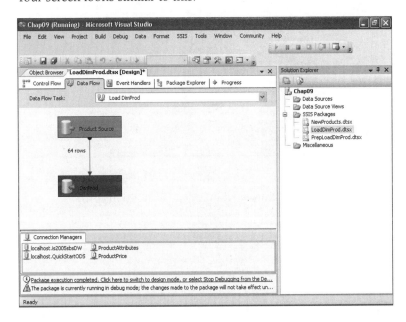

Notice that the Data Flow designer opens and shows that the data flow task successfully selected data from the staging tables but failed when it tried to insert the records into DimProd. The insert failed because the task tried to insert values with the format USD#.00 into the ListPrice column of the DimProd table. This insert failed because the ListPrice column has a numeric data type.

5. On the Debug menu, click Stop Debugging.

6. Switch to SQL Server Management Studio.

7. To view the updated data in the ProductAttributes table:

   a. In Object Explorer, expand QuickStartODS and Tables, right-click dbo.Product-Attributes, and then click Open Table.

   b. To refresh the data in the table, in the Results pane, click the dbo.Product-Attributes tab, and then click the Execute SQL button.

Your screen now looks like this:

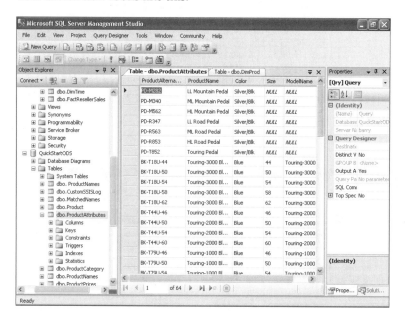

Notice that the ProductAttributes table successfully deleted and then reloaded. Also, notice that the Color column now includes Silver/Blk records.

8. To view the updated data in the ProductPrices table:

    a. In Object Explorer, right-click dbo.ProductPrices, and then click Open Table.

    b. To refresh the data in the table, in the Results pane, click the dbo.ProductPrices tab, and then click the Execute SQL button (exclamation point).

Your screen now looks like this:

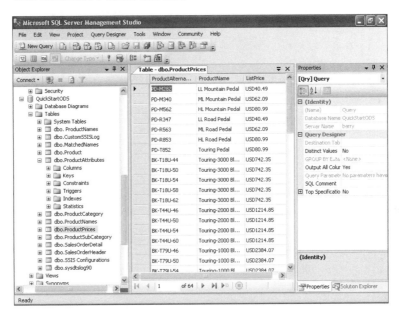

Notice that the ProductsPrices table successfully deleted and then reloaded.

9. To view the updated data in the DimProd table:

    a. In Object Explorer, right-click dbo.DimProd, and then click Open Table.

    b. To refresh the data in the table, in the Results pane, click the dbo.DimProd tab, and then click the Execute SQL button (exclamation point).

Your screen now looks like this:

Notice that the data in the DimProd table successfully deleted, but the load failed, so the table is empty. The failure of the LoadDimProd package has left the data in an inconsistent state.

10. In BIDS, click the Control Flow tab.

11. On the left side of the screen, click Toolbox.

12. In the Control Flow Items group, click Sequence Container, and then drag it into the design environment.

13. In the design environment, right-click the new Sequence Container task and rename it **Process DimProd**.

14. Delete the precedence constraint (green arrow) between the Load Staging Tables task and the Load DimProd task.

15. Click the Delete DimProd task and press SHIFT while clicking the Load DimProd task so that both tasks are selected. Drag both tasks into the Process DimProd container. (The precedence constraint between Delete DimProd and LoadDimProd should remain.)

Your screen should look similar to this:

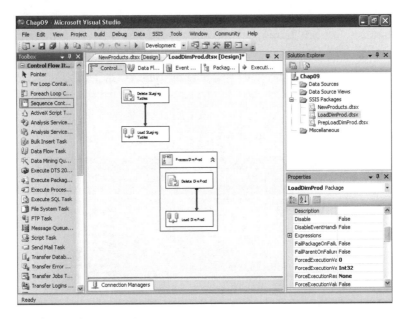

16. Click an empty area of the design pane to deselect the Delete DimProd and LoadDim-Prod tasks.

17. Right-click the Delete DimProd task and click Properties.

18. In the right pane, in the Properties box, locate TransactionOption, and then verify that the column next to it reads Supported.

Your screen should look like this:

19. Right-click the Load DimProd task and click Properties.

20. In the right pane, in the Properties box, locate TransactionOption, and then verify that the column next to it reads Supported.

21. Right-click the Process DimProd sequence container and click Properties.

22. In the right pane, in the Properties box, locate TransactionOption, and then, in the column next to it, click Required.

23. Drag a precedence constraint from the Load Staging Tables task to the Process DimProd sequence container. (Click the Load Staging Tables task, and a new green arrow will appear at the bottom of the box. Drag this new arrow over to the Process DimProd sequence container.)

Your screen should look similar to this:

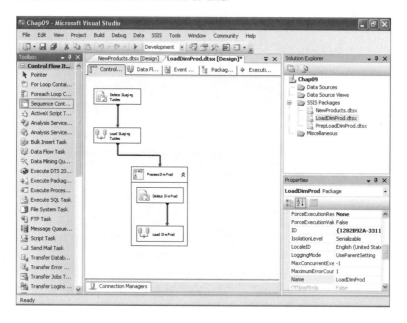

Important   Before executing the LoadDim Prod.dtsx package, ensure that the Distributed Transaction Coordinator (DTS) service is running on your computer. To determine this, click Start, click Control Panel, click Administrative Tools, and then click Services. In the Services console, locate the Distributed Transaction Coordinator service, and then, in the Status column, ensure that the status is Started. If the service is not running on your computer, in the left pane, click Start The Service. Wait for the process to complete, and then ensure that the status is Started.

24. In Solution Explorer, right-click PrepLoadDimProd.dtsx and click Execute Package.

    Wait until the package executes.

    Notice that the package successfully executes.

25. Now switch to SQL Server Management Studio so you can view the table.

26. In SQL Server Management Studio, in the right pane, click the Table – dbo.DimProd tab, and then click the Execute SQL button (exclamation point) to refresh the displayed data.

    Your screen should look like this:

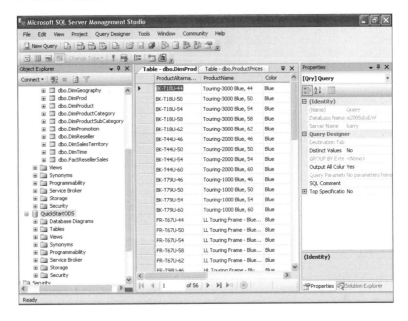

    Notice that the dbo.DimProd table now has data.

    In the preceding procedures, when LoadDimProd failed, the DimProd table was empty. In the next procedure, you will see that even though Load DimProd fails because transactions were implemented, the DimProd table is no longer empty.

27. In BIDS, on the Debug menu, click Stop Debugging.

28. In Solution Explorer, right-click LoadDimProd.dtsx and click Execute Package.

    Wait until the package executes.

Your screen looks like this:

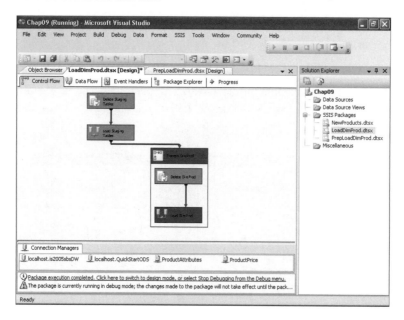

Notice that again the package failed.

29. On the Debug menu, click Stop Debugging.

Now you need to view the DimProd and Product Attributes data tables in SQL Server Management Studio.

30. Switch to SQL Server Management Studio.

31. To view the data in the DimProd table, in the right pane, click the Table – dbo.DimProd tab, and then click Execute SQL.

Your screen looks like this:

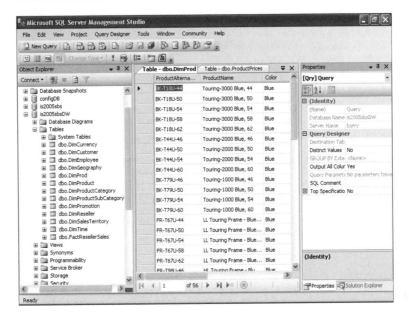

Because Process DimProd ran as a transaction, Delete DimProd was rolled back, so the DimProd table still contains data. This is the data that was in the table before the package ran.

32. To view the updated data in the ProductAttributes table:

   a. In Object Explorer, right-click the dbo.ProductAttributes table in the *QuickStart-ODS* database, and then click Open Table.

   b. To refresh the data in the table, in the right pane, click the dbo.ProductAttributes tab, and then click the Execute SQL button.

Your screen looks like this:

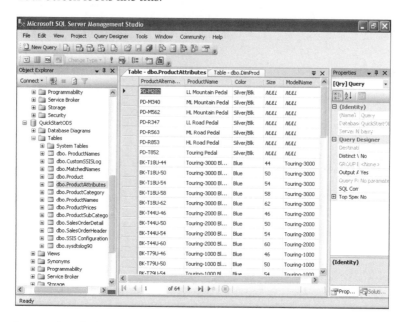

Notice that the ProductAttributes table has Silver/Blk records in it, whereas the DimProd table did not.

Fixing the Error

In the previous exercises, you discovered that the DimProd table successfully deleted, but reload failed. In this procedure, you'll open the ProductPrice table and discover that the dollar amounts are designated using USD, which causes the conversion from Varchar to Money data type to fail. To fix this problem, you enter a new SQL query statement and then execute the LoadDimProd package again. The package fails again because the entire package ran. The ProductPrices table was reloaded, which overwrote the changes you made. This means that you need to restart the package at the point where the error occurred.

Fix the error

1. To view the updated data in the ProductPrices table:

   a. In SQL Server Management Studio, in Object Explorer, right-click the dbo.Product-Prices table in the *QuickStartODS* database, and then click Open Table.

   b. To refresh the data in the table, click the Table – dbo.ProductPrices tab, and then click the Execute SQL button (exclamation point).

Notice that in the ListPrice column, dollar amounts are designated using USD. This causes the conversion from Varchar to Money data type to fail.

2. In Object Explorer, right-click QuickStartODS, and then click New Query.

3. Copy the following SQL script:

```
USE [QuickStartODS]

UPDATE dbo.ProductPrices SET ListPrice = REPLACE(ListPrice, 'USD', '')
```

4. In the right pane, on the localhost.Quic... – SQLQuery1.sql tab, paste the copied script.

5. Click the Execute button to fix the problem.

A Messages tab appears at the bottom of the screen, indicating the number of rows affected.

Your screen looks like this:

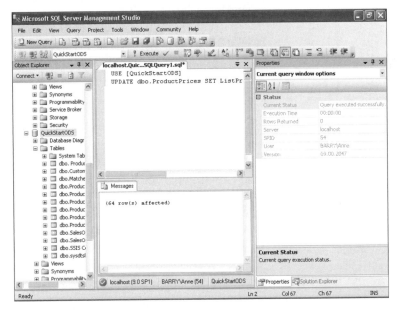

6. To view the updated data in the ProductPrices table:

    a. In SQL Server Management Studio, in Object Explorer, right-click dbo.Product-Prices, and then click Open Table.

    b. To refresh the data in the table, click the Table – dbo.ProductPrices tab, and then click the Execute SQL button (exclamation point).

7. Confirm that the USD prefix has been removed from all values in the ListPrice column.

8. In BIDS, in Solution Explorer, right-click LoadDimProd.dtsx, and then click Execute Package.

   Your screen looks like this:

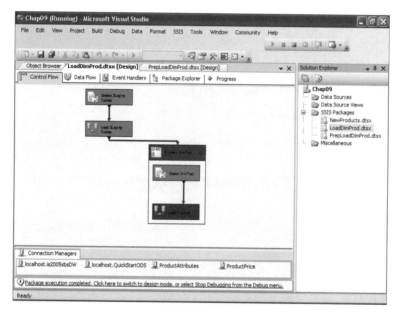

Notice that the package fails again. In the preceding procedure, you ran a SQL statement that removed the USD prefixes from the ProductPrices package. However, when the package ran, the Delete Staging Tables task deleted the records from the dbo.Product-Prices table, and the Load Staging Tables task reloaded the dbo.ProductPrices table with data from the ProductPrice.csv file. This data has the USD prefix on the prices.

9. Switch to SQL Server Management Studio.

10. To view the updated data in the DimProd table:

    a. In Object Explorer, right-click the dbo.DimProd table in the *is2005sbsDW* database, and then click Open Table.

    b. To refresh the data in the table, click the Table – dbo.DimProd tab, and then click the Execute SQL button (exclamation point).

    Notice that the DimProd table is still populated and that it does not have the Silver/Blk records yet. Because the Process DimProd container ran as a transaction, when the Load DimProd task failed, the Delete DimProd task was rolled back. This means that you need to restart the package at the point where the error occurred. In the next exercise, you will configure a checkpoint that will enable you to do this.

11. Switch to BIDS and, on the Debug menu, click Stop Debugging.

Implementing Checkpoints

In the previous procedure, you discovered that you need to restart the package at the point where the error occurred. In this procedure, you'll configure a checkpoint file to restart the package at this point.

Implement a checkpoint file to restart the package at the point of error

1. In BIDS, in Solution Explorer, double-click LoadDimProd.dtsx to open the package in the designer.

2. On the Control Flow tab, right-click anywhere in the package designer and click Properties.

3. Make sure that the LoadDimProd package is displayed in the drop-down list at the top of the Properties pane.

4. In the Properties list, in the left column, click CheckpointFileName, and then, in the right column, click the ellipses button.

5. The Select File dialog box appears.

6. In the Select File box, navigate to C:\Documents and Settings\<username>\My Documents\Microsoft Press\is2005sbs\Chap09\Checkpoints.

7. Select LoadDimProd.txt, and then click Open.

8. In the Properties list, in the left column, click CheckpointUsage, and then, in the right column drop-down list, select IfExists.

9. In the Properties list, in the left column, click SaveCheckpoints, and then, in the right column drop-down list, select True.

10. In the package designer, right-click the Process DimProd container, and then click Properties.

11. Make sure that Process DimProd Sequence is displayed in the drop-down list at the top of the Properties pane.

12. In the Properties list, in the left column, click FailPackageOnFailure, and then, in the right column drop-down list, select True.

13. In Solutions Explorer, right-click LoadDimProd.dtsx, and then click Execute Package.

    Wait until the package executes.

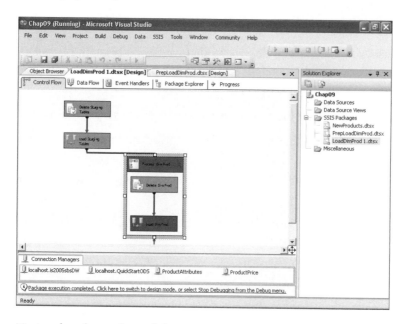

Notice that the package did not execute successfully. The package fails because of the ListPrice column format.

14. On the Debug menu, click Stop Debugging.

15. In Windows Explorer, navigate to C:\Documents and Settings\<username>\My Documents\Microsoft Press\is2005sbs\Chap09\Checkpoints.

Notice the checkpoint file named LoadDimProd.txt file that was created in the Checkpoints folder.

16. In SQL Server Management Server, in Object Explorer, right-click QuickStartODS and click New Query.

17. Copy the following SQL script:

```
USE [QuickStartODS]

UPDATE dbo.ProductPrices SET ListPrice = REPLACE(ListPrice, 'USD', '')
```

18. In the right pane, on the localhost.Quic... – SQLQuery1.sql tab, paste the copied script.

19. Click the Execute button to fix the problem.

Your screen looks like this:

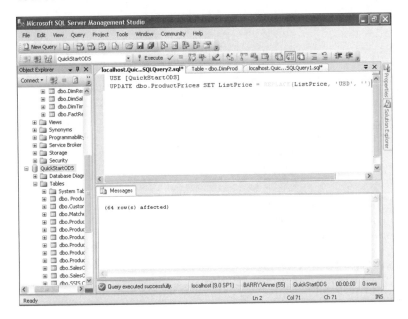

20. To view the updated data in the tables:

    a. In Object Explorer, right-click dbo.ProductPrices, and then click Open Table.

    b. To refresh the data in the table, click the Table – dbo.ProductPrices tab, and then click Execute SQL (exclamation point).

21. Confirm that the USD prefix has been removed from all values in the ListPrice column.

22. In BIDS, in Solution Explorer, right-click LoadDimProd.dtsx and click Execute Package.

23. Wait for the package to execute.

Your screen looks like this:

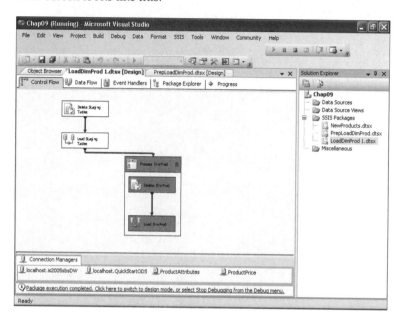

Notice that the Delete Staging Tables and Load Staging Tables tasks did not execute. When the LoadDimProd package executed, it found the LoadDimProd.txt file in the Checkpoints folder. Because this file contained information that told the package that the Delete Staging Tables and Load Staging Tables successfully executed while the Process DimProd sequence container failed, the package executed only the Process DimProd sequence container.

24. In SQL Server Management Studio, click Table – dbo.DimProd and click Execute SQL.

Notice that there are records with Silver/Blk values in the Color column. This means that you have successfully loaded the data from the ProductAttributes.csv and Product-Price.csv files into the DimProd table.

Chapter 9 Quick Reference

To	Do This
Create an *OnPreExecute* event handler	In BIDS, on the Event Handlers tab, in the Executable drop-down list, select NewProducts, and then click OK. In the Event Handler drop-down list, select OnPreExecute. In the Event Handlers design environment, click the blue text that reads "Click here to create an OnPreExecute event handler for executable NewProducts."
Add a task to an event handler	In BIDS, while on the Event Handlers tab, click Toolbox, and then drag the event handler onto the design environment.
Configure a task	In BIDS, double-click the task to open its editor, and then make the configuration changes.
Map SSIS variables to SQL statement parameters	In BIDS, on the Control Flow tab, double-click the SQL task to open its editor. In the Execute SQL Task Editor, click Parameter Mapping, click Add, and then configure the variable.
Create a file system task and a connection manager	In BIDS, while on the Event Handlers tab, click Toolbox, and then drag File System Task onto the designer. Double-click the task and, in the File System Task Editor, type the name, destination connection, and source connection.
Set connection manager settings	In BIDS, in the Connection Managers pane, right-click the connection manager, and then click Properties. In the Properties list, expand Expressions, and then click the ellipses button. In the Property Expressions Editor, change the settings.
Prevent events from escalating to a container	In BIDS, while on the Event Handlers tab, on the SSIS menu, click Variables. In the Variables list, in the Value column drop-down list, change the value.
Change error count properties	In BIDS, on the Control Flow tab, right-click on the design surface, and then click Properties. In the Properties list, locate MaximumErrorCount, and then change the value.

Chapter 10
Securing and Deploying SSIS Packages

After completing this chapter, you will be able to:

- Understand the components of package security and learn to automate package deployment to a server.

- Understand package deployment options: the package deployment utility, command-line options, and package importing and exporting.

- Use role-based security to protect deployed packages for execution and administration.

- Learn to monitor package execution and configure and view SSIS event logs.

Up to this point, you've designed packages in Business Intelligence Development Studio (BIDS) and transformed, imported, and exported small amounts of test data in the development environment. The package designer and development platform does a good job of emulating true package execution, but it isn't the same for at least two reasons. In the designer, a package runs with debugging checks and additional overhead that use up memory and CPU cycles, which can throttle back performance and capabilities. In a deployed server environment, Microsoft SQL Server Integration Services (SSIS) will dedicate more resources to package execution, buffer space, memory allocation, and parallel processing. To get the best performance out of SSIS and to work with large volumes of real business data, you must deploy and execute packages on an enterprise-class production server. In this chapter, you will learn how to make the transition to a deployed server environment.

Security and deployment are managed at the package level. Optionally, you can deploy all packages for a project by building a deployment manifest and using the deployment utility and Package Installation Wizard. A package can be secured by password to protect it from being edited by unauthorized users. Further, information stored within the package can be encrypted. This can be applied to only passwords and other sensitive information or to the entire package.

After a package has been deployed to the server, it can be executed manually or scheduled to run automatically. While a package is executing, you can view its status from SQL Server Management Studio (SSMS). After package execution has completed, you can also use SSMS to view the SSIS logs to obtain detailed information about errors and execution status.

Creating a Deployment Utility

An SSIS project can be configured to prepare packages for server deployment by using a deployment manifest file. This is a convenient method to deploy the packages in a project using the Package Deployment Wizard. You can configure this option in the project properties. To do this from Solution Explorer, right-click the project and select Properties to open the project Property Pages dialog box. Select the Deployment Utility page, and then set CreateDeploymentUtility to *True*.

When you build the project from Solution Explorer or from the Build menu, files are created in the project's Bin\Deployment subfolder, which can then be copied to the target server. Simply double-click the *<project name>*.SSISDeploymentManifest file to launch the Package Installation Wizard. This will install the package to the server with user-selectable options.

Using the Package Installation Wizard

In the following exercise, you will make changes to an existing project to prepare packages for deployment. Setting the project properties to create a deployment utility instructs BIDS to generate a folder containing copies of all packages ready for deployment along with a deployment manifest file when choosing the Build option. You can use this file to launch the Package Installation Wizard to deploy all packages in the project easily to the target SSIS server.

Enable the deployment utility

1. Open the SSIS Sample Solution.sln file located at C:\Documents and Settings\<username>\My Documents\Microsoft Press\is2005sbs\Chap10. This opens BIDS.

2. In BIDS, right-click the SSIS Sample Project name in Solution Explorer, and then click Properties.

3. In the Property Pages dialog box, click Deployment Utility.

4. Change CreateDeploymentUtility to *True*.

5. Confirm that AllowConfigurationChanges is *True*.

6. Note the path for DeploymentOutputPath.

Your screen looks like the following:

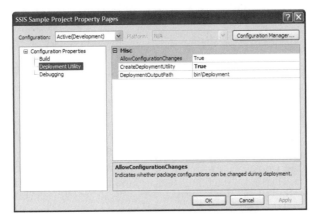

7. Click the OK button to close the Project Property Pages dialog box.

Making these changes to the project sets up the metadata necessary to create a deployment manifest with instructions for package deployment. In BIDS or Microsoft Visual Studio, the Build action performs different functions, depending on the project type. For example, in a custom application project, building the project compiles source code into a binary executable. In an SSIS project, building the project produces an output folder with a deployment manifest and project files ready for deployment.

Build the SSIS Sample Project

1. Right-click the SSIS Sample Project name in Solution Explorer, and then click Build.

> **Note**   The build process creates the .SSISDeploymentManifest file and copies the package files to the Deployment folder to prepare for package deployment.

2. Navigate to the build folder for the project.

3. Using Windows Explorer, locate the project files in the DeploymentOutputPath specified in the project properties. This folder is located at Bin\Deployment, under the project folder.

If you were deploying packages in a production environment, you would copy build files to a production server at this point. For this exercise, you can leave the files in their current location.

4. To start the Package Installation Wizard, double-click the SSIS Sample Project.SSIS-DeploymentManifest file.

5.   Click Next on the Welcome page.

6.   Select SQL Server Deployment, and then click Next.

7.   Specify the target server name: (local).

8.   Select Rely On Server Storage For Encryption.

9.   Click Next three times (keeping the default configuration properties in each page), and then click Finish.

Connect to Integration Services

1.   In SQL Server Management Studio (SSMS), in the Connect To Server dialog box, verify that you are connected to Integration Services.

2.   If not, click the Connect button above Object Explorer, choose Integration Services, and accept the default local server connection.

3.   If launching SSMS for the first time, choose Integration Services from the Server Type drop-down list, select localhost in the Server Name drop-down list, and then click Connect.

> **Note**   After the Connect To Server dialog box closes, you will see Integration Services in the Object Browser with *Running* nodes labeled Packages and Stored Packages. You are now connected to the SSIS server.

Securing a Package

You can protect a package in two ways: by encrypting sensitive information stored in the package definition file and by controlling who has the ability to run or make changes to a deployed package.

You can protect a package so that sensitive metadata, such as connection passwords, is encrypted; or you can encrypt the entire package. You can also use password protection to prevent both modification and execution of the package.

You can use password protection to implement only package definition protection or both package definition and deployed package protection. When deployed to SQL Server, a package can be protected by using role-based security.

Package Encryption

Package definition files contain connection information, user names, and passwords that might be considered sensitive. You can protect this information by encrypting all or part of the definition file with options such as encrypting only sensitive information (that is, connection string passwords) or encrypting the entire package, using the development environment. You can also choose to allow the SQL Server database engine to encrypt the package when it is deployed, using the SQL Server database option. The encryption algorithm can be seeded using a password or a key derived from the developer's Microsoft Windows user account.

Password Protection

You can use password protection to prevent modification and deployment. When you provide a password for the *PackagePassword* property of the package, the development environment will prompt for this password when attempting to open the package file. This, however, does not prevent the file from being opened from the Windows file system. The real value of password protection is when the password is used in conjunction with package encryption. As mentioned previously, the password can also be used to seed the package encryption algorithm, depending on the *ProtectionLevel* property setting.

To enable password protection on a package, right-click anywhere in the package designer, select Properties, and then use the Properties window to set the *PackagePassword* property.

ProtectionLevel Property

All of the security options are controlled by the *ProtectionLevel* property. With the package open in the package designer, you can use the Properties window to set the *ProtectionLevel* property to one of the following values:

- **DontSaveSensitive**   Removes passwords and other sensitive information from the package.
- **EncryptAllWithPassword**   Encrypts all package contents by using a password.
- **EncryptAllWithUserKey**   Encrypts all package contents using a key based on the current Windows user. Only this user will be able to open and make changes to the package.
- **EncryptSensitiveWithPassword**   Encrypts only passwords and other sensitive information in the package by using a password.
- **EncryptSensitiveWithUserKey**   Encrypts the entire package by using a key based on the current Windows user. Only this user will be able to view sensitive information. Another user can modify the package, but sensitive information will not be displayed.
- **ServerStorage**   Encrypts the package contents stored when the package is deployed to SQL Server. The encrypted package is stored in the *MSDB* system database. This option is supported only when a package is saved to SQL Server. Access to the package is controlled using SQL Server database roles.

Role-Based Security

To control who has the authority to run a package or to make changes to a package that has been deployed to the database server, SQL Server 2005 employs role-based security. This form of security is managed by the SQL Server database engine, using database roles in the *MSDB* database. Specific permissions are applied to a package deployed using only the database deployment option.

A package is secured on the server, using database roles defined in the *MSDB* system database. The default roles are db_dtsadmin, db_dtsltduser, and db_dtsoperator. Two levels of permissions are applied to a package: reader and writer. By default, a package reader is any user in the db_dtsadmin, db_dtsltduser, or db_dtsoperator roles; a reader can view and execute a package. By default, a package writer is any user in the db_dtsadmin role; a writer can perform any user or administrative operations, including exporting, modifying, executing, or changing role assignments for a package.

Applying Security

The following exercise will walk you through the process of applying encryption and password protection to a package and then deploying and protecting the package access by using SQL Server role-based security. You will change the protection level of a package to *EncryptAllWithPassword*, prepare a deployment utility, deploy the package to the server, assign reader and writer roles to the package, and then view the default database roles assigned to each.

Change the protection level of a package to *EncryptAllWithPassword*

1. In BIDS, open the ImportCustomers package from Solution Explorer. Make sure that the package name appears in the drop-down list at the top of the Properties window.

2. Locate ProtectionLevel and change the value by selecting EncryptAllWithPassword.

3. Locate PackagePassword and change the value to a password (all lowercase.)

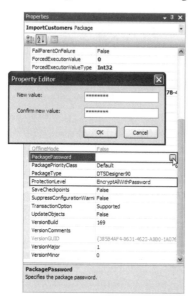

4. Build the project to refresh the deployment manifest.

5. Run the Package Installation Wizard and view the new password option:

    a. Right-click the project in Solution Explorer and choose Build.

    b. Using Windows Explorer, locate the project files in the DeploymentOutputPath specified in the project properties. This folder is located at Bin\Deployment, under the project folder.

    Your screen should look like this:

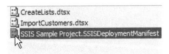

6. Double-click the SSIS Sample Project.SSISDeploymentManifest file to start the Package Installation Wizard.

7. Click Next on the Welcome page.

8. Select SQL Server Deployment, and then click Next.

9. Specify the target server name: (local).

10. Select Rely On Server Storage For Encryption.

11. Click Next.

    Note the new page displayed entitled Encrypted Packages. Enter the password in the Password column and complete the wizard, using the Next and Finish buttons when prompted. View the encrypted package definition.

12. In BIDS, right-click the ImportCustomers.dtsx file in the SSIS Packages folder.

13. Choose View Code.

    Note that the package definition is no longer readable Extensible Markup Language (XML). After the XML header, the rest of the content is displayed on one line.

14. Scroll to the right to reveal the encrypted file content.

15. Close this window when completed.

Assign reader and writer roles to a package

1. In SSMS, verify that you are connected to Integration Services. If not, click the Connect button in the Object Explorer pane, select Integration Services, accept the default local server connection, and then click Connect.

2. Under the Stored Packages folder, expand the MSDB folder to show the ImportCustomers package.

3. Right-click the ImportCustomers package, and then click Package Roles.

4. Note the settings for the Reader Role and Writer Role.

> **Tip** The default setting references multiple preset database roles for the *MSDB* system database. In production, you can assign an existing or newly created database role and then manage user or group membership in this role.

Deployment Options

You can deploy packages either to the file system on the server or into the SQL Server database engine. The SQL Server deployment option writes the package content into the *MSDB* system database. This system database, which exists on every SQL Server, is also used to manage important system objects such as agent jobs, tasks, and backup information. The SQL Server deployment option is the most secure because everything is written to the database catalog rather than to the file system. Packages can be recovered by simply backing up and restoring the *MSDB* database.

Push Deployment

You can push a package to a server by running the Package Installation Wizard (either manually or by opening an .SSISDeploymentManifest file). You can also push a package from SQL Server to another server or to a .dtsx file from within SSMS. A convenient right-click menu option is available in SSMS to import or export a package between servers or package definition files. To push a package to another location, from Integration Services, under the File System or MSDB folder, simply right-click the package and select Export Package.

You have the option to export a deployed package to another SQL Server or to a package file in the file system. You can use the Import Package utility to set the same configuration options as in the BIDS package designer, setting the protection level and a package password.

Pull Deployment

You can also deploy a package from the server in a pull scenario by importing a package within SSMS. In the Stored Packages folder, right-click the server destination (either File System or MSDB) and select Import Package to launch the Import Package utility.

The Import Package dialog box options are nearly identical to those in the Export Package dialog box. You can import a deployed package from another SQL server or from a package file in the file system. Like the export option, you can also set the protection level and a package password.

Managing Packages on the SSIS Server

In the previous exercise, you deployed a package to the database server. In the next exercise, you will redeploy the package to the file system and to the *MSDB* database. You will execute a package from the file system and then monitor running packages.

Import the ImportCustomers package to the file system

1. In SSMS, verify that you are connected to Integration Services. If not, click the Connect button in the Object Explorer pane, select Integration Services, accept the default local server connection, and then click Connect.

2. Expand the Stored Packages folder, right-click File System, and choose Import Package.

3. Set the following properties:

   ❑ Package Location: File System

   ❑ Package Path: C:\Documents and Settings\<username>\My Documents\Microsoft Press\is2005sbs\Chap10\ImportCustomers\Mod10_Project.dtsx

4. Click in the Package Name text box. This sets this property to the designer package name.

5. Click the ellipsis button next to Protection Level. Note the value previously set in the package design. Leave this setting and click the Cancel button to close this dialog box.

6. Click OK.

7. Type the password **password** when prompted.

8. Click OK.

Tip When you import to the File System option, Integration Services stores the package file in a known location on the server (in the \Microsoft SQL Server\90\DTS\Packages folder). You can then access the package without having to know the specific file location.

Import to MSDB

1. Right-click MSDB and repeat the preceding steps to import the same package to the *MSDB* system database but, this time, choose SQL Server For Package Location in the Import Package dialog box.

> **Note**   If the package is already deployed, you will be prompted to overwrite it. Answer Yes if prompted.

2. Complete the steps and note the new package listed on the tree.

Export a deployed package

1. Find the ImportCustomers package in the SSMS Object Explorer under Stored Packages\MSDB.

2. Right-click the package icon and choose Export Package.

3. In the Export Package dialog box, select File System for Package Location.

4. Click the Package Path ellipsis button.

5. In the Save Package To File dialog box, select Desktop and leave all other defaults to save the package, using the default file name ImportCustomer.dtsx.

6. Click Save to save the package file, and then click OK to save and close the Export Package dialog box.

Execute the file system package

1. View the computer's desktop and locate the ImportCustomers.dtsx file.

2. Double-click the file to open Execute Package Utility.

3. Execute the package and view the execution progress. Depending on the speed of your computer, this might take only a few seconds or several minutes to complete. When completed, close the Package Execution Progress dialog box, and then close the Execute Package Utility dialog box.

Monitor running packages

1. Repeat the preceding steps with SSMS and Package Execution Utility open in side-by-side windows.

2. Start the package, and then open the Running Packages folder. If necessary, right-click and choose refresh to see the name of the running package.

Note   The speed of your computer will determine how long this package runs. If the package finishes running before you have a chance to complete the preceding steps, you can extend the running time by creating duplicate copies of the input data files in the project's \Data subfolder. In Windows Explorer, select all of the data files; use the right-click menu to copy and paste options to create duplicate files. Repeat this step if necessary. There is no need to change the default file names.

3. Click the package name on the tree to view the summary page for the package.

4. Click the Report button on the Summary page toolbar.

Note   Selecting the Report option in this view runs a Reporting Services report with summary and detail information about the current package execution.

Note   Keep in mind that SSMS shows only the currently running packages. Some packages can complete in less than a second, and you might not be able to monitor these packages.

5. Close the Execute Package Utility dialog box when completed.

Creating and Applying a Configuration

Use a package configuration to override selected property values stored in a separate file or configuration resource. Typically, this is used to apply properties, such as file paths or connection strings, that would need to be changed when the package is moved to a test or production environment.

Adding a Configuration to the Project

You can add a configuration to the Integration Services project by using the SSIS menu in BIDS.

Use the SSIS BIDS menu to add a configuration

1. Select Package Configurations from the menu.

2. Select the Enable Configurations check box in the Package Configurations Organizer dialog box:

    a. Click the Add button to launch the Package Configuration Wizard.

    b. Click Next, and then view the storage locations and formats in the Configuration Type drop-down list:

        ● XML Configuration File

        ● Environment Variable

        ● Registry Entry

        ● Parent Package Variable

        ● SQL Server

    The values stored in these configurations are applied to the package and component properties when the package is deployed using a deployment utility manifest. You can also apply new property values dynamically to a previously deployed package from a configuration by using Execute Package Utility.

Executing a Deployed Package

You have some choices about how you can execute a package, none of which is very complicated. The easiest method is to locate the package in SQL Server Management Studio Integration Services, right-click the package, and choose Run Package from the menu. This might be simple, but it's certainly not very convenient if you want the package to run every morning at 2 A.M.—especially when you're on vacation in Hawaii!

Fortunately, a package can also be scheduled to run automatically by the server. Typically, you do this by using the SQL Server Agent with a simple command-line script. Using the Agent, the job can be scheduled to run at set intervals. Alerts can be set up to send e-mail, page, or log entries upon success or failure.

Regardless of whether you run the package manually or schedule it to run automatically, you will actually use one of two utility programs:

■ **DTExecUI**   Opens Execute Package Utility in a Windows dialog box

■ **DTExec**   Runs the command-line package execution utility

Running DTExecUI from a shortcut or the command line opens the Windows Execute Package Utility dialog box, as shown in Figure 10-1. This will allow you to specify configurations, optional settings, logging, and execution options on various tabbed property pages in the dialog box. Choosing Run Package within SSMS launches this utility application.

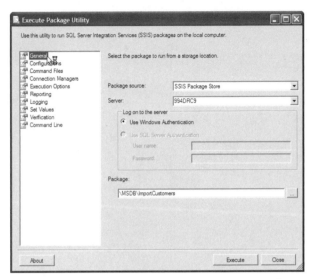

Figure 10-1   General settings using the Execute Package Utility.

Running DTExec from the command line will perform the same operations, using a single command-line string. Although the DTExecUI utility may be dressier, the command-line utility is more versatile and might be preferable in many situations. Using this utility is a convenient way to run a package from a batch or command file.

There is an easy method to assemble the command-line string used to run this utility with all of the necessary options. Run Execute Package Utility (DTExecUI), and then choose all of the appropriate options and execution parameters. On the last tab of this dialog box, labeled Command Line, as shown in Figure 10-2, a text box displays all of the execution options as a command string. Simply copy and paste this string into the command line or to a batch file in Notepad after the text DTExec. It's that easy!

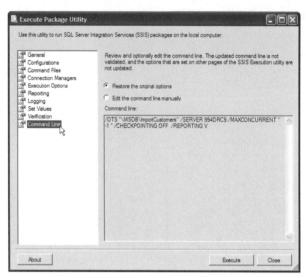

Figure 10-2   Command-line settings using the Execute Package Utility

Monitoring Package Execution and Event Logs

Package execution can be monitored and audited by using three methods, which include active monitoring in SSMS, console reporting in the command window, and viewing execution logs. A number of logging options are available that can be enabled in Execute Package Utility. Logging can be output by using a number of standard logging providers. This requires some planning because this feature requires a connection manager to be defined in the package to handle the logging output. To enable logging, use the logging options to perform the following steps:

- Enable event logging.
- Add logging output in the Execute Package Utility dialog box.
- Set Log Provider.
- Create a package connection manager to output the log.
- Select the connection manager in the configuration string.

The Reporting options page, as shown in Figure 10-3, controls the logging content and specific detail written to the event logs. In addition to the logging information written to a permanent log, you can also control which event information is displayed in the console window while the package is running. Use the reporting options to select console events and to set up console logging.

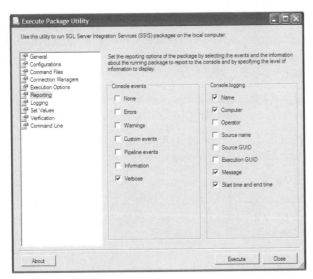

Figure 10-3   Reporting options using the Execute Package Utility

When you run the package from the command line by using DTExec, the selected console logging options are displayed in the console window and can easily be written to a file, as shown in Figure 10-4.

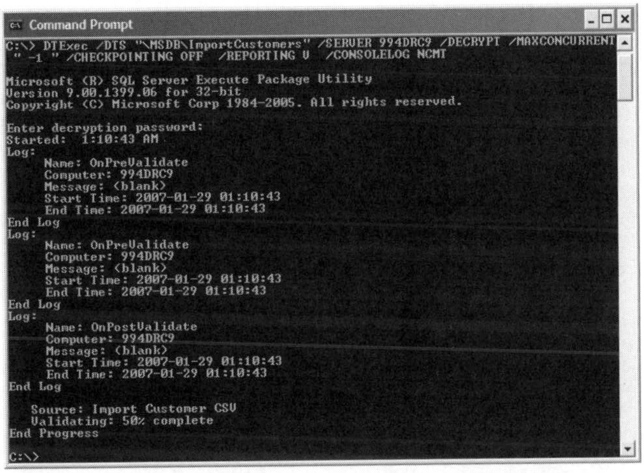

Figure 10-4   Command-line version of the Execute Package Utility

Applying a Configuration

This exercise will lead you through the steps to create a configuration file in which to store alternate property settings. Then you will apply the configuration to a package to control execution under different conditions.

Delete the existing package from SSMS

1. In SSMS, verify that you are connected to Integration Services. If not, click the Connect button in the Object Explorer pane, select Integration Services, accept the default local server connection, and then click Connect.

2. If launching SSMS for the first time, choose Integration Services from the Server Type drop-down list and connect by using localhost as the server name.

3. Expand the Stored Packages folder and the MSDB folder within it to expose the Import-Customers.dtsx package created in the previous exercise.

4. Right-click the ImportCustomers.dtsx package in the MSDB folder and select Delete.

> **Tip**   For the demonstration, you need to delete the deployed package from the server to redeploy an updated package containing the added configuration information.

Add a configuration to the ImportCustomers.dtsx package

1. In BIDS, verify that Chapter 10 Project is open. If not, from the File menu, choose Open, select Project/Solution, and choose the SSIS Sample Solution.sln file.

2. In Solution Explorer, double-click the ImportCustomers.dtsx package to open it in the grid.

3. From the SSIS menu, choose Package Configurations.

4. In the Package Configurations Organizer window, check the Enable Package Configurations check box.

5. Click the Add button to open the Package Configuration Wizard, and then click Next.

6. Ensure that XML Configuration File is selected for the Configuration Type drop-down list.

7. In the Configuration File Name input box, type **ImportCustomersConfiguration**.

8. Click Next.

   This will create a new configuration file with a .dtsxConfig file extension.

9. Maximize the Package Configuration Wizard window to get a better view of the Objects list.

   You are choosing which properties to export to the configuration file. You want two properties to export.

10. In the Executables folder, expand the For Loop Container.

11. Expand the Executables folder.

12. Expand the Find Customer CSV object.

13. Expand the Enumeration Properties folder.

14. Select the check box next to Directory.

15. In the Objects list, scroll to the bottom of the list and expand the Variables folder.

16. Expand MaxLoopCounter.

17. Expand the Properties folder.

18. Select the check box next to Value.

Verify that your screen looks like this:

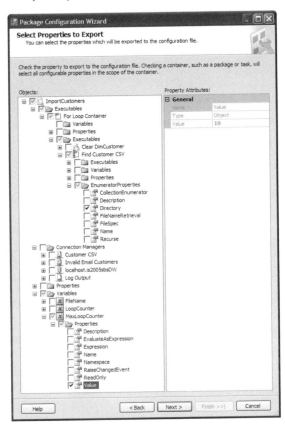

19. Click Next at the bottom of the Package Configuration Wizard dialog box.

20. Accept the default Configuration Name and click Finish to close the Package Configuration Wizard.

21. Click Close in the Package Configuration Organizer window.

22. From the File menu, choose Save All.

Deploy the package

1. In Solution Explorer, right-click the SSIS Sample Project (first item listed on the tree) and click Build.

2. Close BIDS.

Start the Package Installation Wizard

You will deploy the package to SQL Server in the following steps.

1. In Windows Explorer, navigate to the C:\Documents and Settings\<username>\My Documents\Microsoft Press\is2005sbs\Chapter10 folder.

2. Open the Bin\ Deployment folder.

    Here you will see a copy of the configuration file you just created.

3. Double-click the SSIS Sample Project.SSISDeploymentManifest file.

4. In the Package Installation Wizard, click Next.

5. Select the SQL Server Deployment option, and then click Next.

6. Ensure that (local) is listed for the Server Name and click Next.

7. If you are prompted for a package password, type **password**.

8. Click Next to accept the default Folder path for the installation folder.

9. Click Next to start the installation.

    After the package is updated, the Package Installation Wizard will present the configuration settings you exported to the configuration. This is applying the configuration settings.

10. Expand Property to view Loop Counter and Directory Variables. No changes are necessary.

11. Click Next.

12. Click Finish to deploy and apply the configuration settings.

Inspect the alternate configuration files

In this exercise, you will inspect the contents of the two provided configuration files.

1. In Windows Explorer, navigate to the C:\Documents and Settings\<username>\My Documents\Microsoft Press\is2005sbs\Chapter10 folder.

    Notice that there are three .dtsConfig files. Two are alternate copies of the configuration file you created in BIDS. You are going to inspect them both by using Notepad.

2. Locate the ImportCustomersConfiguration (DataFolder).dtsConfig file.

3. Right-click the file and choose Open With.

4. Select Choose Program.

5. In the Open With window, select Notepad from the Programs list.

6. Click OK.

   This is an XML file that holds the configuration information for your deployed package. Notice the new values between the <ConfiguredValue> and </ConfiguredValue> tags.

7. Close Notepad.

8. Right-click the ImportCustomersConfiguration (Empty DataFolder).dtsConfig file.

9. Click Open With and select Notepad.

> **Note**   Notice that the path between the <ConfiguredValue> and </Configured-Value> tags points to a folder that doesn't contain the data files. You will use this configuration and view the results.

10. Close Notepad.

Run the deployed package

1. In SSMS, verify that you are connected to Integration Services. If not, click the Connect button in the Object Explorer pane, select Integration Services, accept the default local server connection, and then click Connect.

2. If launching SSMS for the first time, choose Integration Services from the Server Type drop-down list and connect by using localhost as the server name.

3. Expand the Stored Packages folder.

4. Right-click the MSDB folder and select Refresh to see the newly deployed package.

5. Right-click the newly deployed ImportCustomers package and select Run Package.

6. In the Execute Package Utility dialog box, click the Execute button at the bottom of the window.

7. If prompted for a password, type **password** to continue.

> **Note**   Note that the Package Execution Progress window shows the real-time execution of the package. Note that this package is valid and completes with no warnings or errors.

   Close the Package Execution Progress window when the package finishes running.

8. Close the Execute Package Utility window.

Execute the package by using the configuration files

1. Run the package with two alternate configurations, one at a time:

   You will be prompted for the package password multiple times during this process. In each case, type **password** and click OK to continue.

   a. In the SSMS Object Explorer pane, right-click ImportCustomers under the *Stored Packages* node and select Run Package.

   b. In the Execute Package Utility window, choose Configurations.

   c. Click Add.

   d. Browse to the project folder and select the ImportCustomersConfiguration (Empty Data Folder).dtsConfig file.

   When execution is completed, note how quickly it ran and view the output window to reveal warning messages, which indicate that the import file folder was empty.

Execute the package

1. In SSMS, verify that you are connected to Database Engine. If not, click the Connect button in the Object Explorer pane, select Database Engine, accept the default local server connection, and then click Connect.

2. Browse to the *is2005sbsDW* database and expand the tables.

3. Right-click the DimCustomer table and choose Open Table. A query window opens, revealing no rows in the table.

   The DimCustomer table contains no records because the configuration directed the flat file connection manager to a folder with no files to import.

4. Repeat these steps and add the ImportCustomersConfiguration (Data Folder).dtsConfig configuration file.

5. After executing the package, note that it took longer to run and then view the output. No errors or warnings should be reported.

6. In the query window for the DimCustomer table, click in the results window (center pane), and then click the Execute SQL button on the Query Designer toolbar (the red exclamation mark). The query should return 18,484 rows.

Chapter 10 Quick Reference

To	Do this
Configure a project to create a deployment utility	Right-click the project name in Solution Explorer and choose Properties. In the Property Pages dialog box, set the *CreateDeploymentUtility*, *AllowConfigurationChanges*, and *DeploymentOutputPath* properties.
Create a Configure Deployment Utility manifest file	After configuring the project, right-click the project name in Solution Explorer and choose Build.
Run the Package Installation Wizard	In Windows Explorer, double-click the <project name>.SSISDeploymentManifest file located in the project's Bin\Deployment folder.
Encrypt package contents	Set ProtectionLevel and, optionally, PackagePassword for a package in the Properties window.
Password protect a package	Set PackagePassword for a package in the Properties window.
Apply role-based security to a package deployed to SQL Server	Use SQL Server Management Studio (SSMS) and connect to Integration Services. Expand Stored Packages, the *MSDB* database, and the deployed package name. Right-click the package and choose Package Roles from the menu. Use the Package Roles dialog box to apply the default or specific database roles for the *MSDB* database.
Run a package from SSMS	Right-click the deployed package name under the File System or MSDB folder located under Stored Packages. Choose Run Package from the menu. Use Execute Package Utility to modify options and execute the package.
Run a package from the command line	Run DTExec with the package name and options copied from the Execute Package Utility command-line page.

Chapter 11
Optimizing SSIS Packages

After completing this chapter, you will be able to:

- Generally understand the SSIS engine components and processes.

- Review the memory buffer architecture.

- Monitor package execution trees and their impact on package performance.

- Manage buffer properties.

- Manage task and component parallelism.

- Understanding performance management essentials.

- Use iterative optimization techniques to simplify and tune a package design.

Microsoft SQL Server 2005 Integration Services (SSIS) goes a long way toward ensuring optimal performance with little direct input from the person designing packages. As much as possible, the execution engine will make intelligent decisions about the appropriate use of buffer allocation, memory usage, and whether tasks can be processed in parallel or serial fashion. SSIS also affords many opportunities to affect the way a package executes. A basic understanding of the SSIS run time and data pipeline engines and their core components will help you understand better how system resources are used to perform package execution. The memory buffer architecture allows data flow to be managed in discrete steps as set and row operations. Your choices of tasks, transformations, and precedence constraints will affect the engine's ability to reuse buffers and block related operations only when necessary.

When you design data integration solutions, your design decisions not only determine how successfully your solution meets functional requirements but also how well your solution will perform. To make the right performance design decisions, you need to understand the performance architecture of your data integration tool and, just as important, the techniques that enable you to maximize the tool's use of system resources such as memory, disk or physical storage, and CPU.

SSIS provides full-featured data integration and workflow engines coupled with a rich development environment for building high-performance data integration solutions. SSIS provides a variety of optimization opportunities to help you maximize resource use while successfully meeting the needs of your specific data integration scenario.

SSIS Engine Overview

As you peel back the layers of the Integration Services processing architecture, there are two separate subcomponents that can have a significant impact on performance and package efficiency. These are the SSIS Runtime engine and Data Pipeline engine. It is important to familiarize yourself with the purpose and behavior of these engines to make performance-tuning decisions.

Runtime Engine

The Runtime engine is a highly parallel workflow engine that coordinates the execution of tasks or units of work within SSIS and manages the engine threads that carry out those tasks. For the most part, the performance of the Runtime engine is most heavily influenced by conditions external to SSIS such as the number of available threads, the network bandwidth, and the interaction with external systems such as database servers, File Transfer Protocol (FTP) servers, or e-mail servers. When SSIS runs an Execute SQL task, for example, it sends a call to the target database and then waits for a response from the database server before it continues. In this scenario, the performance of the Execute SQL task is more dependent on the performance of the query execution than on the SSIS Runtime engine.

Data Pipeline Engine

When you use SSIS for data integration, in addition to the Runtime engine, you will use the Data Pipeline engine. The Data Pipeline engine is the underlying counterpart to a special task in SSIS called the *data flow task*. When the data flow task executes, the SSIS Data Pipeline engine extracts data from one or more data sources, performs any necessary transformations on the extracted data, and then delivers that data to one or more destinations.

With data integration solutions, you will likely focus a large part of your performance-tuning time on optimizing the Data Pipeline engine. Like the Runtime engine, the Data Pipeline engine is influenced by external conditions; however, within SSIS, there are a variety of settings that you can manipulate to tune the Data Pipeline engine's performance, based on the requirements of the data integration operations.

Memory Buffer Architecture

A fundamental understanding of the memory management architecture in SSIS will help you make intelligent choices about how to assist SSIS to move data more efficiently through the pipeline. Some transformations require data to be copied or moved from one buffer to another while others do not. Because some transformations depend on the output of others, this can create blocks and bottlenecks in the process. Some operations require that a preceding transformation completely finish its work before it can begin to process any rows. This is said to be a blocking transformation. Other transformations must begin their duty, but rows can begin to flow to another transformation before the entire process has completed. In this case, the operation of the first transformation only partially blocks the second. Finally, there can be data flows and transformations in the package that are not at all dependent on each other and do not block other transformations in the data flow.

Buffer Usage

Behind the scenes, the Data Pipeline engine uses a buffer-oriented architecture to load and manipulate data sets in memory efficiently. The benefit of this in-memory processing is that you do not need to copy and stage data physically at each step of the data integration. Rather, the Data Pipeline engine manipulates data as it is transferred from source to destination.

Buffers are based on design-time metadata. The width of a row determines the size of the buffer. Because buffer space for a data flow task is allocated in a specific size, the number of rows that will fit into a buffer is determined by the number of bytes required for each row. In other words, the smaller the rows, the more rows that can fit into the buffer—and the greater the efficiency of the overall process. Two factors affect row size:

- Number of columns
- Width of each column

Column width is determined by the data type and the number of bytes assigned to fixed-width string types.

Consider the following scenario. Say that a table contains twelve columns consisting of five Int types, three DateTime types, and four 100-byte strings. That's 1,072 bytes per row. Using the default buffer size of ten megabytes, this means that the maximum number of records the buffer can handle is less than ten thousand. If only three columns were actually needed for the transformation (perhaps one of each data type in this example), the number of rows the buffer would accommodate is increased to nearly 40 thousand.

As a rule, select only the columns you need from data sources and assign conservation data types whenever possible. This is a simple matter of specifying columns explicitly in a SQL Select statement. The default lookup query for a data source uses *Select *.* This is because at design time, the package designer gives you all available columns to choose for joins and pass-through. After you have identified the required columns, modify the query to select only the columns that are actually necessary to support data flow operations.

As this data flows through the pipeline, SSIS attempts to reuse data from prior buffers as much as possible when additional operations are performed. How buffers are used and reused depends on the type of transformations that you use in the solution.

Execution Trees

Interrelated components are clustered in a package to form execution trees. Upon careful examination, you will find that some of these source adapters, transformations, and destination adapters might have no dependencies at all. Other components might have fewer linear dependencies than originally thought. Generally, each source adapter will be assigned a separate thread of execution. Destination adapters and asynchronous transformations will also be assigned separate threads. Multithreaded operations have the advantage of using the computer's processor(s) more efficiently with instructions executed in parallel.

Separate memory buffers enable threads to operate on data independently and in parallel. Use the multicast transform to generate multiple buffers. This is one of the easiest and most efficient ways to allocate additional memory buffers and to cast multiple execution threads to use the server's physical resources efficiently to improve performance.

Synchronous and Asynchronous Processing

The synchronous nature of a transformation refers to its row-processing behavior and whether it must first receive all rows from the input before it is able to process and begin returning rows in its output. A truly synchronous transformation processes a row as it flows through its input, performs the transformation, and immediately outputs the row. Synchronous transformations manipulate data that already exists in a buffer faster than a transformation that must copy records into a new buffer.

An asynchronous transformation must wait for all rows or a group of them before it can perform the transformation. This requires management of data in buffer space and blocks the flow of rows to subsequent components in the data flow pipeline. Some transformations must process only groups of rows (for example, all rows matching a value or having a sorted column value) and might exhibit partially synchronous behavior by releasing a group of processed rows for output after transforming the row group.

Streaming transformations (such as Character Map, Conditional Split, Multicast, and Row Count) are faster because they don't require interaction with an external source. By comparison, row transformations such as Lookup, Audit, OLE DB Command, and Slowly Changing Dimension are slower because they do interact with an external source. Asynchronous transformations typically require data to be copied from one memory buffer to another and can have more or fewer output rows than input rows. Some asynchronous transformations that merge data sets to create a data flow that is dissimilar to the source will be slower to process because the data flow blocks subsequent transformations and copies data from one buffer to another.

Data Blocking

Some transformations need partial or complete sets of data to perform their functions. When data in the pipeline is held up by a transformation operation, it blocks the flow of data to subsequent components downstream. As you know, transformation components that depend on each other are synchronous while those that have no direct dependency are asynchronous. Depending on whether the first transformation must process all or part of the data, to pass the data to the next transformation, it will be either a blocking or partially blocking transformation.

Blocking Transformations

Transformations that require all input rows to be read before they can process the data are blocking transformations. These include:

- Aggregation.
- Sort.

The aggregation transformation must read all records to perform a mathematical algorithm and yield a single calculated value. The sort transformation must read records into a separate buffer in the sorted order, which cannot be completed until the last read has been added to the sort stack. Only after these operations have completed will the results flow down the data pipeline to the next transformations or data sources.

Partially Blocking Transformations

Partially blocking transformations are often used to combine data sets. They tend to have multiple data inputs with a resulting output that might have a greater number, a smaller number, or the same number of records than the total number of input records. The transformation(s) on the receiving end of a partially blocking transaction can work with subsets of the total input stream. Because the number of input records will likely not match the number of output records, these transformations are also called asynchronous transformations. Examples of partially blocking transformation components available in SSIS include the following:

- Merge
- Merge Join
- Pivot
- Unpivot
- Union All

- Term Lookup

- Data Mining Query

With partially blocking transformations, the output of the transformation is copied into a new buffer, and a new thread is introduced into the data flow.

Row Transformations

This category of transformations processes data one row at a time. Row transformations are typically considered to be partially blocking because rows are available to downstream components as soon as they flow from the transformation component.

Row transformations include the following:

- Derived Column

- Data Conversion

- Copy Column

- Character Map

- OLE DB Command

- Script Command

These types of transformations are called row transformations because they process data in the pipeline one row at a time. These are also known as synchronous transformations because rows flow to and from the pipeline without completely blocking downstream components. A row transformation also reuses buffers rather than requiring data to be copied to new buffers that would require more memory and processing. It can add or modify columns but will not add additional rows to the pipeline.

Non-blocking Transformations

Because some transformations need to work with only individual field values for rows in the pipeline, they can transform the data row by row. A transformation with this requirement can begin to process data as it flows to it and will make processed rows available down the pipeline as they are processed, and data can stream through this transformation. This process is synchronous and does not block the next transformation in the pipeline.

These transformations either manipulate data or create new fields. Compared with most other transformations, they are fast and efficient.

- Audit

- Character Map

- Conditional Split

- Copy Column
- Data Conversion
- Derived Column
- Multicast
- Percent Sampling
- Row Count
- Script Task
- Import/Export Column
- SCD
- OLE DB Command

Sources

Transformations are not the only components that can be categorized as synchronous or asynchronous. Data sources are a special type of asynchronous component. Each source component automatically creates two buffers: one for the Success output and one for the Error output.

Buffer Settings

Data buffers are managed at the data flow task object level. These settings can be changed in the properties windows by selecting a data flow task in the package designer. Although it can be said that a buffer can be created to manage a new data flow pipeline, this might in fact create multiple buffers. Each physical buffer holds a defined number of rows. A data flow for a large number of rows will overflow to new buffers when the row count exceeds the maximum number of buffer rows or the buffer size exceeds the defined buffer size property settings, whichever threshold is exceeded first.

Blocking operations, such as a sort transformation, will require buffers to contain the entire row set. Non-blocking operations might require enough buffers to manage the flow to and from the transformation but not require the entire row set to sit in memory at one time.

To optimize large result sets, you might set the buffer's maximum number of rows to accommodate anticipated data volume and to work within the server's memory constraints. Transformations that change row value are applied to one buffer at a time. The following properties can be set or adjusted for each data flow task in a package:

- ***BufferTempStoragePath*** Buffer contents can be saved to temporary storage space in the file system. This setting is used to specify one or more folders for these temporary files.

- *DefaultBufferMaxRows* This is the maximum number of rows for each physical buffer allocation. Results larger than this setting will result in multiple buffers.
- *DefaultBufferSize* This setting is for the size of each buffer in the data flow, in bytes. Any value for this property should be divisible by 1,024 and is typically divided evenly into kilobytes (x 1,024) or megabytes (x 1,048,576). The default setting is 10,485,760 or 10 megabytes.

Managing Parallelism

Although the characteristics of package task and data flow transformation execution management are slightly different, each can be either serialized or asynchronous. Synchronous tasks use fewer system resources but might also take longer to process. Any task or data flow transformation can potentially spawn a separate execution thread. The maximum number of concurrent execution threads is controlled at the package level, using the *MaxConcurrentExecutables* property.

The default value of this property is set to -1. A property setting at this value causes the maximum number of executions to be two plus the number of processor cores in the computer. Set this to a different number to reduce or exceed the default. If SSIS runs on a dedicated server and you have a lot of operations that run in parallel, you will likely want to increase this setting if some of the operations do a lot of throttling or waiting for external systems to reply. Alternatively, if you do not have a dedicated SSIS machine and your data integration application runs alongside several other applications, you might need to reduce this setting to avoid resource conflicts.

As you design packages for parallelism, you will need to decide whether to run some or all of the operations in the package in parallel. As with buffer-sizing decisions, decisions about parallelism are best made when you take into account available system resources on your production server.

Data Source Tuning

Relational data sources, whether SQL Server or any other database product, rely on server optimization for peak performance. There are several SSIS features that make this process as efficient as possible, but there is only so much you can do within Integration Services to make queries run as fast as possible. Apply standard database optimization techniques, which might include:

- Designing tables with indexes to support sorting and query joins.
- Creating database objects such as views, stored procedures, and user-defined functions to encapsulate complex queries.

- Minimizing the use of multi-table joins, outer joins, unions, and subqueries where possible.

- Saving index statistics and execute queries ahead of time to cache execution plans.

- Using nondefault locking options to optimize queries when concurrent user access isn't required.

Performance Management

The secret to good performance is often simplicity of design. Extract, transform, and load (ETL) packages are notorious for being convoluted and unnecessarily complicated. Often, as additional requirements crop up during design, it's common simply to add steps that can eventually lead to an overly complicated package that can be difficult to manage and maintain. Before you know it, your package reads from and writes to several staging tables and performs several different and independent transformations. Adhering to the throw-away-your-first-attempt design principle, make a point to review the end-to-end process and look for opportunities to streamline and simplify. It might be necessary to build and test the package more than once to fully understand the processes required to achieve the end goal. Most often, after careful review, you will find better and simpler methods to consolidate the data flow, transformations, and branching logic. Avoid over-design. Not only are too many moving parts difficult to maintain, but more steps often lead to using more buffer space and a slower overall process.

One of the most common trade-off decisions you will need to make is whether to make extensive use of various SSIS transformations or to use a single Transact-SQL statement. Within a single data flow, the difference in performance between these choices might be negligible. However, using tasks, loops, and containers to manage operations that can be performed in a single query will usually be considerably slower. Like using row-by-row cursor operations in a SQL stored procedure, loop containers that initiate a nested data flow can be dreadfully slow, especially when looping through a large number of rows. Consider that each iteration of a data-driven loop requires a separate data source connection, query execution, buffer allocation, and data flow destination to be written and finalized. If it's possible to perform these operations in a single query execution at the data source, SSIS will have far less work to do.

When you truly need to loop through a set of records, the trick is to get the rows of the result set into the workflow to enumerate over those rows and do meaningful work. For example, the meaningful work might be to execute a script task that sends e-mail messages to a large group of recipients. Applications for this integration, however, are limitless. Any time you need to execute a section of work flow per row of a result, this method provides a way.

Here are some examples:

- Sending out e-mail notifications to clients when it's time to renew subscriptions

- Executing subpackages that have been queued up through a management console that stores resulting queue requests in tables

- Processing employee edge events such as birthdays, children turning 18, option expirations, and so on as described in human-resources databases

- Customer relationship management (CRM) stale dates, reminding sales people to contact customers who haven't been contacted within a certain number of weeks

- Processing sales logs to find potential fraud, bad checks, or stolen credit cards

The trick is to get the value of the columns of each row into a form that can be used inside the package. For Integration Services, the way to do that is to change the column values into variables. To do this, you need to take the recordset returned from the SQL task and somehow iterate over it. *ForEachADOEnumerator* was created for just that purpose.

Loops

Although creating a loop seems like a natural approach for many scenarios, it can be very slow and inefficient. Loops are much slower to process than SQL queries, yet they can be more flexible and capable. Even SQL cursor operations can prove to be faster yet might not afford the same opportunity to process business logic and interact with other components. As a rule, keep loops simple and keep the number of iterations as small as possible.

When developing packages, it's important to note that SQL Server Business Intelligence Development Studio (BIDS) runs as a client-side tool. Unlike a package running on the server, data must be pulled to the development machine to be processed. To understand effectively the effects of running a process in a loop, you must first isolate the inefficiencies of the development environment. After this, you can deal with the loop itself. After debugging the package, deploy and test it on the server.

To debug problems with a loop container, it is necessary to isolate the loop from the task running within the loop. To do this, design, test, and optimize the tasks as a single process. Next, create the loop and optimize it to run with nothing in the container or disable the contained tasks. Using this method, it might be possible to eliminate efficiency issues that would otherwise be difficult to track down. The most effective way to isolate a set of tasks from a loop container is to build a separate package and then use an execute package task within the loop.

Because a loop executes multiple instances of a control flow, deepening on the contained tasks, each execution can spawn separate threads. Data flow tasks in the loop can also create multiple connections and buffers, which might, in turn, slow the process significantly. Use SQL Server Profiler and Windows System Monitor to watch these counters under production conditions to get a better idea about the resources a looping process will consume. If you need to loop through records, remember that connecting to data sources in a loop will be very slow. Try reading data into an ActiveX Data Object (ADO) and then looping through the cached data.

Loops introduce more variable conditions than most other package design elements. Understanding the mechanics of the control flow and data flow engines will help, but without a complete understanding of all these elements, sometimes trial and error is the only effective design method. Don't be afraid to experiment; there are many ways to solve a problem.

Flat File Sources

Loading data from text files can be fast because data is stored in an uncomplicated format. Processing the data can be slow because values must be converted from text to specific data types. *FastParse*, a feature of the Flat File Source component, can be used to improve processing performance significantly if values such as dates and currencies are stored in common formats. If this is the case, you can enable the *FastParse* property for those columns that the parsing routine understands. The property is buried a bit in the designer user interface.

After a flat file connection manager has been created, an associated Flat File Data Source adapter can be configured to support this capability. To do this, right-click the adapter and select *Show Advanced Editor*. In the Advanced Editor For Flat File Source dialog box, you would choose the Input and Output Properties tab. On the left side, a tree view list is displayed under Inputs And Outputs. Expand the *Flat File Source Output* node and view the *Output Columns* node. An item is displayed for each of the columns returned by the data source. For each column, you can set properties, using a properties sheet grid displayed on the right side of this tab page in the dialog box window.

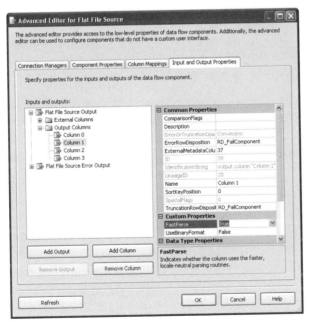

For the columns that are supported, change the *FastParse* property to *True*. SQL Server Books Online contains an extensive list of data types and format string values that are supported. It doesn't perform locale-specific parsing, nor does it recognize special characters in currency data, and it can't convert hexadecimal or scientific notation of numeric values.

Filters and Variables

Filtering data at the source is one of the simplest and most effective ways to optimize package execution. In addition to including only necessary columns in the query explicitly, the query should also exclude unwanted rows. Always filter your data in the Source Adapter rather than filtering it with a Conditional Split transformation component. If your requirements call for transforming multiple pipelines of unique records from a single data source into conditional branches, filter the data at the source first to satisfy all of the branching requirements rather than tossing out unqualified records in a Conditional Split transformation. Suppose a source table contains 500,000 rows, and your package is designed to transform 200,000 of these rows into three separate destinations, using three sets of unique criteria. Allowing 300,000 rows to flow through the package only to be blocked by a Conditional Split transformation would be wasteful. It would make more sense to use a SQL query in the Data Source Adapter with the same filtering criteria as the combined three branches of the Conditional Split transformation. In this example, the WHERE clause of the query might contain three corresponding condition statements separated by using OR logic. It might actually be faster to have three separate Data Source adapters reading from the same table, each using a different SQL query, than to use the Conditional Split transformation at all. If a filtering condition relies on string parsing or pattern matching, Conditional Split would likely be the faster method as opposed to filtering on simple indexed values, where SQL should be more effective. The only way to know for sure is to try both techniques.

Variables provide a way to set values dynamically and control processes in packages, containers, tasks, and event handlers. Variables can also be used by precedence constraints to control the direction of the flow of data to different tasks.

Each container has its own *Variables* collection. When a new variable is created, it is within the scope of its parent container. Because the package container is at the top of the container hierarchy, variables with package scope function like global variables and are visible to all containers within the package. The collection of variables for the container can also be accessed by the children of the container through the *Variables* collection.

Variable scope can affect thread dependency and the memory required to manage object variables and arrays. For this reason, and for manageability, variables should be scoped to the containers in which they are used. Remember that you cannot re-scope a variable once it has been created. To change the scope, the variable must be deleted and then re-created. Because the visibility of a variable is scoped from the top down, variables declared at the package level are visible to all the containers in the package. Therefore, the *Variables* collection in a container includes all the variables that belong to its parent in addition to its own variables. Conversely, the variables contained in a task are limited in scope and visibility and are visible only to the task.

If a package runs other packages, the variables defined in the scope of the calling package are available to the called package. The only exception occurs when a same-named variable exists in the called package. When this collision occurs, the variable value in the called package overrides the value from the calling package. Variables defined in the scope of the called package are never available back to the calling package.

Data Destination Management

As a rule, a package should run as close to the data as possible. A package running on any computer other than the data source or destination is a data client and will move data across a network connection to be processed. This doesn't necessarily mean that all of your packages should be run on the corporate production database servers, but the server hosting SSIS packages should at least have fast network access. A separate subnet from the user community for interserver traffic is typically a good design principle.

The OLE DB provider for SQL Server has a *FastLoad* option that can optimize large insert operations, much like a bulk-load type of insert. To enable this feature, set the *AccessMode* advanced property of the connection manager to *OpenRowset Using Fastload*.

Applying some universal database optimization techniques can help you get the most out of your interaction with SQL Server. Consider the following.

Locking Modes

The default locking mode for inserts takes into account other users who might be working with table data. Because concurrent database access is often not an important factor when transforming data, applying a nondefault table lock when records are inserted can speed things up because the database engine denies concurrent access to the entire table during the insert operation and doesn't have to manage slower row- or page-level locks on the table.

Drop or Disable Indexes

Inserting records into a table that has no indexes or into one in which its existing indexes are disabled can be considerably faster than tables with indexes. A common optimization technique is to drop or disable existing indexes and then to either re-create them or rebuild them. Disabled indexes must be rebuilt to bring them back online. Keep in mind that this applies only to nonclustered indexes. Disabling a clustered index takes the table offline. Index management can be performed in the package by using an Execute SQL task or by calling a maintenance stored procedure on the database server. Although the overall processing time (including index rebuilds) can be longer, using this technique might allow you to complete the package processing faster or to perform other operations while the indexes are being regenerated by the database server.

Use Explicit Transactions

You usually think of transaction processing in a relational database environment as necessary overhead that can threaten performance, but under some conditions, transactions can actually speed things up. When records are inserted (and updated or deleted), new data is written to the database transaction log and then rolled forward into the actual database files in a background process called a *checkpoint*. When multiple data operations are performed, each operation is wrapped in an implicit transaction and must be rolled forward individually. When using a single explicit transaction for multiple data operations, all of the data is written to the transaction log before rolling the rows forward into the database files. By applying these operations in one big explicit transaction, the roll-forward process can complete all at once and in the background after your SSIS package has completed its work.

Performance-Tuning Exercises

The following exercises show how to use optimization options in an SSIS package. The Chap11.sln solution contains five packages that show you different configurations and design options to increment speed when you execute an SSIS package.

The following chart can be used to record the test results for the exercises that follow. If you prefer not to write in your book, a Microsoft Office Excel document named *Chapter 11 Exercise.xls* is provided in the Chap11 project folder to record the execution for each package, according to the following instructions:

Package	Test Criteria	Execution Time
Package 0	Test baseline with default buffer settings and OLE DB destination	
Package 1	Default buffer settings and SQL Server destination	
Package 2	SQL Server destination with elevated buffer settings	
Package 3	Single data flow task with Multicast, Sort, and Union All transformations	
Package 4	Two data flow tasks	

Create a destination table

1. Open Microsoft SQL Server Management Studio and connect to the local database server. Copy the text from this file onto the clipboard, paste it into the SSIS Query window, and use the Execute button on the toolbar.

2. Open a New Query and execute the next script to create the [OLE DB Destination - Test] table. You can find this script in C:\Documents and Settings\\<username>\My Documents\Microsoft Press\is2005sbs\Chap11\Data\ Create OLE DB Destination - Test table.txt.

```
USE is2005sbs
GO
SET ANSI_NULLS ON
GO
SET QUOTED_IDENTIFIER ON
GO
```

```
CREATE TABLE dbo.[OLE DB Destination - Test](
    rowguid uniqueidentifier NULL,
    Name nvarchar(50) NULL,
    CurrencyCode nvarchar(3) NULL,
    CurrencyRateID int NULL,
    CurrencyRateDate datetime NULL,
    FromCurrencyCode nvarchar(3) NULL,
    AverageRate float NULL,
    ToCurrencyCode nvarchar(3) NULL,
    EndOfDayRate float NULL,
    ModifiedDate datetime NULL,
    Expr1 datetime NULL,
    Expr2 uniqueidentifier NULL
) ON PRIMARY
```

Working with Buffer Properties

The first package, Package 0.dtsx, under the Chap11.sln solution shows a simple Data Flow transformation with an SSIS default setting for *DefaultBufferMaxRows* (10,000 rows) and *DefaultBufferSize* (10,485,760 bytes) options in a data flow.

Test execution performance

1. Use Windows Explorer to navigate to the Chapter 11exercise solution folder located at C:\Documents and Settings\<username>\My Documents\Microsoft Press\is2005sbs \Chap11 and open the Chap11.sln solution.

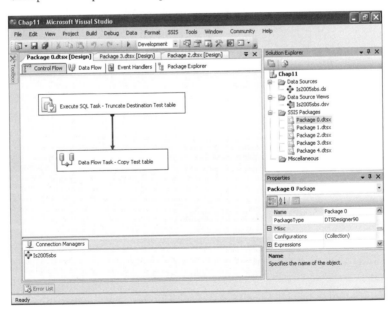

2. Double-click Package 0.dtsx.

3. Right-click Data Flow Task – Copy Test table, click Properties, and then check the values for *DefaultBufferMaxRows* and *DefaultBufferSize* in the properties pane.

4. Right-click Package 0.dtsx and click Execute Package. At the end of the execution, check the *Progress* tab and see the very last line: Finished-.

   It gives you the processing time in seconds (for example, 27.640 seconds). Record this value. Note that the execution time in your development environment will vary based on several factors.

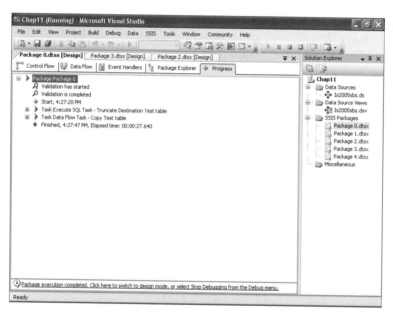

5. On the Debug menu, click Stop Debugging.

Working with a SQL Server Destination

Using an OLE DB data adapter is generally the best option for a package that will run on a separate server than the database (either now or later when the solution is scaled out). However, this flexibility comes at a cost. The SQL Server adapter is optimized to run on the same server as the destination database with improved performance. A SQL Server destination might be the best option if you want to write the result of a data flow to a SQL Server database.

Use a SQL Server connection manager

1. Double-click Package 1.dtsx.

2. On the Control Flow tab, double-click Data Flow Task – Copy Test table in Package 1.dtsx.

   The destination is now a *SQL Server Destination component.* Values for Rows and Buffer-Size are the same as in package 0 (SSIS by default).

3. Execute the package and check its execution time as in the previous package (for example, 21.100 seconds). Record this value and note the difference from the previous trial.

> **Note**   When developing the exercise, this package ran about 25 percent faster than the previous package. Your results might vary, depending on variables in your system configuration.

4. On the Debug menu, click Stop Debugging.

Test *DefaultBufferMaxRows* and *DefaultBufferSize*

1. Double-click Package 2.dtsx.

2. On the Control Flow tab, double-click Data Flow Task – Copy Test table in Package 2.dtsx.

3. In the Properties pane, change *DefaultBufferMaxRows* to **100000** and *DefaultBufferSize* to **30485760** (30 MB). Type only the numbers into the property fields (without commas).

> **Note**   The OLE DB Source component allocates a number of rows close to 100,000 into a buffer, for example, 99,942 rows. It is based on the metadata that SSIS collects about your source data at design time.

4. Execute the package and check execution time (for example, 18.526 seconds). Record this value. Note that the Log Events window is open on the left side of your screen.

> **Note**   If the Log Events window isn't visible by default, you can open it from the View menu by clicking Other Windows and then Log Events.

5. Check the Message column in that Log Events window. It gives you information about the package execution.

6. On the Debug menu, click Stop Debugging.

Design Considerations

The next two packages show you two different designs performing the same functionality but with different execution results.

> **Note** Verify that for Package 3.dtsx and Package 4.dtsx:
>
> BufferMaxRows = 1,000 and BufferSize = 1,048,576. This change in these properties forces SSIS to **auto-optimize** buffer size.

Test a package with blocking transformations

1. Double-click Package 3.dtsx in Solution Explorer to open the package designer.

2. In the Control Flow tab, double-click Data Flow Task – Copy Test table in Package 3.dtsx.

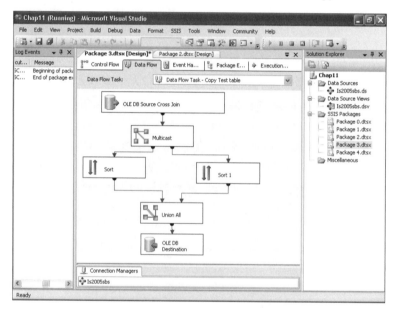

At first glance, it seems to be a parallel package.

> **Note** Remember that a Sort transformation is a blocking transformation, and Union All is a partially blocking transformation.

3. Execute the package.

This might take several minutes to run. While it is executing, switch to the Data Flow tab and watch the row counters.

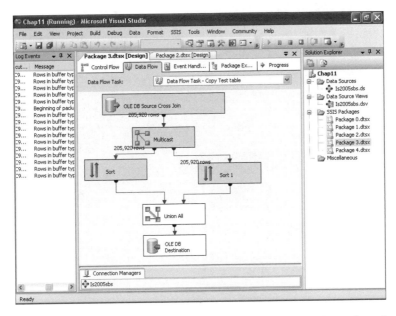

At the beginning, it runs in parallel. The left-side and the right-side output from the Multicast run at the same time. The data flow is blocked until the last record is read from the source because of the Sort transformation.

When both Sort transformations finish reading from the source, only the left side of the data flow runs.

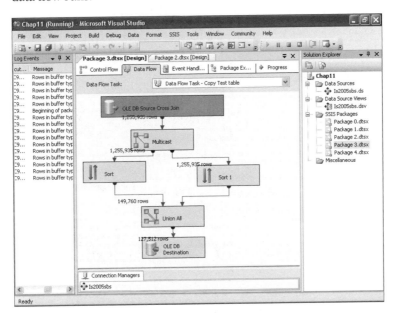

Note the Message column in the Log Events window. SSIS creates new buffers to execute this data flow. After the left-side pipeline finishes writing to the destination, the right side starts loading data to the destination.

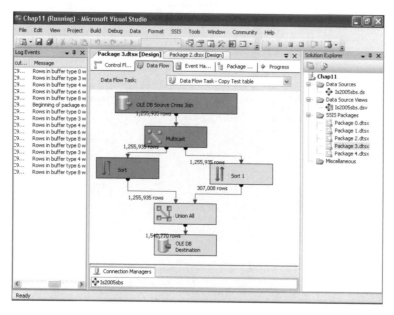

It is apparent that this design is not very efficient.

4. On the Debug menu, click Stop Debugging. Observe the control flow design.

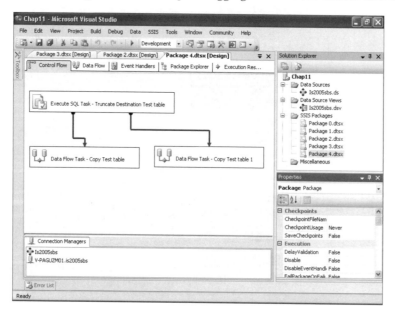

Now you have two data flow components almost identical to each other, one for the left Sort and another one for the right Sort of the data flow in package 3. You would probably think that the processing time for the package would have a direct correlation to the value of data flowing through the package. However, this design runs faster than the previous one. It is a parallel design and a parallel execution.

5. Click the Control Flow tab, and then execute Package 4.dtsx.

6. Note that now the package is executing in parallel. Check both data flows, and you can see how data flows at about the same time in both of the data flow tasks.

7. Monitor the row counts and make note of the time when the package execution completes.

8. On the Debug menu, click Stop Debugging.

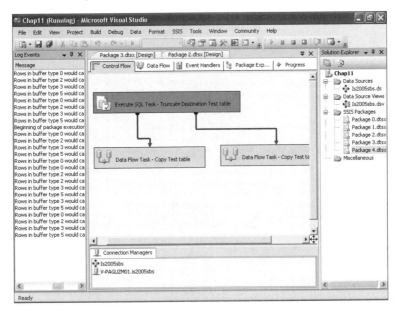

You can check the processing time on the Progress tab and compare it against the previous one in package 3. During the test when designing the exercise, it was at least half of the execution time.

Performance Management

The essence of SSIS performance management is in understanding the mechanics of the processing engine and then making adjustments in the package design to work with these mechanisms. Package design is usually an iterative process that requires several design cycles to discover inefficiencies and to make appropriate design changes. Using the debugging and logging tools, you will learn to work through this process effectively and hone packages into their most simple and efficient form. The following principles define the core components of effective performance management:

- Identifying execution trees
- Reading and understanding execution plans
- Optimization through iterative design
- Effective use of execution parallelism
- Maximizing CPU use
- Performance monitoring
- Using SSIS log reports

Execution Trees

When a data flow begins from a data source and each time the data flow is split into a separate branch, this creates a new execution tree. An *execution tree* can be defined as a segment of a data flow, ending in an asynchronous output. The number of execution threads created for a running package is generally calculated by using the following formula:

Number of threads = Number of sources + Execution trees

Multiple execution trees can be either advantageous or detrimental. Because each execution tree generally creates new buffers and can spawn a new execution thread, this might result in faster, parallel processing at the possible expense of more system resources. Regardless, this is an important system-monitoring metric. To get an accurate log of the execution trees for a package or container, enable the *PipelineExecutionTrees* log event, and then create an event handler, using the techniques you learned in Chapter 9, "Detecting and Handling Processing Errors."

Execution trees demonstrate how your package uses buffers and threads. At run time, the Data Pipeline engine breaks down data flow task operations into execution trees. These execution trees specify how buffers and threads are allocated in the package. Each tree creates a new buffer and thread. When a new buffer is created, additional memory is required to handle the data transformation; however, it is important to note that each new tree also gives you an additional worker thread.

Note that you can display execution trees for your own packages by turning on package logging, enabling logging for the data flow task, and then selecting the *PipelineExecutionTree* event. You will not see the execution tree until you execute the package. It will display in the Log Events window within BIDS.

Execution Plans

Much like the way the SQL Server database engine prepares a query execution plan before each query runs, Integration Services uses a similar approach for package execution. When a package is first executed, an execution plan is generated for each data flow and cached, to be compiled and used internally to optimize run-time execution against SQL Server database objects. The execution plan is a set of lower-level database engine instructions translated from the settings of the data adapters and transformations in a data flow task. It's a form of pseudocode that is translated further into machine-specific instruction code by the Microsoft.NET Framework common language runtime (CLR). In subsequent executions, the compiled execution plan performs the same operations without the added overhead of retranslating the data flow components into instructions. Likewise, data source adapters that execute Transact-SQL statements, stored procedures, or user-defined functions in a SQL Server database benefit from the stored execution plans associated with these objects.

An execution plan provides further insight into which the data flow execution engine operations are to be performed for a given data flow task. Details are provided on individual threads and operation codes. Source threads are generated for data sources; worker threads are created for transformations and all other work. Set the *EngineThreads* property of the data flow task to the number of source threads plus the number of execution trees to ensure that the execution engine has enough threads available to use for optimal processing.

To view an SSIS execution plan, add logging to the package or container and then add the *PipelineExecutionPlan* event for any data flow task you wish to log. The following example is the execution plan logged for a package you will use in a later exercise. Note the metadata for each execution thread and the commands to initiate each component. A SourceThread is created for each data source, and WorkThreads are created for each execution tree in the data flow. Listener objects are defined to coordinate the operations, and buffers are created and managed for each thread. You can see how each transformation is initiated by using various Call commands.

```
SourceThread0
    Drives: 1
    Influences: 5751 5829 6020 6079
    Output Work List
        CreatePrimeBuffer of type 1 for output ID 11.
        SetBufferListener: "WorkThread0" for input ID 5752
        CreatePrimeBuffer of type 3 for output ID 12.
        CallPrimeOutput on component "OLE DB Source Cross Join" (1)
    End Output Work List
End SourceThread0
WorkThread0
    Drives: 5751
    Influences: 5751 5829 6020 6079
    Input Work list, input ID 5752 (1 EORs Expected)
        CallProcessInput on input ID 5752 on component "Multicast" (5751)
            for view type 0
        CallProcessInput on input ID 6080 on component "Sort 1" (6079)
```

```
              for view type 2
      End Input Work list for input 5752
      Output Work List
         CreatePrimeBuffer of type 6 for output ID 6081.
         SetBufferListener: "WorkThread1" for input ID 5895
         CallPrimeOutput on component "Sort 1" (6079)
      End Output Work List
   End WorkThread0
   WorkThread1
      Drives: 5829
      Influences: 5829 6020
      Input Work list, input ID 5895 (1 EORs Expected)
         CallProcessInput on input ID 5895 on component "Union All" (5829)
            for view type 7
      End Input Work list for input 5895
      Output Work List
         CreatePrimeBuffer of type 4 for output ID 5831.
         SetBufferListener: "WorkThread2" for input ID 6033
         CallPrimeOutput on component "Union All" (5829)
      End Output Work List
   End WorkThread1
   WorkThread2
      Drives: 6020
      Influences: 6020
      Input Work list, input ID 6033 (1 EORs Expected)
         CallProcessInput on input ID 6033 on component "OLE DB Destination"
            (6020) for view type 5
      End Input Work list for input 6033
      Output Work List
      End Output Work List
   End WorkThread2
```

A comparison of different prototype packages can help you find inefficiencies in the execution plan. This execution plan created four threads: one SourceThread and three WorkThreads. It also created four buffers.

As a matter of practice, you should also use the SQL Server Profiler to view the behavior of these execution plans on the database server. Evidence of an efficient execution plan will include data selection from pre-existing clustered and nonclustered indexes and efficient join and merge operations using presorted records. Less-efficient operations use operations such as table scans and sorting without the aid of a supporting index.

For SQL queries used in the package, use the Show Execution Plan feature in SQL Server Management Studio. For each operation (whether a read, write, sort, compare, group, join, merge, union, aggregation, or calculation, for example), the database engine will consider different physical operations to process these tasks by using prepared database objects such as tables and indexes. It will use statistics stored with a table or index, which describe characteristics of column values (such as uniqueness, density, and selectivity) to make these choices. For each operation, the plan will estimate the cost of physical disk input/output (I/O), memory, CPU time, and number of rows necessary to process.

Understanding how to use and analyze execution plans is a crucial element of database design and programming; however, the details of this topic are beyond the scope of this book. For more information, read the following topics in SQL Server Books Online:

- "Displaying Graphical Execution Plans" *http://msdn2.microsoft.com/en-us/library /ms178071.aspx*

- "Displaying Execution Plans by Using SQL Server Profiler Event Classes" *http:// msdn2.microsoft.com/en-us/library/ms190233.aspx*

Iterative Design Optimization

At design time, it's very common to define execution trees to match requirements and the designer's thought process. Upon careful review, you can identify unnecessary branches and steps to reduce complexity and improve performance.

The following example shows a data flow with a separate execution tree for erroneous records. Keep in mind that an error can be defined simply as a value that doesn't meet certain criteria. The 10 million rows flowing through the Lookup Error Output pipeline don't meet the same criteria as the 40 million rows flowing through the main pipeline and are corrected by an expression in the Derived Column transformation. These rows flow down the error pipeline and are then joined back to the main pipeline in the Union All transformation. As you see, this data flow task takes 95 seconds to complete.

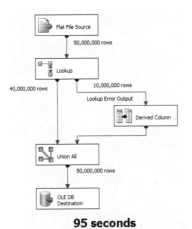

95 seconds

This all seems fine, but it isn't as efficient as it could be. Branching nonqualifying rows to a separate component for correction seems to make logical sense. However, a separate execution tree requires a separate thread and buffers to manage the data. Because the Derived Column transformation can be used to apply conditional logic to rows matching or not matching any criteria, the separate branch wasn't necessary. The next example shows the same package data flow with no error output from the Lookup transformation. As you see, all rows flow through one pipeline. The 10 million rows that were branched off in the previous example are handled in a conditional expression in the Derived Column transformation, and the other 40 million rows simply flow through, unaffected.

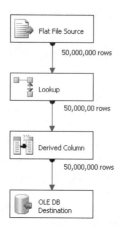

72 seconds

Package redesign can eliminate unnecessary thread and buffers allocation. As a result, it saves memory, disk I/O, and CPU usage. In the preceding example, this step resulted in a 25 percent performance optimization. Imagine how similar efforts could affect the performance of very complex packages with multiple opportunities to save time, effort, and ongoing maintenance costs.

Efficient package design is an iterative process. Be willing to forgo previous thinking to explore alternative solutions.

Logging an Execution Plan

In this exercise, you will view logging options and add an event handler to capture a pipeline execution plan. This package has already been configured for logging. You will review these properties to see where you would make changes in a new package.

View logging options and add an event handler

1. With Package 4.dtsx open in the package designer, view the Properties pane for the package. View the *LoggingMode* property and verify that it is set to *Enabled*.

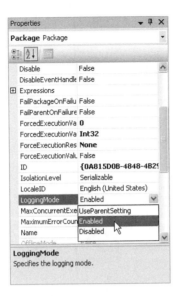

2. Right-click over any white space in the package and select *Logging* from the menu. This opens the Configure SSIS Logs dialog box for the package.

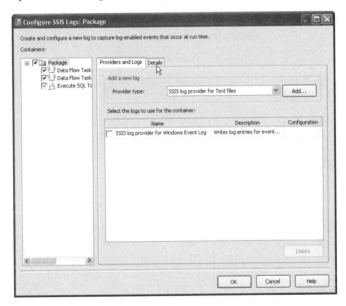

3. Note that a text file log was previously added for this package.

4. Using the object list tree view in the Containers pane of this dialog box, select the first data flow task, and then select the Details tab on the right. A list of events supported by the data flow appears in a check box list.

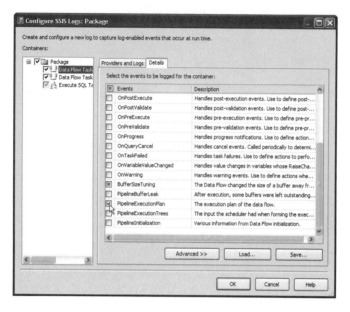

5. Scroll down this list and select the *PipelineExecutionPlan* event.

6. Click the OK button to save changes and close this dialog box.

7. Execute the package and allow it to finish. Stop debugging when execution has completed.

8. The Log Events window is shown on the left side of the package designer. Use this window to find the event named *User::PipelineExecutionPlan*. Double-click this line to open the Log Entry dialog box.

9. View the Message text to review details for the data flow task execution plan recorded in this log event.

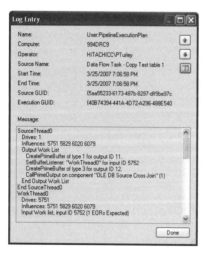

10. Click the Done button to close this dialog box after you have finished reviewing the log event details.

SSIS Log Reports

An effective tool for monitoring the Integration Services logs is a set of Reporting Services reports called the SQL Server Integration Services Log Provider reports. To locate this report pack for download, go to Integration Services Downloads (*http://msdn2.microsoft.com/en-us /sql/aa336314.aspx*) and search for an article titled "Sample SSIS Log Reports using SQL Reporting Services." These reports pull information from the SSIS execution logs and can help you discover useful metadata about deployed SSIS packages such as execution time and error information. Reviewing these reports routinely might be a valuable tool to spot inefficiencies and opportunities for performance tuning.

Chapter 11 Quick Reference

To	Do This
Set *FastParse* on a flat file source	Right-click the Flat File Source adapter and choose Show Advanced Editor. Use the Input and Output Properties tab to set properties for each of the compatible Output Columns.
Enable FastLoad for an OLE DB destination	Open the connection manager properties and select the Advanced properties page. Set the *AccessMode* property to *OpenRowset Using Fastload*.
Change *DefaultBufferMaxRows* and *DefaultBufferSize*	In the Control Flow pane, select a data flow that you want to set. Right-click and click Properties to open the Properties pane. In the Misc category, change *DefaultBufferMaxRows* and *DefaultBufferSize*.
Add a log event to BufferSize Tuning	Select a package you want to log. Go to the SSIS menu in Visual Studio. Select Logging and add a new log as SSIS log provider for Windows Event Log. Select the new log you create, and then choose the package and data flow you want to log. On the Details tab, in the right window, select BufferSize Tuning. Click OK. On the View menu of Visual Studio, select Event Logs under Other Windows.

Part IV
Applying SSIS to Data Warehousing

Chapter 12
Data Warehouse Concepts

After completing this chapter, you will be able to:

- Learn the objectives and characteristics of a functional data warehouse.

- Learn the goals of a business intelligence solution.

- Distinguish the differences between operational and decision support systems.

- Understand the role of data granularity in data warehouse design.

- Define facts, aggregations, and dimensions.

- Discuss proper assessment of data quality, update frequency, and persistence.

- Review ETL architecture options.

Microsoft SQL Server Integration Services (SSIS) will support many different types of database solutions. You might find SSIS useful to import spreadsheet data into your customer management system or to combine invoice records into a central billing system. However, the most common, complete business solution involving significant data transformation is a decision-support data warehouse for reporting and data analysis. As businesses grow and need to analyze and report on more data, a data warehouse becomes necessary to house the increasing volume of data derived from different operational sources. Unlike the occasional need to import and combine data from spreadsheets and other source files, extracting, transforming, and loading data from operational databases into a central data warehouse is a routine business process that must be optimized and performed on a regular schedule.

Data Warehouse Objectives

A *data warehouse* or *data mart*, depending on its size and scope, is a collection of important business data, usually obtained from different sources. For the purposes of this chapter, these terms will refer collectively to any type of decision-support database as a data warehouse.

Raw data or operational transaction data represent the raw material for the information required and desired for a business intelligence solution. Operational data has many characteristics that make it a poor option for direct access within a business intelligence solution architecture. Some of these characteristics include:

- Volatile, changing data values.

- Data that is not maintained for historical reporting.

- Data that is stored only at the detail level, requiring all grouping and aggregation to be performed in live queries.

- Multiple business operational systems not integrated and that must be correlated to expose visibility of the complete business context.

- Proprietary data formats that might be difficult to navigate and access.

These are the primary reasons it is necessary to extract and transform the raw data to be managed into data warehouses. SQL Server 2005 Integration Services provides the ability to extract, transform, and load (ETL) as well as maintain data warehouses. The first consideration of business intelligence (BI) implementation will require access to or creation of a data warehouse that contains the data transformed into BI formats and structures.

One of the most significant differences between a data warehouse and an operational database is that, in a data warehouse, the data isn't perpetually changing. A data warehouse is a read-only copy of integrated operational data. Unlike a transactional or operational system that might be in a state of flux from time to time, the data warehouse is consistent and reliable. If you were to run a report against the live operational invoicing system, you might be reading newly added account changes before credits or adjustments have been applied. If your timing is just right, you might also report on data in the middle of a maintenance routine. Perhaps a group of records has been deleted before correcting records have been inserted or after duplicate records have been added before an operation is completed. Given all of the day-to-day operations in a large business, there is a very good chance that something somewhere in the database will be out of balance.

Operational systems are also big and complicated. To maintain transactional consistency, it is necessary to store records in several different tables related through primary and foreign key relationships. To query even the most simple business information requires several table join operations. These complex queries can be slow and difficult to design and debug. By contrast, a data warehouse structure is simplified and doesn't typically store the same level of detail, which would otherwise be unnecessary for analytical reporting.

Data Warehouse Characteristics

A data warehouse is usually the core component of a BI infrastructure for today's corporations. This chapter will not go into the details of building and maintaining a data warehouse. It is important, however, to look at the characteristics and design considerations that are crucial to BI infrastructure solutions.

The entity-relation diagram, shown in Figure 12-1, illustrates some fundamental characteristics of modern-day data warehouses. Note that the table names are prefixed with Fact and Dim to denote either a business fact or a dimension table.

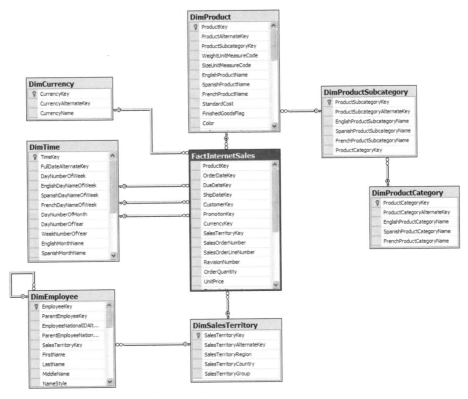

Figure 12-1   Data warehouse database diagram

A data warehouse is implemented as a relational database model and can have different design variations to meet specific business needs. It's not unusual for a data warehouse to store more data than the source systems that feed it. Data cleansing, standardization, and derivation can add to the data volume. Many data warehouses are designed to maintain more historic data than traditional online transaction processing (OLTP) systems. How much *historic data* is required for comparison and trend analysis? Perhaps tens of millions of rows. Even though the data volume might be extremely large, the database model is designed for fast access for reporting.

Data warehouses, if designed and maintained appropriately, provide the most accurate and reliable data for effective reporting and BI solution support. Although the specific purpose and objectives can vary a bit by business need, in general, each data warehouse exhibits the following characteristics.

Providing Data for Business Analysis Processes

A data warehouse is designed for business data reporting. Analytical tools such as key performance indicator (KPI) dashboards, business scorecards, pre-defined reports, and ad hoc reporting systems will read data from either a relational data warehouse or online analytical processing (OLAP) cubes, which in turn aggregate data in the relational data warehouse. SQL Server Analysis Services provides a platform to define multidimensional cubes and pre-defined aggregations. OLAP structures are easy to navigate; queries run with optimal performance and support complex calculations that would otherwise be slow and difficult to perform.

Integrating Data from Heterogeneous Source Systems

Reading data from multiple sources can be difficult and inefficient from a client reporting tool. Not only can this be inefficient from a purely technical perspective, but one of the challenges when combining data from different systems is that the records rarely match up. Data entities from various data sources often have slightly different forms and meanings. For example, the customer records in a company's online shopping system can also contain company employees. The customer records in the customer relationship management (CRM) system might not contain employees but can be commingled with sales leads—contacts that have not yet purchased products. From an enterprise perspective, this raises questions about the definition of a business entity as simple as that of a customer. For example, is an employee a customer if he or she buys a product? Is someone a customer if he or she has expressed an interest but has not made a purchase? Is that person *your* customer if he or she has purchased a product through a vendor? Is a company a customer, or must a customer be a person? And, if a customer is a person (by your definition of the term), who from the purchasing company *is* the customer: the initial contact, the CEO, the administrative assistant who placed the order, or the financial controller who wrote the check? As you can see, there can be many questions, and the answer might be different for the users of different internal systems, all of which deal with customers in a slightly different way. You get the idea. When designing databases and data warehouse systems, similar conversations arise about dozens of different entities.

Combining Validated Source Data

A truly functional data warehouse contains a single location where all of the data, gathered from different sources, has been standardized, cleansed, and validated. A common problem plaguing most businesses is that important business facts are often captured in spreadsheets and small, department-specific databases. Effectively collecting this data is not a trivial feat, yet it can have tremendous business value. Unless data is generated within a unified business application, combining and validating records can also be challenging. Much of this process can be automated but will often require some manual intervention. Business rules must be established to define the criteria for exact matching of duplicate records. Perhaps the combination of first name, last name, and phone number is a reliable indicator that an imported record already exists. But it's the slight misspellings and abbreviations that can be challenging. This is where SSIS transformations such as Fuzzy Lookup can be helpful to populate a list of candidate matches to be reviewed and validated by hand.

Organizing Data into Nonvolatile, Subject-Specific Groups

One common technique for optimizing reporting solutions is to reduce the volume of data in the decision-support database. However, this might not be so simple. To provide the flexibility and detail necessary to satisfy all of the reporting requirements, a decision-support database can actually end up with more volume than some source systems.

One of the important objectives of traditional normalized database design is to reduce data volume size by eliminating redundancy. This is often at the cost of using several related tables to store business facts. In a data warehouse, to reduce complexity and eliminate multiple table joins, redundant records and values might be necessary. Unlike a normalized, transactional database, which might use only one table to manage transaction records, a data warehouse can have details divided into separate fact tables. Several supporting dimension tables surround each fact table to form a star or snowflake schema. A typical data warehouse might be divided into multiple clusters of related fact and dimension tables.

Storing Data in Structures Optimized for Extraction and Queries

Rather than organizing data into many tables with complex relationships, a data warehouse is organized into simple clusters of fact and dimension tables. Reporting data structures are optimized for speed of retrieval rather than to enforce data integrity rules or to reduce redundant values. The relational database engine retrieves data most efficiently when

- Tables are structured and indexed to support queries.

- Records are identified by using simple, numeric keys.

- Records are related using few joins based on indexed, simple keys.

- Record lengths are as short as possible to store necessary values.

- Detail records store only numeric values used to perform aggregations.

A data warehouse is a lean query engine that applies these design principles in their purest forms. Its sole purpose is to allow data to be retrieved from read-only tables, using simple queries. It will support queries returning large volumes of data, grouped and aggregated for reporting.

A relational data warehouse can be used as a stand-alone data solution to address many of the issues normally present when the business relies on operational or transactional databases for reporting analytics. Business reports can be designed to query the relational data warehouse directly.

A relational data warehouse system can also be used as the backbone for an OLAP solution. As discussed briefly in this section, even a relational data warehouse has limits that can be overcome by exposing data through an OLAP system such as SQL Server 2005 Analysis Services, with data presented using business reports, dashboards, and specialized reporting tools.

Data Warehouse Fundamentals

You know that a data warehouse consists of information derived from multiple business operational systems. It should be distinct from the business operational systems that are used to manage day-to-day business operations. As such, it is optimized for reading rather than for inserting, updating, and deleting records. Although these operations are necessary for any data management system, they are secondary to its primary function as a decision-support store of read-only data. Data population and maintenance is performed offline and as part of an automated, bulk process. The data warehouse is also organized for specialized business information analysis and discovery tools. As such, its design is specifically tailored to work with reporting tools and necessary business reporting metrics. It is used to support (or refute) business plans, directions, and actions.

To achieve BI solution capabilities, corporations have deployed technology to collect raw operational business data from across their business systems. This data is then transformed, cleansed, and merged into specialized collection database models. These processes include applying business-specific rules, defining measures, and defining relationships among data sources. A variety of reporting and analytic applications are then used to view and analyze the data in supporting or refuting business decisions.

In the not-so-distant past, it took a lot of effort and technology to accomplish BI solutions. SQL Server 2005 has enabled corporations to design, deploy, and manage BI solutions with relative speed and ease, all from one integrated technology suite.

Business Intelligence Solution Goals

For decades, the computing industry has focused on creating applications to gather input from human users and to collect data from any sources. Now, nearly all businesses have, or have access to, huge repositories of transactions: records of information such as product sales, survey results, phone calls, and the like. In databases, all of these things are stored as simple values in fields and tables. Before these numbers and characters were collected from millions of keyboards and application users, the data was useful information about people, products, and other things that real people cared about. Somewhere along the line, it all got transformed into data and stored in huge databases. One of the most important goals of a BI solution is to retrieve pertinent data out of these enterprise databases. It's to transform all of the right numbers and characters into useful information in such a way that it tells a meaningful story about the information that business leaders need to know to make decisions.

Think about the words business and intelligence and how they should be used together to describe an ideal business environment. Just about everyone can tell sad stories about the inefficiencies and blind direction of many businesses. If business leaders can make informed decisions, completely aware of product demands, customers' needs, competitive forces, sales trends, manufacturing costs, and surpluses and shortages, running a stable and profitable business would be much easier. Customers would want to buy your products and services if they thought your business was intelligent—that the people who ran your company were smart and made intelligent decisions.

A functional business intelligence solution makes this dream a reality by putting relevant, reliable information in front of business information workers and leaders in the right form, at the right level of detail, and at the right time. *Relevant data* means determining the kinds and detail level or granularity of data that is required to support the business analysis.

To design such a solution, it's important to understand the goals of a business intelligence solution. Let's review them.

Combining Relevant Data from Multiple Sources

Source data is transformed into *valid* and *trusted* information. Because data has been reconciled and validated, report data becomes a single version of information. Business users know that this is the point of reference for all other data.

Users understand that the time frames of the information can be current or historic. This enables information users to gain a perspective of the present and the past, so they can understand and respond to trends and variances.

Information is structured according to pre-defined relationships and rules. By conforming to business and industry standards specific to the type of data being presented, users already know how to use and report on information using familiar patterns. They can also make comparisons to information from other sources because it conforms to industry rules and forms.

Providing Fast and Easy Access

How fast is fast enough? Getting data quickly is a very subjective goal. For someone accustomed to waiting all day for an old report to run, a 30-minute query might be just fine from the user's perspective, but the network or database administrator might not be thrilled with the impact it has on servers and the network environment whenever the report runs.

Getting information quickly might not be challenging if this is the only goal. However, getting consistent and reliable information quickly and easily might be another issue. To be useful and trustworthy, information must be of consistent quality. Users are loyal to a system that they can trust and, to earn this status in the minds of users, it is helpful to assure them that data is always accurate and consistent. Business users certainly appreciate a simple, user-friendly interface, but if the system isn't effective enough to deliver the right information quickly—and in a form that is easy to understand—it might as well print hieroglyphics.

There are a lot of different business reporting tools in use today, but many go unused because they are cumbersome for report designers and inconvenient for users. They can also be inefficient or not integrated with other solution components. The kind of solution that users will consistently go to for critical business decisions is obedient to their simple request to provide an answer to a specific question. After posing a seemingly difficult question about the uncertain seasonal sales trends of a particular product commodity, the CEO will be more than cheerful when handed a report that clearly shows the trends for the past ten years based on solid facts and a promising future.

He'll be even more ecstatic to learn that the system, which supports simple, ad hoc queries and elegant reporting, was a thrifty investment. It required only a few brave IT workers who were willing to step outside of their comfort zone and learn to use a new set of tools to build a true data warehouse, automated ETL process, and OLAP reporting cubes.

A solid BI system provides direction. It's fast, reliable, and easy to use, and the data is always clean. In time, business leaders and information users will trust the system with a sense of reverence and respect because it helps executive leaders keep the ship on course and to make course changes only when the compass on the executive dashboard tells them to.

Focus on Decisions

Whereas OLTP business systems are built to store data and update it for running the day-to-day aspects of a business, BI solutions are built to enable decision-making. Operational OLTP systems are good at inserting new records and doing lookups for specific records, but they are not optimized for summarizing that data for analysis. A good BI solution enables users to develop comparisons of information across the organization and over time by consolidating data that might be held in multiple formats on separate systems and by maintaining history more effectively than is often possible in OLTP systems. In addition, a BI solution is optimized for online exploration of large quantities of data through pre-defined relationships and pre-calculated aggregations. SQL Server 2005 includes Analysis Services for this specific purpose. Analysis Services is an OLAP data engine that stores and manages data much differently than the rows and columns of an OLTP database. An OLAP system is almost always used in conjunction with a relational data warehouse. The relational store provides a manageable repository of reliable business data, and the OLAP engine provides an efficient structure for retrieving data designed specifically to meet business reporting requirements. Rather than tables, the OLAP system stores data in multidimensional cubes. Compared with relational table schemas, dimensions and cubes are relatively easy to design and can be adapted to meet changing business reporting requirements.

When relational OLTP databases become large and complicated, retrieving data through complex queries becomes very slow and cumbersome. By contrast, the difference in query performance for a similar OLAP system can be phenomenal. If designed with the business reporting requirements in mind, the degree of query complexity can be reduced exponentially.

Data Granularity

An important consideration in the design of a BI solution is the amount of detail to store. You first need to understand how much data is required to support business decisions. What level of detail is required to analyze trends? You also need to understand what level of data detail is available from your source systems.

When planning for the design of a data warehouse system, understanding the impact of data granularity is one of the most important factors to consider. Operational databases store data at the transaction level, which is one reason they are typically too slow and complex for reporting. When analyzing business data, users will rarely (if ever) need access to the same level of detail, as is recorded in the data source. Trends and comparisons are nearly always performed at some level of aggregation, and different users will need to see data aggregated at different levels. An understanding of this requirement involves two important concepts that this section will cover briefly and only at a high level.

The first concept is the *dimension*. Nearly all data has dimensionality, meaning it can be grouped along different dimensions and at different levels within a single dimension. For example, sales records have an order date dimension that describes when customers placed orders. These records can be grouped at different levels and aggregated by (for example) year, quarter, month, week, or day. By aggregating transactions at the month level, you could report on the transaction count, sales amount sum, or average amount for the month. Other dimensions might include the customer's geography, product category, or customer type. Many of these dimensions can be organized into hierarchies such as the year, quarter, and month for dates; product category and subcategory for products; and country, state, and city for the geography dimension.

The second related concept is the *level of grain*, or *granularity*. Because you typically don't want to store every transaction detail in a data warehouse fact table, each record will represent an aggregation of transactions. For each fact record, one field will store the count or number of orders placed. Another field will store the sum or total purchase amount for orders. The precise level of detail represented by a single record will depend on the detail (or leaf level) of each dimension. Given the dimensions of order date, geography, product, and customer type, a fact table record is the aggregation of values across the lowest level in each of these dimensions. For example, a fact record might represent aggregate values for orders at the day, city, product, and customer type levels.

So how much or how little detail is necessary? The answer to this question is "It depends." If the volume of fact table data negatively affects performance, it would stand to reason that records should be pre-aggregated at a reasonably high level to meet the users' stated reporting requirements without compromising performance. This might solve the immediate problem, but what if the granularity requirements were to change? Say that each fact record contains the sum of the sales amounts and order counts for a month. The data warehouse tables are structured and populated with data to meet the current need but, at some point in the future, users decide they need to drill down to daily sales totals. It would be very difficult, if not impossible, to load a table designed to store monthly sales with daily sales records.

Now, take another approach. Recognizing that the current requirement calls for reporting at the monthly sales level, design the relational data warehouse to store daily sales records, and then design an OLAP cube to aggregate sales at the month level. When the cube is processed, monthly totals are calculated from the data warehouse and stored in the cube. The OLAP engine efficiently stores data with pre-aggregated totals, so no more detail is required. Later, when the requirement changes, you simply add weekly and daily dimension levels to the cube and then reprocess it to load new data. It's true that the size of the cube data has increased, but the impact is far less than it would be if using relational storage. Because the cube was already designed to manage monthly sales data, queries and reports run just as fast as they did previously, but users can also drill down to weekly and daily sales totals much more efficiently than if you had used the relational structure. OLAP cubes allow you to extend this simple scenario across many different dimensions to slice and group data across geography, sales regions, product categories, and many other data attributes, with little impact on performance and query complexity.

Supporting Business Decisions

To design a solution that continues to meet business needs, you have to ask yourself "What do users need now?" and "What will they need in the future?" Regarding future requirements, the next consideration is the tradeoff cost to meet future needs. It's hard to plan for every possible future requirement, but it's quite possible to design a flexible solution to meet most practical needs.

How far and to what level of detail will users need to drill down into the data? For each data dimension, what navigation paths will users naturally follow to discover more detail?

Calculations can be performed on aggregated values to support reporting requirements that make sense only at certain dimensional levels. Different measures might have different granularity. For example, budgeting and forecasting are often performed only at an annual or quarterly level. Actual monthly figures can't be accurately compared with quarterly projections.

Another limitation is that the desired granularity must be supported by source data. In cases in which it is not, values may either be arbitrarily (and inaccurately) derived or simply not provided.

Update Frequency and Persistence

The concurrency of available data in a data warehouse will depend greatly on the frequency of updates from the source data systems. However, updating more often is not necessarily better in all cases. Developers' experience shows that some operational data is in balance only at the close of certain reconciliation cycles. It might be misleading to import new source records in the middle of a sales reporting cycle because the impartial results will be misleading. Time and expenses are often reported at the end of the two-week payroll period, and dissecting data in intervals that are more granular would only prove to be erroneous.

In some cases, it will make sense to import operational data frequently. Near-real-time systems incorporate tight data extraction cycles that populate the data warehouse on an ongoing basis. One caveat in this environment is that users will see slight fluctuations as they view analytic dashboards and reports. Even in the time it takes to run two or three different reports, the data can change enough to create an out-of-balance situation between the reports. This phenomenon is often referred to as *twinkling data*, analogous to counting busy ants in an anthill. Although this situation can be difficult to manage, having up-to-the-hour analytical data can be an important business requirement in your environment. Just be prepared for quite a bit more design work and administrative overhead.

Finally, the opportunity to capture some data from operational sources might be limited as details are purged from the system. You might not be able to get three years' worth of daily data if your operational system maintains only a rolling 13 months' worth of details.

Historical Data

On the other side of the data concurrency equation is how to manage older data. At some point, most data should be retired or archived to prevent excessive or unnecessary data volumes in the data warehouse. In some industries, companies are required to keep records on hand for a period of time. For others, the business requires years of historical data to spot trends and to learn from historical patterns. However, in many business environments, two-year-old data is worthless and an unnecessary commodity for most purposes. Your bank or credit card company isn't likely to provide a two-year-old statement of account activity without digging it out of a vault somewhere (and then only with a court-ordered subpoena).

The challenges associated with keeping both very current data and very old data are not insurmountable. In fact, many improvements were made in the SQL Server 2005 suite to help with these requirements. Federating and partitioning data is the key to maintaining optimal performance with changing and increasing data volumes. SQL Server 2005 Analysis Services, Enterprise Edition, allows a cube consisting of multiple partitions, with portions of the cube stored on separate physical storage devices. Separate physical disks or disk arrays can be managed separately and will improve data throughput. Separate cube partitions do not require separate fact tables in the relational data warehouse, but this can also improve management and performance under the right conditions.

There are technical and practical considerations when deciding on the amount of data required. Optimal storage for performance implications might result from the level of detail desired by the business users. The goal is to strike a balance between business requirements and technical constraints. You could, for example, design a solution that maintains summary information in Analysis Services for fast exploration while keeping detailed-level data in a SQL Server 2005 relational database for targeted queries.

Changing Dimensions

When designing a BI solution, consider the impact of changing data. For example, what happens if you add a new product, or if you change the name of a product or the category to which the product is assigned? How would you handle a customer who is assigned to a different sales territory? Here, you need to make a business decision about how to manage this change in the data warehouse. Do you insert the customer's previous sales into the new territory? Do you track previous sales at their original value and future sales at the new value? Or, do you track at a high level instead? The way that the business needs to respond to these changes will determine the techniques you use to manage these changes in a data warehouse. You might overwrite data in existing records (and thereby lose history), or you might flag the original record as inactive and create a new record that contains the current data (and, consequently, have both the original value as well as the new value). Integration Services includes a special task for managing changing dimensions to meet your specific business requirements.

Surrogate Keys

Surrogate keys are system-generated, redundant, unique keys, redundant because many data source systems include their own keys. Surrogate keys address technical issues encountered with implementing data warehouses from multiple sources and changes over time.

Best practice in designing a data warehouse model is the use of surrogate keys to establish and preserve the relationships among the data. There are several reasons why you want to do this. Some include:

- Source data keys are subject to change in the OLTP applications.
- Some data sources might require that long compound keys and surrogate keys usually use integer format to conserve storage space.
- Combining data from multisource systems might result in duplicate source keys. Traditional identifiers such as social security numbers, universal product codes (UPCs), international standard book numbers (ISBNs), and other assigned code numbers result in duplication (not to mention privacy issues).
- Source data changes can be managed with a new surrogate key preserving original, historical associations.

Surrogate keys are used in a data warehouse to accommodate the technical issues that result from consolidating data from multiple data sources and changes over time. Surrogate keys prevent duplicate key problems from arising if you combine data from multiple sources. For changing dimensions, you can keep historical information by using a surrogate key, such as when you want to track the same customer at two different addresses at different points in time. Finally, if a key changes in the source system, the use of a surrogate key in the data warehouse saves you the effort of rebuilding your database to accommodate the source system changes. You can easily implement surrogate keys by creating an identity column in each of your SQL Server 2005 dimension tables.

Additive Measures

The design of a BI system needs to address the difference between additive measures, which can be stored relationally and then aggregated (either in SQL queries or by Analysis Services when building a cube), and nonadditive measures, which must be handled separately as calculations in Analysis Services. Without storing all of the transaction detail in a relational table, it would be difficult to use nonadditive measures by means of only a relational data warehouse.

This section will look at the difference between additive and nonadditive measures. As you know, an aggregation is the simple calculation of a series of values into a single, scalar value. Common aggregations are summed, counted, and averaged. In less-common cases, aggregation can be the first, last, lowest, or highest value in the series. Aggregation can also be performed using statistical algorithms like standard deviation or variance over the entire range or over a population.

Sums can be calculated from any level. In other words, you can take the sum of a sum and yield an accurate total. The same is true of counts. Once you count something, you can derive a total count by summing all the counts. However, the same is not true of a Distinct Count, in which you do not want to count any duplicate values in the series. If you rolled up your detailed transaction records with order counts at the quarterly level, you could still get an accurate total for the year. Figure 12-2 shows four quarterly sales totals that add up to the total sales for the year.

2003	Qtr 1	3800
	Qtr 2	5300
	Qtr 3	5500
	Qtr 4	4500
2003 Total		19100

Figure 12-2   Quarterly sales sums add up to the sum of sales for the year

Instead of counts and sums, if your measure were the average orders by quarter and, if you are not storing the detailed order records, you could have a problem. Assuming that you have arrived at the quarterly average figure correctly, you cannot use these numbers to calculate an average at the year mark, overall, or at any other level accurately.

If you pre-calculate and store the sum for four quarters, it is easy to add them together to get the annual total. Alternatively, averages cannot be stored and then summed to the annual average. This would give you an average of averages and wouldn't properly account for weightings, as Figure 12-3 shows.

2003	Qtr 1	950
	Qtr 2	1325
	Qtr 3	1375
	Qtr 4	1125
2003 Total		1194

Figure 12-3   The average of averages yields an inaccurate yearly total

In a relational database, you don't typically store a number that can be calculated in real time because it would require redundant data and storage. Analysis Services, by contrast, is focused on analyzing data rather than on storing data, and it is much more efficient at storage, too. During analysis, you need speed, so it is often faster to retrieve a stored aggregated amount, such as sales by quarter, than it is to calculate it on the fly from daily details.

In Figure 12-3, you can see the average sales orders in the four quarters of 2003. Here, the system might store the quarterly average, but it would need to calculate the true average for the annual average rather than to rely on the stored quarterly averages. The 2003 quarterly average is not 1,194, as shown here; it should be computed as 19,100/4 quarters, or 4,775. When designing a BI system, you need to distinguish between additive measures, which can be stored relationally and aggregated by Analysis Services, and nonadditive measures, which must be handled separately as calculations in Analysis Services.

Reviewing an Operational and Database Schema

The best way to see the difference between an operational/transactional database and a decision-support data warehouse database is to diagram a selection of tables. The following exercise will demonstrate some of the structural differences that have been discussed in this chapter. First, you'll create a database diagram of the *is2005sbs* database, a simplified version of the *Adventure Works Cycles* operational database. After that, you will create a database diagram of the *is2005sbs* database, a data warehouse schema based on the same set of sample corporate data.

Using each of these two databases, at the conclusion of this exercise, the objective is to run a query showing the total sales for each store in a specific state or province for a product subcategory and calendar year. Your users want to answer the question, "What were the total Mountain Bike sales for stores in the State of Washington during calendar year 2003?" After diagramming the tables, you will write a query for each database to obtain this information.

Creating a Database Diagram

SQL Server Management Studio includes a database diagramming tool that can be used to view existing tables and their relationships in the form of an Entity Relation Diagram (ERD). Optionally, changes made in a diagram can be captured as Data Definition Language scripts used to persist changes to the actual database schema. The first time a diagram is created, the diagramming tool components are installed.

Create a new diagram for the *is2005sbs* database

1. Using the Object Browser in SSMS, expand Databases and the *is2005sbs* database.

2. Right-click Database Diagrams and choose New Database Diagram from the menu. If this is the first time you have created a diagram, a dialog box might appear, asking if you want to create diagramming objects in the database. If this dialog box is presented, click Yes.

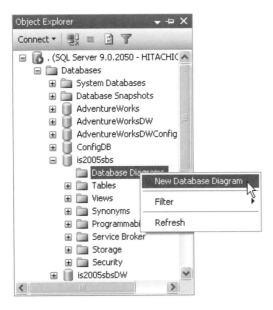

3. The Add Table dialog box displays all of the tables in the *is2005sbs* database. Select the following tables from this dialog box and add them to the diagram:

   ❑ Address

   ❑ Customer

   ❑ CustomerAddress

- ❏ Product
- ❏ ProductSubCategory
- ❏ SalesOrderDetail
- ❏ SalesOrderHeader
- ❏ StateProvince
- ❏ Store

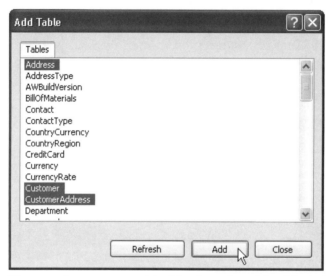

There are three ways to add tables from the Add Table dialog box window:

- ❏ Click a table name, and then click Add.
- ❏ Double-click a table name.
- ❏ Press Ctrl, and then click each table name. Click Add.

4. Close the Add Table dialog box when the tables have been added.

Organize the diagram

1. Resize and rearrange the tables in the diagram to make it more compact and easier to read.

2. To organize these objects automatically, right-click the background of the diagram and choose Arrange Tables from the menu.

It isn't necessary for all of the field names to be visible in a table window. The arrangement of tables is a matter of personal preference.

Tip   Some of the table objects will likely be outside the designer's visible window. To navigate the entire design surface easily, click the compass points icon in the lower-right intersection of the scroll bars. Click, hold, and drag the mouse to move the visible window area to another location within the diagram.

You can rearrange and resize the tables manually to make them easier to read and to understand the diagram.

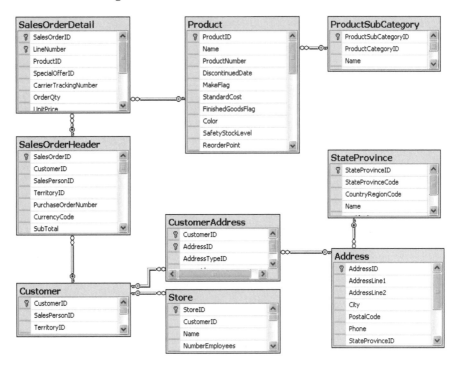

Note the relationship lines between each table. These were added to the diagram because of existing primary and foreign key constraints. Be sure not to delete or change these.

Note   Note that all nine tables are required for the query: The store Name is in the Store table. A store is a type of Customer. The CustomerAddress and Address tables are necessary links to the StateProvince table. The Product table joins SalesOrderDetail (individual sales transactions) to ProductSubCategory, where you will find Mountain Bikes. The SalesOrderHeader contains the OrderDate, which will be used to derive the calendar year, and the SalesOrderDetail contains the LineTotal, which will be used to calculate the total sales amount.

Save the diagram

1. From the File menu, click Save Diagram_1.

2. When prompted, name the diagram **ResellerSales**.

Query the *is2005sbs* database

1. To open a new query window, right-click the *is2005sbs* database in the Object Browser and choose New Query.

2. On the File menu, click File, Open, and then File.

3. Navigate to the C:\Documents and Settings\<username>\My Documents\Microsoft Press\is2005sbs\Chap12\ folder and open Chap12 – is2005sbs Reseller Sales query.sql.

4. This Transact-SQL query references all of the tables you added to the database diagram. Review the syntax of this query:

```
USE is2005sbs

SELECT    Store.Name AS StoreName
        , SUM(SalesOrderDetail.LineTotal) AS SalesAmount
FROM      Product INNER JOIN
          ProductSubCategory
          ON Product.ProductSubCategoryID =
             ProductSubCategory.ProductSubCategoryID
          INNER JOIN SalesOrderDetail
          ON Product.ProductID = SalesOrderDetail.ProductID
          INNER JOIN Customer
          INNER JOIN SalesOrderHeader
          ON Customer.CustomerID = SalesOrderHeader.CustomerID
          INNER JOIN Store
          ON Customer.CustomerID = Store.CustomerID
          ON SalesOrderDetail.SalesOrderID = SalesOrderHeader.SalesOrderID
          INNER JOIN CustomerAddress
          ON Customer.CustomerID = CustomerAddress.CustomerID
          INNER JOIN Address
          ON CustomerAddress.AddressID = Address.AddressID
          INNER JOIN StateProvince
          ON Address.StateProvinceID = StateProvince.StateProvinceID
WHERE     YEAR(SalesOrderHeader.OrderDate) = 2003
          AND ProductSubCategory.Name = 'Mountain Bike'
          AND StateProvince.Name = 'Washington'
GROUP BY Store.Name, StateProvince.Name
ORDER BY Store.Name
```

5. Execute the query by clicking Execute on the SQL Editor toolbar and make note of the time it takes for the query to complete.

   This is displayed in the status bar below the query window. The query returns 15 rows showing the stores and the total Mountain Bike sales in Washington State for calendar year 2003.

Data Warehouse System Components

A common practice and architecture of data warehouse processes includes storing the transaction level data into staging tables. Perform the data staging process to transform, merge, standardize, cleanse, and prepare the data for loading into data warehouse models. Some corporations might create a single enterprise data warehouse as a central repository of all its business data. Subject area subsets of the enterprise data warehouse are often created as data marts to serve departmental and functional area reporting and analysis.

Fact and Dimension Tables

A relational data warehouse consists of two core components called facts and dimensions. Ideally, both of these are simple tables consisting of columns that store either keys or values. A fact table specifically describes a single business fact for reporting and analysis. It stores the actual values for reporting at the least granular level across all possible dimensions. This is very simple in concept. The fact table is related to every corresponding dimension through a foreign key relationship. Foreign keys in the fact table are related to primary keys in each dimension table.

The values stored in the fact table are called measures and are usually aggregated values from multiple detail rows in the operational data source, as shown in Figure 12-4.

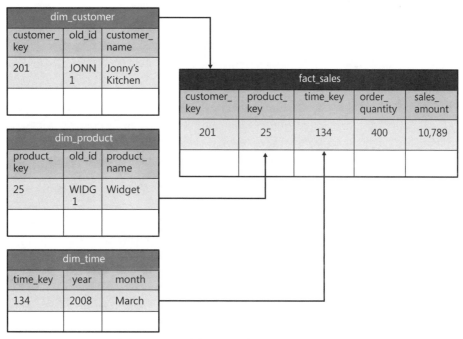

Figure 12-4   Fact and dimension tables related through foreign keys

The grain of the fact_sales table is defined by the lowest level of detail stored in each dimension. The fact table contains the least granular level of values derived from source OLTP systems. Typical examples of this include a Sales Order Fact that might include the dollar value, unit count, and value for a given customer and product on a given date. The customer ID, product ID, and sales date time ID are used to join the fact table to the dimension tables. The customer ID, product ID, and time ID are surrogate keys. The dimension surrogate keys are the unique primary keys for the dimension rows (or members). The fact table keys are foreign keys that identify the corresponding dimension members for the fact.

Dimension Table Characteristics

Dimension tables represent the sets of label lists that can be used to reference the values contained in the fact table. Each row of the dimension table is called a member. Each member represents a unique label for the dimension entities. Each member can have many additional attributes, which are not required to be unique.

For example, a product dimension can include the list of unique products, in which each product is a member of the dimension. Additional attributes can include size, color, weight, and so on, which might not be unique, but provide additional analysis and reporting capabilities. The member attribute, however, must be unique.

Common dimensions include Customer, Product, Geography, and Time. One simple method to refer to the dimension tables is by using the Show Me By tables. This language helps clarify the relationship of a fact and a dimension by allowing the user to ask the data warehouse to show the values by State, by Product, or by Time. Dimensions contain lists of labels for a similar set of characteristics. These characteristics describe business measures. Their purpose is to make the measure more meaningful for the analyst.

The Show Me By tables can also be enabled by dimension hierarchies. Hierarchy levels define values relative to dimension attributes (for example, by size or by color) or via parent-child relationship hierarchies (worldwide total, regional subtotals, divisional subtotals, or entity subtotals). Hierarchies enable powerful ways to aggregate and analyze business data.

Star Schema Dimensions

One of the more popular data warehouse (and data mart) database models is the star schema. The star schema was introduced as a way to organize business data for fast query access. Its design is significantly different from the database models used by OLTP applications. Look at some of the characteristics of the star schema and their effect on SSIS package design. Figure 12-5 depicts a star schema.

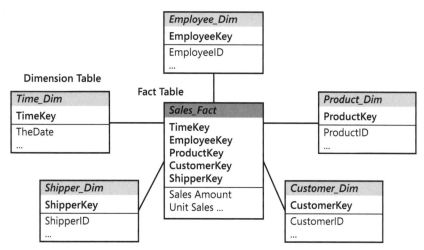

Figure 12-5   Star schema consisting of a fact and multiple dimensions

It's called a star because of its conceptual shape. A star schema relational database model contains one fact table and at least one dimension table. SSIS is used to load data into both fact tables and dimension tables. When using SSIS to maintain star schemas, you need to review the relationships and dependencies between fact and dimension tables to best design the SSIS package control flow and data flow components.

The fact table contains the transaction detail values from source OLTP systems. However, it is common to roll up detail rows to the lowest level. Typical examples include a Sales Order Fact that might include the dollar value and the unit count value for a given customer and product on a given date. The customer ID, product ID, and sales date time ID are used to join the fact table to the dimension tables. The customer ID, product ID, and time ID are surrogate keys. The dimension surrogate keys are the unique primary keys for the dimension rows (or members). The fact table keys are foreign keys that identify the corresponding dimension members for the fact.

Every member of a dimension table is unique to that dimension and identified by the unique surrogate key. Surrogate keys that maintain the relationships between dimension and fact tables is a database model design characteristic, but it is the database design that affects how you design your SSIS packages to load and maintain these tables within the data warehouse. One of the ways used to help optimize the processes required by the SSIS packages for data warehouses is with the use of staging tables.

Snowflake Schema Dimensions

You looked at the star schema model, which involved one dimension table related directly to the fact table. Another version of the model is referred to as a snowflake. This is a hybrid star schema used when a single dimension's attributes are subject to high levels of change (for instance, product line regroupings, renaming categories, and so on). The relationships between these attributes can be maintained while new attribute labels for category or subcategory are supported. The snowflake is quite as common as the star schema, but it's good to know that this type of model is not a problem when the data dictates a little more complexity. Figure 12-6 shows one branch of a simple snowflake schema.

Figure 12-6   Simple snowflake schema

In this database, the related product category, subcategory, and product information are stored in three separate tables. Although this is a typical schema, the same information could be stored in a single table as with the year, quarter, month, and other hierarchy-level values stored in the time dimension table. There are various schools of thought on this and really no perfectly correct answer; the key is to retain simplicity and the ability to maintain the data according to the business need.

Reviewing and Comparing a Data Warehouse Database Schema

The following steps will take you through an exercise similar to the previous one so that you can compare the operational *is2005sbs* database schema to the data warehouse *is2005sbsDW* database schema, using a database entity relation diagram. You will execute a query that will return the same results as before with less effort. As before, this query answers the question, "What were the total Mountain Bike sales for stores in the State of Washington during calendar year 2003?"

Creating a Database Diagram

Using the same technique as you did for the operational *is2005sbs* database, you will create a database diagram for the *is2005sbsDW* database, including the tables needed to run the query.

To simplify many of the data transformation steps thus far, referential constraints and relationships between tables in the *is2005sbsDW* database were removed. This is a common practice when manipulating large sets of data in multiple tables. The process of adding and removing relationships can easily be scripted. You will execute a script to add relationships before creating a diagram and then remove the relationships with a script at the conclusion of this exercise.

Add relationships to the database

1. Using the File > Open > File menu in SSMS, locate and open the Chap12 - is2005sbsDW Add Relationships.sql script file.

2. Execute this script, using the red exclamation icon on the toolbar.

3. Close this tab in SSMS when the script execution has completed.

Create a new diagram for the *is2005sbsDW* database

1. Using the Object Browser in SSMS, expand Databases and is2005sbsDW.

2. Right-click Database Diagrams and choose New Database Diagram from the menu. As before, a dialog box might appear, asking whether you want to create diagramming objects in the database. If this dialog box is presented, click Yes.

3. The Add Table dialog box displays all of the tables in the *is2005sbsDW* database. Select the following tables from this dialog box and add them to the diagram:

   ❑ FactResellerSales

   ❑ DimReseller

   ❑ DimGeography

   ❑ DimProduct

   ❑ DimProductSubCategory

   ❑ DimTime

Note the simplicity of the following diagram compared to the diagram from the "Create a Database Diagram" exercise.

> **Note** It takes only six tables to support the same query in the data warehouse that took nine tables in the operational database. This is because dimension data and business facts have been consolidated.

Save the diagram

1. From the toolbar or File menu, click Save.

2. Name the diagram **ResellerSales**.

Query the *is2005sbsDW* database

1. To open a new query window, right-click the *is2005sbsDW* database in the Object Browser and choose New Query.

2. On the File menu, click File, Open, and then File.

3. Navigate to the C:\Documents and Settings\<username>\My Documents\Microsoft Press\is2005sbs\Chap12\ folder and open Chap12 – is2005sbsDW Reseller Sales query.sql.

4. This Transact-SQL query references all of the tables you added to the database diagram. Review the syntax of this query:

```
USE is2005sbsDW

SELECT   DimReseller.ResellerName
       , SUM(FactResellerSales.SalesAmount) AS SalesAmount
FROM     FactResellerSales INNER JOIN
         DimReseller
         ON FactResellerSales.ResellerKey = DimReseller.ResellerKey
         INNER JOIN DimGeography
```

```
        ON DimReseller.GeographyKey = DimGeography.GeographyKey
        INNER JOIN DimProduct
        ON FactResellerSales.ProductKey = DimProduct.ProductKey
        INNER JOIN DimProductSubCategory
        ON DimProduct.ProductSubCategoryKey =
DimProductSubCategory.ProductSubCategoryKey
        INNER JOIN DimTime
        ON FactResellerSales.OrderDateKey = DimTime.TimeKey
WHEREDimTime.CalendarYear = '2003'
AND DimProductSubCategory.ProductSubCategoryName = 'Mountain Bike'
AND DimGeography.StateProvinceName = 'Washington'
GROUP BY DimProductSubCategory.ProductSubCategoryName, DimReseller.ResellerName
ORDER BY DimReseller.ResellerName
```

5. Execute the query by clicking Execute on the SQL Editor toolbar and make note of the time it takes for the query to complete. This is displayed in the status bar below the query window. The query returns 15 rows showing the stores and the total Mountain Bike sales in Washington State for calendar year 2003. This query should take about two-thirds as long as the first.

> **Note**   Compared with the previous query for the *is2005sbs* database, this query is simpler. It uses fewer tables, and the calendar year value uses an exact value from the DimTime table. The operational database required the year to be derived from the OrderDate datetime type column.

The final step is to set the *is2005sbsDW* database back to its previous state with no relationships. This step is necessary to repeat the exercises for previous chapters.

Reset the relationships for *is2005sbsDW*

1. On the File menu, click File, Open, and then File.

2. Navigate to the C:\Documents and Settings\<username>\My Documents\Microsoft Press\is2005sbs\Chap12\ folder and open Chap12 - is2005sbsDW Remove Relationships.sql.

3. Execute the script, using the exclamation button on the toolbar.

4. Close the script file when execution is complete.

Data Warehouse in Summary

This chapter introduced a lot of concepts about the purpose and function of a data warehouse. These principles apply to any decision-support data structure, ranging from a central corporate data warehouse to a department or subject-specific data mart. You learned that a data warehouse is a relational database designed specifically to support fast queries and reports. As such, the rules of normal form, typically applied in transactional database design to reduce redundancy and enforce data integrity, generally don't apply.

Dimension tables contain descriptive information about the business facts but not the measurable facts themselves. Dimensions are usually organized into hierarchal levels. A fact table contains detail rows, usually aggregated to the lowest level of needed detail across all of the related dimensions. Each fact table describes a specific business fact to help simplify design and to optimize query performance. Fact tables contain only foreign keys related to the dimension tables and measure values used in aggregation. The design characteristics of your data warehouse should support pre-defined business needs such as how future changes to dimension and fact data should be handled. This can be accomplished by storing each change as a separate archived record or by simply discarding previous values and updating a single record.

To design a complete data warehouse, there are many other details to consider, but this chapter has introduced the essential concepts and issues. This should serve as a foundation on which you can build a relational decision-support database to be used for reporting or to populate OLAP cubes for in-depth analysis.

Reset the Relationships for *is2005sbsDW*

> **Note**   The final step is to set the *is2005sbsDW* database back to its previous state with no relationships. This step is necessary to repeat the exercises for previous chapters.

1. Open the script file named Chap12 – is2005sbsDW Remove Relationships.sql, using the File > Open > File menu in SSIS.

2. Execute the script, using the Exclamation button on the toolbar.

3. Close the script file when execution is completed.

Chapter 12 Quick Reference

This term	Means this
Data warehouse	A relational database designed to store management information.
Dimension table	A list of labels that can be used to cross-tabulate values from other dimensions.
Fact table	The relational database table that contains values for one or more measures at the lowest level of detail for one or more dimensions.
Surrogate key	A column in a database dimension table that contains values that uniquely identify each row. Often referred to as the primary key for a dimension.
Foreign key	A column in a database table that contains many values for each value in the primary key column of another database table.
Join	The process of linking the primary key of one table to the foreign key of another table.
Star schema	A database model composed of a fact table and one or more dimension tables. Typically used to model data warehouses and data marts.

Chapter 13

Populating Data Warehouse Structures

After completing this chapter, you will be able to:

- Understand the role of SSIS in maintaining data warehouse models.

- Know when and how to implement staging tables.

- Use SSIS for loading dimension tables.

- Use SSIS for loading fact tables.

Microsoft SQL Server 2005 Integration Services (SSIS) provides a rich set of built-in tasks, containers, transformations, and data adapters that support the development of business applications. Without writing a single line of code, you can create SSIS solutions that solve complex business problems, using extract, transform, and load (ETL) and business intelligence (BI) processes to manage SQL Server databases.

You learned in Chapter 12, "Data Warehouse Concepts," how a data warehouse is often the core component of a BI infrastructure for today's corporations. This book will not get into the details of building and maintaining data warehouses, but it's important to look at some of the characteristics and design considerations that are crucial to BI infrastructures and solutions. Data warehouses are traditionally implemented as relational database models of various design types.

SSIS is used to perform data cleansing, standardization, derivation, and many other transformation tasks. It is not unusual for data warehouses to have more data than the source systems that feed them. But even though the data volume might be extremely large, the database model is designed for fast access for reporting.

Data warehouses, if designed and maintained appropriately, provide the most accurate and reliable data for effective reporting and BI solution support. You will now review data warehouse database models and look at some of the ways SSIS is used to build and maintain data warehouses.

Data Warehouse Characteristics

One of the more popular data warehouse (and data mart) database models is the *star schema* and its use as a way to organize business data for fast query access. Its design is significantly different than the database models used by Online Transaction Processing (OLTP) applications. Look at some of the characteristics of the star schema and its effect on SSIS package design.

It's called a star because of its conceptual shape, illustrated in Figure 13-1. A star schema relational database model contains a fact table (as its center) and at least one dimension table (as a point). SSIS is used to load data into both fact tables and dimension tables. When using SSIS to maintain star schemas, you need to review the relationships and dependencies between fact and dimension tables to design the SSIS package control flow and data flow components most efficiently.

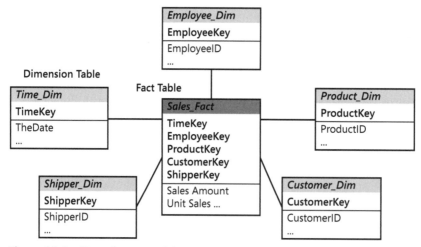

Figure 13-1   Star schema model

The fact table contains the *transaction detail* values from source OLTP systems. Typical examples include a Sales Order fact that might include the dollar value and the unit count value for a given customer and product on a given date. The customer ID, product ID, and sales date and time ID are used to join the fact table to the dimension tables. The customer ID, product ID, and time ID are surrogate keys. The dimension surrogate keys are the unique primary keys for the dimension rows (or members). The fact table keys are foreign keys that identify the corresponding dimension members for the fact.

Every member of a dimension table is unique to that dimension and identified by the unique surrogate key. Surrogate keys that maintain the relationships between dimension and fact tables are a database model design characteristic, and it is the database design that affects how developers design SSIS packages to load and maintain these tables within the data warehouse. One of the ways used to help optimize the processes required by the SSIS packages for data warehouses is with the use of staging tables, the subject of the next section.

Implementing Staging Tables

It is possible to load data directly from the extraction process of data sources into the data warehouse without a separate staging area. In fact, the opportunity to avoid a staging database is even greater when using SSIS, which allows you to apply multiple transformations to data as it passes through memory between the source and the destination. Whether you need to stage the data as part of your ETL process is a common design decision that you have to make.

A common practice and the architecture of data warehouse processes include storing the transaction-level data into *staging tables*. Select source data is loaded into temporary (or persisted) staging tables. The data staging tables become the source data for the next process, where the data is further transformed, merged, standardized, cleansed, and prepared for loading into data warehouse models. Some corporations might create a single enterprise data warehouse as a central repository of all its business data. Subject area subsets of the enterprise data warehouse are often created as *data marts* to serve departmental and functional area reporting and analysis. Figure 13-2 illustrates a common configuration model for staging.

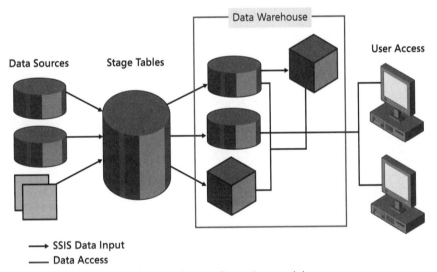

Figure 13-2 Common data staging configuration model

Regardless of the final destination, the staging table provides the fastest and easiest way to extract data from source systems and temporarily store it in a different database where additional transformation, derivation, augmentation, and other tasks can be performed.

Some of the reasons you might want to use staging tables include:

- Only short windows of time are required to extract data from source systems.
- Data from multiple source systems do not exist all at the same time and must be collected at different times and merged once.

- Source data systems might not have changed-data identification, and staging tables enable change detection between existing data warehouse data and the current extract.

- Recovery from failure is typically easier when performed from staging table sources.

- Memory constraints for transformations such as sorting and others might be handled better with disk-based staging.

- Audit tracking and lineage is also more easily managed when data is staged across its various transformations.

- Staging allows for easier surrogate key generation and management for star schema–modeled data warehouses.

Types of Staging Schemes

Once you have decided to stage data for data warehouse maintenance, you can consider various types of staging table patterns. Each affects the design of your SSIS packages and process design. Look at each of these kinds of staging design options and when to use each type.

Staging Data from Multiple Sources

In staging data from multiple sources, the data is temporarily stored in a staging database before the ETL process. SSIS is used to extract the data from the source systems to the staging database. Additional SSIS packages are used to transform the data from the staging database into the final data warehouse database destination. This is a common approach, especially if multiple-source data requires a great amount of standardization, matching, and merging and usually isn't available or doesn't all exist at the same time. Figure 13-3 illustrates multiple-source staging.

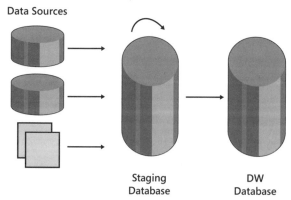

Interactive Extract and Transformation

Data Sources

Staging
Database

DW
Database

Figure 13-3 Staging from multiple sources

Staggered Staging

In staggered staging, the data can be from multiple or single sources. Sometimes the ETL process can be very expensive in terms of processing time, and sometimes you might not have the luxury to repeat the entire process because of a failure at some point during execution. This staging approach allows you to limit recovery reprocessing. Clearly, this approach also results in additional data disk space but enables much greater and faster correction and recovery for high data volumes and long-running SSIS packages. An illustration of staggered staging might look as shown in Figure 13-4.

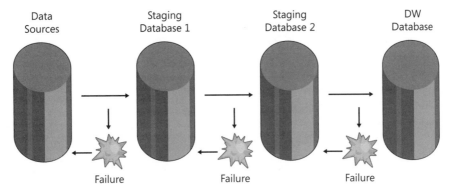

Figure 13-4   Staggered staging model

Persisted Staging

In persisted staging, an archive copy of the staging database is created on a routine basis. The primary reason for using this alternative scheme is to allow auditing of the extract and transformation processes for more than the current period and processing cycle. This allows for smaller data volumes for each current period processing while maintaining previous period processing data lineage for auditing and troubleshooting. An illustration of persisted staging is shown in Figure 13-5.

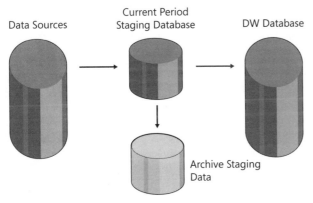

Figure 13-5   Persisted staging model

Accumulated Staging

Ideally, your source application systems can provide a way to determine whether data required for the data warehouse has changed. Then, you could set up a process in SSIS for these data transaction details (inserts, updates, and deletes). In these circumstances, you can use the accumulated staging approach:

- If the source system does not have a built-in delta detection mechanism or changed-data capture capability.

- If the source system does not provide the kind of transaction applied for each delta-detected record.

If your source application system does not have built-in changed-data detection, all the records from the required tables are extracted and compared against the accumulated staging data to determine changes.

If your source application system does have changed-data detection mechanisms and you can extract only the changed and new records, the next step is to determine the transaction type that occurred for these changed records (inserts, updates, or deletes).

For example, in Figure 13-6, when comparing the incoming employee table with accumulated staging, the record EmpId 200 can be determined as *Modified* (changed data for an existing dimension member) whereas the EmpId 202 record can be determined as *Inserted* (a new, previously nonexisting dimension member).

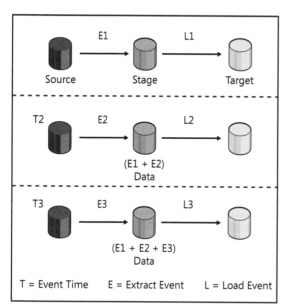

Accumulated Staged Data

EmpID	EmpName	EmpLocal
200	John	New York
201	Mary	Portland

Incoming Staged Data

EmpID	EmpName	EmpLocal
200	John	Redmond
202	James	Seattle

Figure 13-6 Accumulated staging model

Chunked Accumulated Staging

Common in retail or other high transaction-type business data warehouse designs, the chunked accumulated staging scheme enables you to extract a huge volume of data and spread the extract load across the day on the source system. The accumulated information is then transformed and loaded to the destination data warehouse as required by business needs. For example, extraction could happen every hour throughout the day, and transformation and loading could be done once at the end of the day. Figure 13-7 provides an illustration of the chunked accumulated staging approach.

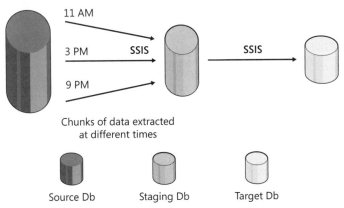

Figure 13-7   Chunked accumulated staging model

Other Destination Considerations

You've just learned various designs for staging data before loading the data warehouse. In some BI and data warehouse database implementations, there can be an additional step that involves distributing the data to separate data marts. For example, the data from the central data warehouse might need to be distributed to data marts at different geographical locations. In some ways, the data warehouse is functioning as a staging area for the distributed data marts. This is not technically a stage, but it still needs to be taken into consideration for choosing appropriate conditions for loading the data warehouse to ensure that it is appropriately populated for destination marts. Figure 13-8 is an illustration of the multiple destination scheme approach.

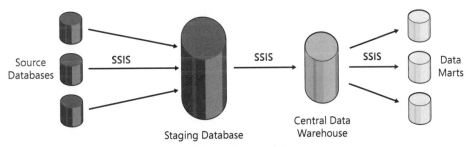

Figure 13-8   Multiple destination with staging model

Managing Dimension Tables Part 1

Earlier in this chapter, you learned about dimension tables within star schema database models. Dimension tables represent distinct lists of members identified by unique primary keys. You also learned in Chapter 12 that surrogate keys are system-generated, redundant, unique keys (redundant because many data source systems include their own keys, often different in value and format). Surrogate keys are used as primary keys for dimension tables. Surrogate keys are important because they address technical issues encountered with implementing data warehouses, especially when these warehouses are created from multiple sources and can have dimensional member changes over time.

One best practice in designing a data warehouse model is to use surrogate keys to define dimension member rows uniquely. Surrogate keys help establish and preserve the relationships within the data in the fact table to all the dimension tables. There are several reasons you want to do this:

- Source data keys are subject to change in the OLTP applications. A surrogate key in the data warehouse would not need to be changed as a result.

- Some data sources might require long compound keys, and surrogate keys are usually in integer format, which reduces database table space and improves table join performance.

- Multisource systems can result in duplicate source keys (SSN, Code_Nbr, and so on).

- Source data changes (for example, Customer location change) can be managed with new surrogate keys, preserving original historic associations.

Surrogate keys are used in a data warehouse to accommodate the technical issues that result from consolidating data from multiple data sources and changes over time. Surrogate keys prevent duplicate-key problems from arising if you combine data from multiple sources. For changing dimensions, you can keep historical information by using surrogate keys, so you can track the same customer at two different addresses at different points in time. Finally, if a key changes in the source application system, the use of a surrogate key in the data warehouse saves you the effort of rebuilding your database to accommodate the source system changes.

Usually, you do not have to deal with surrogate key creation and maintenance for dimension tables within your SSIS design. Surrogate keys are most often defined at the database level and will be generated automatically for each newly inserted dimension member row. You can easily implement surrogate keys by creating an identity column in each of your SQL Server dimension tables.

Note   A common star schema model design includes adding a dummy record member in each dimension. The dummy member is usually the first record whose surrogate key value is zero, called *zero key*. The source application system business key and other attributes are defaulted to NULL or to a default value such as "Not Available." The fact table can contain the transactions from the source application system for dimension members not yet loaded to the database. In such a case, a default key is assumed from dimension (because dimension is not yet populated with the required key) having zero value. This method allows your fact table data to be loaded into the data warehouse, but it doesn't fully solve identifying the fact correctly to the dimension.

When designing SSIS packages used to build and maintain data warehouses or other application databases that require accurate referential integrity, the sequencing of the control flow of the package is critical. Dimension data processing should always be performed before fact table data, as a rule. When maintaining data for fact tables and dimension tables, the order is important because you most often don't want to load fact data that has dimension relationships with members that might not already exist in the dimension tables. In the next demonstration, you will use data staging and learn two ways to manage dimension tables with SSIS.

Loading Dimension Tables by Using a Left Outer Join

Staging tables are often used to collect new data temporarily for data warehouses (DWs). Both fact and dimension tables need to reflect the incoming data accurately. Oftentimes, you might need to configure how to detect new data from existing data already stored in the dimension tables. The following procedures show two procedures you can use when designing SSIS packages for managing dimension table loading. In Part 1 of this procedure, you will learn how to set up a left outer join merge task to detect new data for a dimension update.

Create a new project for dimension table load packages

1. Open Business Intelligence Development Studio (BIDS). On the File menu, select New, and then select Project. Select the Integration Services Project template.

2. Type **Chap13** for the project name. Change the project location to C:\Documents and Settings\<username>\My Documents\Microsoft Press\is2005sbs\Chap13 and confirm that the Create Directory For Solution check box is selected.

3. Click OK to create a new project within BIDS.

4. Right-click Package.dtsx in Solution Explorer and rename it **DW_DimMgmt_1.dtsx**.

5. Drag a data flow task from the Toolbox window onto the Control Flow workspace.

6. Right-click and rename the task **Find New Members Process 1**.

7. Double-click the new data flow task to activate the Data Flow tab.

8. From the Data Flow Sources group in the Toolbox, drag two OLE DB Source objects onto the designer.

9. Right-click and rename the first data source **Stage Customer Table**.

10. Right-click and rename the second data source **Dim Customer Table**.

11. Double-click the OLE DB source named Stage Customer Table. In the OLE DB Source Editor, click New for the OLE DB Connection Manager.

12. If localhost.SSIS DW is in the Data Connections list, select it, and then click OK.

> **Note** If localhost.SSIS DW is not available in the Data Connections list, click New, enter **localhost** for the Server Name, and select SSIS DW in the Select Or Enter A Database Name drop-down list. Click OK, and then OK again.

Add tables to find new dimension members

1. Select [dbo].[DimStageCustomer] from the drop-down list of the Name Of The Table Or The View item and click OK.

2. Double-click the OLE DB source named Dim Customer Table. In the OLE DB Source Editor, verify that localhost.SSIS DW is selected from the OLE DB Connection Manager drop-down list.

3. Select [dbo].[DimCustomer] from the Name Of The Table Or The View drop-down list and click OK.

   Your screen should look like this:

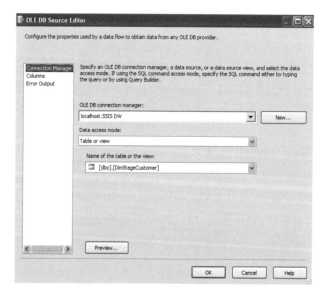

4. Drag two Sort objects from the Data Flow Transformations group in the Toolbox onto the Data Flow designer.

5. Connect Stage Customer Table Data Source to the first Sort task with the green arrow. Double-click Sort Task and select the CustomerKey check box from Available Input Columns.

   Your screen should look like this:

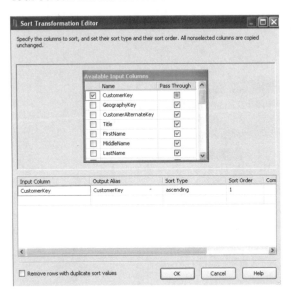

6. Click OK.

7. Right-click and rename the task **Stage Customer Key Sort**.

8. Connect the Dim Customer Table data source to the second Sort task with the green arrow. Double-click the Sort task and select the CustomerKey check box from the Available Input Columns. Click OK. Right-click and rename the task **Dim Customer Key Sort**.

Configure a Left Outer Join Merge join task

1. Drag a Merge Join transformation to the Data Flow designer. Right-click and rename it **Left Outer Join On Customer Key**.

2. Connect Stage Customer Key Sort and Dim Customer Key Sort outputs to Merge Join.

3. In the Input Output Selection dialog box, select Merge Join Left Input from the Input drop-down list.

4. Double-click the Left Outer Join On Customer Key task and change the Join Type to Left Outer Join.

5. Select all the check boxes for the Stage Customer Key Sort columns.

6. Select the CustomerKey check box for the Dim Customer Key Sort column. Scroll to the bottom of the Output Alias list and change the output alias for this column to DimCustomer_CustomerKey.

Your screen should look like this:

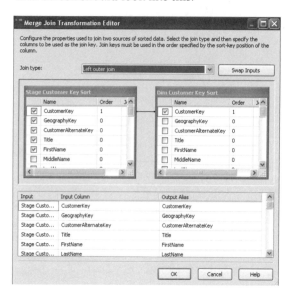

7. Click OK.

Add a conditional split to find new customers

1. Drag a Conditional Split transformation from the Toolbox to the Data Flow designer and attach it to Left Outer Join On Customer Key with the green arrow.

2. Double-click the new Conditional Split and create a new conditional split by typing **New Customers** in the Output Name column. Type into the condition field:

```
ISNULL(DimCustomer_CustomerKey)
```

Your screen should look like this:

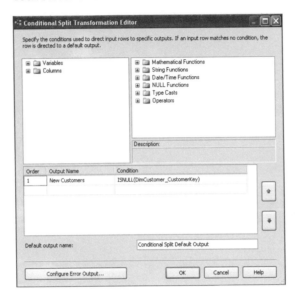

3. Click OK.

Add a flat file destination

1. From the Data Flow Destinations group in the Toolbox, drag a Flat File Destination onto the designer and connect it to Conditional Split, using the green arrow.

2. In the Input Output Selection dialog box, select New Customers as the output and click OK.

3. Double-click the destination task to configure it. Click New to create a flat file connection.

4. Select Delimited for Flat File Format, and then click OK.

5. In the Flat File Connection Manager Name box, type **New Found Customers 1**.

6. Click Browse and navigate to C:\Documents and Settings\<username>\My Documents\Microsoft Press\is2005sbs\Chap13\Data\NewDimCustomers1.txt.

7. Select the Column Names In The First Data Row check box, and then click OK.

8. Check Overwrite Data In File and click the Mappings in the pane on the left.

9. Click OK.

10. Click File, and then click Save All.

11. Right-click the package in Solution Explorer and select Execute the Package.

Your screen should look like this:

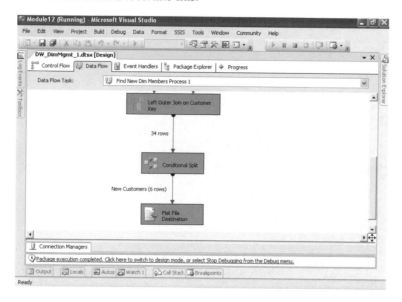

> **Note**   Six new customer rows should have been written to the destination file.

12. Click Stop Debugging from the Debug menu.

13. Double-click Flat File Destination and select Preview to view the data.

Managing Dimension Tables Part 2

In the previous section, you learned to use the Left Outer Join task to detect data changes that could affect your dimension table load processing. The Left Outer Join Merge task is a very powerful way to perform this kind of data inspection. The Left Outer Join Merge task reads all the data to perform the detection of changes. You will now learn an alternative way to perform this dimension data inspection.

Loading Dimension Tables Part 2

In this next procedure, you will learn how to achieve the same results as shown in the previous procedure but using a different technique for finding new dimension members. In the following procedure, you will learn how to use the Lookup task.

Add a new package

1. Right-click SSIS Packages and choose New SSIS Package. Right-click the new package and rename it **DW_DimMgmt_2.dtsx**.

2. Drag a Data Flow task from the Toolbox window onto the Control Flow workspace. Right-click the task and rename it **Find New Dim Members Process 2**.

3. Double-click the Data Flow task to activate the Data Flow tab. From the Data Flow Sources group in the Toolbox, drag an OLE DB Source object onto the designer.

4. Right-click the new OLE DB source and rename it **Stage Customer Table**.

5. Double-click Stage Customer Table and select New to create a new OLE DB connection. Select localhost.SSIS DW and click OK.

6. Select [dbo].[DimStageCustomer] from the drop-down list of Name Of The Table Or The View. Click OK.

   Your screen should look like this:

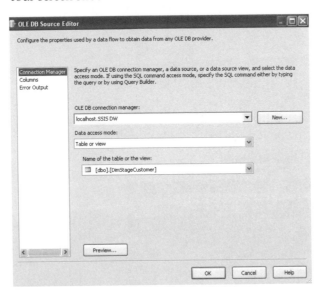

Add a Lookup task process

1. Drag a Lookup task from the Data Flow Transformations group in the Toolbox onto the Data Flow workspace and connect it to the Stage Customer Table data source with the green arrow.

2. Double-click the new Lookup task and select localhost.SSIS DW from the OLE DB Connection Manager.

3. Select the [dbo].[DimCustomer] table as Reference table from the Use A Table Or A View drop-down list.

4. Click the Columns tab and select CustomerKey in Available Lookup Columns. Set Lookup Operation to <add as new column>. Set Output Alias to LookupValue.

Your screen should look like this:

5. Click Configure Error Output and set Lookup Output to Redirect Row. Set the Lookup-Value Truncation column to Redirect Row.

Your screen should look like this:

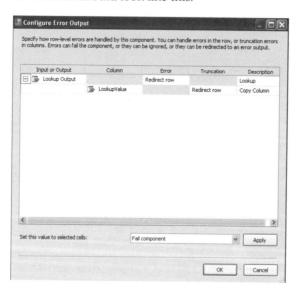

> **Note**   All rows that do not have corresponding rows in the existing dimension table will be redirected to error output.

6. Click OK twice to close the editors.

Add a flat file destination

1. From the Data Flow Destinations group in the Toolbox, drag a Flat File Destination onto the designer and connect it to the red error output arrow from the Lookup task. Click OK in the Configure Error Output window.

2. Double-click the new Flat File destination and click the New button to configure it.

3. Click OK to accept Delimited as the flat file format.

4. In the Connection Manager name field, type **New Found Customers 2**.

5. Click Browse and navigate to C:\Documents and Settings\<username>\My Documents\Microsoft Press\is2005sbs\Data\NewDimCustomers2.txt.

6. Select the Column Names In The First Data Row check box, and then click OK.

7. Select the Overwrite Data In The File check box and click Mappings in the left pane.

8. Click OK.

9. Click Save All on the toolbar to save the package.

10. Right-click DW_DimMgmt_2.dtsx in Solution Explorer and choose Execute Package. Your screen should look like this:

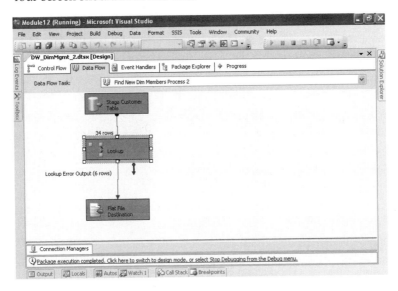

> **Note** Six new customer rows should be written to the destination file.

11. Click Stop Debugging on the Debug menu.

12. Right-click Flat File Destination and choose Edit. Choose Preview to view the data.

13. Click Close and then OK to exit the editor.

> **Note**   Both of these SSIS packages achieve the same result and, usually, you would append the new members directly to the dimension table instead of creating a flat file destination. The second technique (using the Lookup task) is much easier. It is important to remember that using the lookup error output in this manner can be confusing for some users.

Slowly Changing Dimensions

The *slowly changing dimension* (SCD) should technically be called slowly changing attribute because any attribute can be handled differently from any other. There are three logical ways of dealing with a slowly changing attribute, identified by three types:

- **Type 1**   The existing record is updated with the change. Replacing the data is very appropriate if the old data was erroneous, or it is unlikely that the changes will materially affect important analyses. Type 1 slowly changing dimensions do require re-creating any aggregations that would be affected by the change.

- **Type 2**   History is preserved, a new record is added to the dimension, and the old record is marked as inactive and retained with the table. *EndDate* or *IsLatest* attribute columns generally represent the latest record of the dimension member business key. A new surrogate key is created for every change, irrespective of the business key. Type 2 changes can cause a serious inflation in the number of members of a dimension.

- **Type 3**   Type 3 preserves a version of the history by adding it to the dimension record in a different attribute. Typically, there are two states: current and previous. In some cases, you can have four or five states. When the number of defined states is exceeded, previous states are discarded. A Type 3 change does not create a new row, but it does require extra columns in the dimension table schema. As with a Type 1 change, a Type 3 change requires a dimension update, so you need to re-process all aggregations affected after a change.

While loading dimension tables in the data warehouse, you can check for the existence of the new records. If the dimension record already exists, you have a Type 1 or Type 2 effect, depending on the attribute that is changed. If the record does not exist, you can simply add one. In addition, sometimes the record exists in the data warehouse but is no longer in the source database. This signals a logical deletion. Comparing the existence of the values in both the new and old data sets can be slow, particularly when the tables are large.

A good solution is to use a full outer join between the new table and the existing warehouse dimension table, using the business key for the join. You can then determine updates, inserts, and deletes in one query like the following:

```
Select SourceTable Full Outer Join Dim_Table On SourceTable.BusinessKey =
Dim_Table.BusinessKey
```

If the resulting dimension business key is NULL, it means the corresponding record does not exist in warehouse (or that it has expired). In this case, a new record can be inserted into the warehouse table. If the resulting source business key is NULL, it means the corresponding record has been deleted and should be flagged with an *EndDate* in the warehouse table. If neither business key is NULL, it means the corresponding record exists in warehouse and is active. In this case, the appropriate Type 1 or Type 2 processing can be performed as required.

SSIS provides a new Slowly Changing Dimension Wizard as the configuration editor for creating a Slowly Changing Dimension transformation. Building and configuring the data flow for slowly changing dimension data can be a complex task. The Slowly Changing Dimension Wizard offers the simplest method of building the data flow for the Slowly Changing Dimension transformation outputs by guiding you through the steps of mapping columns, selecting business key columns, setting column change attributes, and configuring support for inferred dimension members.

You must choose at least one business key column in the dimension table and map it to an input column. The value of the business key links a record in the source to a record in the dimension table. The transformation uses this mapping to locate the record in the dimension table and to determine whether a record is new or changing. The business key is typically the primary key in the source, but it can be an alternate key as long as it uniquely identifies a record and its value does not change. A business key can also be a composite key, consisting of multiple columns. The primary key in the dimension table is usually a surrogate key, which means a numeric value generated automatically by an identity column or by a custom solution such as a script.

Before you can run the Slowly Changing Dimension Wizard, you must add a source and a Slowly Changing Dimension transformation to the data flow and then connect the output from the source to the input of the Slowly Changing Dimension transformation. Optionally, the data flow can include other transformations between the data source and the Slowly Changing Dimension transformation.

Managing Slowly Changing Dimensions

In this procedure you will learn how to use the new SSIS Slowly Changing Dimension transformation. The transformation will update the Customer Dimension based upon slowly changing dimension changes for Types 1, 2, and 3 changes. You will create a multiple control flow SSIS package that first loads a sample Customer Dimension in a sample database and then uses the Slowly Changing Dimension Wizard to apply updates, additions, and deletions to the sample dimension.

> **Note**   In the next series of steps, you will create a new SSIS package that uses the Slowly Changing Dimension transformation. You will see how this one transformation replaces the majority of the complex tasks and transformations used in the SQL Server 2000 DTS 2000 package designer.

Add a new package for designing a slowly changing dimension process

1. In Solution Explorer, right-click the SSIS Packages folder in the Chapter13 project and select New SSIS Package.

2. Right-click the new package and rename the package **Customers_SCD**.

3. Add a Data Flow task to the Control Flow tab.

4. Right-click the task and rename the task **Create Customer Dim**.

5. On the Data Flow tab, open the Toolbox and, from the Data Flow Sources group, drag an OLE DB Source to the designer.

6. Rename it **Dim Customer**.

7. Double-click the new source to open the editor.

8. Click New to create a new connection manager named **SSIS DW**.

9. Create a new data connection to the server localhost and to the SSIS DW database.

10. Select the [dbo].[DimCustomer] table from the Name Of Tthe Table Or The View in the OLE DB Source Editor dialog box.

11. In the Columns section of the editor, deselect all column check boxes except the following:

    ❑ CustomerKey

    ❑ FirstName

    ❑ LastName

    ❑ BirthDate

    ❑ MaritalStatus

    ❑ Gender

    ❑ EmailAddress

    ❑ YearlyIncome

    ❑ AddressLine1

Your screen should look like this:

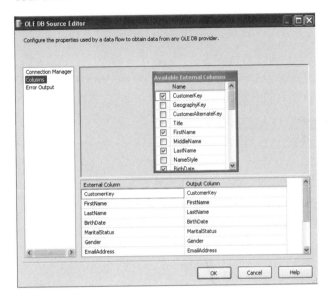

Click OK.

Add a Percentage Sampling transformation

1. Drag a Percentage Sampling transformation onto the Data Flow task grid from the Toolbox.

> **Note**   The Percentage Sampling task will allow you to work with a subset of the Dim-Customer table. The Percentage Sampling and Row Sampling transformations provide very effective means of limiting your data set during prototype package development and testing.

2. Connect an output arrow from the OLE DB Source data adapter to the Percentage Sampling transformation.

3. Double-click the transformation to open the editor.

4. Select 15 percent of rows.

5. Change the sample output name to **Selected Customers** and the unselected output name to **Unselected Customers**.

6. Select the Use The Following Random Seed check box and enter **150**.

> **Note**   Selecting a seed value will enable the transformation always to select the same data set. Although great for development, seed values should not be used in a production environment.

Your screen should look like this:

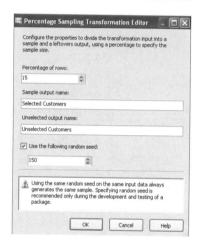

7. Click OK to close the editor.

> **Note**   In the next two steps, you will create a new database (with simple recovery mode) using SQL Server Management Studio (SSMS), and create a new customer dimension table from within a SQL Server Destination from BIDS. These will be used by the package you are creating and will be maintained by a Slowly Changing Dimension transformation.

Connect to SSMS to create a simple database for a new dimension table

1. Start SQL Server Management Studio, and connect to the localhost *is2005sbs* database.

2. In Object Explorer of SSMS, right-click the Databases folder of SQL Server and select New Database.

3. Type the database name: **Customers**.

4. On the Options page, change the Recovery Model to **Simple**.

Your screen should look like this:

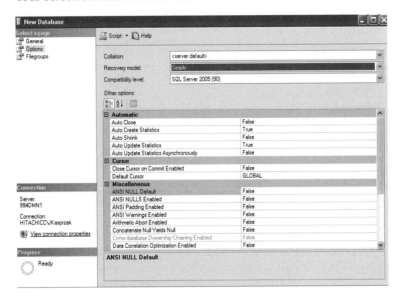

5. Click OK to create the database.

Create a new table within a SQL Server destination

1. Switch back to BIDS and drag an OLE DB Destination object from the Data Flow Destination group in the Toolbox to the designer.

2. Drag an output arrow from the Percentage Sampling transformation onto the SQL Server Destination. Choose the output stream Selected Customers, and then click OK.

3. Double-click the OLE DB Destination data adapter and click the New button to create a new connection manager.

4. Click the New button in the Select Data Connection dialog box to define a new data connection:

    a. Specify the local SQL server as the data source, select Windows Authentication, and select the Customers database.

    b. Click OK twice.

5. Click the New button next to Use A Table Or View in the OLE DB Destination Editor dialog box to create a new table.

6. Make changes to the default Create Table command as indicated by the following bold text. (Change the table name to **DimCustomer** and add the column **CurrentRecord**, as shown here.)

```
CREATE TABLE [DimCustomer] (
    [CustomerKey] INTEGER,
    [FirstName] NVARCHAR(50),
    [LastName] NVARCHAR(50),
    [BirthDate] DATETIME,
    [MaritalStatus] NVARCHAR(1),
    [Gender] NVARCHAR(1),
    [EmailAddress] NVARCHAR(50),
    [YearlyIncome] MONEY,
    [AddressLine1] NVARCHAR(120),
    [CurrentRecord] NVARCHAR(10)
)
```

> **Note**   The *CurrentRecord* field will be used to flag the current version of SCD Type 2 records with a value of *True* and all historical dimension records with a value of *False*. This field should initially be set to *True* for all records because each represents the current record.

7. Click OK.

8. Click Mappings to align the input and destination columns.

   Your screen should look like this:

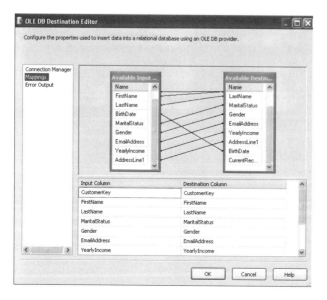

9. Click OK.

> **Note**   In the next steps, you will add a task to initialize the *CurrentRecord* field to *True* for all records. This is performed to identify all the current dimension rows as the most current version. You will use this column to identify which rows have been changed by the Slowly Changing Dimension task.

Initialize the CurrentRecord column for Slowly Changing Dimension reference

1. Click the Control Flow page and add a new Execute SQL Task.

2. Double-click the new SQL task and set the following properties:

   ❑ Name the task **Update CurrentRecord**.

   ❑ Select localhost.Customers as the Connection.

   Your screen should look like this:

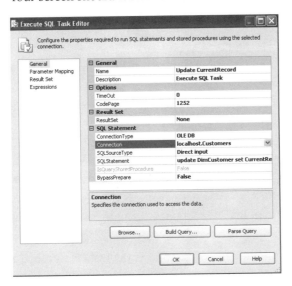

3. In the *SQLStatement* property field, click the ellipses button and type the following SQL Statement:

```
update DimCustomer set CurrentRecord = 'True'
```

Your screen should look like this:

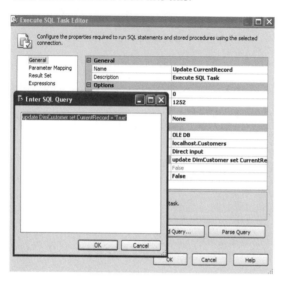

4. Click OK.

5. Add a precedence constraint by dragging the green arrow from Create Customer Dimension to Update CurrentRecord.

Add a new control flow for customer dimension updates

1. On the Control Flow grid, add a new Data Flow task, right-click the task, and rename it **Customer Dim Maintenance**.

2. Add a precedence constraint from the Update CurrentRecord task to Customer Dimension Maintenance.

3. Double-click Customer Dim Maintenance and, on the Data Flow tab, drag a Flat File source from the Toolbox to the designer.

4. Double-click the Flat File Source data adapter and click the New button to create a new connection manager.

5. Name the connection manager **Customer Updates**.

6. Use the Browse button to navigate to the C:\Documents and Settings\<username>\My Documents\Microsoft Press\is2005sbs\Chap13\Data\CustomerUpdates.txt source text file.

Note   This file contains updated customer information. The Slowly Changing Dimension transformation will identify any new information in it and then perform the necessary updates and insertions to DimCustomer.

7. Select the Column Names In The First Data Row check box.

8. On the Advanced tab, correct DataType and OutputColumnWidth for each column, as shown here:

   ❑ CustomerKey: four-byte signed integer

   ❑ FirstName: Unicode string (50)

   ❑ LastName: Unicode string (50)

   ❑ BirthDate: database timestamp

   ❑ MaritalStatus: Unicode string (1)

   ❑ Gender: Unicode string(1)

   ❑ EmailAddress: Unicode string (50)

   ❑ YearlyIncome: Currency

   ❑ AddressLine1: Unicode string (120)

   Your screen should look like this:

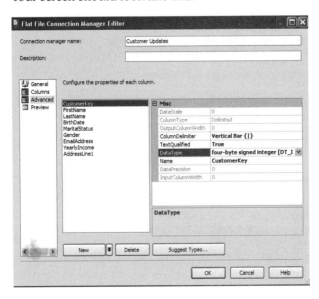

9. Click OK.

10. In the Flat File Source Editor, click Columns to set the mappings.

11. Click OK.

Add a Slowly Changing Dimension transformation

1. Drag a Slowly Changing Dimension (SCD) transformation to the Data Flow grid.

2. Click the Flat File Source data adapter to select it and drag its green arrow onto the SCD transformation.

3. Double-click the transformation to open the Slowly Changing Dimension Wizard.

> **Note**   The Slowly Changing Dimension Wizard will walk you through the steps of identifying the dimension's key fields, which are SCD Type 1 and SCD Type 2. For SCD Type 1 fields, the SCD transformation will update the existing dimension record with any new data. When new data is identified for SCD Type 2 fields, a whole new record is created. A flag field is maintained by the transformation to distinguish the old and new records.

4. Select Customers in the Connection Manager drop-down list and DimCustomer in the Table Or View drop-down list.

5. In the Key Type column, from the drop-down list, select Business Key for CustomerKey.

   Your screen should look like this:

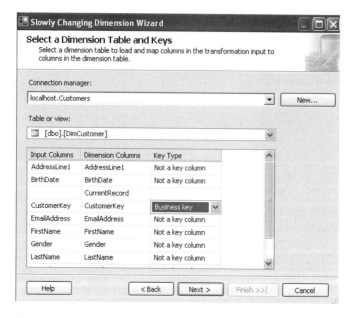

6. Click Next.

> **Note**   This field will be used to join records in CustomerUpdates.txt to those in Dim-Customer. In a production environment, it is unlikely that the customer surrogate key would be stored in the customer update file. Instead, a process would exist within an SSIS package to look up the correct key for existing customer records and generate a key for new records.

7. Add each of the non-key columns by clicking the list box in the Dimension Columns list.

8. In the Change Type list box for AddressLine1, click Historical Attribute.

> **Note**   This column will be treated as SCD Type 2. Any change in value will result in the creation of a new Current record.

9. Identify EmailAddress, LastName, MaritalStatus, and YearlyIncome as changing attributes.

> **Note**   These will be treated as SCD Type 1. Any changes to these columns will result in an update to the underlying record.

10. Select FirstName, BirthDate, and Gender as fixed attributes.

    Your screen should look like this:

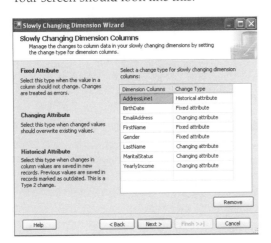

11. Click Next.

12. Clear the check boxes on the Fixed and Changing Attribute Options page.

13. Click Next.

14. Select CurrentRecord in the Column To Indicate Current Record drop-down list.

15. Set Value When Current to True.

    Your screen should look like this:

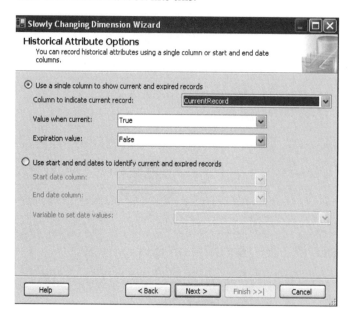

16. Click Next.

17. Clear the Enable Inferred Member Support check box to disable it.

    Your screen should look like this:

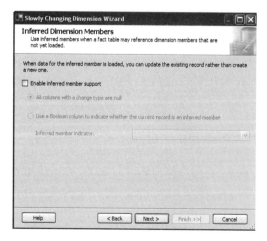

18. Click Next, and then click Finish.

19. Execute the package.

> **Note** The Slowly Changing Dimension Wizard will create three branches in the pipeline from the Slowly Changing Dimension transformation: one to process new records, one to process SCD Type 1 records, and one to process SCD Type 2 records. Three records from CustomerUpdates.txt will travel down the historical attributes path, two records will travel down the changing attributes path, and one new record will be added to the dimension. A total of four new records will be inserted into the dimension.

Your screen should look like this:

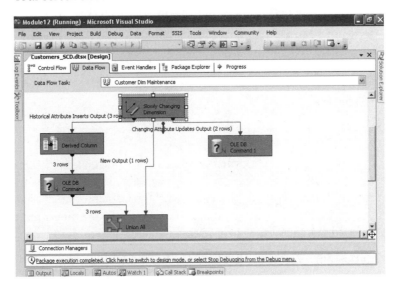

20. Select Stop Debugging.

21. Save the project.

Managing Fact Tables

You've learned that when maintaining data for fact tables and dimension tables, the order is important because you don't want to load fact data that has dimension relationships (foreign to primary key) that might not already exist in the dimension tables. So the order (or control flow) of your data warehouse SSIS packages is important. As a rule, dimension data processing should be performed before fact table data.

Aggregating Data in Fact Tables

Data is generally aggregated to store the summarized information over a period of time of the fact measures such as the number of units of a product sold in a given month. The source for these aggregations is the detailed granular fact, which collects transactional information from the source at regular intervals of time. In some data warehouses, the aggregation is performed directly by the ETL process to move it into an aggregated fact table, where the detailed transactional records do not have any value for the report users. For example, executives might not need to see the number of units sold at the sixth hour of a day.

When fact tables contain transactions for dimension members that have not yet been loaded and without a default member (zero key dimension), the SSIS Load process will usually fail. The failure is triggered by the database, which is forcing referential integrity between the fact transactions and the dimensions. SSIS allows you to configure error handling during package execution. A common practice is to route error records in the SSIS Data Pipeline to error files or tables for further investigation. In the following demonstration, you will learn how to use this helpful capability in SSIS.

Loading Fact Tables

In the next procedure, you will perform a series of steps to create a new SSIS package that loads a fact table. Sometimes fact table sources can contain information that might violate the referential integrity of the DW mode (for example, if the fact table has rows for dimension members that do not exist in the dimensions). The following procedure will show you how to detect and manage loading fact tables that demonstrate this condition.

Add a new package for fact table load processing

1. Right-click the SSIS Packages Folder in the Chap13 project and select New SSIS Package.

2. Right-click and rename the Package **IntSalesFactLoad.dtsx**.

3. Add an Execute SQL task to the Control Flow tab; then right-click the new task and rename it **Clear Staging Table**.

4. Right-click in the white space in the Connection Managers pane at the bottom of the window and select New OLE DB Connection.

5. Select localhost.SSIS DW for the database, and then click OK.

6. Double-click Clear Staging Table and choose localhost.SSIS DW from the Connection drop-down list.

7. In the *SQLStatement* property field, click the ellipses button and type the following SQL Statement:

```
Delete from StageInternetSales
```

Your screen should look like this:

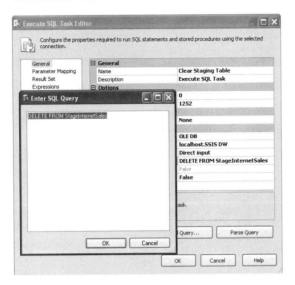

8. Click OK twice.

9. From the Toolbox, drag a Data Flow task to the Control Flow designer.

10. Right-click the new task, rename it **Stage New Internet Sales**, and then connect it to the Execute SQL task by dragging the green arrow from the SQL task to the new task.

11. Double-click Stage New Internet Sales to open the Data Flow tab.

12. Add a Flat File source to Data Flow.

13. Double-click the new source and select New to create a new Flat File connection manager.

14. Type **Internet Sales Extract File** as the connection manager name.

15. Browse to C:\Documents and Settings\<username>\My Documents\Microsoft Press\is2005sbs\Chap13\Data\NewInternetSalesExtract.csv.

16. Select the Column Names In The First Data Row check box and verify that the format is set to Delimited.

17. Click the Columns tab to set the mappings, and then click OK.

18. Right-click the Flat File source and rename it **Internet Sales Extract File**.

Add a Multicast task and an Aggregate task

1. Drag a Multicast task from the Toolbox to the Data Flow and connect the Internet Sales Extract File source to the Multicast task.

2. From the Toolbox, add an Aggregate task to the data flow and connect the Multicast task to it.

3. Double-click the Aggregate task.

4. Click the SONBR (sales order number) column in Available Input Columns to configure the Aggregate task to count the number of distinct new Internet sales orders.

5. Set the output alias to TotalNewOrders.

6. Set the operation to Count Distinct.

   Your screen should look like this:

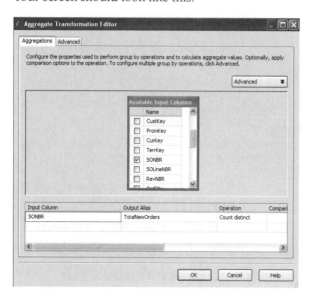

7. Click OK.

> **Note**   You might often want to capture counts and check sums to compare and validate fact tables loading. To accomplish this, you can use the Derived Column task to add aggregate values to the data flow for storing downstream validation.

Add a Derived Column task

1. Drag a Derived Column task to the Data Flow and connect the Aggregate task to it.

2. Double-click the Derived Column task to derive a new column named TotalOrders in the Derived Column Transformation Editor.

3. Click the column's plus sign (+) to expand the available columns.

4. Drag the TotalNewOrders to the expressions position.

Your screen should look like this:

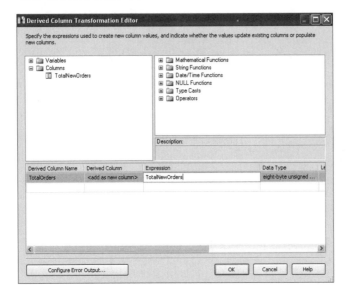

5. Click OK.

6. Add a Flat File destination from the Toolbox and connect it to the Derived Column task.

7. Double-click the new Flat File destination and select New.

8. Accept Delimited as the format and click OK.

9. Name the new connection manager **Total New Orders Check Count**.

10. Browse to C:\Documents and Settings\<username>\My Documents\Microsoft Press\is2005sbs\Chap13\Data\TotalNewIntOrders.txt.

11. Click OK.

12. Click Mappings in the left pane, and then click OK.

Add a Data Conversion task

1. Add a Data Conversion task from the Toolbox and connect it to the Multicast task by dragging the green arrow from the Multicast to the Data Conversion task.

2. Double-click Data Conversion and select the SONBR, CarrierID, and CustPO columns from the Available Input Columns for conversion.

3. Change Data Type to Unicode string[DT_WSTR] for each.

4. Change the length for SONBR to 20 and to 25 for the other two columns.

Your screen should look like this:

5. Click OK.

6. Add an OLE DB destination and connect the Data Conversion task to the new destination.

7. Double-click Destination, configure the destination to use the existing localhost.SSIS DW, and select the [dbo].[StageInternetSales] table from the Name Of The Table Or The View drop-down list.

8. Click Mapping in the left pane.

9. Expand the page for the available input and output columns to view all the columns.

10. Line up the columns from the top down and map columns 1 to 1, 2 to 2, 3 to 3, and so on except for SONBR, CarrierID, and CustPO. (Mapping columns is done by clicking the item in Available Input Columns and dragging it over to the corresponding item in Available Destination Columns.)

11. Map Copy of SOBR, Copy of CarrierID, and Copy of CustPO to SalesOrderNumber, CarrierTrackingNumber, and CustomerPONumber, respectively.

Your screen should look like this:

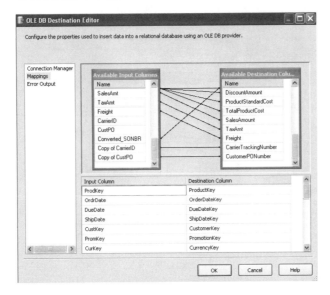

12.   Click OK.

> **Note**   The data flow to load the staging table with the new extract file for Internet sales is complete. Now you need another data flow to load the fact table from the staging table.

Add a new data flow to load the fact table from the staging table

1.   Click the Control Flow tab and add a new Data Flow task.

2.   Right-click the new task and rename it **Load New Internet Sales Facts**. Connect the Stage New Internet Sales data flow task to it.

3.   Double-click the new data flow to go to the design window.

4.   Add an OLE DB data source from the Toolbox for Load New Internet Sales.

5.   Double-click the data source and configure it to use localhost.SSIS DW.

6.   Select the [dbo].[StageInternetSales] table from the Name Of The Table Or The View drop-down list, and then click OK.

Add a variable and a Row Count task

1.   Right-click the designer surface and select Variables to display the Variables tab and add a new variable.

2. Name it **IntSalesCount** and leave all other default values.

Your screen should look like this:

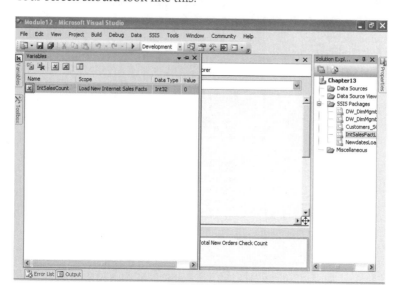

3. Drag a Row Count task from the Toolbox to the Data Flow designer and connect the data source to it.

4. Double-click the new Row Count and configure it to use the *IntSalesCount* variable by typing **IntSalesCount** in the *VariableName* field.

Your screen should look like this:

5. Click OK.

Add an OLE DB destination and configure Error Output

1. Drag an OLE DB Destination from the Toolbox to the Data Flow task and connect the Row Count task to it.

2. Right-click the new destination and rename it **Internet Sales Fact Table**.

3. Double-click the new Destination and configure it to use the localhost.SSIS DW.

4. Select the [dbo].[FactInternetSales] table from the Name Of The Table or The View drop-down list.

5. Change the Rows Per Batch to 1.

6. Change the Maximum Insert Commit Size to 1.

   Your screen should look like this:

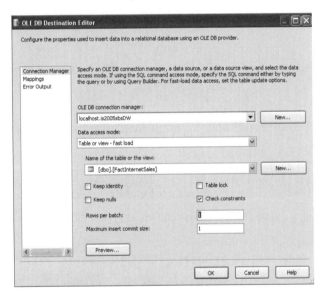

7. Click Mappings.

8. Click Error Output.

9. Set Error for OLE DB Destination Input to Redirect Row.

Your screen should look like this:

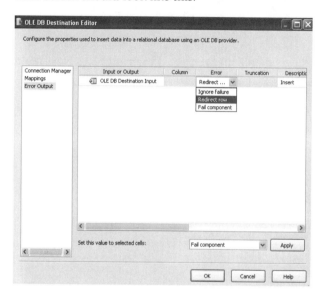

10. Click OK.

11. Add a Flat File destination and connect it to the red arrow from the Internet Sales Fact Table destination.

12. Click OK in the Configure Error Output dialog box.

13. Right-click the new destination and rename it **Load Errors File**.

14. Double-click the new destination and select New to create a new Flat File connection manager.

15. Accept Delimited as the Flat File format and click OK.

16. Name the new connection manager **Load Errors File**.

17. Browse to C:\Documents and Settings\<username>\My Documents\Microsoft Press\is2005sbs\Chap13\Data\ErrorInternetSalesRows.csv.

18. Select Column Names In The First Data Row, and then click OK.

19. Click Mappings in the left pane, and then click OK.

20. Click Save All on the toolbar.

21. Right-click IntSalesFactLoad.dtsx and select Execute Package.

Your screen should look like this:

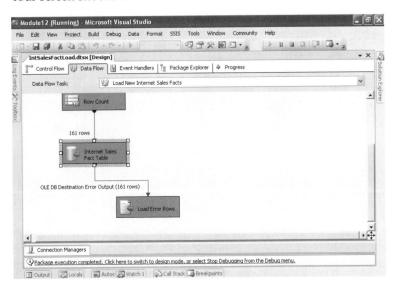

Note   The package fails to load all the rows. The error rows are written to the error file. Upon inspection, the fact sales are for new dates that have not been added yet to the DimTime dimension. The referential integrity of the database prevents these sales facts from being loaded into the DW. The DimTime table needs to be updated first with additional members for the new time frames, and the fact table will need to be reloaded.

22. Click Stop Debugging from the Debug menu.

23. Right-click SSIS Packages in Solution Explorer and select New SSIS Package.

24. Right-click and rename this package **NewDatesLoad.dtsx**.

25. From the Control Flow Items group in the Toolbox, add an Execute SQL task to the Control Flow grid, and then right-click and rename the task **Clear Dates**.

26. Double-click the Clear Dates task and type the following property for the connection: **localhost.SSIS DW**.

27. In the *SQLStatement* property field, click the ellipses button and enter the following SQL Statement:

```
Delete from dbo.DimTime where FullDateAlternateKey > = '9/1/2004'
```

28. Click OK.

29. From the Toolbox, drag a new Data Flow task onto the Control Flow designer. Connect it to the Clear Dates task, and then right-click and rename it **Insert New Additional Dates**.

30. Double-click the new task to open the Data Flow tab.

31. Drag a new Flat File source from the Toolbox onto the Data Flow designer, and then right-click and rename the source **NewDates**.

32. Double-click NewDates and select New to create a new connection manager.

33. Type **NewDates** in the name field.

34. Click Browse and navigate to C:\Documents and Settings\<username>\My Documents\Microsoft Press\is2005sbs\Chap13\Data\NewDates.csv.

35. Select Column Names In The First Data Row, click Columns in the left pane, and then click OK twice.

36. Drag Data Conversion Transformation from the Toolbox to the Data Flow designer and connect the NewDates Flat File source to it with the green arrow.

37. Double-click Data Conversion, select the following from the Input Column Names, and type their properties:

    ❑ EnglishDayName – Unicode String, length = **10**

    ❑ SpanishDayName – Unicode String, length = **10**

    ❑ FrenchDayName – Unicode String, length = **10**

    ❑ EnglishMnthName – Unicode String, length = **10**

    ❑ SpanishMnthName – Unicode String, length = **10**

    ❑ FrenchMnthName – Unicode String, length = **10**

    Your screen should look like this:

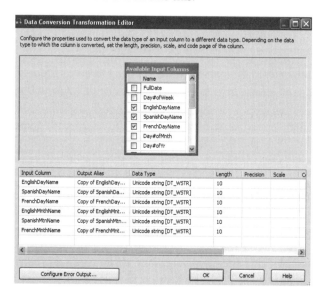

38. Click OK.

39. Drag an OLE DB destination from the Toolbox to the Data Flow designer and connect Data Conversion to it.

40. Double-click the new OLE DB destination.

41. Select Table Or View from the Data Access Mode drop-down list.

42. Select [dbo].[DimTime] from the Name Of The Table Or The View drop-down list.

43. Click the Mappings tab in the left pane, and then map the appropriate columns by selecting the item in the Input Column that corresponds to the OutputColumn.

    Your screen should look like this:

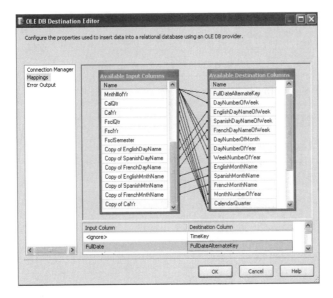

44. Click OK.

45. Execute the NewDatesLoad.dtsx package by right-clicking it and selecting Execute Package.

46. The package adds 668 new dates to the DimTime dimension.

47. Click Stop Debugging from the Debug menu, and then right-click the IntSalesFact-Load.dtsx package and select Execute Package.

> **Note** In this demonstration, all the records for the new Internet sales facts were rejected. Therefore, you can rerun the IntSalesFactLoad.dtsx package from the beginning. Otherwise, you would have had to modify the connection manager for the extract file to point to the load errors file and only rerun the load for the rejected record.

The fact load should have processed 161 rows that represented 62 new distinct orders as counted and stored in C:\Documents and Settings\<username>\My Documents\ Microsoft Press\is2005sbs\Chap13\Data\TotalNewIntOrders.txt.

48. Open SSMS and connect to Database Engine.

49. Click New Query.

50. In the Available Databases drop-down list, select SSIS DW.

51. Type the following query:

```
Select count(distinct SalesOrderNumber) from factinternetsales where orderdatekey =
1159
```

52. Click Execute.

Note   The value returned should equal 62 and match the check value from the staging process.

Your screen should look like this:

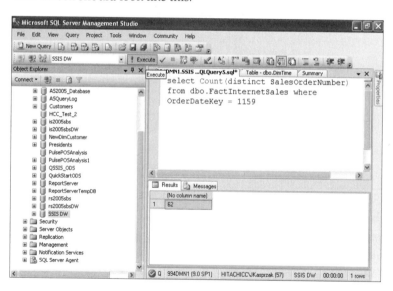

53. Go back to BIDS and save and close the project.

Chapter 13 Quick Reference

This term	Means this
Data warehouse	A relational database designed to store management information distinct from the application data source systems that provide the data.
Dimension table	A list of labels that can be used to cross-tabulate values from other dimensions.
Fact table	The relational database table that contains values for one or more measures at the lowest level of detail for one or more dimensions.
Surrogate key	A column in a database dimension table that contains values that uniquely identify each row; often referred to as the primary key for a dimension.
Foreign key	A column in a database table that contains many values for each value in the primary key column of another database table.
Join	The processes of linking the primary key of one table to the foreign key of another table.
Star schema	A database model composed of a fact table and one or more dimension tables; typically, used to model data warehouses and data marts.

Chapter 14
SSIS General Principles

After completing this chapter, you will be able to:

- Understand package design considerations.

- Understand package component management.

- Understand package component naming standards and policies.

- Understand package deployment management.

This chapter will provide you with some learned techniques, proven best practices, and suggested approaches for your consideration when designing Microsoft SQL Server Integration Services (SSIS) packages and applications. You will most likely discover and define some best practices appropriate for your business requirements, too. The following list identifies the key initial steps for you to follow when designing applications using SSIS.

- Understand your business requirements.

- Understand your business processes.

- Define your package usability.

- Consider future package maintenance.

Before starting your application design, you need to understand the entire picture. When using SSIS for business integration and management applications, it is important to focus on the business requirements first. The next consideration is to understand your source business system's processes and dependencies and your application's need for staging data based upon the business application system processes. You learned in Chapter 13, "Populating Data Warehouse Structures," that there are many approaches and techniques for staging data for a variety of reasons. Only when all your business requirements and system processes are understood, established, and agreed upon should you go forward with designing and developing data migration, integration, and business intelligence (BI) applications. The design should consider the best types of SSIS tasks, components, and control flow processes to make optimal use of all parts of the application.

When you design the application packages for initial use, it is equally important to consider the package design for future maintenance in view of business and application changes. Often, this includes annotations, naming standards for SSIS package components, and other techniques you will learn about later in this chapter.

When using SSIS within data warehouse and BI systems, you also need to decide how to manage dimension tables with surrogate keys. The use of system-generated surrogate keys is a best practices discipline. Once the dimension table management is established, your attention will be focused on the fact tables to determine which level of data granularity is possible and desired.

In Chapter 13, you learned that the SQL Server 2005 SSIS data integration engine and data pipeline constitute a different architecture, requiring a different design strategy than for Data Transformation Services 2000. SSIS can perform data transforms in memory and in parallel, thus enhancing performance. Anytime you can design a package to minimize data writes (other than the final destination, of course), that is best for performance.

Eliminating disk data writes is not always available for your design. You might remember that you sometimes have to stage data that will require intermediate writing to disk. Most often, this is a characteristic of data availability and timing of business processes that provide the data for your application. You need to determine whether staged data needs to be persisted or can be temporarily stored for a specified time frame.

Designing SSIS Packages

When it comes to application development using comprehensive tools such as SSIS, there are usually more ways to design an application than you can count. In the next sections, you will learn an approach to use when starting to design SSIS applications.

OVAL Principles of SSIS Package Design

Created as a development framework for SSIS packages, OVAL principles of package design encompass four facets of SSIS applications. These design considerations include identifying the *Operations* to be performed; the data *Volume* to be processed (in production); the *Application* of the right tools, tasks, sequence, and flow; and *Location*—determining where the SSIS application will run. Each of these facets and its elements is reviewed in the next sections and illustrated in Figure 14-1.

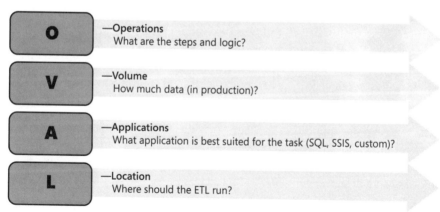

Figure 14-1 OVAL principles of performance

The operations facet of OVAL requires you to consider the steps and logic necessary for your application and how these map to your business processes. You will need to research and understand all operations required. For example, an operations flow can include:

- Opening a transaction on SQL Server.
- Reading data from the text file.
- Loading data into the SSIS data flow.
- Loading the data into SQL Server.
- Committing the transaction.

Beware of hidden operations that might be happening external to your package processing design. Operations often include data conversion and determining when the best time is to perform this operation (that is, in either step 3 or step 10). Some operations might depend on processes external to SSIS, too.

Best practices design concerning data conversion is first to sharpen data types among your data sources and targets to meet your business requirements most efficiently and avoid unnecessary data type conversions. SSIS provides Fast Parse and Suggest Types In Flat File Source that work pretty well. Sometimes, you want to control data type strictly by size for performance processing and storage optimization. A default character size of 50 is often unnecessary, so take the time to reduce character columns appropriately. For example, what data type should you use for numeric data in a range from 1 to 200? Your choices include:

- 4 bytes (real).
- 3 bytes (string).
- 1 byte (byte).

To minimize memory buffers for your data flow and to reduce storage for data, you might opt for the single byte because it takes up the least space. It might seem insignificant to save three bytes, but when accumulating byte savings among numeric and character data, data type is very important and a key performance enhancement when you are dealing with large volumes of data.

The next facet of OVAL after you have defined your operations requirements is volume or, more specifically, how much data in production needs to be processed. The phrase "in production" is key here because often, when developing your application, you are dealing with subsets of production data that will not predict the application performance when executed against production volume data sources. You can also use data snapshots of production databases for your development and testing to simulate and benchmark performance.

Another best practices discipline is to remove redundant or unused columns from your data sources. This sounds obvious, but it is often not performed on the chance that the application might need the data at a future point. Paying the overhead of processing unused data columns through the SSIS engine and data pipeline is usually not worth it. Always use SELECT statements as opposed to tables when configuring a data source. Using a table source configuration is equivalent to using a SELECT * From...Where... statement, which is almost always considered bad practice. SELECT * is your enemy. The WHERE clause is your friend.

Another best practices approach is to remove redundant columns after every asynchronous component. For example, if you have derived new columns from source columns and no longer need the source columns, there is no need to pass these along through the data pipeline. Transformation components with asynchronous outputs are unique because they act as both destination and source components. These types of components receive rows from upstream components and add rows that are consumed by downstream components. No other data flow component performs both of these operations.

The columns from upstream components that are available to a component with synchronous outputs are automatically available to components downstream from the component. Therefore, a component with synchronous outputs does not have to define any output columns to provide columns and rows to the next component. Components with asynchronous outputs, on the other hand, must define output columns and provide rows to downstream components. Therefore, a component with asynchronous outputs has more tasks to perform during both design and execution time.

SSIS provides a Filter task for use in designing applications. If you can filter your rows in the WHERE clause of your data source, that is optimal for your design. Sometimes, however, you might need to filter rows farther into the data flow and, if so, use the Filter task.

In addition to the Filter task, SSIS provides the Conditional Split. Similar to the Filter task, the conditional split can be used to concatenate columns and re-route unneeded rows to optimize your data pipeline performance.

The next facet of OVAL for application design is to consider the application or, more specifically, what application options are best suited for the task to be performed. Should you use a SQL Server 2005 utility such as bulk copy program (BCP), an SSIS package, a custom program, or something else? Choosing which application component isn't always easy or obvious and might require some evaluation, testing, and even a pilot application model.

Given the power and performance of SQL Server 2005, it has become a best practice approach to use the database management system (DBMS) wherever suitable. Rather than reading data from multiple database tables within a single source database and using the Merge Join task within an SSIS package, it is significantly better to create DBMS views or stored procedures and exploit the power of the SQL Server database engine to prepare the data for other SSIS operations. Joining at the database level is one advantage, but you can also take advantage of eliminating Sort tasks, Conditional Splits, and Filter and Derived Columns tasks by including ORDER BY and basic data cleansing using ISNULL, NULLIF, and TRIM options.

Consider whether BCP is good enough for some of your application's data load requirements. The overhead of starting up an SSIS package can offset any performance gain over BCP for small data sets. Obviously, SSIS provides greater manageability and control than the BCP utility, so if control, monitoring, and error handling are key requirements, SSIS packages can be more desirable. Remember, you can generate an SSIS package for Bulk Import by using the Data Import Wizard within Microsoft SQL Server Management Studio.

The final OVAL facet for your consideration is location or, more specifically, deciding where your extract, transform, and load (ETL) and SSIS application packages and other components run. Sometimes, you really might not have many deployment options and, most often, you will need to comply with the SQL Server SSIS production server implementation characteristics of your system architecture. It is important to know whether your application will compete with other applications for resources. Knowing whether data conversion on Server1 will reduce or increase the volume of data transferred across the network could be important. Other considerations might be the impact and overhead of pulling large volumes of text data over for conversion. Your application target database and tables might reside on other servers. It's usually better for your source or target data to be local so that your application is as close to the data as possible to minimize network access. You might have to work with your systems administrator and SQL Server database administrator when determining the best production implementation options for your company.

Wherever you decide to locate your application for production, make sure you have enough memory; disk space; and optimized, stable network resources. If you have to stage data, consider using local RawFiles, if possible. These are specialized, high-performance files that perform faster than writing and reading data from SQL tables.

Sometimes, you will be requested to provide a baseline of your application's resource requirements. You can achieve this by replacing your application destinations with RowCounts, turning on logging, and using Stat Source. Stat Source will provide you with both the pipeline row count and the time it took to process the memory-buffered data. This technique can also help you change components incrementally to see the effects on processing and to optimize slow components for resources available on the production server.

Using SSIS Components in Your Design

Designing your SSIS application for multiple uses is a good way to minimize the number of packages you need to develop. One approach to achieve this is by using variables that can be configured at run time and enabling one package to run in different ways, depending on the variable values.

Input parameters in SQL commands, including queries and stored procedures, are mapped to variables that are created within the scope of the Execute SQL task or within the scope of the package. The values for variables can be set at design time or populated dynamically at run time.

The Execute SQL task uses the SQL syntax in which question marks (?) indicate parameters. For example, the following query uses two input parameters—one for the FirstName column and one for the LastName column—to select rows from the Contact table in the *Adventure-Works* database.

```
Copy CodeSELECT ContactID, Title, FirstName, MiddleName, LastName,
EmailAddress FROM Person.Contact WHERE FirstName=? OR LastName=?
```

If you build the query using the Query Builder that SSIS provides, the question marks are automatically updated with parameter names, making the parameters easier to work with. The following query shows the parameter names.

```
Copy CodeSELECT ContactID, Title, FirstName, MiddleName, LastName,
EmailAddress FROM Person.Contact WHERE (FirstName = @Param1) OR (LastName = @Param2)
```

To set parameter values, each parameter is mapped to a variable. Parameters are order dependent; they are assigned their value in the order that they appear in the query. In this example, the value of the variable mapped to the first input parameter is assigned to the FirstName column, and the variable mapped to the second input parameter is assigned to the LastName column.

There is limited use of variables inside the data flow of your packages, but you can add a variable as a column to the flow as well as parameterize the source query. For example, for the date range in RowChangeDate in the source system, set date range variables in the master package and pass them down to the child package.

When using the Row Count task, you write the row count to a variable. Other than row count, how do you set a variable in the data flow? Not so easily. Often, it is easier to write to a table or to a Recordset Destination and then reference that when needed.

Using Variables

Variables are a way to set values dynamically and control processes in packages, containers, tasks, and event handlers. Also, precedence constraints can use variables to control the direction of the flow of data to different tasks.

Each container has its own *Variables* collection. When a new variable is created, it is within the scope of its parent container. Because the package container is at the top of the container hierarchy, variables with package scope function, such as global variables, are visible to all containers within the package. The children of the container can also access the collection of variables through the *Variables* collection by using either the variable name or the variable's index in the collection.

Because the visibility of a variable is scoped from the top down, variables declared at the package level are visible to all the containers in the package. Therefore, the *Variables* collection on a container includes all the variables that belong to its parent in addition to its own variables.

Conversely, the variables contained in a task are limited in scope and visibility and are visible only to the task.

If a package runs other packages, the variables defined in the scope of the calling package are available to the called package. The only exception occurs when a same-named variable exists in the called package. When this collision occurs, the variable value in the called package overrides the value from the calling package. Variables defined in the scope of the called package are never available back to the calling package.

Using the Lookup Task versus Merge Join

You now know that SSIS is a pipeline architecture to enable high-performance, memory-based transformation processing. Limiting the pipeline to just those columns of data required for the Lookup (that is, not selecting just the table and using a defined SELECT statement) will improve performance and reduce service and system resources. Caching on Lookup components will also improve processing speed. Figure 14-2 shows this principle.

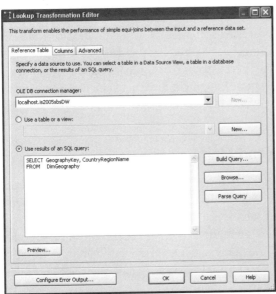

Figure 14-2   Always use the SELECT statement for only the columns you need for the Lookup task

Lookup task components will generally work more quickly than Merge Join components where the two can be used for the same task. There are three configuration modes of operation for a Lookup task:

- Full Cache – for small lookup datasets
- No Cache – for volatile lookup datasets
- Partial Cache – for large lookup datasets

The tradeoff of each approach is always memory usage versus performance. Full Cache is optimal but uses the most memory. Partial Cache configuration uses less memory than Full Cache but affects performance because it takes time to load the Partial Cache because it populates the cache on the fly, using singleton SELECT. No Cache uses no memory but takes the longest. An alternative is to use the Merge Join component instead. The catch is that it requires Sorted inputs, which then must use disk writes.

If possible, avoid using columns that might contain null values in lookup operations. If a column contains null values, configure the Lookup transformation to use an error output that directs rows that have no matching rows in the reference table to a separate transformation output. Alternatively, consider using full caching, which supports lookup operations on null values.

Using Database Snapshots

During testing, you might sometimes need to roll back your databases to their initial states and to perform this in an efficient manner. Using traditional Backup/Restore might also take too long. Long-running transactions are expensive to roll back, too, and the Delete Changes option from the database does not cover all scenarios. SQL Server 2005 provides the new Database Snapshot functionality. Using a specialized log that keeps track of changes—data and metadata—the Database Snapshot performs like an Undo for databases. You can roll back the database by using this log at any time. You might find that Database Snapshots can make development and testing very simple. This technique is a potential best practice for SSIS ETL application development.

Designing for Performance and Maintenance

From an overall package performance perspective, applying your application process to the right component is important. You have learned to use the control flow component for sequencing and to perform multiple iterations of a containerized task (data flow and others). Data flow components are for processing millions of rows of data. Given these combinations, it's important to avoid over-design. Too many moving parts are difficult to maintain and most often result in slow performance. Don't be afraid to experiment; there are many design approaches to meet your processing requirements.

One thing to remember when designing SSIS applications for performance is to maximize parallelism. This can be designed in both control flow and data flow components. Control flow can launch multiple parallel packages, as in the case of master–child designs. Data flow components can parallel-process multiple data pipelines from single data sources or multiple parallel pipelines from multiple data sources.

When using parallel-design techniques, always remember to allocate enough threads for server processing. The *EngineThreads* property is found on the Data Flow task in the control flow component.

There are some SSIS processing tasks that will not always fit parallel design techniques. Figure 14-3 and Figure 14-4 show some ways to use parallel design for different options.

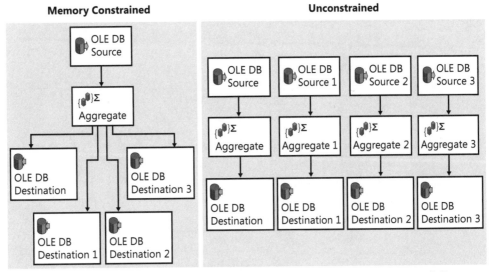

Figure 14-3   Optimizing from constrained to unconstrained processing using parallelism

Reader and CPU Constrained

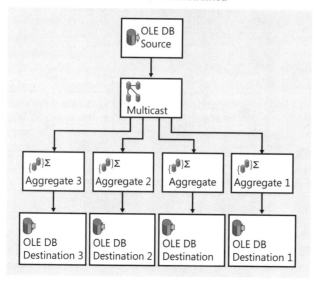

Optimize the slowest

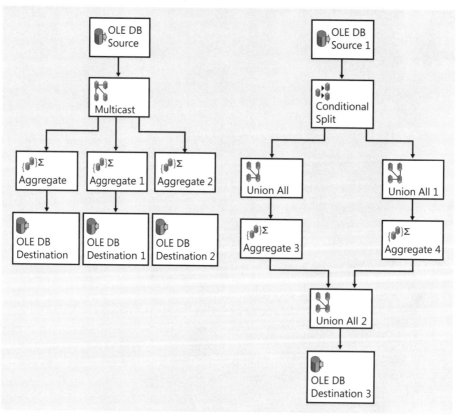

Figure 14-4   Optimizing slowest component using parallelism

Using Fast Parse

Fast parse provides a fast, simple set of routines for parsing data. Fast parse supports only the most commonly used date format representations, does not perform locale-specific parsing, does not recognize special characters in currency data, and cannot convert hexadecimal or scientific representation of integers.

If the data flow in the package requires locale-sensitive parsing, standard parse is recommended instead of fast parse. For example, fast parse does not recognize locale-sensitive data that includes decimal symbols such as the comma, date formats other than year-month-date formats, and currency symbols.

Defining Your Best Practices

Early in your adoption of SSIS for application development, you will want to set your own standard layouts, guidelines, and procedures. Some common best practices design elements for SSIS packages to help make your development process effective, consistent, and easier to maintain include the following:

- Use Row Counts to show whether you have all the rows expected.

- Break out transformation logic specific to your environment.

- Always configure to handle lookup errors (especially for when a fact table business key has no corresponding entry in the dimension table).

- Always perform iterative design and development and testing methodology such as Agile, rapid application deployment (RAD), Extreme, and Microsoft Solutions Framework (MSF), which all promote modularity and short cycles.

- Break complex, multisource, multidestination ETL into logically distinct packages (versus monolithic design).

- Separate subprocesses within a package into separate containers. This is a more elegant, easier way to develop and allows you to disable whole containers simply when debugging.

- Use Script Task/Transform for one-off problems.

- Build custom components to reduce redundant script logic.

Theoretically, you could write one package to do it all. This is not recommended, but if you do, it is best to adopt verbose naming standards for your package elements and comment processes for easier understanding and maintenance.

Rather than create one giant package, many SQL Server SSIS designers create several packages representing distinct, logical units of work. These packages are then called from a master package that acts like the traffic director. The master package contains lots of Execute Package tasks referred to as child packages. A common design approach is to create child packages to process each target table within a multiple-table star schema data model.

Create a Master–Child Package

One way to manage the execution and process of packages is to create a master package that uses the Execute Package task. You can control the sequences of the package execution conditionally. You can even disable select packages from executing, if required. The following procedures show how to create a master package, designed by using SSIS.

Open project and build packages

1. Open the Chp14.sln project in the C:\Documents and Settings\<username>\My Documents\Microsoft Press\is2005sbs\Chap14 folder.

2. The following steps detail creating a new Integration Services Project. Click New, and then click Project from the BIDS File menu. If opening Chp14.sln, these steps will have been completed already.

3. Right-click Package.dtsx and rename this package **MasterPackage.dtsx**.

4. Right-click SSIS Packages and select New SSIS Package. Right-click this package, select Rename, and change the name to **Child1.dtsx**.

5. Right-click SSIS Packages and select New SSIS Package. Right-click this package, select Rename, and change the name to **Child2.dtsx**.

6. Right-click SSIS Packages and select New SSIS Package. Right-click this package, select Rename, and change the name to **Child3.dtsx**.

Add Execute Package tasks

1. Double-click MasterPackage.dtsx and drag an Execute Package task from the Control Flow Items group in the Toolbox to the Control Flow grid.

2. Double-click New Task to edit the properties.

3. Change the name to **Execute Child 1**.

4. Click the Package tab in the list on the left.

5. Set the location to File System.

6. Click in the *Connection* field and select <new connection> in the field drop-down list.

7. In the File Connection Manager Editor, set the Usage type to Existing File. Browse to C:\Documents and Settings\<username>\My Documents\Microsoft Press\is2005sbs\Chap14\Bin and select the Child1.dtsx package file. Click OK twice.

8. Do not change the password.

> **Note**   Note that if the package were password protected, you would need to set the password at this point.

9. Set ExecutionOutOfProcess to False.

10. Your screen should look like this:

11. Click OK.

12. Copy and paste the Execute Child 1 task just below the original task in the same grid.

13. Connect Execute Child1 to the copied task by dragging the green arrow from one to the other.

14. Double-click the newly pasted task and change the task name to **Execute Child 2**.

15. Click the Package tab in the left pane, click in the *Connection* field, and select <New Connection> in the field drop-down list.

16. Set the Usage Type to Existing File, click the Browse button, and browse to C:\Documents and Settings\<username>\My Documents\Microsoft Press\is2005sbs\Chap14\Bin \Child2.dtsx.

17. Click Open, and then click OK twice.

18. Copy and paste the Execute Child 1 task just below the Execute Child 2 task in the same grid.

19. Connect Execute Child 2 to the copied task by dragging the green arrow from one to the other.

20. Double-click the newly pasted task and change the task name to **Execute Child 3**.

21. Click the Package tab in the left pane, click in the *Connection* field, and select <New Connection> in the field drop-down list.

22. Set Usage Type to Existing File, click the Browse button, and browse to C:\Documents and Settings\<username>\My Documents\Microsoft Press\is2005sbs\Chap14\Bin \Child3.dtsx.

23. Click Open, and then click OK twice.

24. Your screen should look like this:

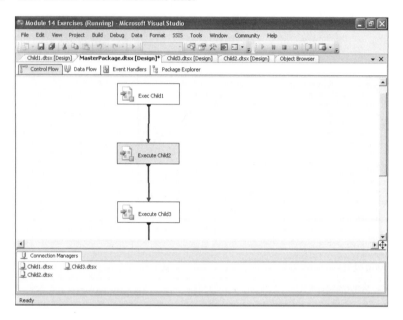

25. Click the Save All button on the toolbar.

Add Data Flow tasks to the child packages

1. Double-click the Child1.dtsx package, and then drag a Data Flow task from the Data Flow Items group in the Toolbox to the Control Flow grid.

2. Right-click the new task and rename it **Child 1**.

3. Double-click the Child 1 task and drag an OLE DB Source from the Data Flow Sources group in the Toolbox to the Data Flow grid.

4. Right-click the new source and rename it **Employees**.

5. Double-click the new source and select New to open the OLE DB Connection Manager.

6. Select localhost.is2005sbsDW from the Data Connections pane and click OK.

7. In the *Name Of The Table Or View* field, select [dbo].[dimEmployee], and then click OK.

Add a Row Count task and variable

1. From the Data Flow Transformations group in the Toolbox, drag a Row Count onto the Data Flow grid.

2. Connect the Employees OLE DB Source to the new Row Count by dragging the green arrow from the source to the transformation.

3. Right-click the Row Count transformation and click Variables. Type the following new variable entries:

   Name: **EmpCount** Scope: **Child1** Data Type: **Int32** Value: **0**

4. Double-click the new Row Count transformation, type **EmpCount** in the *VariableName* field, and then click OK.

5. Your screen should look like this:

6. Double-click the Child2.dtsx package, and then drag a Data Flow task from the Toolbox to the Control Flow grid.

7. Right-click the new task and rename it **Child 2**.

8. Double-click the Child 2 task and drag an OLE DB Source from the Toolbox to the Data Flow grid.

9. Right-click the new source and rename it **Resellers**.

10. Double-click the new source and select New to open the OLE DB Connection Manager.

11. Select localhost.is2005sbsDW from the Data Connections pane and click OK.

12. In the *Name Of The Table Or View* field, select [dbo].[dimReseller], and then click OK.

13. From the Toolbox, drag a Row Count Data Flow transformation onto the Data Flow grid.

14. Connect the Employees OLE DB Source to the new Row Count by dragging the green arrow from the source to the transformation.

15. Right-click the Row Count transformation and click Variables. Type the following new variables:

    Name: **ResellerCount** Scope: **Child2** Data Type: **Int32** Value: **0**

16. Double-click the new Row Count transformation, type **ResellerCount** in the *Variable-Name* field, and then click OK.

17. Double-click the Child3.dtsx package, and then drag a Data Flow task from the Toolbox to the Control Flow grid.

18. Right-click the new task and rename it **Child 3**.

19. Double-click the Child 3 task and drag an OLE DB Source from the Toolbox to the Data Flow grid.

20. Right-click the new source and rename it **Territories**.

21. Double-click the new source and select New to open the OLE DB Connection Manager.

22. Select localhost.is2005sbsDW from the Data Connections pane and click OK.

23. In the *Name Of The Table Or View* field, select [dbo].[dimSalesTerritory], and then click OK.

24. From the Toolbox, drag a Row Count Data Flow transformation into the Data Flow grid.

25. Connect the Employees OLE DB Source to the new Row Count by dragging the green arrow from the source to the transformation.

26. Right-click the Row Count transformation and click Variables. Type the following new variables:

    Name: **TerritoryCount** Scope: **Child3** Data Type: **Int32** Value: **0**

27. Double-click the new Row Count transformation, type **TerritoryCount** in the *Variable-Name* field, and then click OK.

28. Double-click MasterPackage.dtsx.

29. Copy Execute Child 1 – Execute Package, paste it below Execute Child 3, and then connect Execute Child 3 to the new Execute Child 1 – Execute Package 1 by dragging the green arrow from one to the other.

30. Click the Save All button on the Toolbar.

31. Right-click MasterPackage.dtsx in Solution Explorer and select Execute Package.

32. Your screen should look like this:

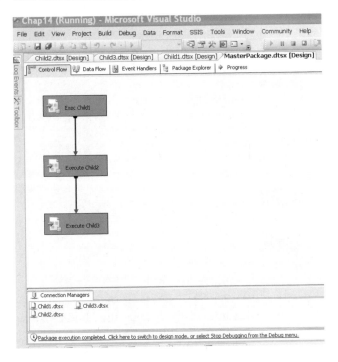

33. Click Stop Debugging from the Debug menu.

Disable an Execute Package task

1. Right-click the Execute Child2 task and select Disable to skip this package in the master package.

> **Note**   When the master package is executed the next time, it will skip this task.

2. Save and execute the package.

3. Your screen should look like this:

4. While the package is executing, click the Progress tab of the MasterPackage.dtsx to view the package execution sequence and see that the Execute Child 2 task has been skipped.

Organizing Package Components

In this section, you will learn the value of managing tasks, containers, sources, destinations, and other components when designing your packages. When you learned how to use BIDS, you learned about SSIS projects and their related components, data sources, data source views, packages, and so on. A best practices approach to SSIS application design is to use separate projects for the following types of applications:

1. Historical loads

2. Unusual events (such as backing out a load)

3. One-time resetting of data

Using Prefixes to Identify SSIS Package Components

A good design and management practice is to develop and use standard naming conventions for all your tasks and other components. You might want to consider using acronyms at the start of the name, and some suggestions for these acronyms are shown here. This approach might not help a great deal at design time when the tasks and components are easily identifiable by the designer, but it can be invaluable at debug time and run-time logging. For example, you can use an acronym such as DFT for a data flow task, so the name of a data flow task that populates a table called MyTable could be DFT Load MyTable. The tables in Figure 14-5 and Figure 14-6 provide a list of possible acronyms.

Task	Prefix
For Loop Container	FLC
Foreach Loop Conatiner	FELC
Sequence Container	SEQC
ActiveX Script	AXS
Analysis Services Execute DDL	ASE
Analysis Services Processing	ASP
Bulk Insert	BLK
Data Flow	DFT
Data Mining Query	DMQ
Execute DTS 2000 Package	EDPT
Execute Package	EPT
Execute Process	EPR
Execute SQL	SQL
File System	FSYS
FTP	FTP
Message Queue	MSMQ
Script	SCR
Send Mail	SMT
Transfer Database	TDB
Transfer Error Messages	TEM
Transfer Jobs	TJT
Transfer Master Stored Procedures	TSP
Transfer SQL Server Objects	TSO
Web Service	WST
WMI Data Reader	WMID
WMI Event Watcher	WMIE
XML	XML

Figure 14-5   SSIS task naming template sample

Component	Prefix
DataReader Source	DR_SRC
Excel Source	EX_SRC
Flat File Source	FF_SRC
OLE DB Source	OLE_SRC
Raw File Source	RF_SRC
XML Source	XML_SRC
Aggregate	AGG
Audit	AUD
Character Map	CHM
Conditional Split	CSPL
Copy Column	CPYC
Data Conversion	DCNV
Data Mining Query	DMQ
Derived Column	DER
Export Column	EXPC
Fuzzy Grouping	FZG
Fuzzy Lookup	FZL
Import Column	IMPC
Lookup	LKP
Merge	MRG
Merge Join	MRGJ
Multicast	MLT
OLE DB Command	CMD
Percentage Sampling	PSMP
Pivot	PVT
Row Count	CNT
Row Sampling	RSMP
Script Component	SCR
Slowly Changing Dimension	SCD
Sort	SRT
Term Extraction	TEX
Term Lookup	TEL
Union All	ALL
Unpivot	UPVT
Data Mining Model Training	DMMT_DST
DataReader Destination	DR_DST
Dimension Processing	DP_DST
Excel Destination	EX_DST
Flat File Destination	FF_DST
OLE DB Destination	OLE_DST
Partition Processing	PP_DST
Raw File Destination	RF_DST
Recordset Destination	RS_DST
SQL Server Destination	SS_DST

Figure 14-6 SSIS component naming template sample

You might also want to take the time to rename all default properties and descriptions for production applications using acronyms. This will help when debugging, particularly if the person doing the debugging is not the person who built the package originally. Some companies standardize naming and annotation, using a *verbose* method with full-named prefixes or suffixes. However, abbreviated forms are very common in programming disciplines. Whichever you choose, be consistent.

Defining Project Folders

When developing projects, you might also want to define a folder structure to keep all related packages and other files organized in the same place. Folder naming and location can be defined and determined based upon your company's needs. You might also want to apply security to these folders to ensure that only authorized SSIS development and administrative personnel have access for adding, updating, and deleting, especially in production environments.

Once you have completed the work to design, develop, and test your application in development and have migrated the application for execution within your production environment, a best practices discipline is to store the solution and project items in a secured Source Code Control system such as Microsoft Team Foundation. If you operate in a multideveloper environment, storing your SSIS application packages in VSS or similar systems enables controlled checkout and check-in of project components to prevent simultaneous modifications and overwrites. Also, VSS offers version control, so you can always retrieve previous versions to see how the project components have changed over time or even restore the project to a specific previous version if required to process data in a historical manner not available in the current production environment.

SSIS packages generate a variety of data files during execution, including Error log files, checkpoint files, error redirect files, and other types of package data files. Defining a standard location and naming convention for these types of components is another best practices discipline for SSIS. There are a number of advantages to this approach. All of your SSIS items (packages, raw files, and so on) will exist in a known, consistent, and secured place. All items of a certain type (for instance, checkpoint files) are stored in the same place. This also allows for consistency across development and production environments.

Other standard best practices are to comment your packages and scripts, using the annotation features within SSIS or directly within your script tasks. In two weeks, even you can forget a subtlety of your design. In the future, watch for new package documenting tools for SSIS from Microsoft.

Managing Performance and Debugging

You learned earlier, in Chapter 2, "Building Your First Package," that BIDS provides a comprehensive design and development platform that includes allowing you to run packages in debug mode and to trace processes and set breakpoints. When you migrate your packages to a production environment, they are executed outside of BIDS.

Managing Buffers and Memory

The SSIS engine and data pipeline uses a memory-based transformation process. The amount of memory used is allocated as buffers and is based on design-time metadata. Buffers are designed to hold the data from the pipeline data rows. This means that the width of a row (sum of size of all columns) affects the number of rows allowed within each buffer. This also means that smaller rows allow for more rows in memory, which means greater processing efficiency. Multiple buffers are allocated for the number of parallel processes in play.

You learned earlier that SSIS tasks include synchronous and asynchronous types. Synchronous task types (Derived Column, Data Conversions, and so on) reuse the same buffers. Alternatively, asynchronous tasks (Sort, Merge, Union, and so on) that must process all the rows before sending them on to the next task require more memory buffers and perform memory copies. Memory copies are expensive, so if you design ways around asynchronous tasks (SQL joins, and so on), you might reduce your application memory resource demand and improve overall performance.

Managing CPU Use

In addition to memory and buffer use, you can take advantage of multithreading SSIS applications to use multiple CPU SSIS servers. Thread allocation is managed by a thread pool distributed between data paths. Each Source can get a thread. Each Execution Path can get a thread, too. You use MaxEngineThreads on DataFlowTask to control parallelism. But remember, you need to have multiple CPU servers to exploit these capabilities.

Managing SSIS Application Deployment

You have learned about the many design considerations for SSIS applications and components. These next sections provide some approaches and techniques for managing and deploying your applications.

Designing for Deployment

Plan early for deployment. When defining your own policies and guidelines, consider simplifying your deployment processes from development to QA to production. List all the areas affected by this migration path.

Some of the considerations you need to address include determining how you will schedule your applications on the production machine. Also, you will need to determine how to synchronize all the SSIS and ETL processes. Deployment considerations most often have to comply with your SQL Server implementation of SSIS, SQL Server, and other production servers and their platform characteristics. Memory and resource use and availability are different between your development and production platforms.

Consider building in your security requirements from the start. Make note of the required production-level execution credentials and other sensitive information. You might need to work with your database administrators to determine who has access to production servers, files, folders, and data sources. You also want to secure the SSIS package components. Just because the database administrators have full control over the databases doesn't mean you will give them the ability to alter packages.

Using SSIS Package Configurations

Build in SSIS package configurations from the start to make things easier later on. Using package configuration is the best option because you will have the ability to reconfigure any component of your application from its development default values and authentication to its production versions.

Package configuration can be accomplished in a variety of ways, from flat files, to XML files, to using SQL Server database tables. One approach is to design the package to read an *environment* variable from the SSIS server operating system to get the location of the config file. The configuration file will provide the SSIS package with the connection string for Config Database and all values required for production execution. Package configuration provides the most flexible deployment process and makes deployment as easy as updating configurations.

Managing Multiple Schemas with SSIS Package Design

Like many SQL Server database environments, the use of database administrator–enforced naming conventions is common. You will want to learn and understand these for use within your SSIS package connection strings and for migration purposes. It is best practice to separate and group database objects visually for easy, fast identification and recognition. A good way to manage this naming standard is to use a scheme such as server.database.schema.object where schema is not a user ID.

Referred to as loose-coupled programming, assigning non-user ID schema names prevents references to named objects from breaking when a user leaves. All the required security mechanisms are still maintained with this approach. Such schemas are securable containers and are easier to manage and modularize. Some examples include:

- dbo.Fact_Sales (Business data)
- etl.Fact_Sales (ETL work table)
- admin.up_SetLogicalDate(@date) (User Procedure)
- util.uf_GetEndOfWeek(@date) (User Function)
- etl.up_TruncateDimDate() (ETL Function)

Logging Reports

SSIS provides a variety of logging for tracing execution, tracking status, and so on. You might need to augment native functionality with custom logging for hybrid applications that combine SSIS packages with custom-coded modules. And although not technically a log, a good practice is always to use the error outputs on transforms to capture anomalies in addition to logging the status of errors during the package execution.

If you have installed SQL Server 2005 Reporting Services in addition to SQL Server and SSIS, you have the ability to generate SSIS server application log reports. SSIS server provides a comprehensive set of logged statistics for application packages it executes. You can obtain these pre-defined reports from the MSDN Web site at *http://msdn2.microsoft.com/en-au/default.aspx*. Search for the SSRS Report Pack, download it to your SQL Server Reporting Services server, and configure it to read your SSIS server event log. A sample SSIS report is shown here.

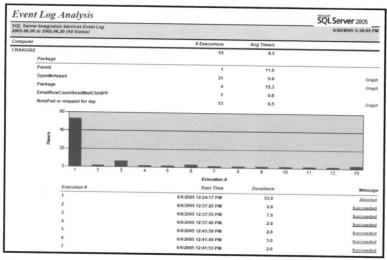

Figure 14-7 A sample SSIS report

Chapter 14 Quick Reference

This term	Means this
OVAL	OVAL is an acronym for the principles of package design for four key facets of SSIS applications. These design considerations include identifying the Operations to be performed; the data Volume to be processed (in production); the Application of the right tools, tasks, sequence, and flow; and the Location—determining where the SSIS application will run.
Synchronous tasks	Transformation tasks that process input rows and send output rows downstream in the data pipeline a row at a time. Examples include derived columns, transformed data types, multicast, and Conditional Split.
Asynchronous tasks	Transformation tasks that process all the input rows before they send output rows downstream in the data pipeline a row at a time. Examples include the Sort task and Aggregate task.
Master–child packages	A design technique used to control package execution sequence, using the Execute Package control flow task. The master package controls the sequence and execution of one or more child packages.

Index

Symbols
.dtsx (DST package) files, 9

A
accessing package variables, 174
accessing SSIS design environment, 242–243
accumulated staging, 372
ActiveX Script Task
    creating a new package with single Active X Script task,
      170–172
    implementing, 169–172
    implementing custom code using, 174
    Script Task and, 139
adding a new package, 380–381
adding a Sequence Container control flow item, 137
adding conditional split to find new customers, 378–379
adding configurations to a project, 297–298
adding connection manager for Fuzzy Lookup input, 138
adding data adapters, 43–49
    OLE DB source data adapters, 43–44
adding error-handling code in Script Task, 146–148
adding Excel connection manager, 65
adding Execute SQL task, 129, 138
adding flat file destination, 379–380, 383–384
adding Foreach Loop containers, 130–132, 138
    Sequence Container – File Exists, 130–132
adding Fuzzy Lookup transformation, 138
adding Lookup task process, 381–382
adding Script Tasks, 137
adding sequence containers, 121
adding SQL Server destinations, 127–129, 138
adding tables to find new dimension members, 376–377
adding variables, 137
additive measures, 353–354
Aggregate task
    adding, 399–400
applying a configuration, 301–306
    adding configuration to the ImportCustomers.dtsx,
      302–303
    deleting existing package from SSMS, 302
    deploying a package, 304
    executing package, 306
    executing package using configuration files, 306
    inspecting alternate configuration files, 304–305
    running deployed packages, 305
    starting Package Installation Wizard, 304
applying precedence constraints, 132–136, 138
    constraint values, 132
applying security, 292–294

assigning a value to variables, 122–123
assigning reader/writer roles to a package, 293–294
asynchronous tasks
    defined, 437
asynchronous transformations, 73, 312
attach_databases.bat script, 4
Audit transformation, 72
Autos window, 194

B
basic error detection and handling, 237–239
    configuring transformation to fail when an error occurs,
      239
    configuring transformation to ignore errors, 239
    configuring transformation to re-route error-causing
      records, 239
    data flow transformations, 239
    metadata lineage, 238
    precedence constraints, 238
    validation, 238
BI architects
    getting started, 2
BI solution goals, 346–348
    combining data from multiple sources, 347
    providing fast and easy access, 347–348
BI solutions
    choosing, 348
    data granularity, 349–350
BIDS, 13–26
    adding a Conditional Split transformation, 112
    adding a connection manager, 112
    adding a Derived Column transformation, 112
    adding a Destination data adapter, 112
    adding a lookup transformation, 112
    adding a Multicast transformation, 112
    adding conditional split transformation, 86–88
    adding connections manager, 82–85
    adding derived column transformation, 89–90
    adding flat file destination data adapter, 92–93
    adding multicast transformation, 95–96
    adding SQL server destination data adapter, 97–99
    creating a data adapter, 112
    creating a data flow task, 112
    creating a Flat File, 112
    creating a task, 112
    creating data adapter, 81–82
    creating Data Flow task, 78–80
    Data Flow designer, 69
    Data Flow Task – Employee List, 19–20

About the Authors

Paul Turley

Paul Turley is an architect for Hitachi Consulting and has been managing and developing business solutions for about 14 years for many companies, such as Hewlett-Packard, Walt Disney, and Microsoft. He manages the BI Training group for Hitachi's national External Education Services. Paul has taught application development and database design courses for a number of colleges and private training facilities. He has been a Microsoft Certified Solution Developer since 1996 and holds MCDBA, MCSD, MCT, MSF, and IT Project+ certifications. Paul has presented at various conferences and industry associations, including Microsoft SQL PASS in 2004, 2006, and 2007. He has authored and co-authored several books for Wrox Press/Wiley Publishing on Reporting Services, Analysis Services, TSQL, and Access. He is the primary author of Beginning Transact-SQL for SQL Server 2000 and 2005 and was the lead author for Professional SQL Server Reporting Services (2000 and 2005). He is also a contributing author for Beginning SQL Server 2005 Administration. He lives in Vancouver, Washington, with his wife, Sherri, four kids, one dog, two cats, and a bird.

Joe Kasprzak

Joseph Kasprzak is a manager of business intelligence (BI) solutions for Hitachi Consulting in Boston. He has over 14 years of comprehensive business, technical, and managerial experience, providing consulting services for clients in the financial services, retail, telecommunications, health care, hospitality, manufacturing, and government industries. He has helped architect, integrate, develop, and manage full life cycle implementations of strategic BI analytical systems. Joe is a leader in providing BI best practices, proven BI methodologies, BI technology assessments, retail marketing analytics, business performance score cards, labor analytics, KPI executive dashboards, corporate performance management and reporting, financial analytics, and database modeling and design. Joe resides seaside in Newburyport, Massachusetts, where he and his wife, Liz, enjoy sailing and local volunteering. Joe holds a Bachelor of Science degree in mathematics/chemistry from Assumption College in Worcester, Massachusetts, and has performed post-graduate studies in computer science at MIT in Cambridge, Massachusetts.

Scott Cameron

Scott Cameron, a Senior BI Architect at Hitachi Consulting, has been developing BI solutions for nine years and has over 20 years' data analysis experience. He has over five years' experience working with SQL Server 2005 BI components and has taught SQL Server BI courses in the United States and Europe. He has experience in the health care, software, retail, insurance, legal, vocational rehabilitation, travel, and mining industries. He has helped several large companies perform their initial implementation of Microsoft Analysis Services 2005 and helped several independent software vendors integrate Analysis Services into their products. He holds a Bachelor of Arts degree in economics and Asian studies from Brigham Young University; his Master of Arts degree in Economics is from the University of Washington. Scott lives in the Seattle, Washington, metropolitan area with his wife, Tarya, and beagles Hunter and Si.

Satoshi Iizuka

Satoshi Iizuka, an engineer with Hitachi Ltd. in Tokyo, has over nine years of database custom development experience and significant BI development experience. He is a member of the Windows COE initiative at Hitachi Ltd., which manages and educates best practices for Microsoft products (including Microsoft .NET technologies). He programs with almost all Microsoft programming languages and Java and is proficient with Microsoft major server products and multiple software development methodologies. He is a Microsoft Certified Systems Engineer (MCSE), Microsoft Certified Database Administrator (MCDBA), and Microsoft Certified System Developer (MCSE) for .NET. Satoshi lives in Tokyo, Japan, with his wife and favorite Nikon cameras.

Pablo Guzman

Pablo Guzman, a BI consultant at Hitachi Consulting, has been developing BI solutions for over seven years. Prior to joining Hitachi Consulting, Pablo worked as a BI consultant for around a year and then worked for three years in a software-development company where he built BI tools for the banking industry. After that, he worked three years at the largest bank in Quito, Ecuador, where he was the BI program manager. He has taught SQL Server BI courses and developed SQL 2005 BI training material. He has engaged with multiple clients in business groups that include data warehousing, IT, insurance, manufacturing, and banking. He has worked in numerous projects that involved performing complex analysis on large data sets. He received an engineering degree in computer and information systems from the National Polytechnic School of Ecuador. Pablo lives in the Seattle, Washington, metropolitan area, where he has been an active volunteer participant in some nonprofit organizations and plays guitar, bass, and drums in several bands in Seattle.

Supporting Author
Anne Bockman Hansen

Anne has ten years' project-based experience in technical writing and editing, instructional design, and project management. She is experienced in designing curriculum for a wide variety of content areas, including Microsoft Windows Server, Windows Small Business Server, Microsoft Exchange Server, SQL Server, and Microsoft Office. She is experienced in designing curriculum for a variety of learning levels, including Web developers, Microsoft Certified Solution Providers, Solution developers, technical implementers and decision makers, corporate developers, site administrators, senior support professionals, and technical consultants. Anne received a Master of Science degree in technical communication from the University of Washington College of Engineering in 1996 and a Bachelor of Science degree in cognitive psychology in 1980. Anne resides in the country in Fall City, Washington, with her husband, Barry.